Inquiry into Philosophical and Religious Issues

Inquiry into Philosophical and Religious Issues

A Practical Resource for Students and Teachers

ROSEMARY LAOULACH

WIPF & STOCK · Eugene, Oregon

INQUIRY INTO PHILOSOPHICAL AND RELIGIOUS ISSUES
A Practical Resource for Students and Teachers

Copyright © 2019 Rosemary Laoulach. All rights reserved. Except for brief quotations in critical publications or reviews, no part of this book may be reproduced in any manner without prior written permission from the publisher. Write: Permissions, Wipf and Stock Publishers, 199 W. 8th Ave., Suite 3, Eugene, OR 97401.

Wipf & Stock
An Imprint of Wipf and Stock Publishers
199 W. 8th Ave., Suite 3
Eugene, OR 97401
www.wipfandstock.com

PAPERBACK ISBN: 978-1-5326-0622-9
HARDCOVER ISBN: 978-1-5326-0624-3
EBOOK ISBN: 978-1-5326-0623-6

Manufactured in the U.S.A.   DECEMBER 10, 2019

This book is dedicated to Samuel, Hope, Summer,
and Jacinta Laoulach.
Also, to Matthew and Nicholas Stejer.

... to be patient toward all that is unsolved in your heart and to try to love the *questions themselves* like locked rooms and like books that are written in a very foreign tongue. Do not now seek the answers, which cannot be given you because you would not be able to live them. And the point is, to live everything. *Live* the questions now. Perhaps you will then gradually, without noticing it, live along some distant day into the answer.

—Rainer Maria Rilke[1]

Thinking itself is a way. We respond to the way only by remaining underway . . . The way of thinking cannot be traced from somewhere to somewhere like a well-worn rut, nor does it all exist as such in any place. Only when we walk it, and in no other fashion, only, that is, by thoughtful questioning, are we on the move on the way.

—Martin Heidegger[2]

I shall argue that cultivated capacities for critical thinking and reflection are crucial in keeping democracies alive and wide awake. The ability to think well about a wide range of cultures, groups, and nations in the context of a grasp of the global economy and of the history of many national and group interactions is crucial in order to enable democracies to deal responsibly with the problems we currently face as members of an interdependent world. And the ability to imagine the experience of another—a capacity almost all human beings possess in some form—needs to be greatly enhanced and refined if we are to have any hope of sustaining decent institutions across the many divisions that any modern society contains.

—Martha Nussbaum[3]

1. Rilke, *Letters to a Young Poet*, 27 (emphasis in original).
2. Heidegger, *What Is Called Thinking?*, 168–69.
3. Nussbaum, *Not for Profit*, 10.

Contents

Permissions | ix
Acknowledgments | xi
Introduction | xiii

Epistemology: How Do We Know What We Know? | 1
Is Religious Faith a Valid Way of Knowing? | 84
How Do We Interpret Sacred Texts? | 144
How Do We Act? An Inquiry of Ethics | 192
How Do We Find Meaning and Happiness? | 276

Bibliography | 377
Index | 399

Permissions

I would like to thank the following individuals and groups for permission to use their material:

"Cynicism about Facts is Symptomatic Not Only of a Cognitive Crisis but of a Wider Moral Malaise" by Rajeev Bhargava. Reproduced with permission by the author.

Extract from *I Met God in Bermuda* by Steven G. Ogden, © 2008 by Steven G. Ogden. Used by permission of John Hunt Publishing.

Scriptures taken from the Holy Bible, New International Version®, NIV®, copyright © 1973, 1978, 1984, 2011 by Biblica, Inc.™ Used by permission of Zondervan. All rights reserved worldwide.

"Understanding Sacred Texts" by the British Library. Used by its permission.

"Praying the Psalms with Jesus" by Michael Fallon, © 2018 by Michael Fallon. Used by permission of Michael Fallon, MSC.

"How to be a Buddhist in Today's World" by the Dalai Lama, © The Office of His Holiness the Dalai Lama. Reproduced by its permission.

"Address of the Holy Father" by Pope Francis. Reproduced with permission by Libreria Editrice Vaticana.

"Thinking about Racism" by Christopher Chaves. Unpublished work reproduced with author's permission.

Extract from "Emotion and Peacebuilding" by Steven Steyl. Unpublished work used by author's permission.

Extract from "What is Scapegoating?" by Arthur D. Colman, © 2019 by Dr.

Arthur D. Colman. Used by author's permission.

"Existentialism and Human Nature" by Lewis R. Gordon. Unpublished work used by author's permission.

I would like to thank the following individuals and groups for permission to use their images:

White Marble Head of a Woman, The Thinker by Rodin, School of Athens by Raphael, Happy Young Man, and Group of Friends Having Coffee all reprinted by permission of Shutterstock.

All other images from sources represented as the public domain.

Every effort has been made to reach copyright holders of reproductions within this book. Please contact the publisher regarding any omissions, so they can be rectified upon further editions or versions.

Acknowledgments

I would like to thank Ryan Wells for his editing. Ryan's professionalism, patience, and expertise were essential in completing this project.

I would also like to thank Dr. Raymond Aaron Younis for his feedback and encouragement, as well as Dr. Matthew Del Nevo for his valuable comments.

Many thanks to the following educators, philosophers, and theologians who in various ways have contributed to the book: Maria Caristo, Michael Davis, Steven Steyl, Stephen Kellett, Dr. Steven Ogden, Dr. Max Deutscher, Fr. Michael Fallon, Dr. Morny Joy, Dr. Lewis R. Gordon, Dr. Antoine Cantin-Brault, Anastasia Yatras, Antoinette Laoulach, and Dr. Christopher Chaves.

Introduction

At school she had trouble concentrating on what the teachers said. They seemed to talk only about unimportant things. Why couldn't they talk about what a human being is—or about what the world is and how it came into being?

JOSTEIN GAARDER[1]

HOW DO WE ENGAGE students in the important questions? *Inquiry into Philosophical and Religious Issues* provides the pedagogical tools of inquiry and philosophy as its main approach. Research has suggested this to be effective in engaging students in deep learning—what is currently termed "meta-cognition." This exploration is based on the premise that if the right questions are posed within a positive learning environment, students can demonstrate a natural ability to wonder and be inquisitive. A setting that challenges preconceived notions allows for intellectual exploration and creativity. The teacher's role will not be one of providing answers, but engendering thoughtful discussion; it can be likened to Socrates' analogy of teaching being a midwife to the truth.

As a resource, *Inquiry* incorporates a student-centered holistic approach to teaching and learning. The book aims to develop the skills of inquiry and critical thinking, while encouraging the ability to reflect and wonder. Its epistemological analysis explores not only the importance of reason in gaining knowledge, but also emotions, intuitions, and imagination. Although the focus is on developing cognitive skills through inquiry, there is also an affective and experimental component. The discussions on happiness, personal meaning, emotions, therapy, and the importance

---

1. Gaarder, *Sophie's World*, 10.

of listening seek to develop life skills, while promoting a level of student well-being.

The book includes a range of activities such as research, listening tasks, group and individual work, essays, presentations, debates, interviews, conferences, and role-play. The activities within each lesson are structured so that the questions posed provide students with the opportunity to integrate their learning through further reflection questions. Stimulus materials stem from philosophy, religion, theology, and psychology, with the inclusion of suggested research tasks for further exploration.

This book—a contribution to the hard work of those educators who have incorporated an inquiry and philosophical approach to education—allows many common questions students ask related to truth, meaning, and happiness to be addressed. The focus is not on information, but rather acknowledging student questions that naturally emerge while they are engaged in religious and philosophical issues. While not claiming to be definitive or comprehensive, *Inquiry* moves away from the content-driven comparative religion and sociological approaches, instead raising important questions within the broad disciplines examined. It should be noted that the scope of the book does not fully explore non-Western perspectives in depth, and teachers are encouraged to draw on knowledge and personal experiences—both the students' and their own—where possible to extend this analysis.

WHY IS THIS BOOK USEFUL TODAY?

Assessing definitively whether young people today are in a worse situation than the previous generation is difficult, yet there are signs that perhaps things are not as they could be. Psychoanalyst and philosopher Julia Kristeva writes, in *New Maladies of the Soul*, about the negative influences of modern society on our psyches.[2] Additionally, Hugh McKay's sociological analysis points to the alienation of individuals from community life.[3] Research from psychology currently suggests that our young people's state of the soul is not as it could be, with conditions such as depression and anxiety prevalent in most Western countries.

If these observations are even partially true, then the role of education is even more crucial. In response to these issues, educators must continually think of creative ways to educate the *whole person*. The approach should lead students to a learning that has personal meaning or internalized knowledge, reflecting what is termed in educational literature as the *Bildung* aspect of

2. Kristeva, *New Maladies of the Soul*.
3. Mackay, *Art of Belonging*.

education.[4] It is here that the wisdom of the ancient Greek philosophers becomes relevant; they understood education as not only for developing the mind, but also the soul.

THIS BOOK MAY BE A USEFUL RESOURCE FOR THE FOLLOWING PROGRAMS

1. Religious education programs wanting to either implement an inquiry-based and philosophical approach, or complement existing curriculums.
2. The Theory of Knowledge course within the International Baccalaureate (IB) Diploma Programme. The exploration of epistemology, ethics and religion addresses relevant issues and questions within this course. Many IB teachers will be familiar with the inquiry approach embedded throughout the book.
3. Gifted and talented programs wanting to provide materials which will stimulate a high level of critical thinking skills.

WHY IS THE STUDY OF EPISTEMOLOGY IMPORTANT?

Epistemological explorations are crucial in formulating core understandings of nearly all topics, including religion, ethics and science because of its foundational nature. In asking epistemological questions, students are able to examine some of the strongly held assumptions and claims to certainty, allowing them to consider different ways of viewing the world. Epistemological questions are asked throughout the book, prompting an examination of claims and basis of knowing. While there are debates about theories of knowledge within philosophy that extend beyond the scope of this book, it focuses here on exploring general (classical) epistemology and commonly posed questions within the epistemology of religion.

INQUIRY-BASED LEARNING

Inquiry-based learning is a process where students are involved in their learning, formulate questions, investigate widely and then build new understandings, meanings and

---

4. Reindal, "*Bildung*, The Bologna Process."

knowledge. That knowledge is new to the students and may be used to answer a question, to develop a solution or to support a position or point of view. The knowledge is usually presented to others and may result in some sort of action.[5]

Inquiry-based learning can be defined as a process of discovery, enhancing creativity and encouraging students to develop and articulate their own thoughts. Inquiry allows students to go deeper in thinking as they explore different levels of understanding about a particular issue or question. Inquiry-based learning is currently evident in activities such as project-based learning, design thinking and action research. There are many benefits of inquiry-based learning demonstrated within educational literature and research shows that applying inquiry-based learning helps students become more creative, positive and independent.[6]

The model of inquiry places the teacher as a facilitator in the learning process. Educators are encouraged to promote risk-taking and discovery in learning. Leading students through inquiry is possibly one of the most important roles a teacher can adopt within the learning process. This approach to teaching and learning is not only a way of elucidating ideas, but also a holistic way of learning which can inspire and "bring forth the person."[7]

> When teaching is too content-based, the education system is basically attempting to stamp this content onto the minds of students, and the education system needs to be an unpleasant regime to do this. Where education is more method-based, more with inquiry, it is doing what its verb form suggests, *educing,* that is to *bring forth*. Not bringing forth this or that bit of information at exam time but bringing forth *the person*.[8]

The inquiry approach has been central in the pedagogy of International Baccalaureate (IB) Diploma Program and the intended focus of the Australian curriculum. Researchers in this field include Mary Hayden and John Thompson, Jennifer Branch and Dianne Oberg, Lyn Erickson, and Kath Murdoch.

---

5. Branch & Oberg, *Focus on Inquiry*, 1.
6. Ibid.
7. Lipman, in Del Nevo, *Continental Community of Inquiry*, 35–36.
8. Ibid.

PHILOSOPHY IN SCHOOLS

> Philosophy actually implies exercising freedom in and through reflection because it is a matter of making rational judgements and not just expressing opinions, because it is a matter not just of knowing, but of understanding the meaning and the principles of knowing, because it is a matter of developing a critical mind, rampart par excellence against all forms of doctrinaire passion. These objectives require time, taking a serious look at oneself, at other cultures and languages. This is a long process that is dependent upon enlightened instruction, upon rigorously putting concepts and ideas into perspective. Philosophy, as a method, as a procedure, as teaching, thus makes it possible to develop each person's skills to question, compare, conceptualise.[9]

There has been significant literature emerging on the educational benefits of teaching philosophy in schools. Some of the researchers in this field include Phillip Cam, Matthew Lipman, Sarah Chesters, Andrea Monteath, Stephen Law and, Martha Nusbaum. Lipman's work, for example, has been influential in developing the community of inquiry.[10] Stephen Law discusses the usefulness of teaching philosophy in helping students to analyse effectively.[11] Philosophy can help develop strong and complex arguments, skills highly desirable in education and the work place.

RELIGIOUS EDUCATION

In recent years some scholars have also incorporated inquiry and philosophy into their approach to religious education. These include the works of Peter Vardy, Robert Kirkwood, and the organization Dialogue Australasia Network, and is both evident in philosophy and philosophy of religion (A-level) courses in England. Other writers have proposed a similar inquiry approach to religious education, including Andrew Wright, James Conroy, Sean Whittle, Clive Erricker, David Torevell, Harvey Siegel, and Graham Rossiter.

Religious education scholar Phillip Barnes argues that students need to be encouraged to think critically about religious issues. He is disapproving

9. UNESCO, *Philosophy*, ix.
10. Lipman, *Thinking for Education*.
11. Law, *Why study philosophy?* 5-8.

of the phenomenological approach to religious education, arguing it implicitly steers away from the important task of engaging students in dialogue and questioning. Barnes proposes that schools should help students make up their own minds on religious ideas and values, rather than be asked to accept blindly the assumptions and ideas presented to them.

> One of the fundamental questions upon which pupils have to make up their own minds is: Is religion true? Does God exist? How do I know? The educational point is that pupils must make up their *own* minds, which means that schools should not determine their answers. Given that decisions about the worth and truth of religion will be made by pupils, either explicitly or implicitly, consciously or unconsciously, whatever happens in schools, it is incumbent upon schools to enable pupils to be critical in reaching their decisions.[12]

HOW TO APPROACH THIS BOOK

The pedagogical approach presented in this book emphasizes that the teacher ought to walk along with students in helping them develop their own thinking and inquiry; in other words, the teacher facilitates. Equally important in the activities included is the ability to listen effectively and respectfully to other people's ideas during discussions. Listening skills will be just as important as talking when it comes to learning. Students are encouraged to note how they are feeling about certain stimuli and explore this in writing, preferably in a journal.

> We know the duties of a host at a dinner party, but what are the duties of a guest? The duty of a guest is to be a good conversationalist–that is, someone well-informed, who can articulate his views, express and explain them, make a case for them, and be prepared to change them if offered better arguments or evidence; but who is also a good listener, who hears what his interlocutors say (not what he thinks they have said), can engage with their views, discuss them, debate them, challenge them if necessary; but along with them seek clarity, understanding, and truth.[13]

---

12. Barnes, "Ninian Smart," 327.
13. Plutarch, paraphrased in Grayling, *The God Argument*, 140.

Complex questions may not have any immediate or definitive answers, leading to an awareness of what many thinkers have termed the *mystery* of life. The process of deep learning over time can make students become more comfortable with what they *do not know*. Students and teachers are called to explore these questions together with inquisitiveness, curiosity, openness, and humility.

The attitudes of wonder and curiosity, effective tools which can lead students into deep inquiry, are encouraged throughout the book. Many philosophers and religious writers adopted an attitude of wonder, with Aristotle writing that "knowledge begins with a sense of wonder."[14] The attitude of wonder can assist in allowing students to ponder complex, open-ended questions such as those related to personal meaning, values, and the origins of the universe. Wonder can encourage the discovery of a student's own voice and ideas, leading them to the ability to think outside the box, in a manner of speaking.[15]

The notion of the teacher as a *learner* is a strong theme within philosophical literature. For example, Martin Heidegger viewed the teacher's role not as one who imposes, but rather enables learning. In *What Is Called Thinking?*, Heidegger proposes—like Socrates and John Dewey—that teaching is not to be seen as an authoritative position, instead placing the teacher as an equal to the student.[16] He argues the teacher has just as much to learn (perhaps even more) than the student.[17] For Heidegger, like Socrates, the relationship between teacher and student is based on genuine respect, and humility on the part of the teacher. It is in this spirit of teaching that the book can be engaged with and practiced.

> The teacher is ahead of his apprentices in this alone, that he has still far more to learn than they—he has to learn to let them learn. The teacher must be capable of being more teachable than the apprentices. The teacher is far less assured of his ground than those who learn are of theirs. If the relation between the teacher and the taught is genuine, therefore, there

---

14. Aristotle, *Metaphysics*, A 2.982b 12–17.

15. The approach of wonder in education is also present within contemporary literature, such as the works of Lipmann and Cam. Also, *Project Zero* (Harvard School of Education) includes "thinking exercises or routines for classrooms known as 'See-think-wonder.'" See also Morrison et al., *Making Thinking Visible*, 55.

16. Heidegger, *What Is Called Thinking?*, 168–69.

17. Ibid.

is never a place in it for the authority of the know-it-all or the authoritative sway of the official.[18]

Arguably, no pedagogy, however conceptually sound, is complete without the *qualitative* relationship between teacher and student. Positive and respectful student-teacher relationships are one of the foundations of teaching and learning. It is this qualitative presence, not easily measured, that provides a space where students feel respected, known, heard, and listened to. Such a space created in the classroom allows students to both take risks in thinking as well as develop a positive sense of self. This process helps to facilitate the development of the whole person.

---

18. Ibid., 15.

Epistemology

How Do We Know What We Know?

Outline

1. Introduction
2. Can we know through wonder?
3. What is the difference between knowledge and wisdom?
4. Socrates—"The unexamined life is not worth living"
5. What can religion teach us?
6. What does it mean to know?
7. Skepticism
8. Thinking "outside the box": Plato's *Allegory of the Cave*
9. Empiricism vs rationalism
10. Three theories of truth
11. Critical thinking
12. Limitations of reason
13. Intuition, emotion, and imagination
14. Scientific knowledge and its limitations
15. Conclusion: The importance of thinking well despite the limitations of reason
16. Main research task
17. Independent research questions

Objectives

At the end of this chapter, students should demonstrate the ability to ask questions, wonder, and think critically about the following:

1. The importance of living an "examined life" through the works of Socrates and Plato.
2. The differences between knowledge and wisdom.
3. The various ways to justify knowledge claims.
4. Critical thinking skills, including examining assumptions, stereotypes, and inductive and deductive reasoning.
5. How science works and some of its limitations.
6. The complexity involved in making any claim or belief.
7. An understanding of bias in knowledge and the importance of developing a healthy skepticism.

INTRODUCTION

> Is there any knowledge in the world which is so certain that no reasonable man could doubt it? This question, which at first sight might not seem difficult, is really one of the most difficult that can be asked. When we have realized the obstacles in the way of a straightforward and confident answer, we shall be well launched on the study of philosophy—for philosophy is merely the attempt to answer such ultimate questions, not carelessly and dogmatically, as we do in ordinary life and even in the sciences, but critically after exploring all that makes such questions puzzling, and after realizing all the vagueness and confusion that underlie our ordinary ideas....[1]
>
> Philosophy, if it cannot answer so many questions as we could wish, has at least the power of asking questions which increase the interest of the world, and show the strangeness and wonder lying just below the surface even in the commonest things of daily life.[2]

1. What does Bertrand Russell claim is the role of philosophy?

---

1. Russell, *Problems of Philosophy*, 5.
2. Ibid., 9.

2. What do you think Russell means by the following phrase, ". . . the power of asking questions which increase the interest of the world, and show the strangeness and wonder lying just below the surface even in the commonest things of daily life."

3. How can asking questions increase our interest in the world?

We rely on experts to give us information which is trustworthy. However, there are many examples in which experts are wrong. Have you ever doubted whether what you were reading or what someone was saying was actually true? How do we make sure that information we rely on is accurate? To what extend can we be totally certain of our own claims?

How we know what we know seems like an odd topic relegated to obscure corners of debate in philosophy. Yet how can we engage in questions of true understanding, including religious faith, ethics, and happiness, without asking this question? In our asking, we begin to discover that the basis on which knowledge is constructed often includes reason, but relies also on other sometimes surprising influences, such as imagination, the senses, language, emotion, and even faith. These factors contribute to our knowledge and understanding of the world, yet their reliability is debated in philosophy.

This chapter begins by exploring some wide topics within general (classical) epistemology and then explores issues and questions commonly posed within the epistemology of religion. The question of *how* we come to believe is complex, yet nevertheless of great importance to understanding the world.

Student Activity—Terminology

Some of the terms below are still debated amongst scholars; however, familiarity with common understandings of the these will assist with engaging in the ideas presented. The Oxford and Webster dictionaries may be a good place to start. Working in student pairs, write down the definitions of the terms below and take turns explaining them to each other:

wonder, contemplation, atheist, curious, religion, humanists, inquirer, theologian, skepticism, dogmatisms, relativism, philosophy, framework, paradigm, assumptions, mystery, *a priori* knowledge, inductive logic, empirical knowledge, deductive logic, rationalism, phenomena.

CAN WE KNOW THROUGH WONDER?

"For wonder is the feeling of a philosopher, and philosophy begins in wonder."[3]

DISCUSSION QUESTIONS

1. What does it mean to wonder? To be curious? To be an inquirer?
2. How can wonder help us to gain knowledge?

Wonder is defined by the Oxford dictionary as a "desire to know something; feel curious."[4] Many philosophers thought wonder was the beginning of learning and considered it an important part of thinking deeply and gaining wisdom:

> For it is owing to their wonder that men both now begin and at first began to philosophize; they wondered originally at the obvious difficulties, then advanced little by little and stated difficulties about the greater matters e.g. about the phenomena of the moon and those of the sun and of the stars, and about the genesis of the universe.[5]

TO WONDER ABOUT THE UNIVERSE

STUDENT ACTIVITY—EXCERPT

Read the extract from *Sophie's World* and answer the questions below:

> The best way of approaching philosophy is to ask a few philosophical questions:
>
> How was the world created? Is there any will or meaning behind what happens? Is there a life after death? How can we answer these questions? And most important, how ought we

---

3. Plato, "Apology," 178.

4. *Oxford Dictionaries, s.v.* "wonder," https://en.oxforddictionaries.com/definition/wonder.

5. Aristotle, *Metaphysics*, A 2.982b 12–17.

to live? People have been asking these questions throughout the ages. We know of no culture which has not concerned itself with what man is and where the world came from . . .

A Greek philosopher who lived more than two thousand years ago believed that philosophy had its origin in man's sense of wonder. Man thought it was so astonishing to be alive that philosophical questions arose of their own accord.

It is like watching a magic trick. We cannot understand how it is done. So, we ask: how can the magician change a couple of white silk scarves into a live rabbit?

A lot of people experience the world with the same incredulity as when a magician suddenly pulls a rabbit out of a hat which has just been shown to them empty.

In the case of the rabbit, we know the magician has tricked us. What we would like to know is just how he did it. But when it comes to the world it's somewhat different. We know that the world is not all sleight of hand and deception because here we are in it, we are part of it. Actually, we are the white rabbit being pulled out of the hat. The only difference between us and the white rabbit is that the rabbit does not realize it is taking part in a magic trick. Unlike us. We feel we are part of something mysterious and we would like to know how it all works.[6]

DISCUSSION QUESTIONS:

1. In pairs or groups discuss following questions:

"How was the world created? Is there any will or meaning behind what happens? Is there a life after death? How can we answer these questions? And most important, how ought we to live?"

Why do you think these questions might be important?

2. What does Gaarder mean by us being the white rabbit?

---

6. Gaarder, *Sophie's World*, 12–13.

3. "We feel we are part of something mysterious and we would like to know how it all works."

Do you agree with Gaarder that the world is mysterious? Explain.

Wonder can be attributed to awe and curiosity. It can connect us to something greater than ourselves. It may be argued that philosophy and religion *arose out of wonder*. Wonder is an attitude which allows a person to ponder and contemplate the universe. As British Philosopher Bertrand Russell (1872–1970) explains below, wonder can liberate us by opening up possibilities and new ways of seeing and understanding the world:

> The value of philosophy is, in fact, to be sought largely in its very uncertainty. The man who has no tincture of philosophy goes through life imprisoned in the prejudices derived from common sense, from the habitual beliefs of his age or his nation, and from convictions which have grown up in his mind without the co-operation or consent of his deliberate reason. To such a man the world tends to become definite, finite, obvious; common objects rouse no questions, and unfamiliar possibilities are contemptuously rejected. As soon as we begin to philosophize, on the contrary, we find, as we saw [in our opening chapters], that even the most everyday things lead to problems to which only very incomplete answers can be given. Philosophy, though unable to tell us with certainty what is the true answer to the doubts which it raises, is able to suggest many possibilities which enlarge our thoughts and free them from the tyranny of custom. Thus, while diminishing our feeling of certainty as to what things are, it greatly increases our knowledge as to what they may be; it removes the somewhat arrogant dogmatism of those who have never travelled into the region of liberating doubt, and it keeps alive our sense of wonder by showing familiar things in an unfamiliar aspect.[7]

What does Russell mean by the "tyranny of custom?" How can philosophy help us keep our sense of wonder alive?

---

7. Russell, *Problems of Philosophy*, 81.

WHAT IS THE DIFFERENCE BETWEEN KNOWLEDGE AND WISDOM?

What is wisdom?

> That man is best who sees truth himself;
>
> Good too is he who listens to wise counsel.
>
> But who is neither wise himself nor willing
>
> To ponder wisdom is not worth a straw.[8]

> ... Are you not ashamed that you give your attention to acquiring as much money as possible, and similarly with reputation and honour, and give no attention or thought to truth [*aletheia*], or thought [*phronesis*] or the perfection of your soul [*psyche*]?[9]

For wisdom is a shelter as money is a shelter, but the advantage of knowledge is this: that wisdom preserves the life of its possessor (Eccl 7:12).

Where is the Life we have lost in living? Where is the wisdom we have lost in knowledge? Where is the knowledge we have lost in information?[10]

DISCUSSION QUESTIONS:

1. What do each of the writers above say about wisdom?
2. Can you think of a person who you believe is wise? What is it that makes them wise?
3. Who can teach us wisdom? How do we attain it?
4. In your opinion, how does knowledge differ from wisdom?

8. Hesiod, in Aristotle, *Ethics*, 67.
9. Socrates, in Plato, "Apology," 29d5–e3.
10. "Choruses from the Rock," in Eliot, *T. S. Eliot*, 107.

Wisdom is understood by religious and philosophical writers, broadly speaking, as that which pertains to right conduct and understanding. To be a wise person one need not only be knowledgeable, but also of good character and able to make effective moral decisions. For both philosophers and the religious, wisdom points not only to knowledge, but also to virtuous actions. The understanding of wisdom for religious thinkers is also associated with spiritual and religious connections with God, the divine, or ultimate reality. For example, in the Judeo-Christian tradition, we see wisdom literature found within sacred text and God is referred to as *Sophia,* meaning "wisdom." From religious and philosophical literature emerge individual figures known for their wisdom and insights called sages, such as Socrates, Solomon, and the Dalai Lama. Can you think of others?

In Greek the first half of the word philosophy, *philo,* means "loving" and *sophia* translates to "knowledge and wisdom."[11] The ancient Greek philosophers understood wisdom as the highest form of knowledge. Living a virtuous life was necessary in gaining wisdom. Virtue was considered a disposition which consistently allowed you to do the morally right action for the right reasons and in a reliable manner.[12] A person cannot act immorally, cause suffering to others, and still be considered wise. Knowledge, for the ancient thinkers, was often connected to how one should live, and as we shall see later on in the book, moral decisions played a primary role.

The claims made by thinkers such as Socrates (470–399 BCE), Aristotle (384–322 BCE), and the English poet T. S. Eliot (1888–1965) above may suggest that the attainment of wisdom may be a challenging yet important goal. The Oxford Dictionary defines wisdom as "The quality of having experience, knowledge, and good judgement; the quality of being wise."[13] Wisdom may imply a different way of thinking that is more than just the accumulation of information or facts. Many writers such as Eliot describe living in the "age of information" as not necessarily leading us to knowledge or wisdom. This critique can challenge us in examining our understanding of knowledge, raising important and complex questions.

---

11. *Etymology Online Dictionary, s.v.* "philosophy," https://www.etymonline.com/word/philosophy.

12. Annas, *The Morality of Happiness,* 3.

13. *Oxford Dictionaries, s.v.* "wisdom," http://www.oxforddictionaries.com/definition/english/wisdom.

Discussion questions

1. Does more information necessarily make us knowledgeable or wiser?
2. Do life experience and age always make people wiser?
3. Is it possible to confuse knowledge with wisdom?
4. How can someone know if they are wise?

Philosophers on wisdom

> Now it is thought to be the mark of a man of practical wisdom to be able to deliberate well about what is good and expedient for himself, not in some particular respect e.g. about what sorts of thing conduce to health or to strength, but about what sorts of thing conduce to the good life in general.[14]

Aristotle made a distinction between practical (*phronesis*) and intellectual (*Sophia*) wisdom. Knowledge of facts useful to living well is required for Aristotle's practical wisdom. Additionally, both knowledge of facts as well as knowing how to use these facts are what makes them practical. Aristotle thought that intellectual wisdom (*Sophia*) was superior to practical wisdom. Intellectual, or contemplative, wisdom was an important tool in exercising reason in thinking about our life. For Aristotle, it was useful in discerning *how* to live well and attain happiness. Intellectual wisdom allows us to reflect on what it means to be happy and live a good life. Aristotle argued that all actions should be aimed at the good life, which is a life lived well. Some of the components which make the good life, according to Aristotle, are pleasure, moral virtue, friendships, good health, sufficient wealth to survive, and a calm mind able to navigate and overcome negative emotions:

> Every person . . . who is in *training for wisdom* . . . chooses neither to commit injustice nor return it unto others . . . As their goal is a life of peace and serenity, they contemplate nature and everything found within her . . . Their bodies remain

---

14. Aristotle, *Nichomachean Ethics*, VI, 1140a–1140b.

> on earth, but they give wings to their souls, so that rising into the ether, they may observe the powers which dwell there, as is fitting for those who have truly become citizens of the world. Such people consider the whole world as their city, and its citizens are the companions of wisdom; they have received their civic rights from virtue . . . they train themselves to be indifferent to indifferent things; they are armed against both pleasures and desires, and, in short, they always strive to keep themselves above passions . . . they do not give in under the blows of fate . . . [15]

Philo of Alexandria (20 BCE—50 CE), inspired by the Stoic philosophers, writes that wisdom involves treating others justly as well as living in peace and serenity. The Stoics believed the person who is wise is able to live on earth with all its challenges, and also to transcend it. This is possible by seeing events from a broader perspective. The Stoics believed in fate, and when tragedies or misfortunate occurred, they encouraged being indifferent and detached. As we shall discuss further in chapter 5, a wise person is able to rise above their passions and negative emotions in order to achieve a tranquil mind. This equilibrium allows a person to subsequently deal calmly with all the challenges life presents. Contemporary French philosopher Pierre Hadot claims the Stoics advocated a way of life which transformed the individual. He describes the Stoics as advocating an approach to living that is part of spiritual exercise. Wisdom, he argues, is a way of life that results in inner peace, freedom, and an awareness of a "cosmic consciousness," or "broader perspective." Regarding the philosophy of the Stoics, Hadot states, "Wisdom, then, was a way of life which brought peace of mind (*ataraxia*), inner freedom (*autarkeia*) and a cosmic consciousness."[16]

1. Can you think of examples of practical and intellectual wisdom? Do you agree with these distinctions?
2. Does wisdom include the ability to understand and see things from a "broader perspective?" What do you think this means?

Modern conceptions of wisdom

Robert Nozick (1938–2002) described wisdom as a complex way of knowing that has practical application to daily living and allows us to make good

---

15. Philo, *On the Special Laws*, 2, 44–48 (emphasis in original).
16. Hadot, *Philosophy as a Way*, 265.

decisions. It can give us the necessary tools in gaining judgement and insight into the challenges of life related to personal goals, relationships, and other circumstances we encounter:

> Wisdom is not just one type of knowledge, but diverse. What a wise person needs to know and understand constitutes a varied list: the most important goals and values of life—the ultimate goal, if there is one; what means will reach these goals without too great a cost; what kinds of dangers threaten the achieving of these goals; how to recognize and avoid or minimize these dangers; what different types of human beings are like in their actions and motives (as this presents dangers or opportunities); what is not possible or feasible to achieve (or avoid); how to tell what is appropriate when; knowing when certain goals are sufficiently achieved; what limitations are unavoidable and how to accept them; how to improve oneself and one's relationships with others or society; knowing what the true and unapparent value of various things is; when to take a long-term view; knowing the variety and obduracy of facts, institutions, and human nature; understanding what one's real motives are; how to cope and deal with the major tragedies and dilemmas of life, and with the major good things too.[17]

Psychological understandings of wisdom

> Wisdom is one of those qualities that is difficult to define because it encompasses so much, but which people generally recognize when they encounter it. And it is encountered most obviously in the realm of decision-making. Some psychologists claim that wisdom involves an integration of knowledge, experience, and deep understanding that incorporates tolerance for the uncertainties of life as well as its ups and downs. There's an awareness of how things play out over time, and it confers a sense of balance. It can be acquired only through experience, but by itself experience does not automatically confer wisdom. Only now are researchers beginning to look

---

17. Nozick, *The Examined Life*, 269.

into the social, emotional, and cognitive processes that transmute experience into wisdom.

Wise people generally share an optimism that life's problems can be solved and experience a certain amount of calm in facing difficult decisions. Intelligence—if only anyone could figure out exactly what it is—may be necessary for wisdom, but it definitely isn't sufficient; an ability to see the big picture, a sense of proportion, and considerable introspection also contribute to its development.[18]

Discussion questions

1. What are the main components of wisdom described above?
2. Compare the approaches to wisdom discussed. What are the similarities and differences between the various perspectives?

Student Activity—Homework

Ask three to four people the following questions: What does it mean to be a wise person? Where do we learn wisdom? You may choose to interview a parent, guardian, grandparent, teacher, or friend. Share your responses in class.

Student activity—Research

1. Research wisdom from a religious or philosophical perspective. You may choose to focus on a particular religious or philosophical text. For example, the Bible or Stoic philosophy. Include the following:

    a. What are the features of wisdom described?
    b. What characterises a wise person?
    c. Is wisdom related to personal qualities, actions, or both?
    d. How is wisdom connected to moral acts?

---

18. "Wisdom," para. 1.

2. Study a sage (contemporary or historical person). This may be from a religious, philosophical, scientific, or artist context. Identify and discuss *why* you think the individual is wise. For example, you may study Socrates or the Dalai Lama.

Record your findings and present them to the class.

"THE UNEXAMINED LIFE IS NOT WORTH LIVING" —SOCRATES

I say that it is the greatest good for a man to discuss virtue every day and those other things about which you hear me conversing and testing myself and others, for the unexamined life is not worth living.[19]

The Greek philosopher Socrates stressed the importance of an examined life. He argued that what distinguishes humans from animals is their ability to think. He called himself a "midwife to the truth," viewing himself as someone who helped people give birth to ideas, metaphorically speaking. He did this by posing provocative questions in order to encourage people to think critically and reflectively about their ideas and assumptions. Socrates proposed a dialectic method which included the process of examining and cross-examining in order to arrive at truth, or to at least expose falsehood. This is known as the Socratic method, and in Hellenistic Greek is *elenchus*, meaning "inquiry" or "cross-examination." It is also referred to as the maieutic method.[20]

Socrates on wisdom

Socrates' questioning technique was aimed at prompting people to examine their opinions more closely. He sought to ask people on *what basis* they held their beliefs. Socrates observed that the majority of people in Athens believed things which they did not examine. People were like sheep, following the opinions of the majority without question. Socrates claimed he did not intend to impart knowledge, but rather to encourage people to gain clarity

19. Plato, "Apology," 38a.
20. "Socrates," *Internet Encyclopaedia of Philosophy*.

into the reasons that formed their beliefs and to examine them critically. He believed that thinking critically about opinions allowed a person to live a good life, one that could lead to wisdom and happiness. "[I] sought to persuade every man . . . that he must look to himself and seek virtue and wisdom."[21] Socrates claimed that all wisdom came from virtue.[22] As mentioned earlier, the ancient Greek philosophers considered the notion of virtue as a disposition which included the presence of morally right action, for the right reasons consistently, and in a reliable manner.[23] An ignorant person was one who lacked knowledge of virtue or morals and the ability to distinguish between good and evil. Socrates argued that an understanding of morals was essential to the attainment of wisdom, which he considered the highest form of knowledge.

Socrates observed that many in his society who claimed to be wise were not. For Socrates, wisdom was achieved by not only understanding virtue, but also the limitations of knowledge. Ultimately, Socrates was sentenced to death for corrupting the minds of the youth. We are able to read Socrates' ideas through the works of his student, Plato. The Socratic approach has influenced much of Western philosophy and culture, and his ideas have become foundational in fields of study as broad as education, law, and therapy.

21. Plato, "Apology," 1:418.
22. Ibid., 1:413.
23. Annas, *The Morality of Happiness*, 3.

Student activity: Video and podcast

Watch the video on Socrates, "Philosophy: A Guide to Happiness—Socrates on Self-Confidence."[24]

Also, listen to the podcast *Philosophy Now*, specifically "Socrates: Man and Myth,"[25] and answer the following:

1. Identify and discuss the main claims made by Socrates on the importance of thinking independently and examining life. Do you agree with these claims?
2. Write a response on one or more of the ideas you found to be interesting and challenging.

Student activity: Homework:

Ask three to four people the following question: Is the unexamined life not worth living?

You may choose to interview a parent, guardian, grandparent, teacher or a friend. Share your responses in class.

WHAT CAN RELIGION TEACH US?

---

24. https://www.youtube.com/watch?v=_gVyEOefhIQ
25. https://philosophynow.org/podcasts/Socrates_Man_and_Myth.

Student Activity: Definition

What is religion?

Write your own definition. Research one or two definitions of religion and summarise the main ideas.

We will be exploring further the nature of religion in the book; however, these extracts are for you to read in order to start you thinking about this topic. Contemporary American religious scholars John Haught and Timothy Beal define religion in the following ways below.

> Religion "shows up" in an especially clear way at those points where we experience the "limits" to our ordinary life and thought. It is at these limits that we begin to feel the presence of the unknown in an exceptional way. And it is at the limits of life and thought that we may locate with some precision how religion fits into the texture of human existence... Religion is the most explicit way in which human beings have expressed their cherishing of the unknown... What distinguishes religion from ordinary life and consciousness is its explicit openness to an other-than-ordinary dimension of reality for which we can probably find no better word than "mystery"... Rudolf Otto writes that religious people always and everywhere have felt a "numinous" (holy) presence of inexhaustible mystery lurking behind, beyond or in the depths of ordinary things, persons and events. He defines this intuited dimension of otherness as a *mysterium tremendum et fascinans*... Religion, then, may be understood here as a special discernment of and response to *mysterium*.[26]

> In what sense is religion a kind of *binding* (from the Latin, *religare*) a being bound to a web of principles, doctrines, certainties, and in what sense is it a *process of reading again*, as Cicero suggested (*relegere*, "to read over again [and again]"), a continuing engagement with texts, a way of articulating, by reading/writing, the most profound questions about life and death, identity and otherness? Is religion about asserting answers or crafting questions?[27]

26. Haught, *What is Religion?*, 158–59.
27. Beal, "Opening," 1.

Student activity

1. Look up the meanings of key words and phrases and write down their meanings.
2. Can you identify common themes and differences in the definitions above?
3. What words or phrases do you find interesting or puzzling?

John Haught and Timothy Beal point to religion as:

- responding to the limits of ordinary life and thought
- cherishing the unknown and mystery of life
- responding to the mystery of life
- "binding" to a set of principles, doctrines, or certainties
- crafting questions

Discussion questions

1. What do you think of the above descriptions of religion by Haught and Beal?
2. Can you think of examples for any of the above points?
3. Explain the following claim, ". . . And it is in the limits of life and thought that we may locate with some precision how religion fits into the texture of human existence . . ."
4. What is the definition of "holy"?
5. How is religion about "crafting questions?"
6. How does wonder relate to the "unknown and mystery of life?"

What can we learn from religion?

Religious faith has many manifestations. There are people of sincere piety for whom the religious life is a source of deep and powerful meaning. For them and for others, a spiritual response to the beauty of the world, the vastness of the universe, and the love that can bind one human heart to another feels as natural and necessary as breathing. Some of the art and music has been inspired by faith counts amongst the loveliest and most moving expressions of human creativity. It is indeed impossible to understand either history or art without an understanding of what people believed, feared, and hoped through their religious conceptions of the world and human destiny. Religion is a pervasive fact of history and has to be addressed as such.[28]

Contemporary English philosopher A.C. Grayling claims that religion has provided deep meaning, inspiring creative and artistic expression throughout human history. Professor of Religious Studies June O'Connor states that religion has had, and still remains, an enormous influence in our culture through the arts, literature, history, politics, science, economics, and psychology:

> ... I believe that it's simply impossible to be a well-educated person without learning about how religion has, throughout history, consequentially shaped the human story in almost every culture. And I believe that the sacred texts of all the great religions should be introduced to students with reverence and intellectual insight. Students simply cannot know art without reflecting on the influences of religion—from the Hindu cave paintings to Buddhist art to the temples of ancient Greece to Michelangelo to the great cathedrals of the Middle Ages that so inspired Henry Adams and Marc Chagall. They cannot know literature without understanding how religion has shaped the world's great writers, from Homer and Euripides of ancient Greece to the writers of our day, from T. S. Eliot to John Updike to I. B. Singer. Students cannot understand music without grasping the power of religion that inspired performers and composers from Hildegard, the great twelfth-century nun/composer, to Leonard Bernstein. Virtually every discipline has been influenced by religion. In psychology, we have William James' landmark study, *The Varieties of Religious Experience*, and in sociology we have Max Weber's classic work, *The Protestant Ethic and the Spirit of Capitalism*. And, of course, there's no conceivable way for students to understand

---

28. Grayling, *The God Argument*, 1.

the conflicts in the Middle East or Northern Ireland, or our own history here in the United States, without understanding the consequential role of religion.[29]

Student Activity: Research

1. According to Grayling and O'Connor, list the areas of knowledge and inquiry in which religion has made a significant impact.
2. Select and research one of the examples of religious influence and its contribution to an area of knowledge listed above and research. For example, you may focus on Max Weber's religious influences on economics, Marc Chagall's on art, or T. S. Eliot's on literature. Present your research findings to the class.

If the above scholars are correct, religion can inspire us to wonder. It can engage us in the mysteries of the universe and propel us to contemplate them. Religious writers can prompt us to view the world as sacred and imbued with meaning. While atheists and humanists may claim we can appreciate the world as meaningful without religion—a valid position—religious thought for centuries has nevertheless provided an intellectual, cultural, and artistic framework of personal meaning for millions. As we shall explore in chapter 2, this framework is vast, encompassing centuries of thinking from across the globe.

There are many scholars, as we shall explore in the next chapter, that have put forward rational justifications in support of religious faith. These include Arabic scholars such as Avicenna (970–1037) and Christian scholar Thomas Aquinas (1224–1274). Modern thinkers such as philosopher Richard Swinburne propose an inductive argument for the existence of God. Swinburne argues that, based on current evidence regarding how the universe works, there is a high probability of God's existence. There are others who claim that religious faith is not irrational, but beyond reason. Some have proposed that religious faith is known *intuitively*. Theologian Paul Tillich proposes that God is the existential core of a person's being, arguing in favour of religious experience as a justification for religious claims.

---

29. Boyer, "Why Study Religion?," para. 27.

STUDENT REFLECTIONS

WHAT ARE YOU NOW WONDERING ABOUT?

- What ideas or questions are you wondering about as a result of these lessons?
- Have these lessons made you think differently? Explain.
- What have you found challenging, provocative, or intriguing?

WHAT DOES IT MEAN TO KNOW?

In philosophy, the study of knowledge is called epistemology. The Greek word *episteme* means "to know."[30] Epistemological issues have been debated for centuries by philosophers. Beliefs are deemed true if they represent reality. However, can we be sure that our beliefs are correct in depicting things *as they are*? How much can we rely on other people's opinions and conclusions? What about our own senses, what we hear and see? Is our own reasoning sufficient? You may respond by saying that a belief is true if there is solid evidence or reasoning to support it. Although this is a legitimate response, supporting claims with evidence is not as easy as it seems; philosophers frequently have pointed out some complexities and problems.

Throughout philosophy's history of epistemology, some philosophers thought knowledge was derived from what we experience through our senses, such as sight and touch—known as the basis of empirical knowledge—while others believed that our mind, or reason, was the source of knowledge, known as rationalism. German philosopher Immanuel Kant (1724–1804) believed that knowledge was derived from both our senses and reason. Some philosophers such as Bertrand Russell understood the importance of intuition for our understanding of basic concepts that underpin our knowledge.

STUDENT ACTIVITY—DISCUSSION QUESTIONS

Respond in words or illustrations.

1. What does the phrase "to know" mean?

---

30. *Oxford Dictionaries*, s.v. "epistemology." http://www.oxforddictionaries.com/definition/english/epistemology.

2. When you think of the word "knowledge," what image or word comes to mind?

3. Can a robot know or think?

4. In what ways does an animal know? Is it the same or different for a human?

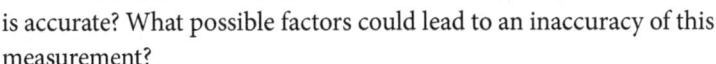

5. What is the difference between opinion and knowledge?

6. French philosopher and mathematician Rene Descartes (1596–1650) challenges us with the following questions:

    • Can we trust what we see, hear, and touch?

    • How do you know for certain what you see in front of you is real? What tells you this?

    • How can you be sure that right now you are not dreaming? What tells you this?[31]

7. English philosopher David Hume (1711–1776) poses the question: Does the future necessarily resemble the past?[32] What do you think? Can we be certain that the sun will rise tomorrow? How do we know this?

8. What constitutes a fact? For example, to what extent can we be sure that the Nile river is 6,690km long?[33] How can we be sure that this measurement is accurate? What possible factors could lead to an inaccuracy of this measurement?

9. What then do we mean by the term "evidence?"

---

31. Descartes, *Meditations on First Philosophy*, 23.
32. Hume, *An Enquiry Concerning Human Understanding*, 17–18.
33. http://www.infoplease.com/ipa/A0001779.html.

The infinite regress argument

A fact is defined by the Oxford English Dictionary as "A thing that is known or proved to be true."[34] For a belief to be justified, there needs to exist evidence based on good reason. However, evidence also must be believed, requiring more evidence to support the first set of evidence, and so on infinitely with no foundational basis. This infinite regress argument shows the difficulty in gaining a solid basis in our beliefs. When exploring the connections between our beliefs and the reasons that support them, we can see an ongoing endless chain of contingency. In the earlier example of the Nile river, if we believe that it is 6,690km long, we must also believe that the people taking these measurements had reliable instruments and were in a stable mental and physical condition to record the measurements accurately. Additionally, what if there was a bias of some kind which affected their results? Perhaps one of the surveyors had a thousand-dollar bet with another that the Nile was not longer than 6,700km; if so, the distance of 6,690km would appear suspect. This questioning of alleged facts, if applied to every other set of data for Earth's topography, can throw into disarray what anyone knows about our planet, the chain continuing infinitely back in time with no solid and irrefutable evidence to justify belief of anything. This is the infinite regress argument. Do we therefore doubt everything in life, or dismiss this argument as a nonsensical waste of time? As we shall see further on, a number of thinkers have responded to the infinite regress argument.[35]

SKEPTICISM

> You must realize that it is not our intention to assert that standards of truth are unreal (that would be dogmatic); rather, since the Dogmatists seem plausibly to have established that there is a standard of truth, we have set up plausible-seeming arguments in opposition to them, affirming neither that they are true nor that they are more plausible than those on the contrary side, but concluding to suspension of judgement because of the apparently equal plausibility of these arguments and those produced by the Dogmatists. (*PH* II 79; cf. *M* VII 444)[36]

---

34. *Oxford Dictionaries*, s.v. "fact." http://www.oxforddictionaries.com/definition/english/fact.

35. For further research on epistemic or infinite regress see McCain, "Epistemic Regression Problem."

36. Morison, "Sextus Empiricus," sect. 4.1, para. 4.

To what extent can we be sure of anything?

The problems with infinite regress led to skepticism. Sextus Empiricus (AD 160–210) was a philosopher who adopted skepticism and claimed that due to the infinite regress problem, knowledge was ultimately unattainable, and justification not possible. Sextus challenged those who had a dogmatic approach to knowledge, claiming to have attained the truth. He argued that for every claim made, there can also be evidence put forward to refute it, forming an ongoing chain of claims and counterclaims.

Some tenets of skeptical arguments include the following:

- On what grounds can we be sure we exist?
- How can we be certain our beliefs are true, as they are based on other assumptions and beliefs of which we can never be totally certain?
- Beliefs cannot be certain because evidence and justification for them are inadequate.
- We cannot know anything for certain; therefore, we cannot know anything.

Not all philosophers have adopted the form of skepticism outlined above—there are moderate skeptics who acknowledge the difficulty in attaining certainty, but do not conclud that it is impossible to attain knowledge. Moderate skeptics such as Socrates claimed that knowledge is possible despite the difficulties and complexities in justifying claims. Skepticism within philosophy is understood as a general approach encompassing an attitude of doubt and investigation. Skepticism in it various forms has existed within philosophy throughout its history. In the ancient world, schools advocating skepticism were known as the Academic and Pyrrhonian, beginning approximately in the third century BCE.

Relativism

Relativism is also advocated by Protagoras (490–420 BCE) and Montaigne (1533–1592). Protagoras stated, "Man is the measure of all things," meaning knowledge is understood as relative to each person. As will be discussed further in chapter 4 on ethics, relativism is the belief that there are no absolute truths, only different points of view. Truth, according to this approach, is contextual; it depends on culture, history, and perspectives. Knowledge is understood as different for everyone and largely determined by worldviews or structures of the mind and language.[37] Moderate forms of relativism claim that something can be true in one culture or worldview and yet unknowable within another.[38] Relativists argue that cultures have different outlooks which can never be understood within a different context.[39] However, there are those like Plato (whom will be discussed further on) that disagree with the position of relativism, arguing there are universal components of human perception and language.

For further research on skepticism and relativism, the following links may be useful:

1. BBC—In Our Time: Scepticism[40]
2. Wi-Phi, Open Access Philosophy, PHILOSOPHY—Epistemology: The Problem of Skepticism[41]
3. BBC—In Our Time: Relativism[42]

Discussion questions

1. Do you agree/disagree with the main ideas of skeptical arguments? Give your reasons.
2. What would be the benefits of adopting a skeptical approach to knowledge?
3. Can you identify any counterarguments?
4. Is the position of relativism plausible? What are its strengths and limitations?

Extension student activity—
Research one or all of the following:

1. Contemporary American philosopher Edmund Gettier proposed a response to the infinite regress problem; research and summarize his main ideas. This link may be a place to start: Wi-Phi, Open Access

---

37. McInerney, *Introduction to Philosophy*, 63.
38. Ibid.
39. Ibid.
40. Bragg, "BBC Radio 4—In Our Time," podcast, *Scepticism*, 2016, http://www.bbc.co.uk/programmes/b01kblc3.
   41. http://www.wi-phi.com/video/problem-skepticism.
   42. https://www.bbc.co.uk/programmes/p003hyc8.

Philosophy, PHILOSOPHY—Epistemology: Analyzing Knowledge #1 (The Gettier Problem) [HD][43]

2. What are some differences between moderate and other forms of skepticism?

3. Research a philosopher who advocated skepticism or relativism. Some examples include the Sophists (i.e. Protagoras), Zhuang Zhou (369-286 BCE), Pyrrho (361-270 BCE), Socrates, Arcesilaus (316-240 BCE), Carnedeas (214-129 BCE), Cicero (106-43 BCE), Sextus Empiricus (AD 160-210), Montaigne, Richard Rorty (1931-2007) and Jacques Derrida (1930-2004).

Summarise their main ideas and write an appraisal of their work. You may present your findings to the class.

How did Rene Descartes dispute the skeptical argument?

Descartes' Meditation II: Of the Nature of the Human Mind; and That It Is More Easily Known Than the Body.

> I suppose, then, that all the things that I see are false; I persuade myself that nothing has ever existed of all that my fallacious memory represents to me. I consider that I possess no senses; I imagine that body, figure, extension, movement and place are but the fictions of my mind. What, then, can be esteemed as true? Perhaps nothing at all, unless that there is nothing in the world that is certain. But how can I know there is not something different from those things that I have just considered, of which one cannot have the slightest doubt? Is there not some God, or some other being by whatever name we call it, who puts these reflections into my mind? That is not necessary, for is it not possible that I am capable of producing them myself? I myself, am I not at least something? But I have

43. http://www.wi-phi.com/video/analyzing-knowledge-part-1-gettier-problem.

already denied that I had senses and body. Yet I hesitate, for what follows from that? Am I so dependent on body and senses that I cannot exist without these? But I was persuaded that there was nothing in all the world, that there was no heaven, no earth, that there were no minds, nor any bodies: was I not then likewise persuaded that I did not exist? Not at all; of a surety I myself did exist since I persuaded myself of something [or merely because I thought of something]. But there is some deceiver or other, very powerful and very cunning, whoever employs his ingenuity in deceiving me. Then without doubt I exist also if he deceives me, and let him deceive me as much as he will, he can never cause me to be nothing so long as I think that I am something. So that after having reflected well and carefully examined all things, we must come to the definite conclusion that this proposition: I am, I exist, is necessarily true each time that I pronounce it, or that I mentally conceive it.[44]

Student activity—Excerpt and Video

Read the extract above from *Meditations II* and listen to this link on Descartes (Alain de Botton, *The School of Life—Descartes*[45]). Summarise his main ideas.

Rene Descartes, like the skeptics, doubted everything. He applied the method of doubt and questioned all his assumptions. Descartes ultimately doubted whether he could be certain he existed. He questioned the reliability of his senses to tell him the truth and thought it could be possible that he was merely in a dream. Unlike the skeptics, who claimed that our inability to be certain meant we cannot know anything, Descartes eventually came to the realization that our reason and thinking was a justification for knowledge and certainty. He concluded that there was something irrefutably doing the doubting, and that something he was certain of was *his thinking*. Descartes claimed what he was certain of was that his *thoughts existed*—famously stating, "I think, therefore I am."[46]

---

44. Descartes, *Meditations on First Philosophy*, 63.
45. https://www.youtube.com/watch?v=CAjWUrwvxs4.
46. Descartes, *Meditations on First Philosophy*, 63.

Discussion questions

1. What are the main claims presented by Descartes?
2. Can our senses deceive us as Descartes describes above?
3. Does the existence of thoughts really "prove that we exist?" Explain.
4. How has Descartes' rationalism influenced our approach to knowledge today? Give examples.
5. What are some limitations to his claims?

THINKING "OUTSIDE THE BOX"— PLATO'S *ALLEGORY OF THE CAVE*

What do you think the phrase "to think outside the box" means?

To think outside the box can be understood, broadly speaking, as an analogy meaning to question our assumptions. It could imply asking questions and going beyond what is in the box, namely our assumptions and beliefs. Discerning our assumptions—that is, what is in the box—is the first important step in this process. Logically, we cannot go beyond the ideas and perspectives within the box unless we understand what is in it, so to speak. This task in thinking requires much more than lip service, but a profound questioning of all that we take for granted and assume to be true and real. If we are serious about this task, the box which is familiar to us must be unpacked, layer by layer, so that we can think outside it. This task is not easy, as philosophers have testified, requiring time, deep thinking, and courage, as exemplified in the life of Socrates.

Discussion questions

Let's for a moment ponder this question of what is in the box. What are some current assumptions or beliefs we have, personally or collectively, that we claim to be true which, if we bring to the light or reason and examine closely, may be found to be false or only partially true?

Some examples include:

1. "If I don't pass my exams I will be considered not intelligent and will be a failure in life."
2. Or collective beliefs such as:
   - Happiness is based only on what is pleasurable or feels good for me.
   - Technological devices have increased our ability to think critically.
   - The only way to solve crime is to lock people in prisons.

Philosopher of science Thomas Kuhn (1922–1996) points out that our emotions can hinder us from questioning our assumptions and seeking new ways of thinking outside the box.[47] He emphasizes the importance of acknowledging the emotional reactions we attach to ideas, and what stops us from being open to new ways of thinking.

If we were to identify some commonly held assumptions today, they might include science as the only way to gain truth or that the progress of technology is the proper way forward for society. Do you agree that these are beliefs we currently hold and assume to be true? Are there examples that show how these claims might not be true?

What is crucial in our thinking are the skills to discern what the underlying assumptions actually are. If the discernment above is correct, that these are pervasive assumptions about science and technology, then we must examine them intelligently. To do otherwise would mean to negate the process of thinking outside the box and to remain within the box's ideologies and beliefs. It can be argued that only when we are able to examine our assumptions and beliefs can we truly say we are thinking critically. This process of examining our assumptions or thinking outside the box, as we shall see further on, can be likened to Plato's *Allegory of the Cave*—of existing in the dark within our illusions, trapped and unable to see the light of reason.

Student activity—Video

You may be familiar with the film *The Matrix* based, in part, on Plato's Cave. Watch the scene concerning the red pill and the blue pill.[48] Which pill would you take, and why?

---

47. Kuhn, *Structure of Scientific Revolutions*.
48. https://www.youtube.com/watch?v=ytftrd6rxps.

Illusion or reality? Plato's Cave

STUDENT ACTIVITY—EXCERPT

Read the following allegory and summarize the main points:

BOOK VII OF THE REPUBLIC—THE *ALLEGORY OF THE CAVE*

[Socrates is speaking with **Glaucon**]

[Socrates:] And now, I said, let me show in a figure how far our nature is enlightened or unenlightened:—Behold! human beings living in a underground den, which has a mouth open towards the light and reaching all along the den; here they have been from their childhood, and have their legs and necks chained so that they cannot move, and can only see before them, being prevented by the chains from turning round their heads. Above and behind them a fire is blazing at a distance, and between the fire and the prisoners there is a raised way; and you will see, if you look, a low wall built along the way, like the screen which marionette players have in front of them, over which they show the puppets.

[Glaucon:] I see.

And do you see, I said, men passing along the wall carrying all sorts of vessels, and statues and figures of animals made of wood and stone and various materials, which appear over the wall? Some of them are talking, others silent.

You have shown me a strange image, and they are strange prisoners.

Like ourselves, I replied; and they see only their own shadows, or the shadows of one another, which the fire throws on the opposite wall of the cave?

True, he said; how could they see anything but the shadows if they were never allowed to move their heads?

And of the objects which are being carried in like manner they would only see the shadows?

Yes, he said.

And if they were able to converse with one another, would they not suppose that they were naming what was actually before them?

Very true.

And suppose further that the prison had an echo which came from the other side, would they not be sure to fancy when one of the passers-by spoke that the voice which they heard came from the passing shadow?

No question, he replied.

To them, I said, the truth would be literally nothing but the shadows of the images.

That is certain.

And now look again, and see what will naturally follow if the prisoners are released and disabused of their error. At first, when any of them is liberated and compelled suddenly to stand up and turn his neck round and walk and look towards the light, he will suffer sharp pains; the glare will distress him, and he will be unable to see the realities of which in his former state he had seen the shadows; and then conceive someone saying to him, that what he saw before was an illusion, but that now, when he is approaching nearer to being and his eye is turned towards more real existence, he has a clearer vision—what will be his reply? And you may further imagine that his instructor is pointing to the objects as they pass and requiring him to name them—will he not be perplexed? Will he not fancy that the shadows which he formerly saw are truer than the objects which are now shown to him?

Far truer.

And if he is compelled to look straight at the light, will he not have a pain in his eyes which will make him turn away to take and take in the objects of vision which he can see, and which he will conceive to be in reality clearer than the things which are now being shown to him?

True, he said.

And suppose once more, that he is reluctantly dragged up a steep and rugged ascent, and held fast until he's forced into the presence of the sun himself, is he not likely to be pained and irritated? When he approaches the light his eyes will be dazzled, and he will not be able to see anything at all of what are now called realities.

Not all in a moment, he said.

He will require to grow accustomed to the sight of the upper world. And first he will see the shadows best, next the reflections of men and other objects in the water, and then the objects themselves; then he will gaze upon the light of the moon and the stars and the spangled heaven; and he will see the sky and the stars by night better than the sun or the light of the sun by day?

Certainly.

Last of all he will be able to see the sun, and not mere reflections of him in the water, but he will see him in his own proper place, and not in another; and he will contemplate him as he is.

Certainly.

He will then proceed to argue that this is he who gives the season and the years, and is the guardian of all that is in the visible world, and in a certain way the cause of all things which he and his fellows have been accustomed to behold?

Clearly, he said, he would first see the sun and then reason about him.

And when he remembered his old habitation, and the wisdom of the den and his fellow-prisoners, do you not suppose that he would felicitate himself on the change, and pity them?

Certainly, he would.

And if they were in the habit of conferring honours among themselves on those who were quickest to observe the passing shadows and to remark which of them went before, and which followed after, and which were together; and who were therefore best able to draw conclusions as to the future, do you think that he would care for such honours and glories, or envy the possessors of them? Would he not say with Homer,

Better to be the poor servant of a poor master, and to endure anything, rather than think as they do and live after their manner?

Yes, he said, I think that he would rather suffer anything than entertain these false notions and live in this miserable manner.

Imagine once more, I said, such a one coming suddenly out of the sun to be replaced in his old situation; would he not be certain to have his eyes full of darkness?

To be sure, he said.

And if there were a contest, and he had to compete in measuring the shadows with the prisoners who had never moved out of the den, while his sight was still weak, and before his eyes had become steady (and the time which would be needed to acquire this new habit of sight might be very considerable) would he not be ridiculous? Men would say of him that up he went and down he came without his eyes; and that it was better not even to think of ascending; and if any one tried to loose another and lead him up to the light, let them only catch the offender, and they would put him to death.

No question, he said.

This entire allegory, I said, you may now append, dear Glaucon, to the previous argument; the prison-house is the world of sight, the light of the fire is the sun, and you will not misapprehend me if you interpret the journey upwards to be the ascent of the soul into the intellectual world according to my poor belief, which, at your desire, I have expressed whether rightly or wrongly God knows. But, whether true or false, my opinion is that in the world of knowledge the idea of good appears last of all, and is seen only with an effort; and, when seen, is also inferred to be the universal author of all things beautiful and right, parent of light and of the lord of light in this visible world, and the immediate source of reason and truth in the intellectual; and that this is the power upon which he who would act rationally, either in public or private life must have his eye fixed.[49]

Student activity—Video

Watch the following video from TED Talks and summarise the main ideas: "Plato's *Allegory of the Cave*—Alex Gendler."[50]

From ignorance towards "true" understanding

Plato, a student of Socrates, thought that knowing was more than just conforming to popular opinion, which could be fraught with illusions, but rather truths based on reason and true knowledge. As illustrated in the allegory, humans are attached to their views of the world, but when examined closely, these ideas turn out to be mere illusions. Plato argued that the use of reason is an important tool in deciphering whether our assumptions are true or illusory. He proposed that those who were enlightened were to instruct the prisoners still in the cave. In many of his dialogues, Socrates thought that the prisoners had to think for themselves. Plato's *Allegory of the Cave* describes steps from opinions to true knowledge or, put another way, from ignorance to enlightenment.

In *The Republic*, Plato argued that truth is not found in the material world through our senses, but rather discovered in the ideas within our minds. What Plato highlights in this allegory is that there are truths beyond the mere level of physical appearances—truths he termed as the Ideal Forms, (see the discussion on Plato in chapter 5). Plato's *Allegory of the Cave* has been used widely by writers and artists as a metaphor in exploring questions about truth.

---

49. Plato, *Republic*, Book VII, para. 1–92 (emphasis added).
50. https://www.youtube.com/watch?v=1RWOpQXTltA.

EPISTEMOLOGY

Student activity — Reflections

a. Write or draw the steps that Plato describes above. How does someone proceed from ignorance to enlightenment, or from opinions to true knowledge?

b. Write your own interpretation of the *Allegory of the Cave*. Give a modern-day example of proceeding from illusions to enlightenment or true understanding.

Discussion questions

1. To what extent is Plato's allegory useful in exploring questions about truth?
2. Where do we ask questions about truth today? Give examples.
3. Should education teach students to search for truth? How?
4. When you think of the term "reason," what comes to mind? How do you define reason?
5. Is reason the same or different to the terms "reflection," "thinking," "logic," "dialectic," or "cognition?"

RATIONALISM VS EMPIRICISM

Justified true belief

What are some of the ways we can justify, or give reasons for, our beliefs and respond to the skeptical argument? Socrates, in the *Theaetetus*, addressed the claim that "knowledge is true belief."[51] What does this mean? What are some of the problems in justifying our beliefs?

You may have an understanding that to believe something you must show *good reasons* as to why you think it is true. For example, if you believe that Siberia is extremely cold, you would need to have evidence, perhaps from a reliable textbook or reputable website. Maybe you have actually experienced very cold weather in Siberia firsthand. While you can assert that the weather in Siberia is extremely cold, you cannot be *totally certain*, as David Hume points out, that these conditions will not change in the future

---

51. Chappell, "Plato on Knowledge," para. 9.

(this is discussed further in the science section). Philosophers differ on the *level of certainty* required for justification. Descartes claimed that we need total certainty, while others like John Locke (1632–1704) have argued that *strong evidence* is required as a justification for beliefs, but *not total certainty*.[52]

Some philosophers, like Aristotle, attacked the skeptics by arguing that not all claims need to connect to other reasons, or propositions; neither do they need to be proven and instead are *self-evident*. Some knowledge, he claimed, must be independent of demonstration.[53] Aristotle argued that all knowledge to some extent must rest on *first principles*. This view is known as foundationalism:

> "... not all knowledge is demonstrative" (i.e., not all knowledge is based on an argument from other things known), and that some knowledge must be "independent of demonstration."[54]

Is knowledge gained by reason or through our senses?

As alluded to earlier, rationalism is the view that reason is the source of all knowledge. The alternative perspective is empiricism, which claims that knowledge is derived solely from our sense experiences.[55] This is an ancient debate which has its origins with the ancient Greek thinkers.

---

52. Locke, in McInerney, *Introduction to Philosophy*, 43.
53. Aristotle, *Posterior Analytics*, I.3,2.
54. Ibid., I.3.
55. Markie, "Rationalism vs. Empiricism."

Raphael's School of Athens. Raphael depicts Aristotle's hands pointing to the physical dimensions of the earth and implying the importance of sense experiences, Plato points upward to the eternal ideas of the Forms.

Plato, in some of his dialogues, adopted a rationalist view and believed that reason was universal and objective. In *The Republic*, he claimed that this universalism is found in the unchanging, eternal, and perfect Forms mentioned in the allegory. Knowledge is essentially innate, and we are able *to know* or understand these objective realities by drawing them out through the use of reasoning. Continental rationalists Descartes, Baruch Spinoza (1632–1677) and Gottfried Leibniz (1646–1716) further developed Plato's ideas. These philosophers claimed that certainty in knowledge is possible from the application of deductive reasoning, allowing principal truths to become self-evident:[56]

> The senses, although they are necessary for all our actual knowledge, are not sufficient to give us the whole of it, since the senses never give anything but instances, that is to say particular or individual truths. Now all the instances which confirm a general truth, however numerous they may be, are

56. McInerney, *Introduction to Philosophy*, 43–45.

not sufficient to establish the universal necessity of this same truth, for it does not follow that what happened before will happen in the same way again.... From which it appears that necessary truths, such as we find in pure mathematics, and particularly in arithmetics and geometry, must have principles whose proof does not depend on instances, nor consequently on the testimony of the senses, although without the senses it would never have occurred to us to think of them...[57]

Aristotle took the empirical view, claiming that our understanding of the world has its origins through our observations derived through our senses. We are born into the world with a *blank slate* and through our sense experiences can attain knowledge. British empiricist John Locke (1632-1704), David Hume (1711-1776), and George Berkeley (1685-1753) further developed this concept, and modern scientific knowledge is predominately derived from an empirical approach.

Student activity—Questions

Read the following quotes and answer the questions below:

> The mind being every day informed, by the senses, of the alteration of those simple ideas, it observes in things without; and taking notice how one comes to an end, and ceases to be, and another begins to exist which was not before; reflecting also on what passes within itself, and observing a constant change of its ideas, sometimes by the impression of outward objects on the senses, and sometimes by the determination of its own choice; and concluding from what it has so constantly observed to have been, that the like changes will for the future be made in the same things, by like agents, and by the like ways, considers in one thing the possibility of having any of its simple ideas changed, and in another the possibility of making that change; and so comes by that idea which we call power.[58]

> What is perhaps the most interesting form of the debate occurs when we take the relevant subject to be truths about the external world, the world beyond our own minds. A full-fledged

---

57. Leibniz, *New Essays on Human Understanding*, 150-51.
58. Locke, *An Essay Concerning Human Understanding*, 219-20.

rationalist with regard to our knowledge of the external world holds that some external world truths can and must be known *a priori*, that some of the ideas required for that knowledge are and must be innate, and that this knowledge is superior to any that experience could ever provide. The full-fledged empiricist about our knowledge of the external world replies that, when it comes to the nature of the world beyond our own minds, experience is our sole source of information. Reason might inform us of the relations among our ideas, but those ideas themselves can only be gained, and any truths about the external reality they represent can only be known, on the basis of sense experience.[59]

Rationalism and empiricism, so relativized, need not conflict. We can be rationalists in mathematics or a particular area of mathematics and empiricists in all or some of the physical sciences. Rationalism and empiricism only conflict when formulated to cover the same subject. Then the debate, Rationalism vs. Empiricism, is joined.[60]

Student questions

1. Explain the differences between how a rationalist and empiricist approach their understanding of the external world beyond the mind.
2. What does the following mean: "Rationalism and empiricism only conflict when formulated to cover the same subject?"

This epistemological debate between empiricism and rationalism as a source of knowledge has also extended into metaphysical arguments. The topic of metaphysics concerns itself with abstract concepts beyond the physical world, such as what time is and the creation of the universe. These ideas will be important for our discussions in chapter 2, when we explore some of the arguments for the existence of God. Rationalists such as Descartes have presented metaphysical theories which claim that God is known only by reason.[61] Empiricists like Hume claimed that these concepts of God's existence are just speculation and that trying to describe a reality

---

59. Markie, "Rationalism vs. Empiricism," 8–9.
60. Ibid.
61. Descartes, *Meditations on First Philosophy*.

beyond our sense experience is not sufficient justification for God. German philosopher Immanuel Kant argued that metaphysics, by definition, cannot rely on empiricism for justification, for its very nature is not physical but metaphysical, and therefore must be beyond experience:

> The very concept of metaphysics ensures that the sources of metaphysics can't be empirical. If something could be known through the senses, that would automatically show that it doesn't belong to metaphysics; that's an upshot of the meaning of the word "metaphysics." Its basic principles can never be taken from experience, nor can its basic concepts; for it is not to be physical but metaphysical knowledge, so it must be beyond experience.[62]

Other sources of knowledge:
Language, intuition, emotion, and imagination

Language: Ludwig Wittgenstein (1889–1951) claimed that language was important in conveying knowledge. He argued that language provided the parameters with which we understand the world.[63]

Intuition, Emotion, Imagination: Many existential philosophers such as Karl Jaspers (1883–1969) claimed that reason is limited in gaining knowledge and emphasized the importance of intuition, emotions, and imagination.

Faith: Theologians, mystics, and religious writers such as Gabriel Marcel (1889–1973) claimed that faith is a way through which we attain knowledge.

These epistemological tools will be further explored, and despite their limitations still provide means in which we can attain knowledge and understanding. These ways of knowing give rebuttal and response to the skeptical argument which claims that knowledge is not possible.

---

62. Kant, *Prolegomena to Any Future Metaphysics*, Preamble, I, 7.
63. Wittgenstein, *Tractatus Logico-Philosophicus*.

THREE THEORIES OF TRUTH

In epistemology, there are three categories applied to how knowledge is constructed, known as the Three Theories of Truth.

1. Correspondence
2. Coherence
3. Pragmatic

Read the outline of these categories and answer the questions below.

Correspondence Truth

Statements are true if they correspond to fact. True statements must correspond to something knowable in the world. For example, the statement "Milk chocolate is dark brown" is only true if, and only if, milk chocolate is actually dark brown.

> A belief is true when there is a corresponding fact and it is false when there is no corresponding fact.[64]

Coherence Truth

A statement is true if it fits into our overall belief systems. For example, if someone states that they saw "a fairy in the room who told them to dance," we would generally assess this claim's validity on the grounds that it fits into other beliefs. These may include the belief in fairies, as well as the belief in supernatural powers. Hence, we can reject or accept claims if they do not cohere, or fit, with the rest of our other beliefs.

> Subjective confidence in a judgment is not a reasonable evaluation of the probability that this judgment is correct. Confidence is a feeling, which reflects the coherence of the information and the cognitive ease of processing it. It is wise to take admissions of uncertainty seriously, but declarations of high confidence mainly tell you that an individual has contrasted a coherent story in his mind, not necessarily that the story is true.[65]

---

64. Russell, *Unpopular Essays*, 71.
65. Kahneman, *Thinking, Fast and Slow*, 212.

Discuss the preceding claim. Do you agree? Explain.

Pragmatic Truth

A claim is true if it works in practice. Likewise, a proposition is true if it is useful. Philosopher and psychologist William James (1842–1910) argued that an idea is true so long as the belief is useful to our lives. For example, if the hypothesis of God works satisfactorily, broadly speaking, it must then be *true*. Therefore, the importance of objective truth is replaced by usefulness.[66]

Can you think of examples in which these theories apply to different disciplines? What are some of their advantages and disadvantages?

STUDENT REFLECTIONS

WHAT ARE YOU NOW WONDERING ABOUT?

- What ideas or questions are you wondering about as a result of these lessons?
- Have these lessons made you think differently? Explain.
- What have you found challenging, provocative, or intriguing?

CRITICAL THINKING

With the emergence of social media, we have seen the rise of true, as well as fabricated, information. Bold claims can emerge and quickly gather momentum, only to be revealed as falsehoods made by dubious sources, while the impacts of those false claims often cannot be undone. Many have observed that modern society has neglected open and transparent discussion about important issues, calling it the era of "post-truth." In 2016, the Oxford Dictionary Word of the Year was "post-truth," defined as "relating to or denoting circumstances in which objective facts are less influential in shaping public opinion than appeals to emotion and personal belief."[67] If these observations are correct, then the need to discern fact from opinion is

---

66. James, *Varieties of Religious Experience*, 397–98.
67. "Word of the Year 2016 Is . . ." para. 1.

just as important as it was during Plato's era. How do we discern truth from falsehood? This task necessitates a well-developed ability to *think critically*. The skills of critical thinking use reason as tools that can help in examining false claims, identifying weak arguments, and discerning facts from opinions.

Activity: Test your thinking skills

Fact or opinion

State whether the following statements are facts or opinions. Discuss in groups.

1. Ice cream is better than chips
2. World War 1 started in 1914
3. Love is stronger than hate
4. Lisbon is the capital of Portugal
5. Smoking is bad for your health
6. Evolutionary theory is reliable knowledge
7. We always learn from the mistakes of history
8. London is cold in the winter
9. Intelligence is based on a person's ability to recall information and facts
10. The use of herbal and natural remedies for illness is ineffective

What are the differences between fact and opinion?

Write responses to the statements below. You will need to explain your reasons and some may require research:

1. Soccer and tennis both use balls
2. Democracy is preferred over dictatorship
3. It is wrong to hit children
4. Rome is the capital city of Italy
5. Racism is based on fear, false stereotypes and assumptions
6. The Black Death originated in Europe

7. Julian Assange and Edward Snowden are villains
8. Scientific knowledge is based on facts
9. In a democratic country, competing for resources and looking after individual self-interests leads to a happy society
10. People in Australia are more likely to die from a bee sting than a terrorist attack
11. The *UN Declaration of Human Rights* states that all countries are required to provide protection to asylum seekers fleeing from persecution, and therefore they are not *illegal* under international law
12. Eating a protein-rich diet is good for your health
13. All laws are moral
14. The people who live in Amsterdam are very friendly
15. The media presents facts

REFLECTION QUESTIONS:

- Why do you think it is sometimes difficult to distinguish between fact and opinion? Give examples.
- Can facts change? Give an example.

More exercises—Fact or fiction?

Examine whether the following statements are based on false assumptions and limited evidence. State your reasons with appropriate examples and remember to define your terms.

1. All English people drink tea
2. Leaders are wise
3. The majority is always right
4. French cheese is better than Italian bread
5. World War 2 began in 1939
6. People believe in God because they are insecure and need comfort
7. Girls are more intelligent than boys
8. Most people who are rich are happy

9. Unemployed people are lazy
10. China has a population of over one billion people
11. Migrants take jobs and burden economies
12. People who show humility are weak
13. All people think freedom is important for a happy life

Why can it be difficult to distinguish between facts and assumptions? A fact is defined as "a thing that is known or proved to be true."[68] An opinion, on the other hand, is "a view or judgement formed about something, not necessarily based on fact or knowledge."[69] As we saw earlier, Plato thought it was important not to base our knowledge on opinions, but rather on facts or true propositions. Strong emotions, whether conscious or unconscious, can influence our thinking. This can result in claims based on false assumptions.

Student activity: Media

To what extent can the media influence assumptions? Can you think of one example?

Activity

Research an article which includes obvious false assumptions, summarise the main ideas, and answer the following questions:

- Why is it important to identify assumptions?
- Can you think of assumptions which have led to stereotypes?
- To what extent can assumptions come to be perceived as "facts?" Can you think of historical or contemporary examples? Are there any ethical or moral implications?
- How does emotion play a role in forming assumptions and stereotypes?

---

68. *Oxford Dictionaries*, s.v. "fact." http://www.oxforddictionaries.com/definition/english/fact.

69. *Oxford Dictionaries*, s.v. "opinion." http://www.oxforddictionaries.com/definition/english/opinion.

DISCUSSION QUESTIONS

1. Why do you think it is important to think well and with clarity? This is sometimes referred to as thinking independently and critically.
2. What are some of the things that stop us from thinking independently or with clarity?

LOGIC

Logic is the formal study of reasoning. Logic allows us to assess information we encounter and evaluate whether it is valid and true, as well as establish rules that guide decision-making. There are primarily two types of logic: deductive and inductive logic.

Deductive logic

Deductive logic begins with a set of statements or assertions called premises. Reasoning is then applied to the premises to arrive at a conclusion based on those premises. Each step of this process has its own set of requirements that determine the step's quality, as discussed below. Deductive reasoning draws from the *general* to the *specific*. The following is a basic example to illustrate the process of deductive logic:

> Premise: A is B
>
> Premise: B is C
>
> Conclusion: Therefore, A is C.

Using that formula of two premises with the resulting conclusion, but with observations, is:

> Premise: All men are mortal
>
> Premise: Socrates was a man
>
> Conclusion: Socrates was mortal

These three-part deductive arguments are called *syllogisms*. A syllogism is an efficient device for illustrating logical reasoning. Important to note is that there are further types of deductive logic; however, only some basics will be covered within this section.

True Premises

In a syllogism, or any more complex deduction, the premises are either *true or false*. This truth-or-falsehood evaluation is applied to the premises and differs from *validity*, discussed below. For the purpose of these exercises, whether a premise meets the criteria required to be called true will need to reflect reality, or the state of affairs in the world.

Validity

Validity is the process of concluding something—an argument—from the premises *necessarily*, regardless of the premises being true or false. An argument may be valid—the conclusion correctly being surmised from the premises—with premises that are false (this distinction between truth and validity is important and often confused).

For example:

>Premise: All wallabies play the harmonica.
>
>Premise: Harold is a wallaby.
>
>Therefore, Harold plays the harmonica.

The first premise of this syllogism is false since wallabies, to everyone's reasonable knowledge, do not play harmonicas. However, the argument is still *valid* since the conclusion that Harold plays the harmonica necessarily follows from the premises given.

Can you think of your own examples?

Invalid Argument

Some arguments appear valid at a glance, but are actually invalid due to the *structure* of the argument. For example:

>Premise: If it is raining then the ground is wet.
>
>Premise: The ground is wet.
>
>Conclusion: Therefore, it is raining.

In this example, the ground may still be wet for factors other than rain, such as water from a sprinkler. The first premise does not state that the ground is *only* wet when it rains. Therefore, this is an invalid argument. Often, structures of arguments appear simple and quite possibly valid due to language; however, they often are invalid.

Can you think of your own examples?

A Sound argument

An argument is *sound* if the premises are true and the argument is valid, resulting in a true conclusion. Therefore, soundness is simply a concept that acknowledges all steps of the argument have succeeded. Using the first syllogism: "All men are mortal" is a true premise; "Socrates was a man" is a true premise; "Socrates was mortal" is the conclusion of an argument possessing validity; therefore, the argument has satisfied all requirements for being sound.

Can you think of your own examples?

Inductive logic

Inductive logic is the reasoning process that uses *specific* premises to support a *general* conclusion. Unlike deductive logic, in inductive logic it is possible that, despite the truth of the premises, the conclusion can be false. Inductive arguments are based on inferences and analogies from the observed world. We see patterns, make analogies (i.e., create comparisons to similar things and situations), and infer conclusions from these observations. These conclusions facilitate predictions about the future based on the patterns observed.

Inductive reasoning is required in practical daily living. For example, someone may find the neighbor's dog friendly and playful, pat him on a regular basis, and conclude that he is a safe pet, just like other docile dogs observed. Or, there may be black clouds in the sky before leaving the house and, due to past experiences of such clouds indicating rainfall, one may infer the same will occur and therefore take an umbrella. However, these observations make inferences and analogies with the past which are not conclusive, as the dog may bite one day and the clouds may pass.

For example:

> Every swan observed has been white.
>
> Therefore, *all* swans are white.

For a long time, Europeans believed from observation that all swans were white, until black swans were discovered in Australia, thus disproving this theory. In inductive reasoning, the premises are intended to support the conclusion. As stated, induction begins with a specific example and moves towards a general conclusion.

Can you think of another example of inductive reasoning used in your daily life?

Generalisations about particular groups of people may generate stereotypes as well as strong emotions. As a simple example, if someone has a negative experience with a person from France and, as a result, selectively notices that French people are not very pleasant, then they may conclude that *all* French people are rude. Inductive reasoning can lead to generalisations and false assumptions, which generate stereotypes that have moral implications. Inductive logic can, through the use of inferences and analogies, provide *probability*, but not certainty.

What is the difference between inductive and deductive reasoning?

This link may be of help in answering this question: "Deductive vs Inductive Reasoning."[70]

Informal Fallacies

The word "fallacy" is defined as "A failure in reasoning which renders an argument invalid."[71] Identifying fallacies greatly helps in discerning true from false, and good versus bad arguments. Logicians have observed many fallacies people make and have categorised the more common types. Although there are arguably hundreds of fallacies, the following are a few of the most common:

Ad Hominem: attack on the person

This common fallacy is where the person is attacked and not the argument presented. Central ideas are ignored or minimized with an emphasis instead on personal qualities or information that is irrelevant to the argument. Perhaps a person's dress or personal life is pointed out as being significant,

---

70. Crossman, "What's the Difference?," https://www.thoughtco.com/deductive-vs-inductive-reasoning-3026549.
71. *Oxford Dictionaries, s.v.* "Fallacy," https://en.oxforddictionaries.com/definition/fallacy.

rather than the merits of the argument presented. For example, Jude is a politician who presents an argument as to why the government should intervene in controlling house prices in order to reduce the financial pressures on families. Her opponent responds without addressing the argument, but instead attacks her character—"Jude was investigated for tax fraud last year and also has been accused of having an affair with a minister. What would she know about politics?" Here, we see an attempt to avoid debating the actual argument by mentioning her personal character instead, as a diversion.
Can you think of other examples?

Appeal to Authority

Accepting an argument based on authority and not the merits of relevant reason or evidence is a common fallacy. If an authoritative institution such as the government states something is true, it may be believed because of their stature of importance rather than the nature of the evidence presented. Military leaders might claim that decreases in defense spending inevitably will lead to international conflict and, therefore, a proposed defence budget should be approved. Such arguments may be persuasive due to the positions held by the speakers, and not on the strength of the arguments.
Can you think of other examples?

Correlation versus Causation

Often when two events occur concurrently, causation rather than correlation is attributed. When events take place that frequently, or always, precede other events, a natural assumption is to view the first event as the cause of the second, but there is not necessarily a causal relationship. For example, "Every autumn in North America, birds start flying south and then winter comes. Therefore, we can prevent winter if we stop the birds from flying south."
Can you think of other examples?

Ad Ignorantiam

Ad ignorantiam is claiming something is true because it cannot be disproven or that it is false because it has not been proven 100 percent true. The lack of knowledge to justify or refute can be used to either assert a truth or deny a strongly supported argument. For example, "No one has proven that ghosts do not exist, so ghosts must exist" attempts to claim a truth from a lack of disproof. This is sometimes known as trying to prove a negative. The second type of this argument is shown in an example like the following: "There is not absolute, complete agreement that global warming exists, so we cannot conclude that it, indeed, does exist."

Can you think of other examples?

Strawman

Distorting and misrepresenting a person's argument, then attacking that fabrication—rather than the actual claim—is a strawman fallacy (imagine a scarecrow-type of figure that can be pummelled and easily defeated). For example, Clyde the politician may support stricter rules on bank loans for business investment. His opponent could respond with, "Clyde is against providing jobs and keeping food on families' tables. I, however, am for supporting workers and family stability." In this example, Clyde was criticized with a strawman argument. His position on bank loans has nothing to do with opposing jobs and families, but his opponent infused this assumption into the response and easily refuted it. The strawman fallacy is one frequently used in politics.

Can you think of other examples?

Loaded or Complex Question

A question that has inherent assumptions, nuances, or biases is known as a loaded question.

Try to answer the question, "Do you still cheat on exams?" with a "yes" or a "no." Either answer implies you have regularly cheated on exams at some point. This fact is assumed in the question proposed yet would first need to be established before the question would make sense.

Can you think of other examples? Is this devise used as a component in other types of fallacies? Why is learning about fallacies important? How does language influence fallacies?

Student Activity

Research other logical fallacies and come up with your own examples. Work individually or in pairs.

These links may be useful: "Logically Fallacious" and "Owl English Purdue."[72]

Student Activity — Critical Thinking

Read the following article and answer the critical thinking questions:

Cynicism about facts is symptomatic not only of a cognitive crisis but of a wider moral malaise

Rajeev Bhargava OCTOBER 15, 2017 00:15 IST UPDATED: OCTOBER 14, 2017 21:16 IST

I've heard it said that facts are unimportant, that only public opinion matters, implying that political action or public policy must be guided not by facts but by the opinion of the people. An even more pernicious claim is also made that there are no facts in the world, only biased interpretations and subjective opinions.

Both these strange claims have alarming practical consequences. Imagine if you've just been robbed, and go to the police station to register a complaint. And the policeman horrifies you with the response, "I don't think this is a fact, it's only your opinion." Worse, imagine if you went to a doctor complaining of chest pain, and the doctor says, "I don't consider this a fact, its only your biased view." If you are really having a heart attack, well then, good luck!

Indifference to or denial of facts is more common in public life. Governments refuse to face uncomfortable facts and deny them forcefully—high unemployment, the economy's downward spiral, violations of rights, scandals. Such refusal to acknowledge facts has terrible consequences too; not addressing the problem of unemployment can lead to social unrest, violence, even terrorism.

Simple and complex facts

---

72. https://www.logicallyfallacious.com/tools/lp/Bo/LogicalFallacies/1/Ad-Hominem-Abusive, and https://owl.english.purdue.edu/owl/resource/659/03/.

How are facts accessed or established? Not all facts have the same form. Some are simple, while others have an increasing degree of complexity. The more complex a fact, the harder it is to establish and the greater the room for ambiguity and multiple descriptions. Consider the following: John F. Kennedy (a) died, (b) was assassinated. It was easy to establish that he died. But more information and time were required to establish his assassination by Oswald—corroboration by several witnesses, films, forensic evidence. But why did Oswald do it? It is claimed that he acted willingly or unwittingly at the behest of the CIA. But to establish this fact—the motive—is more difficult, and never conclusively established. But even here there are better and worse arguments, and as in legal judgements, its facticity is grounded not in evidence alone but in reasons. Facts here are whatever has the best argument on its side. But comparing and ascertaining the validity of all reasons takes time, effort, skill. And we may still not come to a definitive conclusion. So, the issue is not the existence of facts but that where multiple agents are involved with complex collective motivations, it is hard, even for educated persons, to directly access facts. Perhaps facts such as the bad state of the economy fall in this category.

Furthermore, when vested interests muddy the waters by planting misleading information, spreading lies, deliberately creating a fog around the event—as the tobacco industry once did—then facts become extremely elusive. Such a condition of opaqueness has penetrated so deep in societies in recent times that it has become our default position, part of our second nature to be sceptical about all factual claims. Living in a world of radical uncertainty, in the era of "post-truth," we don't know who to trust to get facts. How then does one get out of this conundrum?

Age of domain expertise

We once lived in a society where knowledge was believed to be inherited, not socially acquired, and in some domains so socially insignificant that it was considered no knowledge at all (farming, weaving, singing). In any case, a select group acquired sole authority to pronounce on what the truth is in all domains—experts we totally trusted. As this society disappears, we find ourselves in an exactly opposite condition where we make radical self-reliance our ideal, and the easy availability of information on the Internet breeds the delusion that we can be experts in everything. Alas, when we are unable to achieve this, we plunge into a state of radical uncertainty, unreliability and mutual distrust. Mercifully, these are not the only options. I believe it best to recognise that knowledge in contemporary societies is evenly distributed, with a more complex cognitive division of labour, and that expertise now is more democratised than ever before. All of us are skilled at something, experts in some small, specialised domain. We acquire the ability, through formal or informal training, to recognise or establish facts in the many domains that make up our social world. Economists might know more about the aggregate state of the agriculture sector but farmers know crops and the conditions under which they grow. In knowledge of the social world, therefore, we must aspire to a mixture of self—and other-reliance and provide alternating and reciprocal leadership in fact-acquisition. Facts and social trust are related and crucial to the working of society.

What happens when experts themselves have conflicting views? Here individual accomplishments count. Some within each of these expert domains are hardworking and sincere, avoid self-deception, recognise their failures and work to overcome their flaws. Such people, with intellectual virtues and strength of ethical character, usually accomplish more. Our best bet, therefore, is to rely on the more accomplished people in each domain. All teachers are not selling ideologies; some are better than others at providing an empathetic, wide-ranging perspective on an issue. Likewise, not all doctors are trying to make a quick buck. Some willingly tell you when you don't need any treatment and when you need diagnostic tests to identify what treatment you need. This is also true of media persons, lawyers, bureaucrats, electricians, shopkeepers, businessmen, perhaps even politicians!

We all benefit if governments are guided by public opinion grounded in the best available facts provided partly by experts in each of the relevant domains. But the identification of facts is impossible without mechanisms to identify reliable experts, and social trust more generally. Conversely, cynicism about facts is symptomatic not only of a cognitive crisis but of a wider moral malaise.Critical Thinking [73]

Questions:

1. Does the article come from credible sources? For example, is it written by experts in the field?
2. Are there any images or language which could potentially influence your views, e.g., sensational headlines, photos, statistics, or direct quotation?
3. What is the main argument or claim?
4. What evidence or examples are used to support the main argument?
5. Evaluate the validity of the evidence. Is it reliable and appropriate to the argument?
6. Does the article present other points of view or claims?
7. Are the main terms and concepts clearly defined? If so, what are these?
8. Is the argument self-confirming? For example, does it select evidence to support its view?
9. What fallacies, if any, can you identify? Choose from those listed earlier and discuss the reasons for your choice.
10. In your opinion, is this a good article? Explain.

Student activity

Study three short articles from a range of sources. Some suggestions include:

1. Tabloid article
2. Newspaper article

---

73. Bhargava, "Facts Matter Even More."

3. An article from a journal, good website or textbook considered reputable

Answer the critical thinking questions for each of the articles. Compare and contrast the sources. The following resources may be useful:

1. BBC, CNN, ABC, SBS, *The New York Times*.
2. "The Rise and Rise of Fake News"—*BBC Trending*.[74]
3. "Scientists Consider Fake News Vaccine"—*BBC News*.[75]
4. "The Proliferation of Fake Style Facts."[76]

LIMITATIONS OF REASON

To what extent can reason and logic attain knowledge and truth?

Formal logic and reasoning provide tools which allow us access to a vast amount of knowledge about ourselves and the world around us. The skills within logic can assist in identifying assumptions, biases, stereotypes, and conclusions by others. It is important, however, to note that the term "reason" has many associative terms such as "concepts," "logic," "cognition," "reflection," "thinking," "rationality" and "the dialectic." These terms are used somewhat interchangeably.

The nature of reason is a contested issue within philosophy and theology, one worth further debate and exploration. There are many philosophers and theologians who have discussed the limitations of reason. Scottish philosopher David Hume was an empiricist who argued that while reason allows us knowledge about mathematical truths, these are only ideas understood or known within the mind and do not allow us access to the external world.[77] He argued that we cannot be certain whether our ideas are evident in the external world.[78] Hume stated that while we might seem to observe causal links between events in the external world, we cannot be sure these observed patterns will be repeated. Thus, he challenged the inductive method of proceeding from the particular to a generalization. Hume concluded that we cannot guarantee that the past will resemble the future.

---

74. http://www.bbc.com/news/blogs-trending-37846860.

75. http://www.bbc.com/news/uk-38714404.

76. https://www.washingtonpost.com/posteverything/wp/2016/12/07/the-proliferation-of-fake-stylized-facts/?tid=hybrid_collaborative_2_naandutm_term=.2148E02E56C0.

77. McInerney, *Introduction to Philosophy*, 55.

78. Ibid., 55–56.

Hume also argued that reason is not totally reliable since it is influenced by emotions; reason is not immune to emotions, but rather it *directs* reason:[79]

> Reason is, and ought only to be *the slave* of the passions, and can never pretend to any other office than *to serve and obey* them . . .[80]

Immanuel Kant's (1724–1804) famous work, *Critique of Pure Reason*, discusses—as the title suggests—both the nature and inevitable limitations of reason.[81] What Kant concludes is that while reason is valuable in gaining knowledge (for example, in thinking about science and ethical issues) it cannot, by its nature, extend its inquiry in understanding to *all* of reality or phenomena.[82] Reason can only ascertain things it is capable of dealing with. That is, we cannot know of the "universe in its totality," as we do not have *access* to it in our experience.[83] Relying on the experiences and observations of others will give us a measure of *some certainty* of the event, but *not total certainty*.[84] Kant argued that our minds categorize our experiences of the external world, and that our understanding of concepts and principles is determined by our experiences of the world.[85] However, we cannot have total access to all experiences within the external world, or the "whole universe in its totality." Therefore, there are objects which are *beyond our cognition* and experience. As contemporary philosopher Raymond Younis points out, while analogy or inductive inferences help us bridge such gaps in our knowledge, complete certainty is unattainable.[86]

> Human reason admits of limits but not of bounds, namely, it admits that something indeed lies without it, at which it can never arrive, but not that it will at any point find completion in its internal progress . . . Natural science will never reveal to us the internal constitution of things . . . Reason through all its concepts and laws of the understanding which are sufficient to it for empirical use, that is within the sensible world, finds in

---

79. Ibid., 322.
80. Hume, A *Treatise of Human Nature*: II.iii.3, 414–15 (emphasis in original).
81. Kant, *Critique of Pure Reason*.
82. Younis, "These Ultimate Springs and Principles," 317–34.
83. Ibid., 319.
84. Ibid., 321, 324.
85. Younis, "These Ultimate Springs and Principles," 319.
86. Ibid., 324.

it no satisfaction, because ever recurring questions deprive us of all hope of their complete solution.[87]

German philosopher Theodore Adorno (1905–1969) argued that knowledge in the West adopts an emphasis on what is termed as "instrumental reasoning." By this he means a way of thinking which places a high importance on logic, analysis, and abstract reasoning.[88] He argued that this seeks to reduce thought to systems and measurements, resulting in reality as "quantifiable, calculable and known."[89] The purpose of reasoning, he argued, is to acquire facts for the sake of "systematizing knowledge."[90] Adorno proposes a more intuitive and creative approach to knowledge which does not need to construct principles and universal concepts, but rather a more open-ended method. Adorno argues that instrumental reasoning limits our understanding of the world by reducing it to facts and universal systems.

Some religious writers also debate how reasoning is applied, especially in the light of faith and religious experience. Christian theologian Thomas Aquinas (1225–1274) argued that reason is important as it can provide a justification for God's existence, most famously employed in his Five Proofs essay.[91] However, he points out that ultimately to *know* truth or God, we rely on "revelation." Revelation, within the religious context, is a *knowing* that transcends reason, often likened to an *intuitive* sense of reality. This reality is a *knowing* based on a connection with the divine experienced by many people within religious traditions. This experience has a long history and tradition which has attempted to *explain and systemise* this phenomenon. Religious teachings and dogma are therefore ways of describing, through reason, the experience of the divine and transcendence which many over millennia have attested to.

However, despite the limitations of reason in gaining total knowledge, one can argue that reason still remains a useful tool in assessing truth claims. Even if limits in what it *cannot tell us* are identified, the processes of reasoning and thinking (in its various forms, e.g., logic, reflection) nevertheless remain invaluable and necessary tools for discernment.

---

87. Kant, *Prolegomena to Any Future Metaphysics*, 100–1.
88. Adorno and Horkheimer, *Dialectic of Enlightenment*.
89. Walker, *Slow Philosophy*, 61.
90. Ibid., 62.
91. Aquinas, "Summa Theologiae," 1a, q.2, art.3.

STUDENT REFLECTIONS

What are you now wondering about?

- What ideas or questions are you wondering about as a result of these lessons?
- Have these lessons made you think differently? Explain.
- What have you found challenging, provocative, or intriguing?

INTUITION, EMOTION, AND IMAGINATION

> Man is a rational animal—so at least I have been told. Throughout a long life, I have looked diligently for evidence in favor of this statement, but so far I have not had the good fortune to come across it . . . though I have searched in many countries spread over three continents.[92]

Do you agree with Russell's observations? Is it difficult to find humans acting rationally? Give examples.

Discussion questions

In groups/pairs, discuss the following and summarise the ideas in your notebook.

1. In what areas would reason and logic be limited in gaining knowledge?
2. In what areas of life do we rely on intuition, emotions, and imagination, rather than reason and logic?
3. Are our emotions a component of our reason, or are they separate?
4. Do women experience emotions differently than men do? Explain.

---

92. Russell, *Unpopular Essays*, 71.

Intuition, emotion, and imagination

- To what extent is imagination more powerful than reason? Can reason and imagination enrich each other, or are they opposed? Explain.
- Is imagination similar or different to intuition and emotions? Explain.
- Identify an artwork (i.e., book, painting, film) and describe how imagination is used.

Science and imagination

> ... according to Popper's methodology, every recognition of a truth is preceded by an imaginative preconception of what the truth might be—by hypothesis such as William Whewell first called "happy guesses" ... most of the day-to-day business of science consists in making observations or experiments designed to find out whether this imagined world of our hypothesis corresponds to the real one. An act of imagination, a speculative adventure, thus underlies every improvement of natural knowledge.[93]

Karl Popper (1902–1994), a philosopher of science, argued that imagination plays a crucial role in our understanding of the world and in the scientific process.

Do you agree/disagree with this observation? Explain.

Do you know of any scientific discoveries that emerged from intuition or imagination? Explain how this may happen.

DISCUSSION QUESTIONS

1. To what extent is knowledge in science and the arts the same or different? Discuss.
2. Is scientific knowledge more reliable in telling us the truth than the arts? How?
3. Can you think of examples of how and when creativity was used within science?

93. Medawar, *The Limits of Science*, 51.

Student activity: Video

Watch "Martin Luther King—I Have A Dream Speech—August 28, 1963"[94] and respond to the following questions:

1. What is Dr. King's main message?
2. How does he use both reason and imagination in his speech?
3. Does this speech have sound arguments, just good rhetoric, or both?
4. What impact does this have on the tone and overall message of the speech?
5. In this example, do you think the use of imagination was useful? If so, what impact did it have? Explain.
6. Can you think of examples when imagination may be harmful or result in negative consequences?

Reflection question

To what extent can imagination *teach us* anything about human nature, creativity, and/or knowledge?

How can we know through intuition?

Discussion questions

1. What role does intuition play in gaining knowledge?
2. Can a scientist talk seriously about intuition?
3. Are women more intuitive than men?
4. Is intuition related to or independent of reason?

94. https://www.youtube.com/watch?v=vP4iY1TtS3s.

We are all familiar with the term "gut feeling," a type of understanding about something that cannot be logically explained. For example, when meeting someone for the first time, we may have a positive or negative intuitive sense about the person which we do not immediately know the reasons for. The Oxford Dictionary defines intuition as, "The ability to understand something instinctively, without the need for conscious reasoning. A thing that one knows or considers likely from instinctive feeling rather than conscious reasoning."[95] Can our intuitions always be reliable? Are some people innately more intuitive? Is intuition purely instinctive or does it relate to prior knowledge? In a general sense, the topic of intuition can be understood within the context of:

1. the acceptance of universal, broad concepts such as that found in logic and mathematics
2. new discoveries about the world
3. social relations and morality
4. being related to prior knowledge
5. being related to sense perception and feelings

As Henri Bergson notes:

> It follows from this that an absolute could only be given in an *intuition* while everything else falls within the province of *analysis*. By intuition is meant the kind of *intellectual sympathy* by which one places oneself within an object in order to coincide with what is unique in it and consequently inexpressible. Analysis, on the contrary, is the operation which reduces the object to elements already known, that is, to elements common both to it and other objects.
>
> To analyze, therefore, is to express a thing as a function of something other than itself. All analysis is thus a translation, a development into symbols, a representation taken from successive points of view from which we note as many resemblances as possible between the new object which we are studying and others which we believe we know already. In its eternally unsatisfied desire to embrace the object around which it is compelled to turn, analysis multiplies without end

---

95. *Oxford Dictionaries*, s.v. "intuition." https://en.oxforddictionaries.com/definition/intuition.

the number of its points of view in order to complete its always incomplete representation, and ceaselessly varies its symbols that it may perfect the always imperfect translation. It goes on, therefore, to infinity. But intuition, if intuition is possible, is a simple act.[96]

How does Bergson describe intuition?

Intuition and knowledge

To what extent is intuition important in understanding the world? Is our understanding of basic concepts based on intuition?

We may have answered the skeptic earlier that we are not merely living a dream because intuitively we know that our experience of reality is a distinct experience from dreaming and therefore true. There are many philosophers who describe intuition as necessary in our understanding of how the world works in the general sense, as well as laws which govern the universe. For example, we apply the use of logic in our understanding of the laws of nature, yet we cannot *prove* that logic works, but rather accept it as intuitively true. As Locke has noted:

> Sometimes our mind perceives the agreement or disagreement of two ideas *immediately*—by themselves, without the intervention of any other ideas. I think we may call this *intuitive knowledge*, for in it the mind isn't trying to prove or explore anything, but simply perceives the truth as the eye perceives light, just by being directed towards it. Thus the mind perceives—by bare intuition, without the intervention of any other idea—that white is not black, that a circle is not a triangle, that three are more than two and equal to one plus two. This kind of knowledge is the clearest and most certain that human frailty is capable of. Knowledge of this kind is irresistible: like bright sunshine it forces one to perceive it immediately, as soon as the mind looks that way; and it leaves no room for hesitation, doubt, or further enquiry because the mind is *filled* with the clear light of it. All the certainty and evidentness of all our knowledge depends on this intuition. The certainty it brings is so great that no-one can imagine—and so

---

96. Bergson, *Introduction to Metaphysics*, 2 (emphasis in original).

> no-one could ask for—a greater. A man cannot conceive himself capable of a greater certainty than to know that a given idea in his mind is such as he perceives it to be; and that two ideas between which he perceives a difference *are* different and not precisely the same.[97]

Locke claimed that intuition is an independent mode of understanding and different from sense perception, which allows us to comprehend concepts or self-evident truths. For example, although we know through our sense of hearing that we can receive sound, we comprehend through intuition that circles are not squares. "Thus the mind perceives—by bare intuition, without the intervention of any other idea—that white is not black, that a circle is not a triangle, that three are more than two and equal to one plus two."[98] Some propositions are understood through intuition alone while other claims are drawn from conclusions made from intuitive premises. That means we may have an intuitive understanding of concepts which we then logically demonstrate. Often intuition works alongside reason. There are examples where intuition creates theories and new ways of understanding the world. For example, Galileo and Einstein had a strong intuition of their original ideas, which were later developed through logic and empirical testing.

> Some propositions in a particular subject area . . . are knowable by us by intuition alone; still others are knowable by being deduced from intuited propositions. Intuition is a form of rational insight. Intellectually grasping a proposition, we just "see" it to be true in such a way as to form a true, warranted belief in it . . . Deduction is a process in which we derive conclusions from intuited premises through valid arguments, ones in which the conclusion must be true if the premises are true. We intuit, for example, that the number three is prime and that it is greater than two. We then deduce from this knowledge that there is two. Intuition and deduction thus provide us with knowledge *a priori*, which is to say knowledge gained independently of sense experience.[99]

How is intuition related to sense experience in the above quote?

---

97. Locke, *An Essay Concerning Human Understanding*, Essay IV ii 1 (emphasis in original).

98. Ibid.

99. Markie, "Rationalism vs. Empiricism," 3–4.

Bertrand Russell points out that intuition is the source of our knowledge. He argues that intuition is able to connect what we experience in the world through our senses to reason, or *a priori knowledge*—deductive reasoning independent of experience. Russell believed that we are able to understand particulars, or "things in the world," only in reference to universal concepts. A universal concept can be defined as "Relating to or done by all people or things in the world or in a particular group; applicable to all cases."[100] As Russell further stated:

> Thus our intuitive knowledge, which is the source of all our other knowledge of truths, is of two sorts: pure empirical knowledge, which tells us of the existence and some of the properties of particular things with which we are acquainted, and pure *a priori* knowledge, which gives us connexions between universals, and enables us to draw inferences from the particular facts given in empirical knowledge. Our derivative knowledge always depends upon some pure *a priori* knowledge and usually also depends upon some pure empirical knowledge.[101]

Explain Russell's understanding of intuition.

Intuition and the divine

> "An equation for me has no meaning . . . unless it expresses a thought of God."[102]

Srinivasa Ramanujan (1887–1920) was a self-taught—or inspired—mathematician and regarded as a genius. He came from India and had no formal education, yet was accepted to Cambridge University England (awarded honorary titles) based on his deep and rare understanding of complex mathematical concepts. When asked how he was able to come up with his

---

100. *Oxford Dictionaries*, s.v. "universal." https://en.oxforddictionaries.com/definition/universal.
101. Russell, *Problems of Philosophy*, 76.
102. Ramanujan, in Kanigel, *The Man Who Knew Infinity*, 7.

discoveries, Ramanujan attributed intuition and the Hindu gods helping him, rather than logic or a formal education.

Student activity—Film:

Watch *The Man Who Knew Infinity*. How does Ramanujan explain his discoveries?

Srinivasa Ramanujan

Student reflection questions

1. Can you recall a time when you had an intuitive insight which seemed to emerge spontaneously? How did you make sense of this experience?
2. What are some limitations or problems in using intuition for understanding?
3. Is logic or intuition more important for new discoveries?
4. Can intuition be religious? Explain.

Intuition in morality and relationships

Intuition plays a large role in our interpersonal interactions with others. Much of our understanding of other people is not only rational, but also based on intuition. Many of us intuitively *know* that killing and stealing are wrong. This knowing is not based on rational arguments or proofs, but rather a felt sense. There are philosophers who claim that morality is based on intuition. For example, some philosophers, such as Aristotle, argue that humans possess an intuitive ability to grasp moral principles. This concept is known within philosophy as *synderesis* and is defined as "the intuitive ability to grasp moral principles, defined as the 'inborn knowledge of the primary principles of moral action.'"[103]

1. Does intuition guide our moral actions? Explain.
2. What are some of the limitations in basing moral justification on intuition?

Can we learn intuition?

Many researchers have pointed out the intuition of expertise becomes more reliable the greater practice they have in their specific field.[104] For example, within the context of counselling, the intuition of the therapist is crucial in trying to understand the underlying issues of clients. While information and logic may be useful, often the unsaid and unknown are more crucial. However, being able to identify these complex issues, some argue, would require experience in the field. Experience allows the therapist to test intuition with past experiences of similar cases to the one presented. This may suggest that intuition is not independent of, but rather connected to, subject-specific knowledge and, therefore, reason.

1. To what extent is intuition important in our relationships and understanding of other people?
2. Do you think that intuitive insights are independent of, or connected to, prior knowledge?

Intuition and bias

> Most of us are healthy most of the time, and most of our judgements and actions are appropriate most of the time. As we navigate our lives, we normally allow ourselves to be guided by impressions and feelings, and the confidence we have in

103. https://www.merriam-webster.com/dictionary/synderesis.
104. Kahneman, *Thinking, Fast and Slow*, 24.

> our intuitive beliefs and preferences is usually justified. But not always. We are often confident even when we are wrong, and an objective observer is more likely to detect our errors than we are.[105]

Some psychologists tell us our intuitions may not all be that accurate. For example, we may confuse intuitive insights with associations to past memories, experiences, and beliefs.[106] Daniel Kahneman, a researcher in psychology, has spent many years studying decisions and intuition and claims that despite our deeply held confidence in our intuitive beliefs, they can be wrong.[107] Kahneman distinguishes two levels of thinking called Type 1 and Type 2. In Type 1 thinking, there are automatic, quick, effortless, and unconscious associations. Perception, impressions, feelings, and *intuition*, he claims, are in this category. Type 2 is thinking that is controlled, conscious, and logical. Kahneman argues that much of our thinking is a mixture of both. Type 2 usually adopts impressions and suggestions from Type 1, which are then synthesised and turned into beliefs that are not always justified. Kahneman's studies have shown that beliefs based on impressions and intuition, despite their cohesive feelings of correctness, can turn out to be wrong:[108]

> You have to think of [your associative memory] as a huge repository of ideas, linked to each other in many ways, including causal links and other links, and activation spreading from ideas to other ideas until a small subset of that enormous network is illuminated, and the subset is what's happening in the mind at the moment. You're not conscious of it, you're conscious of very little of it.
>
> Coherence means that you're going to adopt one interpretation in general. Ambiguity tends to be suppressed. This is part of the mechanism that you have here that ideas activate other ideas and the more coherent they are, the more likely they are to activate each other. Other things that don't fit fall away by the wayside. We're enforcing coherent interpretations. We see the world as much more coherent than it is . . . What's

---

105. Ibid., 4.
106. Newell, "Explainer," para. 3.
107. Kahneman, *Thinking, Fast and Slow*, 24–25.
108. Kahneman, *Thinking, Fast and Slow*.

interesting is that many a time people have intuitions that they're equally confident about except they're wrong.[109]

Discussion questions

1. How does Kahneman define intuition?
2. What does Kahneman mean by "coherent interpretations?"
3. If Kahneman is correct about intuition, what implications does this have on our understanding of its role in decision-making?
4. Compare Kahneman's understanding of intuition to the philosophical approach mentioned earlier. What are the differences?
5. How does Kahneman's description differ from that of the religious intuition of Ramanujan?

Extension student activity — Research

Choose one of the following:

1. Research the understanding of intuition from a philosophical or psychological perspective. For example, you may research the works of philosophers such as Immanuel Kant, Baruch Spinoza, John Locke, or Bertrand Russell on intuition. Or, explore the concept of synderesis as understood by a particular philosopher such as Thomas Aquinas.
2. Alternatively, study the works of Daniel Kahneman or another researcher on intuition.
3. Explore the discoveries of Srinivasa Ramanujan. Explain how religious intuition led to his discoveries.

    Record your findings and present them to the class.

---

109. Kahneman, in Popova, "How Our Minds Mislead Us," paras. 8, 11.

SCIENTIFIC KNOWLEDGE AND ITS LIMITATIONS

Subjective versus objective knowledge

Hypothetical: Car accident

There was a car accident in London on Sunday afternoon in which a woman driving a car hit a dog and stopped her car to check on the dog. A second car then struck the woman's car and did not stop. Both the woman and the dog were injured. A witness saw the accident and a police officer arrived at the scene afterward to take a report.

From the list below, who is able to tell us the *most truth* about the accident and *why*?

- victim
- witness
- policeman
- dog.[110]

Discuss this with your partner and/or class. What issues does the above example raise?

Why are there difficulties in deciding between the options presented?

If you are the officer taking notes for the accident report, what questions would you ask?

Add the following facts and discuss how they affect the report:

- The witness speaks only broken English.
- The woman has been in numerous car accidents, but has not been cited for a traffic violation.
- The witness is the owner of the dog and is visibly upset.

---

110. This example is taken from Antony Ibrascinao's course, "Philosophy and Theology," Sydney College of Divinity, 1994.

Discussion questions

1. In your opinion, who had the most objective account of the accident? Explain your reasons.
2. What does this example reveal about the *nature of truth*?
3. In your opinion, is truth objective, subjective, or both? Explain.
4. What does it mean to say science provides objective as opposed to subjective truth?

Does science exist only in the mind?

Student activity: Excerpt

Read the following from *Zen and the Art of Motorcycle Maintenance* by Robert M. Pirsig, and answer the questions below:[111]

> "The problem, the contradiction that scientists are stuck with, is that of mind. *Mind* has no matter or energy, but they can't escape its predominance over everything we do. Logic exists in the mind. Numbers exist only in the mind. I don't get upset when scientists say that ghosts exist in the mind. It's that *only* that gets me. Science is *only* in your mind too, it's just that that doesn't make it bad. Or ghosts either."
>
> They are looking at me so I continue: "Laws of nature are human *inventions*, like ghosts. Laws of logic, laws of mathematics are also human inventions, like ghosts. The whole blessed thing is a human invention, including the idea that it isn't a human invention! The world has no existence whatsoever outside the human imagination. It's all a ghost, and in antiquity it was recognised as a ghost—the whole blessed world we live in. It's run by ghosts. We see what we see because ghosts show it to us, ghosts of Moses and Christ, and Buddha, Plato, Einstein and so on. Isaac Newton is a very good ghost. One of the best. Your 'common sense' is nothing more than

---

111. Pirsig, *Zen and the Art*, 32–33 (emphasis in original).

the voices of thousands of these ghosts from the past. Ghosts and more ghosts. Ghosts trying to find their place among the living."

John looks too much in thought to speak. But Sylvia is excited. "Where do you get these ideas?" she asks. I am about to answer, but do not. I have a feeling of having pushed it to the limit, maybe beyond, and it is time to drop it.

Discussion questions

1. Do ideas exist inside or outside the mind?
2. Are laws invented or do we discover them?
3. Pirsig uses the analogy of ghosts to describe many of our laws and human inventions. Is this an effective analogy?
4. How would Plato respond to Pirsig's ideas?
5. What do you think a scientist today would say to the claim that "science is only in the mind?"

Science

Science is a vast field of study which observes the natural world and, through an exhaustive process, makes conclusions based on these observations. Science is defined by the Oxford Dictionary as, "The intellectual and practical activity encompassing the systematic study of the structure and behaviour of the physical and natural world through observation and experiment."[112] Science consists of a body of knowledge and a specific method used to obtain knowledge known as the scientific method. Through this method, science attempts to describe how the world works by discovering regular patterns in the natural world that may result in scientific laws through the use of inductive logic. The discipline of science uses this empirical approach to produce a body of objective knowledge outside the influences of human expectations, assumptions, and bias.

---

112. *Oxford Dictionaries*, s.v. "science." https://en.oxforddictionaries.com/definition/science.

How does science work?

Student activity—Observation questions

1. Think about the last scientific experiment you engaged in at school. Can you describe what you did? What process were you involved in?
2. Describe what the scientist is doing in this picture.

3. What *processes* is he using to gather information or examine the data or evidence in front of him? What ways of knowing is he using? How will he use this information?

From the exercises above and your own research, answer the following questions:

- What is the scientific method? Identify some of the processes involved in the scientific method. You may illustrate your response in a diagram.
- What are the ways of knowing used by scientists?
- Explain how inductive logic is used within the scientific method.
- Can you think of some limitations in using the inductive method in science?

Some limitations of the scientific method

Science has made incredible discoveries in numerous areas of study, explaining much of the physical world, and has provided innumerable positive benefits in nearly all fields of study. However, the scientific method is not without its problems and limitations.

Science and the Problem of Induction

> Hypotheses always remains hypotheses, that is, suppositions to complete certainty of which we can never attain.[113]

> The conclusions of science make no pretence to being more than probability.[114]

Science operates by inductive reasoning. Scientists observe the natural and human world, identify patterns, and form hypotheses to be tested. Scientific conclusions eventually arise from this process. Yet those conclusions are still not irrefutable. A classic example is the observation of swans mentioned earlier, where all observed swans in the known world were white. Understandably, the scientific conclusion was that the species of swans was white and for many years, scientists accepted this conclusion—until a black swan was discovered. This example shows that our observations may provide a generality, but this generality is not always conclusive. We may observe many similar patterns in the natural and human world, and yet we cannot be totally certain that they apply generally. Many philosophers and scientists have identified the limitations of induction. David Hume argued that scientific thinking is based on the assumption that the *past will resemble and predict the future*. Hume argued that there is no evidence to support this claim:

> ... the supposition that, *the future resembles the past,* is not founded on arguments of any kind, but is deriv'd entirely from habit, by which we are determined to expect for the future the same train of objects, to which we have been custom'd.[115]

Confirmation Bias—
Do We See Only What We Want to See?

When looking for evidence to prove a hypothesis, scientists look for facts to support their ideas. However, many have identified flaws in this process when scientists only observe and document supporting data. American researcher Dr. John William Money (1921–2006) chose to focus on selective evidence in order to suit his own hypothesis about gender identity. His bias and emotional attachment to the outcomes of his experiment meant that

---

113. Kant, in Medawar, *The Limits of Science*, 41.
114. Pearce, in Medawar, *The Limits of Science*, 41.
115. Hume, *A Treatise of Human Nature I*, 134 (emphasis in original).

he was not able to be objective in his analysis of the observations of gender qualities in young children who had gender reassignment surgery. Thomas Kuhn argued that much of science is slow to change and evidence is often selectively observed due to the emotional attachments and biases of the scientist. Karl Popper (1902–1994), a philosopher of science, attempted to address this problem, stating that scientists should not seek evidence to support their hypotheses, but rather evidence to *dispute it*. Popper's falsification argument states that once the theory cannot be refuted with evidence, only then it can be *tentatively* accepted. Popper claimed that no scientific theory should be viewed as absolute, but instead needs be open to evidence that can refute.[116]

STUDENT ACTIVITY: VIDEO

For further ideas on Dr. Money and Karl Popper, the following resources may be useful.

1. BBC Horizon, "Dr Money and the Boy With No Penis."[117]
2. BBC Radio 4, "Karl Popper's Falsification."[118]

CAN WE MAKE ACCURATE PREDICTIONS ABOUT HUMAN BEHAVIOR?

How do we account for the complexity of human character and behavior? The study of science is divided between natural science and human science (also known as social science). Human science applies the scientific method to fields of study that involve human behavior, which many say leads to significantly less certain conclusions compared to the natural sciences. The unpredictability of human behavior, the problems of sample sizes, expectations, and bias in questionnaires are some of the issues that are faced when applying the scientific method within the human sciences. Disciplines such as psychology, sociology, anthropology, and economics contrast significantly with physics, chemistry, geology, and biology because they often base predictions of future human behavior on data that represents current behavior. Human science also faces problems of cultural bias and observations

---

116. Popper, *Conjectures and Refutations*.
117. https://archive.org/details/DrMoneyAndTheBoyWithNoPenis
118. https://www.bbc.co.uk/programmes/p02yvk9n.

affecting data. Many have argued that applying scientific analysis to human behavior does not easily result in reliable outcomes.

> A social scientific scrutiny of the human, rather than natural, world doesn't easily lend itself to generalizable laws, cast-iron predictions, nor can it always preserve a distinction between fact and value.[119]

For further research, you may want to look at the Hawthorn effect in psychology, or the finding of quantum mechanics on the observer effect. The film, *What the *Bleep* Do We Believe?* depicts the observer effect.

Student activity—Research

Scientism: Study the main components of scientism and write up a summary.

This video may be helpful: "The Limits of Science—A Critique of Scientism."[120]

Questions:

1. What is scientism and logical positivism?
2. List some of the limitations of scientism.
3. According to scientism, how does science adopt presuppositions?
4. How is science self-refuting?

Can science tell us the whole truth?

Today there is a widely held assumption that science is more reliable than other subjects in telling us the truth. There is also belief that the scientific way of thinking can be applied to *all* areas of knowledge. Science is often viewed as objective, accurate, and generally able to provide a reliable source of evidence. While this may often be the case, as science has provided us with reliable and pragmatic knowledge, there are scientists and philosophers who do not agree with this assumption. Some criticisms of science include its dogmatic views in claiming to explain how the world works *in its totality*. Some critics of science include Immanuel Kant, David Hume, Bertrand Russell, Karl Popper, Thomas Kuhn, Paul Feyerabend, Alfred Whitehead, Peter Medawar, and Max Wilber.

119. Marar, "Why Does Social Science?," para. 11.
120. https://www.youtube.com/watch?v=pYq5IItUvFM.

> It is important to realize that science does not make assertions about ultimate questions—about the riddles of existence, or about man's task in this world. This has often been well understood. But some great scientists, and many lesser ones, have misunderstood the situation. The fact that science cannot make pronouncements about ethical principles has been misinterpreted as indicating that there are no such principles.[121]

What does Popper mean by "The fact that science cannot make pronouncements about ethical principles has been misinterpreted as indicating that there are no such principles."[122]

Scientism

Scientism began in the twentieth century with the logical positivism movement which claimed that all knowledge can only be understood within science. However, some limitations of scientism include presuppositions which critics deem questionable. These presuppositions include: 1) That observation is reliable, and 2) that there exist regularities within the universe, both of which are accepted as true in order to begin a scientific inquiry.[123] These assumptions or presuppositions which begin scientific experiments are not "proven" or tested by science.[124]

SCIENTISTS CRITIQUING SCIENCE

> It is not to science, therefore, but to metaphysics, imaginative literature or religion that we must turn for answers to questions having to do with first and last things. Because these answers neither arise out of nor require validation by empirical evidence, it is not useful or even meaningful to ask whether they are true or false . . . there is no limit upon the power of science to answer questions of the kind science *can* answer.[125]

What does Medawar say about the role of science?

---

121. Popper, "Natural Selection and the Emergence," 342.
122. Ibid.
123. Academy of Ideas, "Limits Of Science", Medawar, *The Limits of Science*.
124. Ibid.
125. Medawar, *The Limits of Science*, 60.

In certain ways, science has attempted to explain the nature and complexities of human experiences. Certain emotions can be detected in brainwaves and mental stress manifests in observable physical symptoms. Yet many have argued that while science might attempt to show emotional states and their connection to human behavior, it cannot adequately address these, nor can it provide sufficient responses to questions of meaning and purpose. Professor Peter Medawar and psychologist Carl Rogers illustrate below some of the limitations of science, noting that science is not the only method of gaining truth, but one of many ways to knowledge, and therefore truth:

> The model of a precise, beautifully built, and unassailable science (which most of us hold consciously and unconsciously) becomes, then, a limited and distinctly human construction, incapable of precise perfection. Openness to experience can be seen as being fully as important a characteristic of the scientist as the understanding of research design. And the whole enterprise of science can be seen as but one portion of a larger field of knowledge in which truth is pursued in many equally meaningful ways, science being of those ways.[126]

PHILOSOPHERS CRITIQUING SCIENCE

> Moreover, nothing entitles us to assume that man has a nature or essence in the same sense as other things. In other words, if we have a nature or essence, then surely only god could know and define it, and the first prerequisite would be that he be able to speak about a "who" as though it were a "what."[127]

What do you think the German-born philosopher Hannah Arendt (1906–1975) means by speaking about a "who" as though it were a "what?" Explain.

There are many philosophers who argue that to understand who a human being is—our essence—we need to move beyond scientific analysis. Philosophers known as phenomenologists, such as Edmond Husserl (1859–1938), Martin Heidegger (1889–1976), and Maurice Merleau-Ponty (1906–1961), argued that the scientific method does not provide an adequate and conclusive description of human experience. Broadly speaking, phenomenologists attempted to examine "phenomena" or "the world as it

---

126. Rogers, *A Way of Being*, 238.
127. Arendt, *The Human Condition*, 10.

appears to us" without "imposing" a theory.¹²⁸ These philosophers proposed that in order to have an adequate understanding of the human person and their deep essence or being, we need to extend our inquiry beyond the sciences. These philosophers were interested in exploring the nature of human experiences and studying how humans both understand and interact with the world.

> Rather than conducting experimental analysis of an objectified world, this tradition focused its attention on "being" itself, on the lived world of human experience, on its unceasing ambiguity, its spontaneity and autonomy, its uncontainable dimensions, its ever-deepening complexity.¹²⁹

Student activity: Podcast

Listen to the following podcast on Merleau-Ponty's understanding of phenomenology: "Katherine Morris on Merleau-Ponty on the Body."¹³⁰

1. Who is Maurice Merleau-Ponty?
2. Explain how Merleau-Ponty describes the lived human experience through our bodies.

Maurice Merleau-Ponty

128. Moran, *Introduction to Phenomenology*.
129. Tarnas, *The Passion of the Western Mind*, 374.
130. http://philosophybites.com/2016/03/katherine-morris-on-merleau-ponty-on-the-body.html.

EXTENSION ACTIVITY—RESEARCH TASK

Research one area of inquiry and summarize its main ideas. If possible, present your findings to the class. Suggested topics:

- Methodology: the scientific method
- Problems of induction, Karl Popper on falsification, Thomas Kuhn on paradigm shifts
- Differences between the human and natural sciences
- Problems of accuracy within social sciences, i.e., questions, sample sizes, observer effect, etc.
- The positive contributions of science to knowledge—for example, explaining how the world works and the pragmatic benefits
- Critique of scientism from phenomenologists such as Edmond Husserl, Martin Heidegger, and Maurice Merleau-Ponty.
- Paul Feyerabend's (1924–1994) critique of science.

CONCLUSION

In order to understand knowledge, philosophers have traditionally taken to Plato's definition that states, "knowledge is justified true belief."[131] This involves notions of belief, truth, and justification. Beliefs, hence, can be accepted as true when they can show things as they really are. There are three categories in assessing the validity of beliefs: correspondence theory argues that beliefs need to *correspond* with reality; coherence theory claims that beliefs are to *fit into other beliefs*; and pragmatic theory states the truth of beliefs are in their *usefulness*.[132]

The purpose of a justification is to demonstrate how our beliefs are true. This is generally attributed to good reasoning. The degree of evidence or reason needed in order to support a justification for knowledge is disputed amongst philosophers. Some, like Descartes, argue that one needs to be *absolutely* certain. Others such as Locke, claim that strong evidence is sufficient without acquiring *total certainty*.

Empiricism and rationalism are schools of thought offering differing theories in relation to sources of knowledge. Rationalist thinkers claim that knowledge derives from reason which, broadly speaking, can attain

---

131. McInerney, *Introduction to Philosophy*, 61.
132. Ibid., 61.

certainty. Self-evident truths can be drawn from logical arguments, good reasoning, definitions, and principles.[133] Empiricists claim that ideas are only relevant in order to understand connections within the mind.[134] What they claim is that knowledge is not certain and is derived originally not from thought, but our sense experiences of the external world.

> The five major ways of building up justified beliefs are: sense perceptions, forming generalisations from sense perceptions, forming and testing hypotheses, deducing conclusions from other justified beliefs and learning about a subject from the reports of other people. [135]

Providing adequate justification for beliefs is a complex task; it requires all of the above to be applied diligently. Those advocating skepticism argue that because we cannot rely on firsthand evidence and require secondary sources, our senses are not reliable and therefore our knowledge can never be certain. Our lack of certainty, skeptics claim, means we cannot attain knowledge. Descartes refuted this claim, stating that our *thinking* allows us to make justifications for knowledge.

Hume was an empiricist who questioned causation and induction, claiming there are no reasons to think one event necessarily causes another, thereby undermining inductive generalizations.[136] He argued that there is no reason to assume the past will resemble the future.

Relativism is the belief that there are no absolute truths, only different points of view. Knowledge and truth, according to this understanding, are contextual and dependent on culture, history, and perspectives.[137] However, many disagree with the position of relativism, arguing that there are universal components of human perception and language independent of cultural context.

The importance of thinking well is just as important today as it was in the time of Socrates. Philosopher Hannah Arendt argued that the defining quality of a person is *their ability to think well*.[138] This thinking, she argued, involved the ability to distinguish between what is right and wrong. In thinking well, Arendt states people are better able to make moral decisions. The lack of independent thinking, Arendt suggests, allowed many within

133. Ibid., 61–63.
134. Ibid., 62.
135. Ibid.
136. Ibid., 63.
137. Ibid.
138. Arendt, *Eichmann in Jerusalem*.

the Nazi party to follow orders without question, which ultimately led to the massive scale of evil committed in the Holocaust, which she termed as the "banality of evil." Arendt describes Adolf Eichmann, a Nazi war criminal, as someone who was "swept away unthinkingly by what everyone else does and believes in."[139] She states:

> Is our ability to judge, to tell right from wrong, beautiful from ugly, dependent upon our faculty of thought? Do the inability to think and a disastrous failure of what we commonly call conscience coincide? . . . An answer, if at all, can come only from the thinking experience, the performance itself, which means that we have to trace experiences rather than doctrines.[140]

> Just as terror, even in its pre-total, merely tyrannical form ruins all relationships between men, so the self-compulsion of ideological thinking ruins all relationships with reality. The preparation has succeeded when people have lost contact with their fellow men as well as the reality around them; for together with these contacts, men lose the capacity of both experience and thought. The ideal subject of totalitarian rule is not the convinced Nazi or the convinced Communist, but people for whom the distinction between fact and fiction (i.e., the reality of experience) and the distinction between true and false (i.e., the standards of thought) no longer exist.[141]

While we may use our reason to examine various claims related to propaganda, racism, or certain ideologies, reason in and of itself can only take us so far.[142] The use of reason to examine truth claims is not always able to predict or help us to arrive at complete truths. In the end, there are limitations to what we can fully know through reason:

---

139. Arendt, "Thinking and Moral Considerations," 445.
140. Ibid., 418, 426.
141. Arendt, *Origins of Totalitarianism*, 474.
142. Magee, *Ultimate Questions*, 16.

In our attempts to understand the universe we cannot get outside the empirical world. In our attempts to understand ourselves as human beings we cannot get outside ourselves as human beings. This is not, and I hope obviously not, to say that we cannot understand anything. But it is certainly to say that we cannot understand everything.[143]

Many philosophers would strongly reject the notion that the claim made above necessarily leads to an absence of thinking, but what perhaps it can lead to is a thinking that requires a different, broader context. This limitation to our reasoning, and by extension our knowledge, does not necessarily need to be understood as a human defeat or limitation to our progress. Rather than diminish our understandings of reality, limits can help us deepen our knowledge. Limits can, if we have the intellectual imagination (as Bryan Magee puts it) to conceive them, potentially keep us from arrogance and self-righteousness. Our awareness of what we cannot know has the potential in developing a sense of humility and wisdom, as exemplified in the life of Socrates, propelling us to pursue further questions with curiosity and a sense of wonder.

LOOKING FORWARD: IS RELIGIOUS FAITH RATIONAL?

Limitations to our reasoning, and by extension to our knowledge—sometimes referred to as "mystery"—are evident in the works of many philosophers, theologians, scientists, and thinkers who recognise the frontiers of what we know. Mystery was illustrated earlier in Jostein Gaarder's *Sophie's World* as enveloping the white rabbit. Karl Jaspers and French philosopher Jacque Maritain (1882–1973) understood the awareness of this mystery and the limitations of philosophical reasoning as leading to a profound personal experience of God.[144]

How do we interpret this limitation to our knowledge? Can we understand it? Can the presence of mystery lead us to subsequently infer that there is a creator or God? Does this mystery necessarily (logically or empirically) demonstrate God's existence? What is the nature of justifications used by people who believe in God? While the unknown, many argue, does not necessarily prove God's existence, some claim that it does *point* to the existence of the divine or transcendent. These are questions which people

143. Ibid.
144. Jaspers, *Way to Wisdom*.

have debated for millennia and which are not easily answered; however, we will explore some of these perspectives in the next chapter.

MAIN RESEARCH TASK

Write an essay, deliver a presentation, or debate on the following:

1. It is important to examine our lives
2. Wisdom should be taught in schools
3. Wonder is the origin of knowledge
4. Intuition is a valuable way of knowing
5. Technology facilitates critical inquiry
6. Skepticism is necessary in gaining knowledge
7. Scientism is a limitation to progress in knowledge
8. Humility leads to true understanding

INDEPENDENT RESEARCH QUESTIONS

1. In considering some of the limitations of science, what implications does this have regarding research in the human or social sciences?
2. To what extent can the scientific method ensure certainty regarding human behavior?
3. Are intuition and imagination more important than reason in gaining knowledge?
4. How can gender differences affect knowledge? Do men and women think differently?
5. How are both dogmatism and relativism problematic in their approaches to knowledge?
6. Is total certainty in knowledge possible?

What are you wondering about?

- What are you wondering about as a result of these lessons?
- What did you find interesting or intriguing?
- Have these lessons made you think differently about certain ideas or issues? Explain.
- What further questions do you have?
- In years to come, what might you remember from these lessons?

Is Religious Faith a Valid Way of Knowing?

Outline

1. Introduction
2. How is religious faith understood?
3. Traditional arguments: cosmological, ontological, wager, and teleological arguments
4. Contemporary debates
5. Religion and science
6. Other debates
    a. The problem of evil and suffering
    b. Miracles as a justification for religious faith
    c. Logical positivism
7. Religious experience as a justification for faith
8. Objective and subjective truth
9. Relational aspect of faith
10. Main research task
11. Independent research questions

Objectives

At the end of this chapter, students should demonstrate the ability to ask questions, wonder, and think critically think about the following:

1. Some traditional and nontraditional arguments for the existence of God
2. Examples of contemporary debates about religious faith
3. Distinctions made between religious and scientific claims
4. Understanding the ways of knowing which are used to justify religious faith

INTRODUCTION

> He understood the conflict of faith, the necessity of belief fighting the voice of experience. The voice that always urges the faithful—the *questioning* faithful—to adapt their beliefs to the world they inhabit, their culture. Christianity is based on faith, but if you study its history you see that it's had to adapt itself over and over with great difficulty in order that faith might flourish. That's a paradox and it can be an extremely painful one: on the face of it, believing and questioning are antithetical. Yet I believe they go hand in hand. One nourishing the other. Questioning may lead to great loneliness, but if it coexists with faith—true faith, abiding faith—it can end in the most joyful sense of communion.[1]

What does this passage say about religious faith?

> There is a place where we are always alone with our own mortality, where we must simply have something greater than ourselves to hold onto—God or history or politics or literature or a belief in the healing power of love, or even righteous anger. Sometimes I think they are all the same. A reason to believe, a way to take the world by the throat and insist that there is more to this life than we have ever imagined.[2]

What does this quote tell us about the human desire to believe in something greater than ourselves? Do you agree?

Since the beginning of civilization, we know that humans have thought there is something more than the physical world in which they live. Ancient

---

1. Scorsese, in Endō and Johnston, *Silence*, viii; (emphasis in original).
2. Allison, in Putnam, *Cambridge Companion to William James*, 96.

cultures worldwide believed there were powers in control of an existence they themselves often could not affect, causing rain to fall and crops to grow, but also drought and famine. It is likely that the belief in an otherworldly force or being—albeit in many varied forms—that persists to this day sprang from observation of the surrounding world. Yet despite the fact that today science can explain how rain falls and crops grow, researchers suggest that well over half of the world's population claims to be religious.[3] In countries where religion is outlawed, like China, we see a growing rise in religious adherents.[4]

Clearly, religious belief has not disappeared. How do we explain this phenomenon? Are religious people all deluded, as some atheists claim? Is religious belief genetic? Can modern science explain it? It is important to note that these questions about genes and physics come from an empirical way of seeing the world and therefore seek answers within this framework. Questions about the origins of the universe are not bound to science, but rather have been debated by philosophers and religious writers for centuries and are known as metaphysical questions. Metaphysics is broadly defined as "The branch of philosophy that deals with the first principles of things, including abstract concepts such as being, knowing, identity, time, and space,"[5] and includes the investigation into God's existence.

Student activity—Terminology

Some of the terms below are still debated amongst scholars; however, familiarity with some common understandings of the these will assist with engaging in the ideas presented. The Oxford and Webster dictionaries may be a good place to start.

Working in student pairs, write down the definitions of the terms below and take turns explaining them to each other:

theism, transcendent, pantheism, imminent, deism, omnipotent, polytheism, agnosticism, atheism, cosmological, metaphysics, teleological, subjective, objective, ontology, religious faith, evidentialism, Reformed epistemology, foundationalism.

---

3. Mackay, *Beyond Belief*, 3–5. See also Lugo, "Global Religious Landscape"; Bowker, *Oxford Dictionary of World Religions*; Harper, "84 Percent Of The World"; "World Factbook—Central Intelligence Agency."

4. Mackay, *Beyond Belief*, 3–5.

5. *Oxford Dictionaries*, s.v. "Metaphysics." http://www.oxforddictionaries.com/definition/english/metaphysics.

HOW IS RELIGIOUS FAITH UNDERSTOOD?

To begin this topic, we must first ask what we mean by existence. As you have learned from the epistemological section, there are many ways to justify claims of knowledge—what we determine to be true or existing. Does this question of God's existence pertain to the five senses, reason, logical arguments of induction and deduction, intuition, personal experience, or empirical evidence? Does it point to objective or subjective truth? Or both? To what extent can personal, spiritual, or religious experience be a justification? How do we make sense of the various terms used for the "mystery" discussed in chapter 1, also known as transcendence or God in religious writings?

What do we mean by the term "God?"

DISCUSSION QUESTIONS

1. Where does the idea of God come from?
2. Is God different than a god?" Can there be more than one God, or is that a contradiction?
3. Can we know there is a God or not? How have people over history approached this question?

When exploring the nature and understanding of God, we are faced with challenging and complex questions. The word "God" has for centuries conjured various notions and ideas. What do we mean when we refer to God? Are the terms used by religious people such as God, the divine, nirvana (Buddhism), Ultimate Reality (Hinduism), Allah (Islam), and Yahweh (Judaism) referring to the same or a different reality? By "God," do we mean a benevolent being who created the world, but is now not involved in order to allow for free will (deism)? Or perhaps a belief in God or a deity who intervenes in the universe (theism)?[6] Maybe "a doctrine which identifies God with the universe or regards the universe as a manifestation of God" (pantheism)?[7] Is God a projection of human subjective imaginations, or an objective phenomenon? Or something else?

---

6. *Oxford Dictionaries, s.v.* "Theism." https://en.oxforddictionaries.com/definition/theism.

7. *Oxford Dictionaries, s.v.* "Pantheism." https://en.oxforddictionaries.com/definition/pantheism.

The term "God" or "gods" is defined according to a particular religious tradition: for example, in Christianity, the term "God" is used, while for Hindus, references to "gods" are made in their belief system. In religious writings, terms such as "transcendence" and "immanence" are two modes for understanding God, the divine, mystery, the ineffable, or ultimate reality. Transcendence is a broad concept; understood as incomprehensible and beyond the world, it points to God or mystery. It can be defined as "Beyond or above the range of normal or physical human experience. Surpassing the ordinary; exceptional; existing apart from and not subject to the limitations of the material universe. It is often contrasted with immanent."[8] In Latin, transcendent means "climbing over." The word immanent, however, is slightly different, referring to the experience of the divine "within" a closeness to the divine.[9] It is important to note that in philosophy the term "transcendent" also touches on metaphysics.

Student activity

Match the statements below with the following terms:

Theism, pantheism, deism, immanence, and transcendence

1. God is the supreme creator and in control of the universe.
2. Through God's grace I experience peace and joy.
3. By following the teachings of Buddhism, I experience enlightenment and inner peace.
4. I see God when I gaze into the night sky or listen to the wind.

Pluralism: Do all religious traditions point to the same or different reality?

Religions differ in how they express notions of transcendence, the divine, or God. Religious traditions have for millennia developed notions of the divine or ultimate reality through their teachings and practices, resulting in both ideological and cultural differences. So, do the various religious traditions point to the same reality?

---

8. *Oxford Dictionaries*, s.v. "Transcendent." https://en.oxforddictionaries.com/definition/transecendent.

9. *Oxford Dictionaries*, s.v. "Immanent." https://en.oxforddictionaries.com/definition/immanent.

IS RELIGIOUS FAITH A VALID WAY OF KNOWING?

Philosopher of religion John Hick (1922–2012) states all religious traditions point to "the same reality."[10] An advocate of pluralism, he proposes that all religions point to the same concept, which differ in expression according to their particular traditions. He argues that our interpretation of ultimately reality, the ineffable or God, is determined by our cultural conceptual frameworks.[11] For example, the "ineffable"—which he defines as beyond the human scope of concepts—is experienced differently for Jews, Muslims, Hindus, and other religions. Essentially, reality is therefore the same, but experienced differently depending on the individual's particular religious tradition.

> . . . that there is an ultimate reality, which I refer to as the Real . . . which is in itself transcategorial (ineffable), beyond the range of our conceptual systems, but whose universal presence is humanly experienced in the various forms made possible by our conceptual-linguistic systems and spiritual practices.[12]

What do you think of the pluralism advocated by John Hick?

What are the justifications made for religious faith?

Religious faith can be defined as, "Relating to or believing in a religion: (of a belief or practice) forming part of someone's faith in a divine being."[13] Critics of religion claim that religious faith is irrational, with little justifiable evidence, rejecting its legitimacy as a valid way of knowing. A common critique is one supporting evidentialism, which is based on the notion that a "belief is justified only if it is proportioned to the evidence . . . and it implies that full religious belief is justified only if there is conclusive evidence for it."[14]

---

10. Meister, *Introducing Philosophy of Religion*, 31.
11. Ibid., 31.
12. Hick, *Interpretation of Religion*, xix.
13. *Oxford Dictionaries*, s.v. "Religious faith." https://en.oxforddictionaries.com/definition/religious faith.
14. Forrest, "Epistemology of Religion," 1.

DISCUSSION QUESTIONS

1. Does religious faith need to be justified by evidence? If so, what kind of evidence is required to justify religious faith? Is it the same as, or different from, science?
2. Can divine revelation or inspiration be a valid justification for religious faith? Can this be considered a "type of reason?"
3. What is your own understanding of God or gods?
4. What arguments could you put forward in favour of and against religious faith?

As discussed in the epistemology chapter, what is understood as reasonable evidence is contested in philosophy. We saw the limitations of using reason in arriving at absolutely conclusive evidence. Through the problems of induction, for instance, it was evident that total certainty was not possible. For example, for the past 100 years it has snowed in Siberia and it will most probably snow again the next winter, a fact not of total certainty, but rather high probability.

Some philosophers and theologians have proposed that faith is not irrational and have made connections between faith and reason. These thinkers have demonstrated the existence of God through reasoned arguments such as the works of Thomas Aquinas, as well as the Kalam argument, among others. English philosopher Richard Swinburne proposes an inductive argument for the existence of God, arguing that based on evidence of how the universe works, there is a high probability of God's existence.

Some claim that religious faith does not require evidence because it is known intuitively. Others have claimed that religious faith is not irrational, but beyond reason. American philosopher Alvin Plantinga argues that it is rational to believe in God despite the lack of conclusive evidence. Platinga rejects the notion of evidentialism defined earlier, claiming that its assumptions are flawed. He argues that much of what counts as evidence under this approach cannot be conclusive or logically proven.

There are those who have critiqued the conceptual and abstract understanding of religious faith, positing an existential approach which focuses on personal meanings. Some of these thinkers include Rudolf Otto, Søren Kierkegaard, Karl Jaspers, and Simone Weil. These philosophers have proposed the value of some religious and mystical experiences as providing a

IS RELIGIOUS FAITH A VALID WAY OF KNOWING?

valid justification for religious faith.[15] For example, philosopher and psychologist William James argues that religion provides positive psychological needs through religious experiences and therefore serves a practical purpose. This chapter briefly presents these various perspectives on religious faith, which the reader is encouraged to further explore and discuss. It includes an introduction to some traditional and nontraditional arguments as epistemological questions continue to guide the inquiry.

DISCUSSION QUESTIONS

1. How did the world begin? Did it appear from nothing or did it have a first cause? Or did the world always exist?
2. Is reason a useful justification for religious faith? Are there other ways of knowing better suited to answer this question? Explain.
3. To what extent can we explore the question of religious faith outside the lens of science?

TRADITIONAL ARGUMENTS USING REASON AS A JUSTIFICATION FOR RELIGIOUS FAITH

STUDENT PROMPTING ACTIVITY—VIDEO:

Watch the following video, "PHILOSOPHY—Religion: Reason And Faith [HD]."[16]

What connections does Greg Ganssle make between faith and reason?

HOW DID THE WORLD BEGIN?

Human curiosity and inquiry naturally ask questions pertaining to identity such as who we are and how we got here. These questions were echoed by the Greek philosopher Xenophanes (570–478 BC), who proposed that something must have created the world. This *something* was a single God, according to Xenophanes, rather than *many* that were reflected in pagan

---

15. Gellman, "Mysticism," 30.
16. https://www.youtube.com/watch?v=MTPHXNMi9tA.

belief in his time, and this God was immaterial and must have always existed.[17]

Today, many of us think of the Big Bang as creating the universe. However, we may naturally wonder, as scientists do, *who or what* created the Big Bang? Did something always exist? Does matter need a cause, or can it come from nothing? Some scientists argue for the need of a cause, whilst others claim it is possible for something to come from nothing. These questions lie at the base of what is known as the cosmological argument.

Discuss the questions posed above. How did the world begin?

Cosmological argument—Causation

The cosmological argument is the idea that nature depends on something independent of itself for its existence and that the chain of cause and effect had a first cause. Many thinkers over the years have explored this fundamental argument.

THE KALAM ARGUMENT—
ISLAMIC SCHOLARS IN THE MUSLIM GOLDEN AGE

The conclusion that the universe must have a beginning arose in the Muslim world during its Golden Age (ca. 1000–1350 CE), a period of investigation and flourishing enlightenment similar to Europe's Renaissance.[18]

---

17. Tarnas, *The Passion of the Western Mind*, 45.
18. Gutas, in Janssens and De Smet, *Heritage of Avicenna*, 81–97.

A number of prominent luminaries living primarily in the economic and cultural centre of Baghdad used what is known as the Kalam argument (Kalam translates to "speculative theology" in Arabic) in determining a finite beginning to the universe. The Kalam argument uses a logical proof to identify the contradiction in an existence comprised of cause-and-effect events that would have an infinite timeline (referred to as infinite regress in chapter 1). Scholars such as Ibn Sina (ca. 970–1037 CE), Ishâq al-Kindî (ca. 800–870 CE), and Abû Hamid al-Ghazâlî (c.1056–1111) concluded that there must be a beginning and therefore a cause to  the universe, the cause being God. Some scholars attribute the influence of these ideas to the readings of Aristotle's work on cosmology, particularly his theory of the Prime Mover. The Kalam argument has experienced contemporary resurgence with American Christian philosopher William Lane Craig.

For further research, these links may be useful:

Bragg, Melvyn. "Al-Kindi, In Our Time—BBC Radio 4," *BBC*, 2012.[19]

Bragg, Melvyn. "Al-Ghazali, In Our Time—BBC Radio 4," *BBC*, 2015.[20]

Perry, John, and Taylor, Ken. "Islamic Philosophy." *Philosophy Talk*. Podcast audio, Nov. 18, 2007.[21]

---

19. http://www.bbc.co.uk/programmes/b01k2bv8.
20. http://www.bbc.co.uk/programmes/b055j9rv.
21. https://www.philosophytalk.org/shows/islamic-philosophy.

Thomas Aquinas (1224–1274)
Christian Western thinking

First Cause is a term introduced by Aristotle and used in philosophy and theology. Aristotle noted that things in nature are caused and that these causes in nature exist in a chain, stretching backward. The cause of the cat you see today, for example, was its parent cats, and the cause of those parents were the grandparent cats, and so on. The same for the oak tree you see; it was caused by an acorn from a previous oak tree, which in turn was caused by an acorn tree from a previous oak tree, and so on, stretching back to whenever. The central question about such causal chains, raised by Aristotle and others, is whether they must have a starting point. Aristotle, and others following him, claim that the answer is yes, i.e., that there must be a First Cause because such causal chains cannot be infinite in length. Aristotle referred to the First Cause also as the "Prime Mover" that is a deity of "pure form" without any potentiality, but theists such as Thomas Aquinas identify this First Cause with God in Christianity, and use this argument, usually known as the "argument from causation," as an argument for the existence of God. This argument was the second of Aquinas' "Five Ways' of proving (he thought) the existence of God.[22]

Thomas Aquinas further developed the cosmological argument. A significant influencer on Christian thought, he wrote extensively on the topics of faith and reason, applying these to prove the existence of God. Like Aristotle and proponents of the Kalam argument, Aquinas observed that the natural world had order based on cause and effect.[23] Each action was caused by a previous action which set it into motion. Drawing on Aristotle's ideas,

---

22. "First Cause," para 1.
23. Ibid.

IS RELIGIOUS FAITH A VALID WAY OF KNOWING?

Aquinas argued that reality did not engage endlessly in the action of cause and effect, but rather there was a first cause which put an end to the infinite regress. Aquinas calls this the first cause—referred to as the Unmoved Mover or Prime Mover by Aristotle—that presence which does not need a cause, as it was the *cause of all causes*. Aquinas claimed this first cause which started the motion of all cause and effect was initiated by God:

> There are five ways of proving there is a God: . . . The first and most obvious way is based on change. For certainly some things are changing by something else. The second way is based on the very notion of agent cause. In the observable world causes are found ordered in series: we never observe, nor ever could, something causing itself, for this would mean it preceded itself, and this is not possible. But a series of causes can't go on for ever, for in any such series an earlier member causes an intermediate and the intermediate a last (whether the intermediate be one or many). Now eliminating a cause eliminates its effects, and unless there's a first cause there won't be a last or an intermediate. But if a series of causes goes on for ever it will have no first cause, and so no intermediate causes and no last effect, which is clearly false. So we are forced to postulate some first agent cause, to which everyone gives the name God.[24]

What do you think of the ideas presented by Aquinas? Do you agree? Explain.

Can you think of counterarguments?

One of the objections to Aquinas' argument is whether the universe needs a first cause. Could it have existed indefinitely? If there is a first cause, does this necessarily prove the existence of the Judeo-Christian God? Do we even need to ask these questions about how the world came into existence and instead accept that it just exists? Philosopher Bertrand Russell points out, "I see no reason whatsoever to suppose that the total has any cause whatsoever . . . I should say the universe is just there and that's all."[25]

Student activity—Research

Islamic cosmology:

24. Aquinas, "Summa Theologiae" 1a, q.2, art.3.
25. Russell, in Meister, *Introducing Philosophy of Religion*, 70.

Research Ibn Sna, also known as Avicenna (AD 980–1037), an Islamic philosopher and theologian who used reason to develop the cosmological argument within Islam's Golden Age.

This link may be a useful start: Melvyn Bragg, "Avicenna, In Our Time—BBC Radio 4," *BBC*, 2007.[26]

Compare and contrast to Hindu cosmology.
This link may be a useful start: Melvyn Bragg, "Hindu Ideas Of Creation, In Our Time—BBC Radio 4," *BBC*, 2015.[27]

An article for further reading is: "Big Questions Online—Can Cosmology Prove or Disprove Creation?"[28]
    Record your findings and present them to the class.

Extension—Student activity:

What are some similarities and differences between the cosmological arguments of the Kalam argument and Aquinas?

Ontological, wager, and teleological arguments

Read the following extracts, highlighting key words, and respond to the activity below.

Anselm—Ontological argument

> For I do not seek to understand in order to believe; I believe in order to understand. For I also believe that "Unless I believe, I shall not understand.[29]

> Truly there is a God, although the fool has said in his heart, There is no God.

---

26. http://www.bbc.co.uk/programmes/b008551t.
27. http://www.bbc.co.uk/programmes/b03k289f.
28. https://www.bigquestionsonline.com/2017/10/02/can-cosmology-prove-disprove-creation/
29. Anselm, *Proslogion I*, 53.

AND so, Lord, do you, who do give understanding to faith, give me, so far as you knowest it to be profitable, to understand that you are as we believe; and that you are that which we believe. And indeed, we believe that you are a being than which nothing greater can be conceived. Or is there no such nature, since the fool has said in his heart, there is no God? (Psalms xiv. 1). But, at any rate, this very fool, when he hears of this being of which I speak—a being than which nothing greater can be conceived—understands what he hears, and what he understands is in his understanding; although he does not understand it to exist.

For, it is one thing for an object to be in the understanding, and another to understand that the object exists. When a painter first conceives of what he will afterwards perform, he has it in his understanding, but be does not yet understand it to be, because he has not yet performed it. But after he has made the painting, he both has it in his understanding, and he understands that it exists, because he has made it.

Hence, even the fool is convinced that something exists in the understanding, at least, than which nothing greater can be conceived. For, when he hears of this, he understands it. And whatever is understood, exists in the understanding. And assuredly that, than which nothing greater can be conceived, cannot exist in the understanding alone. For, suppose it exists in the understanding alone: then it can be conceived to exist in reality; which is greater.

Therefore, if that, than which nothing greater can be conceived, exists in the understanding alone, the very being, than which nothing greater can be conceived, is one, than which a greater can be conceived. But obviously this is impossible. Hence, there is doubt that there exists a being, than which nothing greater can be conceived, and it exists both in the understanding and in reality.[30]

1. What do you think Anselm is trying to say about religious faith?
2. What are the connections between belief and understanding?

30. Anselm, *Proslogion II*, 54.

3. Do we understand first then believe, or believe then seek understanding? Explain.

Paley—design (Teleological argument)

Consider William Paley's 1867 watchmaker argument:

> [S]uppose I found a watch upon the ground, and it should be inquired how the watch happened to be in that place, I should hardly think . . . that, for anything I knew, the watch might have always been there. Yet why should not this answer serve for the watch as well as for stone [that happened to be lying on the ground]? . . . For this reason, and for no other; namely, that, if the different parts had been differently shaped from what they are, if a different size from what they are, or placed after any other manner, or in any order than that in which they are placed, either no motion at all would have been carried on in the machine, or none which would have answered the use that is now served by it.
>
> Every indicator of contrivance, every manifestation of design, which existed in the watch, exists in the works of nature; with the difference, on the side of nature, of being greater and more, and that in a degree which exceeds all computation. I mean that the contrivances of nature surpass the contrivances of art, in the complexity, subtlety, and curiosity of the mechanism; and still more, if possible, do they go beyond them in number and variety; yet in a multitude of cases, are not less evidently mechanical, not less evidently contrivances, not less evidently accommodated to their end, or suited to their office, than are the most perfect productions of human ingenuity.[31]

Does a world with intricate design necessarily need an intelligent maker? How else might we explain it?

---

31. Paley, *Natural Theology*, 1, 13.

Is Religious Faith a Valid Way of Knowing? 99

Pascal's (Wager Argument)

> "God is, or He is not." But to which side shall we incline? Reason can decide nothing here. There is an infinite chaos which separates us. A game is being played at the extremity of this infinite distance where heads or tails will turn up . . . Which will you choose then? Let us see. Since you must choose, let us see which interests you least. You have two things to lose, the true and the good; and two things to stake, your reason and your will, your knowledge and your happiness; and your nature has two things to shun, error and misery. Your reason is no more shocked in choosing one rather than the other, since you must of necessity choose . . . But your happiness? Let us weigh the gain and the loss in wagering that God is . . . If you gain, you gain all; if you lose, you lose nothing. Wager, then, without hesitation that He is. Let us see. Since there is an equal risk of gain and of loss, if you had only to gain two lives, instead of one, you might still wager. But if there were three lives to gain, you would have to play (since you are under the necessity of playing), and you would be imprudent, when you are forced to play, not to chance your life to gain three at a game where there is an equal risk of loss and gain. But there is an eternity of life and happiness.[32]

What motivates Pascal to believe in God? Is it a sense of wonder and awe, or fear that he might lose out? Or be punished? Can you relate to Pascal's line of thinking?

We project our own wishes and imagination in creating a God—Ludwig Feuerbach (1804–1872)

> Therefore, God is an existent, real being, on the very same ground that he is a particular, definite being; for the qualities of God are nothing else than the essential qualities of man himself . . .[33]

How does Feuerbach understand God?

---

32. Pascal, *Pensées*, 233.
33. Feuerbach, *Essence of Christianity*, 251.

Student Activity—Comprehension

Respond to the following, working in pairs or individually:

1. In each of the passages above, research the meanings of key words or phrases.
2. Identify the main claims used for the justification of God in each of the extracts.
3. Discuss the similarities and differences between the arguments presented.
4. What ways of knowing are used for the justification of faith in each of the passages? Can you think of limitations and strengths of each argument?

You may want to use the following resources: Philosophy of Religion: The Ontological Argument; The Cosmological Argument; The Teleological Argument[34]

Your discussion and research may lead you to some of the following:

St. Anselm (1033–1109)

St. Anselm asserts God's existence by proposing an ontological argument. Ontology can be defined as a "particular theory about the nature of being or the kinds of things that have existence."[35] Anselm proposes that we need to think of the greatest and most perfect being imaginable. If this being has all the desirable attributes and not existence, it cannot be the most perfect. Something that exists is most perfect and greater than that which does not exist. Therefore, the greatest and more perfect, which is God, must exist.[36] St.

---

34. http://www.philosophyofreligion.info/theistic-proofs/the-teleological-argument/.

35. *Merriam-Webster Dictionary*, s.v. "Ontology." https://www.merriam-webster.com/dictionary/ontology.

36. Anselm, *Proslogion*.

Thomas Aquinas disagreed with Anselm's argument as it jumped from the conceptual to the ontological order. It is important to keep in mind that Anselm wrote within a medieval scholastic culture where the belief in a God was generally accepted. He argued that in order to fully know God, we first had to have faith. Anselm's linguistically intricate deductive argument aligns with his known outlook of "faith seeking understanding" and facilitated religious belief in connecting with philosophical reasoning.

BLAISE PASCAL (1623–1662)

Blaise Pascal argued that we cannot prove God's existence. He states that arguments for and against God are equally valid, and therefore, we cannot be certain of either. Pascal thought that to live in a world *as* if God exists leads to greater benefits. First, we would be happier in this life, and second, judgement would be more favorable upon death. Overall, the benefits of believing outweighed not believing. He concluded that ultimately, religious belief is a calculated gamble with better odds towards belief. His theory is widely known as Pascal's wager.

LUDWIG FEUERBACH (1804–1872)

Ludwig Feuerbach argued that there is no reason for a belief in God and that humans project their own needs in constructing an image of God. Humans identify all the positive qualities of perfection, intelligence, and goodness, then project through imagination an image of God which they can trust and believe.[37] For Feuerbach, God was nothing more than a fulfillment of human wants and needs.

---

37. Kirkwood, *Looking for Proof of God*, 20.

William Paley (1743–1805)

William Paley argued that the universe's complexity and intricate design, like a watch, possessed extreme order. He concluded that this purpose, design, and order within creation had to have a creator. This order, Paley argued, did not emerge by chance, but was rather created by a designing mind, which he claimed to be God.

Student activity—
A conversation with some great scholars

- Form groups of four to five and research one of the following people: Avicenna, St. Thomas Aquinas, Anselm, Pascal, Feuerbach, Paley, or another cosmologist from another religious tradition.
- One of the members of the group will then be chosen as a representative to be included on a panel in order to join a conversation.
- The focus question in conversation is, "How is the existence or nonexistence of God understood through reason?"
- Each of these speakers will give a three-to-six-minute initial speech, then all will engage in a conversation directed by a chairperson.
- The chairperson (a teacher or student) will be responsible for steering the conversation and asking relevant questions.
- Time will be allocated to the audience (rest of the class) to ask questions from the scholars on the panel.

Student Reflections

What are you now wondering about?

- What ideas or questions are you wondering about as a result of these lessons?
- Have these lessons made you think differently? Explain.
- What have you found challenging, provocative, or intriguing?

CONTEMPORARY DEBATES

There is a high probability that God exists—Richard Swinburne

Oxford scholar Dr. Richard Swinburne uses inductive reasoning to argue that, based on the current evidence of how the universe works, there is a high probability of God's existence. He bases his argument on some of the following points:

1. There is matter in the universe rather than nothing and it behaves according to a few simple laws.[38]
2. The level of order and deep structure which forms the fundamental basis of our universe is presupposed by science.[39]
3. This order and simplicity has persisted throughout time.
4. This order includes regularities, which he claims are not random or accidental, such as the periodical table of elements, but rather *point* to a purpose, design, intelligence, and power beyond the natural world. We cannot expect this order and regularity to emerge from its own accord, which therefore requires a maker, suggesting a high probably of God's existence.[40]

Swinburne points out that much of our knowledge from science is based on probability, not certainty. He also argued that theories and predictions cannot exist within a vacuum unless there is something constant outside it to formulate the theories. Swinburne claims that while science can describe and explain the regularities within the universe it cannot explain *why* there are these laws. Swinburne also observed other factors which increased the probability of God's existence; these included the awareness of morality amongst humans, religious experiences, and the evidence of some miracles:

> . . . I have urged that various occurrent phenomena are such that they are more to be expected, more probable, if there is a God than if there is not. The existence of the universe, its conformity to order, the existence of animals and humans with moral awareness, humans having great opportunities for co-operation in acquiring knowledge and moulding the universe, the pattern of history and the existence of some evidence of

---

38. Swinburne, *The Existence of God*, 328–54.
39. Ibid., 328–54.
40. Ibid.

miracles, and finally the occurrence of religious experiences, are all such as we have reason to expect if there is a God, and less reason to expect otherwise.[41]

Do Swinburne's observations warrant the probability of God's existence? Explain.

Some have argued that Swinburne's ideas are similar to Paley's design argument. Do you agree?

If Swinburne is understood correctly above, there may be some limitations to his argument. First, some maintain there is a multiple universe theory within physics which states there are different sets of matter, not one. Second, it is possible that the natural ordering of matter can be caused by natural rather than supernatural causes. Third, some have argued that subjective religious experience cannot be inferred to an objective reality; in other words, a person's experience of God cannot tell us anything objective and is therefore an insufficient proof of God's existence.

Student activity—Research

Study the works of Swinburne on the "existence of God" argument and answer the questions below.
The following videos may be useful:
Richard Swinburne: On Arguments for God's Existence[42]
Richard Swinburne: The Existence of God.[43]
Richard Swinburne: On arguments for Atheism.[44]

Discussion questions

1. Are Swinburne's claims of probability convincing? Explain.
2. What are some limitations to his argument?
3. From the terms mentioned, what understanding of God does Swinburne adopt? For example, theistic, pantheistic, etc.

---

41. Ibid., 328.
42. https://www.youtube.com/watch?v=y52I3aNbMYg.
43. https://www.youtube.com/watch?v=ALwlAetJWvs.
44. https://www.youtube.com/watch?v=oh6IwNlEQ2g.

4. How does Swinburne make the connections between faith and reason?

Belief in God is rational and justifiable—Alvin Plantinga

American philosopher Dr. Alvin Plantinga argues that a belief in God is rational and justifiable. He is critical of evidentialism which, as defined earlier, includes the view that a "belief is justified only if it is proportioned to the evidence . . . and it implies that full religious belief is justified only if there is conclusive evidence for it."[45] Platinga argues that evidence, within this model, can never be *conclusive*. Evidentialism, or what is also termed by scholars as foundationalism, seeks to gather evidence on the following grounds:

1. Incorrigible: beliefs are relevant to personal experience; for example, I feel joy, or I see a desk in front of me.

2. Self-evident: beliefs are based on logic or mathematical truths; for example, 1+1 = 2, or a bachelor is an unmarried man.

3. Evident to sense experience: beliefs based on one of more of the five senses; for example, I feel wet or I smell curry.[46]

Philosophers advocating classical foundationalism believe that in order to form a reasonable belief, two out of three experiences listed above must be demonstrated. Platinga, like other philosophers, has critiqued this approach, arguing that the components listed above do not provide a strong enough basis for belief. He argues that much of what counts as "evidence" under this approach cannot be logically demonstrated. For example, as discussed in chapter 1, personal experience and our senses are not always reliable, so self-evident truths cannot be proven and are therefore self-refuting.[47]

What Platinga and other thinkers such as reformed epistemologists have proposed is that while rational positions formed from basic beliefs are feasible, they need not conform to the above criteria.[48] These "basic" beliefs, Platinga argued, can be in themselves justified; for example, I can see that

---

45. Forrest, "Epistemology of Religion," 1.
46. Meister, *Introducing Philosophy of Religion*, 161–62.
47. Plantinga and Wolterstorff, *Faith and Rationality*, 59–63.
48. Ibid., 59–63.

a book or flower is a basis for a justified belief. What he calls "basic and proper" beliefs do not need to refer to other beliefs:[49]

> Although beliefs of this sort are typically taken as basic, it would be a mistake to describe them as *groundless*. Upon having experience of a certain sort, I believe that I am perceiving a tree. In the typical case I do not hold this belief on the basis of other beliefs; it is nonetheless not groundless. My having that characteristic sort of experience ... plays a crucial role in the formation of that belief. It also plays a crucial role in its justification.[50]

Platinga is attempting to broaden the category of foundationalism to also include the belief in God. He argues that the belief in God is not very different to basic beliefs like, "I live in a certain country, am a certain age and I had eggs for breakfast." Platinga claims that a belief in God can be part of what he deems "properly basic belief," an "immediate and direct" belief which does not need further justification.[51] Additionally, Platinga proposes that humans naturally have an innate awareness of the divine.

Discussion questions

1. Identify the main arguments put forward by Platinga. Are they convincing? Explain.
2. What are some limitations to his argument?
3. Can a belief in God be the same as other "basic beliefs" we hold, as suggested by Platinga?
4. To what extent can God be known through an intuition or feeling? Is this adequate justification? Why do some people experience this and not others?

People who believe in God are deluded—Richard Dawkins

In his book *The God Delusion*, Dr. Richard Dawkins argues that religious faith is based on false assumption and erroneous justification. Dawkins is

49. Ibid., 79.
50. Ibid., 79 (emphasis in original).
51. Ibid., 87–91.

a biologist, an advocate of evolutionary theory, and a well-known critic of religion. He proposes that, based on scientific evidence, there is no proof of God's existence. He also goes on to say that people who believe in religion and God are, in fact, deluded.

> I shall define the God Hypothesis more defensibly: *there exists a superhuman, supernatural intelligence who deliberately designed and created the universe and everything in it, including us.* This book will advocate an alternative view: *any creative intelligence, of sufficient complexity to design anything, comes into existence only as the end product of an extended process of gradual evolution.*[52]

Do you agree with Dawkin's claims?

What do you think Dawkins might mean by a "creative intelligence?"

Does a "creative intelligence" necessarily need to come into existence as the end product of evolution?

Dawkins is using science, and in particular his evolutionary biology framework as a justification for his claims about God. Many philosophers and religious writers have critiqued Dawkins. One could dispute the claim made by Dawkins, that the emergence of a creative intelligence does not necessarily need to come into existence as the end product of evolution. Additionally, Dawkins does not solve the issues of *what* created the biological and evolutionary system.

Richard Dawkins

---

52. Dawkins, *The God Delusion*, 31 (emphasis in original).

> ... I don't believe in an old man in the sky with a long white beard. That old man is an irrelevant distraction and his beard is as tedious as it is long. Indeed, the distraction is worse than irrelevant. Its very silliness is calculated to distract attention from the fact that what the speaker really believes is not a whole lot less silly ... I am not attacking any particular version of God or gods. I am attacking God, all gods, anything and everything supernatural, wherever and whenever they have been or will be invented.[53]

What is your opinion of the quote above?

We may call into question Dawkins' depiction of how people imagine a higher being. Can we say definitely that a belief in a "white bearded man" is true for all religious beliefs about God? This view may be depicted in Hollywood and perceived within religious fundamentalist views, but it is not part of mainstream religious and theological beliefs. Many religious writers have described Dawkins' depiction of God as inadequate.

> Religion ... has certain ideas at the heart of it which we call sacred or holy or whatever. What it means is, "Here is an idea or a notion that you're not allowed to say anything bad about; you're just not. Why not?—because you're not!"[54]

Dawkins includes in his work comments arguing that religion is a closed system not open to question or criticism. Certainly, there are instances of coercion today and throughout history to abstain from religious criticism due to its perceived sanctity, which may not be justified. However, debates and differences of opinion amongst many theologians, religious scholars, and philosophers make this claim suspect.

The notion of holy or sacred

The term "sacred" or "holy" has a meaning, which in the context of religious writings possesses a component of a deeper mystery not acknowledged by Dawkins. As discussed in chapter 1, this mystery points to the limitations of knowledge and reason argued by many well-known philosophers such as Kant and Hume, rather than something that is not to be questioned,

---

53. Ibid., 36.
54. Ibid., 20.

as implied by Dawkins. Although the word "mystery" can be defined as a problem to be solved, it can also mean a presence which permeates the universe independently of the discoveries of science. It is this latter use that religious writers have adopted. For religious writers, this sense of mystery which pervades the universe in a broad sense is understood to have characteristics of the sacred or holy.

Do you agree/disagree with the counter arguments presented? Explain.

> God is a delusion—"a psychotic delinquent" invented by mad, deluded people. That's the take-home message of *The God Delusion*. Although Dawkins does not offer a rigorous definition of a "delusion," he clearly means a belief that is not grounded in evidence or, worse, that flies in the face of the evidence. Faith is "blind trust, in the absence of evidence, even in the teeth of evidence." It is a "process of non-thinking." It is "evil precisely because it requires no justification, and brooks no argument." These core definitions of faith are hardwired into Dawkins' worldview and are obsessively repeated throughout his writings. It is not a Christian definition of faith but one that Dawkins has invented to suit his own polemical purposes. It immediately defines those who believe in God as people who have lost touch with reality—as those who are *deluded*.[55]

According to Alister E. McGrath and Joanna Collicutt McGrath, what does Dawkins mean by the phrase, "religious people are deluded?"

Do you agree/disagree with the claims made about Dawkins? Explain.

The Mystery

As alluded to, the term "mystery" used by many philosophers is not a problem to be solved, but a pervading presence which induces awe and wonder. For example, in chapter 1, the mystery in *Sophie's World* was the world depicted outside the rabbit's snug fur. As philosophers, religious writers, and scientists have recognised, this mystery is not easily explained though language yet remains a powerful phenomenon. Albert Einstein (1879–1955) states the following:

---

55. McGrath and McGrath, *The Dawkins Delusion*, 1 (emphasis in original).

The most beautiful and deepest experience a man can have is the sense of the mysterious. It is the underlying principle of religion as well as of all serious endeavour in art and science. He who never had this experience seems to me, if not dead, then at least blind. To sense that behind anything that can be experienced there is a something that our minds cannot grasp, whose beauty and sublimity reaches us only indirectly: this is religiousness. In this sense I am religious. To me it suffices to wonder at these secrets and to attempt humbly to grasp with my mind a mere image of the lofty structure of all there is.[56]

Albert Einstein

Dawkins points out that Einstein never subscribed to the notions of a personal God attributed in theistic religious traditions. However, in Einstein's attempt to understand the universe, he wrote about religious feelings experienced in what he sensed was an "expansive mystery" within the universe, unfathomable to the human mind. As discussed in chapter 1, there are many religious writers who argue that religion *is a response* to this mystery which pervades the universe. They describe mystery as a presence which is

56. This article is a speech by Albert Einstein to the German League of Human Rights, Berlin, in the autumn of 1932. This short speech appears in White and Gribbin, *Einstein*, 262.

powerful and embedded within a sense of the sacred. Scholars Rudolf Otto (German; 1869–1937) and Mircea Eliade (American; 1907–1986) describe the religious response to this mystery. Otto illustrates below the experience as powerful and spiritual, or numinous (in Latin, *mysterium tremendumet fascinas*), and like Einstein, he states that it induces a sense of fear, awe, and ecstasy.[57] Eliade describes Otto's experience of the mysterious in the following way:

> . . . Otto sets himself to discover the characteristics of this frightening and irrational experience. He finds the *feeling of terror* before the sacred, before the awe-inspiring mystery (*mysterium tremendum*), the *(majestas)* that emanates an overwhelming superiority of power; he finds *religious fear* before the fascinating mystery (*mysterium fascinans*) in which perfect fullness of being flowers. Otto characterizes all these experiences as numinous (from Latin *numen*, god), for they are induced by the revelation of an aspect of divine power. The numinous presents itself as something "wholly other" . . . something basically and totally different.[58]

DISCUSSION QUESTIONS

1. What are some common features of the term "mystery" described by Einstein, Otto, and Eliade?
2. What do you think Dawkins would say to both of these descriptions?

---

57. Eliade, *The Sacred and the Profane*, 9–10.
58. Ibid, 9–10; (emphasis in original).

RELIGION AND SCIENCE: CAN THEY COEXIST?

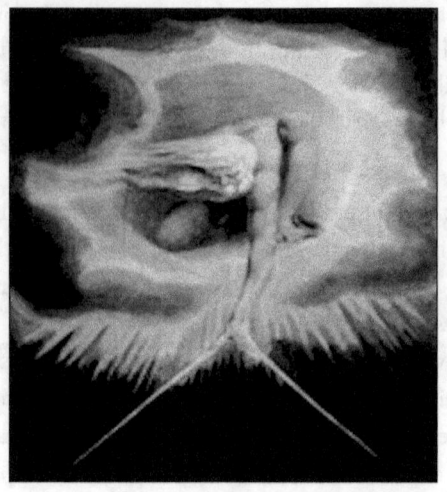

Ancient of Days (1794) William Blake

STUDENT ACTIVITY—VIDEO

Watch the following debate between Dawkins and a Jesuit priest.

1. "Star Talk S01 E05—Richard Dawkins"[59]

DISCUSSION QUESTIONS

1. Identify the claims made by defenders of science and religion.
2. Who is telling the *most* truth and why? Explain.

---

59. https://www.youtube.com/watch?v=7_zezmQrkec.

Are religious and scientific truths different?

Scientific/Historical Truths	Religious/Spiritual Truths
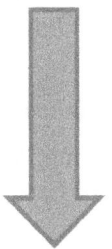	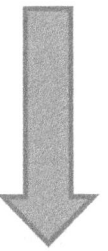
Knowledge is derived from applying the SCIENTIFIC METHOD.	Philosophical arguments (REASON) positing the existence of God.
	First Cause (Aquinas) and Kalam argument (al Ghazali and al-Kindi).
	RELIGIOUS EXPERIENCE is also a justification for religious faith (i.e., James).
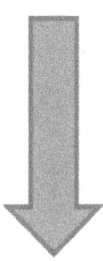	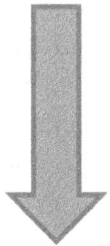
Hypothesis, observation, theory, and inductive and deductive reasoning are used as ways of knowing (or justification). There is EMPIRICAL framework in understanding reality.	Reason, intuition, experience and emotion as ways of knowing (or justification). Many theologians and some philosophers argue that religious faith is not irrational but rather understood as beyond our reasoning capacity. STORIES, MYTHS, and PARABLES are used to convey moral and religious truths.

What do you think of the distinctions made above? Do you agree/disagree? Explain.

Student activity — Video and excerpt

Palaeontologist Stephen Jay Gould (1941–2002) claimed that science and religion can coexist. Read the following article and watch the YouTube links included, and then summarise the main arguments.

1. "Gould's NOMA—A Thorough Analysis (Part 1) Revisited."[60]
2. "Stephen Jay Gould's Concept of Non-Overlapping Magisteria (NOMA)."[61]
3. "Science, Fate and Religion."[62]

Student activity — Research

Can there exist a synthesis between science and religion?

Select one of the following thinkers, and then research and present their ideas:

Pierre Teilhard de Chardin (1881–1955), Alfred Whitehead (1861–1947), Stephen Hawking (1942–2018), Ken Wilber (b. 1949), and Stephen Jay Gould (1941–2002).

Pierre Teilhard de Chardin

Student activity 2 — Debate

Debate the following: Religion and science can coexist.

---

60. https://www.skepticink.com/tippling/2014/11/01/goulds-noma-a-thorough-analysis-part-1-revisited/.
61. https://www.youtube.com/watch?v=yVd6MDLSYVA.
62. https://www.youtube.com/watch?v=D12OQ3MvaT8.

OTHER DEBATES

What do the presence of evil and suffering pose to the understanding of God or the divine?

Many religious scholars have understood the divine as *powerful, a creator, perfect,* and *loving*. However, these notions have caused problems and have raised challenging questions throughout history. If God created the universe and is all powerful and loving, how does God allow suffering and evil? There are various responses to the problem of evil. For example, some religious writers argue that God abstains from interference with the world to allow human freedom, and as a result evil and suffering occur because of the choices humans make. This theological approach is known as deism. Murders and wars, for instance, are a result of human free will and not brought about by God. If your understanding of God or the divine is immanent, then humans become responsible for evil actions and not God.

Student activity: Video

Watch the following YouTube video that shows the arguments about the problem of evil presented by philosopher Greg Ganselle (Yale University) and summarise the main ideas:

"Problem of Evil Part 1."[63]

For a further development of these arguments, you may watch parts 2 and 3 of this series.

Scholar and Anglican priest Dr. Steven Ogden explores the issues of human suffering and evil. He argues that the God of hard theism is no longer tenable.[64] As defined earlier, this is a belief in a God or gods that are distinct or separate from humans and who are in control of events within the world. This notion of God lends itself to exclusion and control that cannot adequately address the issue of evil and suffering in the world. Ogden claims that many people, mostly outside the church (including fundamentalist Christians), still think of God as the *old man in the sky*. This view of God, he argues, is not in line with current theology which over the years has had to rethink its understanding of God in order to address the issue

---

63. http://www.wi-phi.com/video/problem-evil-part-1.
64. Ogden, *I Met God in Bermuda*, 9–13.

of suffering and evil. For example, how does God successfully answer some prayers and not others? How can God fail to intervene in numerous wars, tsunamis, and other extreme tragedies in our world?

In his book, *I Meet God in Bermuda,* Ogden draws on the works of well-known Christian theologians such as Karl Rahner and Paul Tillich to propose an understanding of God which accommodates for both God's "absence" as well as God's "presence."[65] He argues that the experience of God is about *grace*, or "divine power," which arises in sometimes unexpected places and, although it is experienced in short moments, grace can leave a permanent transformative change.[66]

Ogden stresses the importance of relationships and shared human experience as an approach to finding new ways to talk about God which do not omit the issue of suffering.[67] He suggests that religious communities must debate, explore, and discuss openly these complex and important questions without resorting to simplistic conclusions. Ogden's suggestions here are useful in helping tackle complex issues that do not have easy answers.

Student activity: Excerpt

Read the following extract from the book, *I Met God in Bermuda,* by Dr. Steven Ogden, and answer the following questions:

1. What does Ogden suggest are the main problems inherent in the notion of a theistic God, as depicted by an *old man in the sky* or what he terms the "Car Park God?"
2. What problems does Ogden identify are present within the fundamental approach to religion?
3. According to Ogden, what could the "God of the twenty-first century" look like?
4. What ideas or questions did you agree/disagree with? Explain.
5. Are there ideas that you found interesting, puzzling or challenging? Explain.

> At 3am on Australian television, on any given day, there is usually at least one televangelist on air, in full flight, called something like Leroy van Bank. Typically, the way Leroy

---

65. Ibid., 64–75.
66. Ibid.
67. Ibid., 107, 122.

speaks about Jesus, God and the Devil is truly cringe worthy. He believes that the mythological figure of the Devil actually exists and his audience squeals with delight every time the Devil's name is mentioned. The audience's response to the Devil's name is like children at a pantomime, who greet the arrival of the moustachioed villain with rapture, as his sinister presence heightens the dramatic tension. In both situations, Leroy's and the pantomime, the tension seems more satisfying than the promise of its resolution. However, in Leroy's situation, there is every chance that vulnerable people are being disturbed and manipulated by this perverse form of hero-worship, which finds its focus in the enduring fascination with Leroy and the Devil (followed by Jesus and God in that order).

In terms of my concerns, the problem is the prevalence in tabloids and on television of the fire and brimstone anti-heroes of the religious right, who give the false impression that all Christians are like this. For instance, eminent biologist Richard Dawkins uses Leroy-like images to represent and condemn mainstream Christianity when he writes statements like, "the miracle-wreaking, thought-reading, interventionist, sin-punishing, prayer-answering God of the Bible."

In terms of baggage, another issue needs to be named. In the last decade or so, a number of clergy in the US, Australia, Europe and elsewhere have been convicted for offences relating to child abuse. While the majority of clergy are innocent of such appalling acts, we were all part of an inward-looking culture that fooled ourselves into believing that acts like these could never happen in the Church. There is a theological dimension here too, which propagates an idealized view of the Church and the Christian family. The idealized view is misleading, dishonest and dangerous. It is the kind of view that presumes God is in heaven and all is well, so consequently, we do not need to exercise wisdom and discernment in either our faith communities or our families. We are Christian and evidently Christian families are perfect families.

This toxic combination of a heavenly God, removed from earthly realities, with a naive and over-confident Church proved diabolical. There is no doubt that a certain way of idealizing God, clergy and Christian families helped to create this dangerous in-house culture as we did not feel obliged to take the normal precautions or set the standards, which were observed in society at large.

In short, this is just some of the contemporary baggage that comes with the word *God*. In an honest and transparent approach to today's big issues, these negative associations need to be named, as the process of naming may help some people discover that there is a life-affirming alternative to Leroy van Bank's life-denying pathology. However, while mainstream Christianity is radically different from Christian fundamentalism, there is a certain view of God, which they hold in common. This is the God of extreme or hard theism, the old man in the sky.

The God of hard theism is rightly linked to the Crusades, antisemitism, witch hunts, the Inquisition, racism and sexism. This is not to say that God or religion or individual Christians singlehandedly caused these events. These events have many interrelated causes. However, the God of hard theism lends itself to human attempts to control and exclude others. This is the God who rules, judges, punishes, saves and intervenes in world events at will. I call this *the Car Park God*. I have heard people say that they prayed to God, as they were racing to get to a meeting, and He got them a car park. While this type of prayer surfaces mainly in fundamentalist circles, for many of us there is the temptation to resort to the Car Park God under duress (as in the evening before an examination).

However, there is a profound issue at stake here and this is the failure of this God to intervene successfully for millions of innocent people. Where was the Car Park God at Auschwitz? This failure is a constant source of sadness, anger, bewilderment, disillusionment and cynicism for the inestimable casualties of human history. It raises the theological question of our day: Where is God? Where is God in the earthquakes, floods, fires, famines and plagues of history? Where is God in the sacking of Constantinople in 1204 (when Christians slaughtered Christians)? Where is God in the Holocaust? Where is God in September 11, Iraq, the Sudan or Zimbabwe?

However, before we can even begin to approach these hard questions, there are a number of preliminary problems that need to be raised.

The first problem could be glibly described as a public relations exercise, but it is ultimately about relevance. The second and related problem has to do with re-interpreting the meaning of God and Jesus, which is my main focus. The first problem has to do with the fact that many people outside the Church think Christians worship something like the old man in the sky. For many practicing Christians, the experience of suffering has brought about a radical rethinking and re-casting of God. We no longer worship this God. But this is not the impression the wider community has of the Church. This is partly due to the Church's retention of ancient language and rituals, so that while the meaning of its symbols has changed, the archaic forms have remained the same. From the outside, this is confusing. Personally, I find the experience of the shared meal of bread and wine a life-giving experience (also referred to as Holy Communion, Eucharist or the Mass). From the outside, it may seem a quaint, meaningless, even ghoulish ritual, especially if it is assumed it is done for the benefit of soothing a cartoon-like wrathful God. This has not been helped by the fact that some churches are not good at the kind of hospitality that fosters understanding, participation and inclusion.

The impression that Christians are appeasing a punitive God is reinforced by the tendency of leading Christian fundamentalists to monopolize the media limelight. This is compounded by the media's fascination with the absurd, eccentric and offensive actions and pronouncements of fundamentalists. Consequently, it is hard for people not to associate the word God with such baggage. It is like a psychologist saying to her students, "Don't think about camels." Naturally, we cannot get those darn camels out of our heads. Likewise, whenever God is mentioned, we cannot get the old man with the beard on a throne in the sky out of our heads. The second problem relates to the on-going task of rethinking and re-describing God, Jesus and the Church. There is a risk here. What if God cannot be re-claimed? Nonetheless, I work on the assumption that faith is renewed by taking a risk and addressing rather than suppressing questions and that the process of addressing questions is a profound expression of faith itself.

The current invitation to explore, to make the journey, is not an excuse for shoddy thinking or sloppy writing; as I will try to explain and justify claims clearly and fairly. The exploratory nature of the work itself reflects something of the search for faith. It presumes that if Christianity is going to be relevant in the twenty-first century, then it has to address the big issues of the day, seriously and adequately. It has to be accountable. The big issues in the real world demand this kind of accountability. I distance myself completely from any form of fundamentalism. Nonetheless, the meaning of the term *fundamentalism* is hard to define in strict terms. Suffice to say, fundamentalism here refers to religious fundamentalism in general, and Christian fundamentalism in particular. There are considerable differences between Christian fundamentalism and mainstream Christianity. Naming and addressing these differences may help some people find or reclaim another view of God and even experience good religion.[68]

Extension student activity

You may research these links to see how the issue of human suffering and evil is further explored:

a. "What Does it Mean to Have Free Will?"[69]
b. "Classical Theism 7 (Atheistic Arguments from Evil)"[70]

Can miracles be a defense for religious faith?

A miracle can be understood as an event that both countervails the laws of nature as we understand them and is not verified by science. Examples of miracles are found throughout ancient writings. For example, in the Bible

---

68. Ogden, *I Met God in Bermuda*, 9–11 (emphasis in original).
69. https://www.bigquestionsonline.com/2017/10/11/what-does-mean-have-free-will/.
70. http://www.wi-phi.com/video/classical-theism-7-atheistic-arguments-evil.

we know Jesus healed the sick. Some Protestants hold that the only miracles are those in the Bible. Others claim to have experienced miracles today, like being cured of incurable illnesses through divine intervention.

There are many who have debated both for and against the legitimacy of miracles. One of the critics was Scottish philosopher David Hume, who claimed that a belief in miracles was irrational with little justifiable evidence. While Hume did not dispute that unexpected things can happen, he nevertheless thought it inaccurate to assume a cause-and-effect nature. In other words, while there might be events which appear contrary to the laws of nature, they cannot be attributed to divine causes or miracles.

Student activity 1—Research Task:

Research miracles.

a. What are miracles and how do we define them?

b. Explore people who have written on miracles, i.e., David Hume and others.

c. You may also include accounts of people who claimed to have experienced miracles.

d. Write up a table and include points in favor and against the belief in miracles.

e. In your opinion, to what extent is the belief in miracles a justification for religious claims?

Student activity 2—Debate

Debate the following topic: Belief in miracles is a valid justification for religious claims.

If you cannot explain something in language, does it, therefore, not exist?

Logical positivists are a movement of philosophers who emerged in the middle of the eighteenth century, arguing that if something cannot be explained in a proposition it does not exist. A claim is only true if it can be put into language and empirically verified. As we have discussed, religious writers have had difficulty describing the transcendent, God, or ultimate reality in language, arguing that its depth, breadth, and complexity makes it difficult to define concisely in words. Austrian-British philosopher Ludwig Wittgenstein (1889–1951) alludes to the "unknown" or "mystery" as not able to be expressed in language. As he famously put it, "Whereof one cannot speak, thereof one must pass over to silence."[71]

Do you agree with logical positivists that something is only true if it can be put into language and empirically verified? What might be some benefits in the approach of logical positivism when exploring issues of truth?

While there are debates on how we understand and define transcendence as divine, God, Yahweh, or ultimate reality, some commonly understood attributes to the divine *point* to having the following characteristics:

1. nonmaterial
2. invisible
3. spiritual being

Can you think of examples of these attributes being illustrated in films or books? What are some limitations and strengths to these concepts?

STUDENT REFLECTIONS

WHAT ARE YOU NOW WONDERING ABOUT?

- What ideas or questions are you wondering about as a result of these lessons?
- Have these lessons made you think differently? Explain.
- What have you found challenging, provocative, or intriguing?

---

71. Wittgenstein, *Tractatus Logico-Philosophicus*, 149.

RELIGIOUS EXPERIENCE AS A JUSTIFICATION FOR RELIGIOUS CLAIMS

> My religion consists of a humble admiration of the illimitable superior spirit who reveals himself in the slight details we are able to perceive with our frail and feeble minds.[72]

> ... the most important truths cannot be reached by any amount of common sense or scientific observation, nor by logical thought, but only by insights and intuitions that are driven forward by intense concentrations of feeling. Of these the question can always be legitimately asked: "But how can we be sure this is valid and not misleading?" At that point the whole armoury critical appraisal should be brought to bear on them. But critical thinking alone, analytic thinking alone, cannot answer our questions ...[73]

What do Albert Einstein and Bryan Magee say about the capacity of reason?

TO WHAT EXTENT IS REASON RELIABLE IN REVEALING TRUTH?

Limitations of reason have been part of a long debate within philosophy and theology. At the end of chapter 1, Kant's and Hume's explorations of these limitations for gaining total knowledge were discussed. While such restrictions of reason do not necessarily imply logically or empirically that there is a God, they open up the possibility of such discussions. What the boundaries of reason can offer are the plausibility of other ways to understand knowledge beyond the scope of reason. Robert Kirkwood explains this further through his analogy that proving God's existence with the human mind is like trying to prove the existence of water with a metal detector—it is simply the wrong instrument.[74]

If Kirkwood is correct that in reason alone we are not capable of fully understanding God, *what tools do we need?*

William James (1842–1910) was an American professor of physiology, psychology and philosophy. The extract below is taken from his well-known text, *The Varieties of Religious Experience*:

---

72. Einstein, in Barnett, *Universe and Dr. Einstein*, 109.
73. Magee, *Ultimate Questions*, 97.
74. Kirkwood, *Looking for Proof of God*, 38.

I had spent the evening in a great city, with two friends, reading and discussing poetry and philosophy. We parted at midnight... My mind, deeply under the influence of the ideas, images, and emotions called up by the reading and talk, was calm and peaceful. I was in a state of quiet, almost passive enjoyment, not actually thinking, but letting ideas, images, and emotions flow of themselves, as it were, through my mind... Di-

William James

rectly afterward there came upon me a sense of exultation, of immense joyousness accompanied or immediately followed by an intellectual illumination impossible to describe. Among other things, I did not merely come to believe, but I saw that the universe is not composed of dead matter, but is, on the contrary, a living Presence; I became conscious in myself of eternal life. It was not a conviction that I would have eternal life, but a consciousness that I possessed eternal life then; I saw that all men are immortal; that the cosmic order is such that without any peradventure all things work together for the good of each and all; that the foundation principle of the world, of all the worlds, is what we call love, and that the happiness of each and all is in the long run absolutely certain. The vision lasted a few seconds and was gone; but the memory of it and the sense of the reality of what it taught has remained during the quarter of a century which has since elapsed. I knew that what the vision showed was true. I had attained to a point of view from which I saw that it must be true. That view, that conviction, I may say that consciousness, has never, even during periods of the deepest depression, been lost.[75]

1. What do you think of the experience above? Can you relate to some or parts of this experience?
2. To what extent can this experience be described as religious?

---

75. James, *Varieties of Religious Experience*, 7–8.

3. Can personal experience be a valid justification for religious faith? Discuss.

Student Activity — Video

Watch this video on William James—"William James and the Sick Soul"[76]—and answer the following questions:

1. How is religious experience described?
2. What is the "healthy-minded" view presented?
3. According to James, what is the purpose of religion?

> The central thesis of this book is that experiential awareness of God, or as I shall be saying, the *perception* of God, makes an important contribution to the grounds of religious belief. More specifically, a person can become justified in holding certain kinds of beliefs about God by virtue of perceiving God as being or doing so-and-so. The kinds of beliefs that can be so justified I shall call "M-beliefs" ("M" for *manifestation*). M-beliefs are beliefs to the effect that God is doing something currently vis-a-vis the subject—comforting, strengthening, guiding, communicating a message, sustaining the subject in being—or the effect that God has some (allegedly) perceivable property—goodness, power, lovingness. The intuitive idea is that by virtue of my being aware of God as sustaining me in being I can justifiably believe that God is sustaining me in being.
>
> The chief aim of this book is to defend the view that putative direct awareness of God can provide justification for certain kinds of beliefs about God. In this chapter I will set the stage for that defense by explaining how I am thinking of (putative) direct awareness of God, what its crucial features are, what territory it covers, over what important differences it ranges, and on which stretches of the territory we will be concentrating. I shall illustrate all this by a sample of reports

---

76. https://www.youtube.com/watch?v=fLUBcOXI5pU.

of such experiences, drawn both from "professional" contemplative mystics, and from humble laypersons.[77]

How does William Alston describe religious experience above?

American philosopher William Alston (1921–2009) argued that religious faith is rational and justified. His work explores the reliability of perception and personal experiences as a justification for religious claims.[78] There are many philosophers and theologians, as we shall see further on, in various ways, who have also defended the evidential value of religious and mystical experience.[79]

Søren Kierkegaard (1813–1855)

God is not man, and man is not God. And the gulf between them cannot be bridged by dialectical thinking. It can be bridged only by a leap of faith, by a voluntary act by which man relates himself to God and freely appropriates, as it were, his relation as creature to Creator, as a finite individual to the transcendent Absolute.[80]

What does the above quote mean?

Søren Kierkegaard, a Christian philosopher and one of the founders of existentialism, argued that while reason is important, it could not help us understand God or the relationship between humans and the divine. Kierkegaard was not totally opposed to reason; he understood the benefits of the Socratic method in its ability to allow individuals to think and take responsibility for themselves.[81] However, he argued that reason alone could not provide us with the evidence needed for faith—only lived experience could. Kierkegaard thought that becoming a Christian was not just accepting certain conceptual rational ideas or conventions, but rather one of a *constant process* in becoming a Christian person. Christian faith was more than

---

77. Alston, *Perceiving God*, 1, 9 (emphasis in original).
78. Ibid., 1, 9.
79. Gellman, "Mysticism," 30–31.
80. Copleston, *History of Philosophy*, 336.
81. Ibid., 336.

attending mass—it included a dynamic and passionate personal experience of God continually emerging. An individual *becomes* a Christian by making challenging decisions which are in line with our most true authentic self.[82]

Kierkegaard thought that when we are in touch with our "authentic selves" we find God.[83] This subjective experience, or the "inner life" cannot be articulated or systemized in concepts, according to Kierkegaard. He was not a relativist, but rather wanted to emphasize the importance of the individual as the focus of knowledge, as opposed to the objective and conceptual frameworks which he thought dominated academia and scholarship in the West.

Kierkegaard pointed out that life was made of many uncertainties, unknowns and paradoxes; for example, we may think about our personal future yet we can never be certain about it. Kierkegaard stated there is what he termed an "objective uncertainty" within reality.[84] Despite this uncertainty, what may seem an uncomfortable realization is an opportunity for individuals inwardly to live a "passionate faith."[85]

> Faith is precisely the contradiction between the infinite passion of the individual's inwardness and the objective uncertainty. If I am capable of grasping God objectively, I do not believe, but precisely because I cannot do this I must believe. If I wish to preserve myself in faith I must constantly be intent upon holding fast to the objective uncertainty, so as to remain out upon the deep, over seventy thousand fathoms of water, still preserving my faith.[86]

Discussion questions

1. What does Kierkegaard mean by the leap of faith?
2. How does he view reason in relation to faith?
3. According to Kierkegaard, how does a person become a Christian?

---

82. McDonald, "Søren Kierkegaard," 21.
83. Ibid., 21.
84. Kierkegaard, *Concluding Unscientific Postscript*, 182.
85. Ibid., 182.
86. Ibid.

Karl Jaspers (1883–1969)

> In the philosophical transcending of question and answer we arrive at the limit, at the stillness of being.[87]

Karl Jaspers' philosophical explorations led him to believe in God. An existential German philosopher, he concluded that reason was limited in providing answers to questions related to personal meaning. Jaspers proposed that only when we transcend rational thinking and the world of objects do we discover a deeper reality, which is God.[88] He states that our understanding of God is not through teaching or dogma, but emerges from the silence of our own being, the immanent dimension alluded to earlier. Jaspers viewed the arts as an important vehicle for not only transforming the self, but also as a way of knowing or experiencing the divine.

DISCUSSION QUESTIONS

1. What do you think it means to "transcend questions and answers?"
2. What could the term "stillness of being" refer to?
3. Can there be a realm of experience which transcends reason? Explain.

Simone Weil (1909–1945)

Well known French philosopher Simone Weil, a contemporary of philosopher Jean-Paul Sartre (1905–1980), also had a similar realization in her philosophical explorations, claiming that her religious experiences came as somewhat of a surprise and an unexpected realisation.

> In my arguments about the insolubility of the problem of God I had never foreseen the possibility of that, of real contact, person to person, here below, between a human being

---

87. Jaspers, *Way to Wisdom*, 49.
88. Ibid., 49.

IS RELIGIOUS FAITH A VALID WAY OF KNOWING? 129

> and God. I had vaguely heard tell of things of this kind, but I had never believed in them. In the *Fioretti* the accounts of apparitions rather put me off if anything, like the miracles in the Gospel. Moreover, in this sudden possession of me by Christ, neither my senses nor my imagination had any part; I only felt in the midst of my suffering the presence of a love, like that which one can read in the smile on a beloved face.[89]

For Weil, God was not understood by grasping anxiously to attain knowledge, like learning facts for an exam or accumulating savings in a money box. She proposed that we must *wait* for insights and ideas to be *revealed*. We understand God, she argued, by adopting a contemplative and unhurried attitude—what she termed as "waiting for God"[90] in order for knowledge and understanding to be discovered. This notion is more like an intuitive sense of knowing, something that may come spontaneously, as she describes in the quote above. Like Jaspers, Weil experienced God most profoundly through music:

> This movement of descent, the mirror of grace, is the essence of music... The rising of the notes is a purely sensorial rising. The descent is at the same time a sensorial descent and a spiritual rising. Here we have the paradise which every being longs for: where the slope of nature makes us rise towards the good... A double movement of descent: to do again, out of love, what gravity does. Is not the double movement of descent the key to all art?[91]

DISCUSSION QUESTIONS

1. Is intuition a valid justification for knowing something? Explain.
2. Can you give an example of having an intuition which revealed something to you? For example, you may sense something about someone you first meet. How much do we use our intuition when we encounter people?

89. Weil, *Waiting for God*, 27.
90. Weil, *Waiting for God*.
91. Weil, *Gravity and Grace*, 137.

3. To what extent is intuition a justification for religious experience and/or claims?
4. Both Jaspers and Weil argued that art, such as music, is important in understanding ourselves and experiencing God. Could they be correct?
5. Was there a time you listened to music, read a book, saw a film or artwork, or danced and had an experience which led you "out of yourself"? Explain.

OBJECTIVE AND SUBJECTIVE TRUTH

Student activity—Research task

1. Research and write in your own words the meanings of the following terms: theorizing, theoreticians, abstraction, generalities, particulars, objectivity, subjectivity, subjectivism.
2. To what extent do the concepts above apply to the study of science and religion? Discuss.

Discussion questions

1. Is it possible to understand reality outside our own subjective experience?
2. Which is more important: objective or subjective truth? Explain.
3. How do these concepts affect our understanding of God?

You may want to refer to the objective/subjective stimulus exercise in chapter 1.

As discussed in chapter 1, German philosopher Immanuel Kant attempted to bridge rationalism and empiricism, arguing we are preprogrammed with a set of rules within our mind to structure our experiences. Kant termed this *a priori* knowledge, existing within our own minds and independent of any experience, yet giving structure to the external world in order for us to understand it. Our own minds, therefore, have the innate capacity to comprehend the world and our sense experiences. Knowledge is therefore gained not only from something out there during our experiences in the external world, but also by our reason.

Existentialism

Kierkegaard, Jaspers, Weil, and other philosophers moved away from what they viewed as excessive rationality and its understandings of God that had previously dominated Western thought.[92] Some of these existentialist thinkers emerged from World War Two Europe and needed to make sense of the immense suffering that resulted. They looked for answers to the extreme atrocities which much of society could not find in the conceptual and theoretical frameworks of traditional philosophy, the sciences, or the intellectual world. Many of these thinkers explored metaphysical and ethical questions in order to find the answers as to why such a large-scale evil was committed. Broadly speaking, these thinkers are known as the *continental philosophers*. Although their work is not always considered amongst traditional arguments, their explorations of epistemology, personal meanings, and ethics are worth considering in our explorations of religious faith.[93] What most of these thinkers argued is that our understanding of knowledge cannot be completely understood objectively. In order to understand the objective, they argued, we need to understand ourselves and human experiences. This became the focus of a study called *phenomenology*, which can be defined as "an approach that concentrates on the study of consciousness and the objects of direct experience."[94] Many continental philosophers who were also phenomenologists argued that the rational and conceptual are limited in fully understanding human experiences as they are always unique to each individual. Their focus was on exploring the nature and complexity of human experience. As we shall explore further, what is distinct in the approach of some of the thinkers is knowledge, or knowing, as having a *relational* component.

Do you agree with claims that the rational and objective/conceptual approach favored by the sciences and some philosophers is limited in conveying meaning about our own subjective experiences? Discuss.

---

92. Joy, *Continental Philosophy*, 8.
93. Ibid.
94. *Oxford Dictionaries*, s.v. "Phenomenology." http://www.oxforddictionaries.com/definition/english/phenomenology.

Martin Heidegger (1889–1976)

German philosopher Martin Heidegger challenged much of the central ideas of analytical philosophers and scientists. His epistemological position was that humans have the ability to draw out meanings and understand reality presented to them without the conceptual representations and scientific theories which have dominated Western philosophy and contemporary knowledge.[95] Heidegger attempted to remove the gap between the subjective and objective phenomena. He was critical of the approach to knowledge that advocated excessive rationalism and proposed a return to a holistic emphasis in our understanding of the world and ourselves.[96] He rejected the abstract and conceptual discussions of many philosophers, such as Aristotle, and modern science, arguing that these were limited in fully understanding nature and the complexity of human experiences. Heidegger thought that the use of logic in both the sciences and philosophy did not reveal to us adequately the nature of ourselves or, in other words, our *true essence*.

> Whence do the sciences—which necessarily are always in the dark about the origin of their own nature—derive the authority to pronounce such verdicts? Whence do the sciences derive the right to decide what man's place is, and to offer themselves as the standard that justifies such decisions?[97]

WHAT IS IT TO EXIST AND BE?

As discussed in chapter 1, epistemology in the West has tended to focus on the question of what it is *to know* and *how we know*. Heidegger was interested in exploring the question of *what it is to exist* and be a human person, rather than what it *is to know*. The question of what it is *to be a human*, he argued, was also of great interest to the ancient Greek philosophers.

---

95. Heidegger, *Poetry, Language, Thought*, xvi–xvii.
96. Heidegger, *What Is Called Thinking?*
97. Ibid., 43.

IS RELIGIOUS FAITH A VALID WAY OF KNOWING? 133

Which is a more important question—what *is it to know* and how we know, or what it is to *exist* and be a person?

> Basically, all ontology, no matter how rich and firmly compacted a system of categories it has at its disposal, remains blind and perverted from its ownmost aim, if it has not first adequately clarified the meaning of Being, and conceived this clarification as its fundamental task.[98]

Heidegger contributed to the field of philosophy called ontology, which can be understood as an inquiry that explores the "nature of being."[99] The word "being" is defined by the Oxford Dictionary as "The nature or essence of a person."[100]

What does it mean to explore "the nature or essence of a person?"

Heidegger claimed that all concepts and systematic frameworks were limited in fully describing the "essence" of the human person or their experiences. He was interested in describing the nature of the human person and their experiences in the world. Heidegger explained the structures that make up the human person (which he called "Dasein") without theories which, he argued, can be prone to error. His analysis of Dasein comprised his first major work, the massive treatise *Being and Time* (1927).

Heidegger explored many existential themes, such as how to live an authentic life which is true to oneself, personal freedom, death, and the nature of thinking. He observed that awareness of death induces anxiety, which he argued many of us attempt to escape or avoid. However, the reality of our inevitable death, he states, can challenge us to ask important questions about the meaning of life. Heidegger encouraged people not to shy away from these questions of meaning, but rather to embrace and attempt to answer them.

What are your thoughts about death? Do they generate some unease or anxiety?

Can awareness of our imminent death cause us to ask questions about meaning as Heidegger is suggesting?

---

98. Heidegger, *Being and Time*, 31.

99. *Oxford Dictionaries*, s.v. "Ontology." http://www.oxforddictionaries.com/definition/english/metaphysics.

100. *Oxford Dictionaries*, s.v. "Being." http://www.oxforddictionaries.com/definition/english/metaphysics.

What is Thinking?

For Heidegger, thinking was not a means to end, nor a grasping after some end, but rather a *way of being in the world*, stating that, "For it is the same thing to think as to be."[101] Heidegger thought that it was important for humans to clarify a sense of meaning and "presence" in the world they inhabited. This task was not an easy one, requiring openness, questioning, and deep listening. Heidegger placed an emphasis on the importance of emotions, senses, and intuition as epistemological tools which are not removed from thought or the rest of our being. As a phenomenologist, Heidegger wanted to understand reality and our experiences as they "truly are," without concepts and theories, and to see "things in themselves."[102] He argued that we can achieve this task by opening up to our whole being and human spirit in order to understand the world around us. When we allow reality to be "as it is" from this perspective, our thinking emerges.[103]

> Most thought-provoking in our thought-provoking time is that we are still not thinking.[104]

What do you think of the distinctions in thinking made by Heidegger? Is it true that we are "not thinking?" What could Heidegger be referring to here?

Heidegger argued that people in the modern world "flee from thinking." For him, thinking meant *meditative thinking*. He claimed that we are dominated by *calculative thinking* in the modern world. Our preoccupation with technology and a fast-paced society has left us feeling dislocated from our true authentic selves.[105] He observed that people in the modern world had lost touch with themselves—their *essence*.[106] Heidegger suggested it is necessary to be aware of these influences so that we can become free of them.

Calculative thinking is evident mostly in the domains of measurement, logic, and analytic research—thinking used mostly within the sciences.

---

101. Heidegger, *What Is Called Thinking?*, 240.
102. Ibid., 211.
103. Ibid.
104. Ibid., 6.
105. Ibid.
106. Heidegger, *Basic Writings*, 332.

This type of thinking, he claimed, does not help us understand our deepest selves or essence; only meditative thinking does. Meditative thinking is slow, reflective, and open-ended, encompassing not just our thinking, but our whole being; a type of thinking open to the arts, our intuition, and emotions. Heidegger claimed thinking is a way of life and demands us to be attentive listeners, open and receptive to things presented to us as opposed to a grasping after knowledge or ideas. Heidegger argued that while calculative thinking has its place in the world of research and serves practical applications in a range of areas, it should not dominate our way of being in the world, nor should it replace meditative thinking:

> Calculative thinking computes. It computes ever new, ever more promising and at the same time, more economic possibilities. Calculative thinking races from one prospect to the next. Calculative thinking never stops, never collects itself. Calculative thinking is not meditative thinking, not thinking which contemplates the meaning which reigns in everything that is.[107]

Do you think meditative thinking as described Heidegger helps us understand ourselves better than calculative thinking? Explain.

Does a scientist think differently to a poet?

Heidegger does not articulate his understanding of God adequately and has been critiqued by some scholars for his vagueness and subjectivism. However, his ontology has been influential in the writings of many existential philosophers and religious writers. He is seen as the source philosopher for the twentieth-century movements of existentialism, existential phenomenology, structuralism, and post-structuralism (i.e., philosophical post-modernism associated with deconstruction). What is useful for this discussion is Heidegger's challenge to some of the assumptions of objectivity, theoretical constructs, and scientism. He provides a way of thinking and questioning the nature of subjective and objective reality—all of which are relevant to our understanding of knowledge, truth, and transcendence.

---

107. Heidegger, *Philosophical and Political Writings*, 89.

DISCUSSION QUESTIONS

1. What could be the meaning of the phrase, "our whole being" or "heart?"
2. Is Heidegger correct that the sciences cannot fully understand the human person in regard to their "deep essence" or what a human person is at their core?
3. Do you think it is important to explore issues of meaning or the essence of a human being? Explain.
4. Are Heidegger's distinctions between meditative and calculative thinking relevant today? How?
5. Why do you think some religious writers have been interested in Heidegger's ideas?

STUDENT REFLECTIONS

WHAT ARE YOU NOW WONDERING ABOUT?

- What ideas or questions are you wondering about as a result of these lessons?
- Have these lessons made you think differently? Explain.
- What have you found challenging, provocative, or intriguing?

RELATIONAL ASPECT OF RELIGIOUS FAITH

... If I face a human being as my *Thou*, and say the primary word *I Thou* to him, he is not a thing amongst things, and does not consist of things ... I do not experience the man to whom I say *Thou*. But I take my stand in relation to him, I the sanctity of the primary word. Only when I step out do I experience him once more ... Even if the man to whom I say *Thou* is not aware of it in the midst of his experience, yet relation may exist. For *Thou* is more than *It* realizes. No deception penetrates here; here is the cradle of Real Life.[108]

What do you think the above quote means?

Does knowing or knowledge have a relational aspect? How does this connect to how we experience or understand God?

Martin Buber (1878–1965)

Martin Buber is a Jewish philosopher who connects our relationships with others to our experience and understanding of the divine. He argues that it is respectful dialogue with others that leads us to an experience of transcendence, or God. In his famous book *I and Thou,* Buber distinguishes two types of relating that he observed in modern culture: the *It,* which is objectifying and using people as a means to get something from them—what he describes as viewing them as "things"—and the *I-Thou,* which involves a dialogue of deep listening and presence with the *other.* When we are able to be present with the other and really listen, we see people as human beings with unique qualities and human dignity, not as objects or things we can exploit for our own purposes. It is a way of relating to others with our "whole being" which, he argues, is inherent in our nature. Through this way of relating, Buber states that we recognize something of the transcendent in them, and experience it ourselves through such encounters.

Discussion questions

1. What do you think of Buber's distinctions between "It" and "Thou?" Do we treat people as "things" or as objects, rather than people? Give examples.
2. What skills or qualities do we need in order to relate to people, as Buber is suggesting?

In the English-speaking domain, philosophy of religion is principally identified with

---

108. Buber, *I and Thou*, 14–16 (emphasis in original).

> analytic philosophy, where the universal presumptions of an abstract reason, especially with reference to matters of belief and justification, have dominated . . . In this tradition, truth pertains to an objective frame of reference, which is based on logical arguments and processes of verification. As a result theists and atheists have debated long and often, according to tenets of propositional argumentation, with occasional forays into symbolic logic, on the particular merits of their positions on the above issues. . . . [For these reasons] Epistemology has been found wanting in its avoidance of the interrelatedness of mind and body, reason and emotion, of abstract and concrete.[109]

> What you call religious philosophy is a philosophy that has an opening toward religion. But I shall, at the same time, resist identification of a God who is named and prayed to in the Psalms and in the prophecies, with the word "God" in philosophy, which is the presupposition of a particular culture that is no longer ours . . . what we name God in philosophy is not somebody to whom we can pray, it is not somebody with whom we can enter into a personal relation, but a concept.[110]

What do you think the quotes above mean?

Morny Joy

Dr. Morny Joy, a philosopher of religion, argues above that traditional discussions of abstract reasoning concerning the proofs of existence are limiting. She claims that truth understood in terms of an "objective frame of reference, based on logical arguments and processes of verification" has dominated much of the discussion of epistemology as well as the existence of God. Joy moves away from such traditional discussions and explores phenomenology, hermeneutics, and ethics, informed by the work of the French philosopher Paul Ricoeur (1913–2005). The emphasis in this approach is focused on understanding knowledge, where "knowing" can be described as having a *relational* component to other human beings.

---

109. Joy, *Continental Philosophy*, 1, 7.
110. Ricoeur, in Raynova, "All that Gives Us," 683–84.

Joy proposes an integrated approach to knowledge, connecting mind, body, reflection, and emotions, allowing us to relate to other people in a positive way. Rather than focusing solely on reason and abstract ideas—removed from interpersonal dimensions—Joy includes wisdom and reflection on experiences that involve our bodies, emotions, and relationships with others.

Ricoeur proposes a way of relating to others based on mutual respect and recognition. Other people are to be respected as entitled to the same dignity and esteem as someone would grant themselves.[111] Ricoeur suggests that a person ought to recognize others as not merely existing for that person's benefit, but rather as equally deserving of respect *in their own right*, i.e., I esteem others as I do myself yet recognize that they are also different to myself.[112] Ricoeur's book, *Oneself as Another*,[113] which has influenced Joy's work, has profound implications for our understanding of ethics and human beings' relationships with each other in this world, as well as for how we understand God.[114]

> I cannot myself have self-esteem unless I esteem others *as myself*. "As myself" means that you too are capable of starting something in the world, of acting for a reason, of hierarchizing your priorities, of evaluating the ends of your actions, and having done this, of holding yourself in esteem as I hold myself in esteem.[115]

Discussion questions

1. Can you think of examples of how you might relate to others in the way described by Joy?
2. To what extent can an epistemology including mind, body, and emotions lead to a more ethical approach in relating to others?
3. Can Joy's ideas have implications on how we understand God or the divine? Explain.

---

111. Joy, "Paul Ricoeur, Solicitude, Love," 94.
112. Ibid., 91.
113. Ricoeur, *Oneself as Another*.
114. Joy, *Continental Philosophy*, 17–37.
115. Ricoeur, in Joy, "Paul Ricoeur, Solicitude, Love," 90.

4. Do you agree/disagree with the ideas of Joy? Explain.

Student Activity: Reflection and research

1. How much do positive relationships contribute to our understanding of transcendence? Discuss in reference to either Joy or Buber.
2. Do these ideas of existentialism agree with or contradict the main tenets of religious ethical teachings? Explain with an example from one religious tradition.

CONCLUSION

In order to adequately understand religious claims, we need to go back to the classic epistemological question raised: Where and how do we find truth? Is truth to be found in the realm of the subjective or objective? While personal experience can be problematic in the justification of religious belief, we cannot ignore its importance for attaining knowledge and meeting existential concerns. Perhaps the challenge is maintaining a balance between the two dimensions: the objective, which includes the theoretical, abstract, and reasoning; and the subjective, including personal experiences such as those present within mystical writings. Holding the tensions between the two in dialogue acknowledges that each dimension contains aspects of truth and justification in our understanding of knowledge, the world, and notions of the transcendence. In considering our justification for knowledge we may be wiser to be mindful of the many ways of understanding knowledge and, therefore, truth. While reason can take us a long way in understanding truth, reason also has its limitations. Some scientists and atheists may argue that if God cannot be proven by reason or science, religious claims become irrelevant. Many religious scholars, however, debate the legitimacy of reason to adequately understand all of reality. As we have seen, atheists, scientists, and religious scholars raise questions which are not completely resolved. In our search for truth, we may be better equipped by embracing humility in the face of larger questions that remain to a large extent a mystery.

MAIN RESEARCH TASK

Select one area of interest from either the suggested topics or questions listed below.

Become the authority and give a lecture to your class.

Make sure you are familiar with the main terms listed at the start of the chapter.

Suggested topics:

1. Design Argument
2. Cosmological Argument
3. Ontological Argument

Suggested focus questions:

1. Discus the Kalam argument. To what extent is it convincing?
2. Select one cosmological argument from the Christian, Jewish, Islamic, Hindu, Buddhist, or Sikh traditions. Alternatively, you may research the cosmology of an indigenous religion such as that of the Maori, Native American tribes, the Celts, Aboriginal culture, Ryukyuan people, or another of your choosing. Discuss the main ideas. What are its attributes?
3. Explore Rudolf Otto's or William James' work on religious experience as a justification for religious claims.
4. Discuss how one of the following thinkers explores the question of God's existence through their existentialism. To what extent can this be a legitimate justification for religious faith? Søren Kierkegaard, Jacques Maritain, Karl Japers, Simone Weil, Gabriel Marcel, C. S. Lewis, or Paul Tillich.
5. Discuss some of the main issues concerning suffering and the problem of good and evil.
6. To what extent can miracles be a justification for religious faith?
7. Is God a projection of our own needs and wishes? (For example, Ludwig Feuerbach)
8. Explore the criticism of religion by a contemporary atheist, such as Daniel Dennet, Christopher Hitchens, or Richard Dawkins. What are the strengths and limitations to their arguments?
9. To what extent can a synthesis exist between religion and science? Discuss.
10. What are the views of Sam Harris on religion?

11. Karen Armstrong claims religion essentially is about action and compassion. Do you agree?
12. How do Hindus' and Buddhists' beliefs differ from monotheistic religions?
13. To what extent is religious pluralism possible? (For example, John Hick)

EXTENSION TASK—STUDENT ACTIVITY—CONFERENCE

Organize a philosophy and theology conference. The topic is *The belief in God today is redundant*.

Work in groups and select an individual as your representative to summarise your main ideas in a speech of about six to ten minutes to the class.

There is a question-and-answer period allocated in which the audience may ask anyone in the entire group about anything concerning this topic.

INDEPENDENT RESEARCH QUESTIONS

1. What are Friedrich Nietzsche's critiques of monotheism?
2. Discuss Richard Rorty's philosophy of religion. What are some of its strengths and limitations?
3. Explain the genetic arguments for the existence of God. What are some of their strengths and limitations?
4. What are neuroscientists saying about religion and/or religious experience? Is it convincing? What epistemological issues does this research raise?
5. To what extent is there a high probability that God exists? (Richard Swinburne's argument of probability)
6. Explore the feminist approach to the philosophy of religion: For example, discuss the works of Pamela Sue Anderson, Rosemary Radford Ruther, Morny Joy, Julia Kristeva, Nancy Frankenbury, or Grace Janyze.
7. Alvin Platinga proposes that a belief in God can be rational without evidence. Discuss.

Choose one of the topics above, research and present it to the class. Include the following:

1. Summarise the main ideas.
2. Define the main concepts.
3. Outline briefly the historical context from which these concepts emerge.
4. What are some limitations or criticisms of the arguments?
5. What did you find interesting? What were you surprised by?

STUDENT REFLECTIONS

What are you now wondering about?

1. What are you wondering about as a result of these lessons?
2. Did you find anything interesting or intriguing? Explain.
3. Have these lessons made you think differently about certain ideas, issues, or questions? Explain.
4. What further questions do you have?
5. In years to come, what might you remember from these lessons?

How Do We Interpret Sacred Texts?

Outline

1. What is a sacred text?
2. Introduction
3. How do believers within the same religious tradition differ in their approach to sacred texts?
4. To what extent can we say that sacred texts are true?
5. Interpretation of sacred texts
6. Critical method
7. What way of knowing is best suited in approaching the reading of sacred texts?
8. Main research task
9. The role of community in interpreting sacred texts and religious faith
10. Fundamentalism
11. Independent research questions

Objectives

At the end of this chapter, students should demonstrate the ability to ask questions, wonder, and think critically about:

1. the use of reason as a way of understanding sacred texts, including an introduction to the biblical critical method, discussing the importance of context, literary style, history, and the author's intention.

2. reading sacred text as a spiritual and poetic work which invites readers to a "listening" of the text using emotion, senses, imagination, and intuition.
3. personal experiences revealed in sacred texts. The aim is to understand sacred texts as not purely historical, but also as fulfilling spiritual and existential needs.

Student Activity: Terminology

Some of the terms below are still debated amongst scholars; however, familiarity with common understandings of these will assist with engaging in the ideas presented. The Oxford and Webster dictionaries may be a good place to start.

Working in student pairs, write down the definitions of the terms below and take turns explaining them to each other:

sacred, religious tradition, exegesis, androcentric language, translations, eisegesis, spiritual scholars, hermeneutics, redaction criticism, theologians, aesthetics, historical criticism, parables, existential, patriarchal, oral tradition, paradox, divinity, myths, ambiguous, fundamentalism, ineffable, synthesis, monotheism, translation, enlightenment, objectivity, justification, literal, subjectivity, Hebrew Scripture, inspiration, complexities, Old and New Testament, limitations, deconstructed.

> I think when people usually use the word "sacred," they're trying to give over a sense of untouchability or utter reverence we have to have towards something. That we take it to be true, eternal and we can't question it, we can't criticise it, we have to take it as the final authority.—Julian Baggini[1]

What does the quote above mean? Do you agree?

WHAT IS A SACRED TEXT?

Student Activity: Define

1. What does the term "sacred" mean to you?

---

1. Baggini, "Understanding Sacred Text, Activities and Questions," 9.

2. Research the original meaning or the etymology of the word "sacred."

Discussion questions

Read the following statements to questions that were asked by the British Library of people from a range of backgrounds and faiths. Discuss these in groups or pairs:

What is sacred?
"... the problem with this word is that it seems to set the Bible and other sacred writings apart from us, as something to be venerated, treated with awe and respect. And I understand the Bible to be a book that is relevant to our everyday lives."[2]—Morna Hooker, Christian educator

How would you describe the word 'sacred?" What is it that makes the holy or sacred stand out from the "profane?"
"Sacred is to surrender to a deity or to a text from the deity."[3]—Muhammad Yazdani, Muslim educator
He explains that the text from a deity, God, must not have anything added to it by humans and that sacred means absolute belief in God and the text.

Do you think it could be possible to see something as sacred at the same time as seeing it as part of everyday life?
"Sacred translated means holy, and holy means to me different. It's something which is not mundane . . . We talk about life being sacred it's because it's different—human life is different to other forms of life because we have a soul. That's what I mean by holy."[4]—John Williams, Christian Educator
"In Hebrew, the word for sacred is *kodesh*, it's a word that's often translated to mean holy, but actually it means separate or distinct or other."[5]—Gila Sacks, Jewish educator

2. Ibid., 2.
3. Ibid., 9.
4. Ibid.
5. Ibid.

INTRODUCTION

Sacred texts within all religious traditions have been used over the millennia in numerous ways, from sources of hope to tools of oppression. Their vast appeal and historical development make them extremely important and influential, yet not so easily interpreted. Sacred texts from the world's various religions have throughout history captured the imagination and interest of believers, as well as artists, philosophers, and theologians.

How do we adequately read and understand these important writings which are foundational in establishing religious beliefs? What ways of knowing can we use to understand them? This chapter presents two approaches in understanding sacred texts: first, the critical method and then subjective readings of the writings. Both its historical and spiritual natures will also be explored. While there is more of an emphasis on the Christian tradition, students are encouraged to extend their analysis to other religious traditions whenever possible.

A range of approaches to interpretation, including fundamentalism, orthodoxy, and liberalism demonstrate that interpretations of a text can vary, even within the same religious tradition. Similarly, scholars also differ in their approach to reading sacred texts. This introduction aims to encourage thinking about the topic beyond a simplistic view. It seeks to develop religious literacy and to gain an understanding of approaches scholars use in order to thoughtfully engage in discussion on religious faith.

Student Activity: research

1. List the names of the ancient texts for each of the religions below:

   Judaism

   Christianity

   Islam

   Hinduism

   Buddhism

   Sikhism

2. Draw a timeline which illustrates the emergence of sacred writings from the religious traditions above.
3. For each sacred text write something about their historical origin.
4. Choose one sacred text and describe the *process of translation*.

a. What was the original spoken language?
b. Describe the process of translation.
c. How many languages was it translated from before the first English version emerged?
d. What other factors and processes were involved?

As a start, you may read the article below and summarize the main ideas:

Brennan Breed, "How Was the Bible Written and Transmitted?"[6]

What do you think are some problems associated with the process of translation and interpretation?

Some useful websites include:

British Library Online Gallery[7]
BBC Schools—Religion[8]

Discussion Questions

In groups or pairs, discuss the following statements from the *British Library: Understanding Sacred Texts* interviews:[9]

"As a non-believer, I have no problem if my conscience disagrees with a religious text, because I think I can learn from religious texts, but I don't take them to be final authorities . . ."[10]—Julian Baggini, atheist philosopher

"I've got the right to argue with the text and that's okay, that's allowed."[11]—Gila Sacks, Jewish educator

---

6. http://www.bibleodyssey.org/tools/bible-basics/how-was-the-bible-writen-and-transmitted.
7. https://www.bl.uk/learning/resources/pdf/sacredactandquest.pdf.
8. http://www.bbc.co.uk/schools/religion/.
9. "Understanding Sacred Texts."
10. Ibid., 5.
11. Ibid.

"If a passage from Scripture does not seem to make sense, this is because the reader does not understand rather than because the passage cannot be understood."[12]—Muhammad Yazdani, Muslim educator

"We can use the Bible as a guide to how we live, provided we don't expect it to answer everyday problems that confront us."[13]—Morna Hooker, Christian educator

HOW DO BELIEVERS WITHIN THE SAME RELIGIOUS TRADITION DIFFER IN THEIR APPROACH TO SACRED TEXTS?

The spectrum of religious belief

According to statistics, there are approximately 2.2 billion Christians, 1.6 billion Muslims, 1 billion Hindus, 376 million Buddhists, 20 million Sikhs, 13 million Jews, 7 million Baha'i, 4 million Jianists, and there are others as well.[14] Within these religious traditions are different perspectives from scholars and religious believers on how sacred texts are interpreted. The following diagram highlights within religious traditions ways in which people interpret sacred writings. Although it is important not to make definitive generalizations, below are some common characteristics which may help us understand the wide range of different perspectives amongst believers within religious communities and traditions. Important to note is that *not all* people within religious communities share the exact same views.

12. Ibid.
13. Ibid.
14. "Global Religious Landscape," para. 2, and Meister, *Introducing the Philosophy of Religion*, 6.

	Fundamentalist	*Orthodox*	*Progressive/Liberal*
SACRED TEXT	Literal interpretation of sacred texts. For example, stories in Genesis are understood as historical events.	People are in general agreement with mainstream teachings on interpretations of the text.	Sacred texts are understood and read within the context of their culture and time.
TRADITION	Tendency to maintain status quo of traditions at all costs, and are not open to change.	Not opposed to change, nor as receptive as their liberal members. Generally known as traditional in their views.	Tradition is maintained only if it is meaningful. Generally receptive to new forms and structures within the religious tradition and are therefore open to change.
MODERN SOCIETY AND CULTURE	Very little dialogue or openness to modern culture and ideas.	Dialogue and exchange ideas within the modern world. However, would probably rely more on leaders within their religious community for guidance on such matters.	Pursuing dialogue with modern culture and ideas. Often find ways of engaging with the culture while making intellectual and creative links to the religious tradition.

Reflection questions

1. What do the statistics about religious affiliation mean? How are they useful?
2. What could be the purpose of publishing such statistics?

Student activity: Interview

Interview an adult from one of the religious traditions and ask them the following questions:

1. How do you understand sacred texts? Are they literal, historical, the word of God, poetry, a combination, or other?
2. Do you belong to a religious community? If so, how does it help you interpret a sacred text?
3. Is the religious tradition or community that you belong to open to various interpretations of sacred writings? Does it try and interpret writings according to modern times or people's needs?
4. How does the reading of sacred text help shape a person's spirituality? Explain.

TO WHAT EXTENT CAN WE SAY THAT SACRED TEXTS ARE TRUE? INTERPRETATION OF SACRED TEXTS

Spoken or written statements often have very different meanings based on how the audience infers meaning. For example, most legal systems have an entire area—the judicial branch—dedicated to interpreting existing texts of laws, facts, and legal opinions. Sacred texts also lead to differing views, resulting in debates and controversy. So, how can we interpret sacred texts adequately? As the skeptic argued in chapter 1, can we be sure that any of our interpretations are true? How can we be sure that we are interpreting the writing on this page correctly? Have you ever been misinterpreted or misunderstood? The answer is most likely yes. Were Jesus or Siddhartha Gautama misunderstood by people? Again, likely they were, yet this does not suggest we must abstain from making *any* claims regarding sacred religious writings. We just need to be mindful and aware of the limitations and complexities involved in any interpretations.

STUDENT REFLECTIONS

WHAT ARE YOU NOW WONDERING ABOUT?

- What ideas, issues, and questions are you wondering about as a result of these lessons?
- Have these lessons made you think differently about certain ideas, issues, or questions? Why?
- What questions or ideas did you find interesting, challenging, or intriguing? Explain.

Discussion questions

In groups or pairs discuss the following statements from the *British Library: Understanding Sacred Texts* interviews.[15]

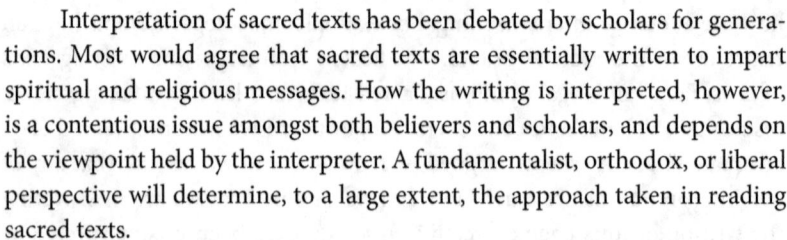

1. How does a person decide what a passage from a religious text means? What would they need to consider? What questions would they need to ask?

2. Do you think religious people should ignore passages that do not seem relevant for the modern world? How can they decide what is relevant?

3. If a passage can be interpreted in a variety of ways, does this mean that the sacred text has less authority?[16]

Interpretation of sacred texts has been debated by scholars for generations. Most would agree that sacred texts are essentially written to impart spiritual and religious messages. How the writing is interpreted, however, is a contentious issue amongst both believers and scholars, and depends on the viewpoint held by the interpreter. A fundamentalist, orthodox, or liberal perspective will determine, to a large extent, the approach taken in reading sacred texts.

Are sacred texts literal?

Historical accounts

Some believe that God or the divine acted in history, and that the events depicted in sacred texts are historical fact. The texts are interpreted literally as true, without metaphorical meanings. The Oxford Dictionary defines "literal" as "Taking words in their usual or most basic sense without metaphor or exaggeration: representing the exact words of the original text."[17] For example, The Genesis accounts of creation and the parting of the Red Sea in the Hebrew Scriptures are understood as historical events where God acted within history.

---

15. "Understanding Sacred Text," Theme 3.
16. Ibid.
17. *Oxford Dictionaries, s.v.* "literal." http://www.oxforddictionaries.com/definition/literal.

Metaphorical accounts

Those who advocate a liberal and mainstream approach understand the text as containing some history, but predominantly expressing religious and spiritual truths in the form of stories, myths, and parables. From this perspective, authors are not viewed as historians, but rather as wanting to convey their own spiritual experiences and insights. This position maintains that while there are passages written as historical events, they were not all essentially written for that purpose, but rather to impart spiritual insights. Some passages in the Bible, such as St. Paul's writings, were written to inspire and encourage religious communities in their faith. From this perspective, biblical stories are more like theological reflections (i.e., thoughts about faith) rather than historical descriptions.

When you read sacred writings, if you are asking if the texts are true in a historical sense—that is, did the events happen as depicted in the text—the answer is "yes" and "no." Some events we know from various ancient sources did occur. For example, Roman (Tacitus) and Jewish (Josephus) historians show evidence that Jesus was a historical figure. The Hebrew Scripture story of Jonah and the Whale, according to most scholars, was exaggerated in order to convey a religious and spiritual message. The story of Siddhartha Gautama's temptation by a group of women is debated on its historical accuracy. Yet such stories remain a *useful narrative* in conveying central religious themes, such as desire and detachment.

Scholars mostly agree that stories were passed on through an oral tradition and eventually written. Ancient cultures used the medium of stories to convey important moral and religious truths. These writings were collated and preserved within the various religious traditions over many years. People collectively have found these texts to be useful in providing personal and existential meaning. The texts also provide moral guidance and teachings.

What has caused problems over time with all sacred texts is their literal interpretation. While different understandings and meanings are unavoidable, some interpretations are problematic. Literal interpretations of texts have resulted in extreme and rigid views, sometimes causing negative consequences. This is often the stance present within religious fundamentalism, which will be discussed later on.

STUDENT ACTIVITY—RESEARCH:

1. Read the Bible's Genesis account of creation below.
2. Use the links below to write a summary of the different interpretations of this account.
3. To what extent is the Genesis account of creation true? Write your response.

Creation story—Genesis chapter 1

In the beginning God created the heavens and the earth. Now the earth was formless and empty, darkness was over the surface of the deep, and the Spirit of God was hovering over the waters. And God said, "Let there be light," and there was light. God saw that the light was good, and he separated the light from the darkness. God called the light "day," and the darkness he called "night." And there was evening, and there was morning—the first day. And God said, "Let there be an expanse between the waters to separate water from water." So God made the expanse and separated the water under the expanse from the water above it. And it was so. God called the expanse "sky." And there was evening, and there was morning—the second day. And God said, "Let the water under the sky be gathered to one place, and let dry ground appear." And it was so. God called the dry ground "land," and the gathered waters he called "seas." And God saw that it was good. [18]

---

18. Gen 1:1–9 (NIV).

HOW DO WE INTERPRET SACRED TEXTS?

Included below are links demonstrating *different* interpretations of Genesis. Watch and identify the differences:

Rabbi Arthur Green: "A Contemporary Jewish Theology of Creation."[19]
Rob Bell: "Beginning In the Beginning."[20]
Dr. Rowan Williams: "Do You Believe that Adam and Eve Is Literally True?"[21]
MSNBC: "Literal vs 'Poetic' Interpretation of the Bible."[22]
"The Creation Story—Fact or Fiction?—Pastor Elbert Moralde."[23]

Student activity: Debate

The Genesis account of creation is true.

Alternative student activity: Interviews

1. Forms groups of four to five.

2. In your groups, research the works of one of the following people: Rabbi Arthur Green, Rob Bell, Dr. Rowan Williams, Ken Ham, and Elbert Moralde.

3. Select one person in your group to be a representative. This person will be on a panel to be interviewed on the truth of the Genesis account of creation.

4. Some of the questions which might be posed for the panel to answer include the following:

   - Is the creation story historical, metaphorical, or both?
   - What kind of truth does the story present?
   - What relevance does it have to religious faith today?

5. The discussions will be directed by a teacher and two to three students.

19. https://www.youtube.com/watch?v=PaVO3drLoV8&t=22s

20. https://www.youtube.com/watch?v=2CwMOcMDjhc.

21. http://www.faradayschools.com/re-topics/re-year-10-11/questions-to-the-archbishop-dr-rowan-williams/.

22. http://www.msnbc.com/msnbc/watch/literal-vs-poetic-interpretation-of-the-bible-137777219903.

23. https://www.youtube.com/watch?v=xHoZ5BVjJ30.

6. The class will have time to ask questions.

CRITICAL METHOD: TO WHAT EXTENT CAN WE USE REASON TO ANALYZE SACRED TEXTS?

From your study of epistemology, you can appreciate the complex process of interpretation and attaining total objectivity, even in traditionally empirical fields such as science. As the biblical scholar Anthony Thiselton states in his book *Hermeneutics*, "Are the meanings of the texts 'constructed' by the readers or are meanings 'given' through the text by the author?"[24] We will explore both approaches to this question, as well as Thiselton's additional distinction between *explanation* and *understanding* of sacred texts.[25]

This section will explore how Christian scholars have attempted to understand meanings in the Bible by applying modern biblical criticism. Thiselton's distinction of explanation in regard to the text refers to this critical process. Many parallels also apply to sacred texts of other religious traditions.

The critical method or analysis of the Bible was formalized by scholars in the sixteenth century. It involved what is termed as *exegesis*, Greek for "to lead out of."[26] The word "critical" gives us a clue as to evaluation, inquiry, analysis, and what is involved. A different approach which is also discussed is *eisegesis*, which involves a personal subjective reading *into* the text, as opposed to the exegesis process of reading *out of* the text.[27] "Hermeneutics" is the term used to define the broader category that includes both exegesis *and* eisegesis, examining influences and philosophical approaches which underlie this communication between author, text, and reader.[28]

---

24. Thiselton, *Hermeneutics*, 2.
25. Ibid., 9.
26. Hayes and Holladay, *Biblical Exegesis*, 5.
27. Ibid., 17.
28. Thiselton, *Hermeneutics*, 4.

Biblical criticism

Biblical criticism (exegesis) is an attempt to infer from the text the meaning of the Bible. There are many branches of inquiry within this field, including historical, textual, literary, narrative, traditional, and redaction criticism. When examining the Bible using the critical method, some of the following factors are considered as possibly influencing the text:

- *Author*: What are the author's *perspectives* influencing the writings?
- *Time and historical context*: What are significant historical events which influenced the author's writings? (historical criticism)
- *Sociological context*: What was the nature of society and how was it structured? For example, what was the gap between rich and poor? What were the roles of women and children?
- *Writing style (genre)*: How does the style of writing influence the message? For example, is a story intended for literal translation or rather for providing metaphorical and allegorical significance?
- *Audience:* Who was the text intended for? For example, was it written for a community in Rome, the Empire's capital, or Jerusalem, an outlying city permeated with rebellion and discord? The aim will determine the form/style and what ideas are included.
- *Redaction*: Was the text edited or changed for a particular purpose? Who edited the text and for what purpose? Can we identify the author's ideology and bias? (redaction criticism).[29]

All of these factors are important in helping scholars better understand the text and the intention of the author.

> What is the literal sense of a passage is not always as obvious in the speeches and writings of the ancient authors of the East as it is in our own times. For what they wished to express is not to be determined by the rules of grammar and philology alone, nor solely by the context. The interpreter must go back wholly in spirit to those remote centuries of the East and with

---

29. Hayes and Holladay, *Biblical Exegesis*.

the aid of history, archaeology, ethnology and other sciences, accurately determine what modes of writing the authors of that period would be likely to use, and in fact did use.

For the ancient peoples of the East, in order to express their ideas, did not always employ those forms or kinds of speech which we use today; but rather those by the men of their time and centuries . . . The investigation carried out on this point during the past forty or fifty years . . . has more clearly shown what forms of expression were used in those far-off times, whether in poetic description or in the formulations of laws and rules of life or in recording the facts and events of history.[30]

Historical criticism

Discuss the following question:

> To what extent can knowledge of historical events allow a greater understanding of any sacred text? Give examples (you may choose to draw from any religious tradition).

As with any ancient writing, historical context is important. In order to understand the meanings of sacred texts we need to carefully consider the society and culture from which they emerged and the historical events that influenced the authors' writings. It is important to know what issues the writers were dealing with. Were they writing in a time of a war, drought, or prosperity? Knowing their situations when writing helps us understand what factors could have influenced the texts.

Ancient people of the Middle East lived in societies which are very different from the ones found in modern times. Mostly agrarian economies were dominated by strong empires, slavery was a norm, infant mortality was high, and daily life was predominantly patriarchal.[31] For example, the Hebrew people were nomadic and, like most civilizations during that time, were involved in conflict with various tribes.[32] This is evident in the Hebrew Scriptures' references to war and violence. Throughout the time that Jesus lived, the Jews were under the rule of the Romans.

30. Boadt, *Reading the Old Testament*, 13.
31. Hayes and Holladay, *Biblical Exegesis*, 15.
32. Pope Pius XII, in Boadt, *Reading the Old Testament*, 13.

Ancient cultures worldwide had references and understandings of God, as well as some type of divinity, throughout history.[33] Most scholars attempt to make sense of these historical events in light of the writing within the texts.

Discussion questions

Discuss the quotes below in groups:[34]

... the more we understand the context in which those texts were written, and the more we understand the kind of problems which the people who wrote them were facing, the easier it is to understand the real significance of those texts.[35]—Morna Hooker, Christian academic

... as modern people, we read these texts and we need to understand about their history, and where they come from, the social background—all these things are important.[36]—Julian Baggini, atheist philosopher

"In religious texts, you have to read between the lines."[37]—Harry, young Jew

---

33. Ibid., 13.
34. "Understanding Sacred Text," Theme 3.
35. Ibid., 8.
36. Ibid.
37. Ibid.

160 INQUIRY INTO PHILOSOPHICAL AND RELIGIOUS ISSUES

STUDENT ACTIVITY: A DAY IN THE LIFE OF . . .

Write a short diary entry for one of the religious founders below:

1. Moses
2. Jesus
3. Muhammed
4. Siddhartha Gautama
5. Gur Nanak

Include the historical context which surrounded these religious leaders. Make reference to relevant historical events and religious festivals, as well as social and cultural aspects.

EXTENSION QUESTION—STUDENT ACTIVITY,
DISCUSS THE FOLLOWING:

1. Is it possible to transcend the factors of history and culture? To what extent are these factors important in influencing people's ideas? Explain.

2. To what extent can individual reasoning (and/or in this case divine inspiration) transcend the influences of culture and history, or are we *determined by them*? Give your reasons.

STUDENT REFLECTIONS

WHAT ARE YOU NOW WONDERING ABOUT?

- What ideas, issues, and questions are you wondering about as a result of these lessons?
- Have these lessons made you think differently about certain ideas, issues, or questions? Why?
- What questions or ideas did you find interesting, challenging, or intriguing? Explain.

Language

Another approach in understanding the meaning of texts is to explore the language used. Austrian-British philosopher Ludwig Wittgenstein (1889–1951) argued that to comprehend the meaning of language you must figure out what words meant within the "language game,"[38] meaning within the particular context from which they originated. For example, when we try and understand the works of Shakespeare, we attempt to understand what the words or phrases would have meant to Shakespeare and his readers. The phrase taken from Antony III, "Though you can guess what temperance should be, You know not what it is,"[39] needs to be understood within the cultural and societal context. So, what does it mean? As Wittgenstein argues, words have a life and meaning within the context in which they were

---

38. Wittgenstein, *Philosophical Investigations*, 7, 19, 47.
39. Newell, *Shakespeare and the Human Mystery*, 39.

written and need to be understood within that, rather than imposing our own meanings on the words.[40] Biblical scholars, when attempting to apply literary criticism, do just what Wittgenstein proposes—explore the meaning of words "within the life and society of the author" in order to understand the message and intention of the author.

Student activity—Discuss the following question and write a response:

How can an understanding of what words meant in a particular culture or historical time help understand the meaning of a text? Give examples. You may refer to any ancient text.

Contradictory statements in the text

> And when the Lord your God has delivered them over to you and you have defeated them, then you must destroy them totally. Make no treaty with them, and show them no mercy. Do not intermarry with them. Do not give your daughters to their sons or take their daughters for your sons, for they will turn your children away from following me to serve other gods, and the Lord's anger will burn against you and will quickly destroy you. This is what you are to do to them: Break down their altars, smash their sacred stones, cut down their Asherah poles and burn their idols in the fire.[41]

> The Lord is gracious and compassionate, slow to anger and rich in love. The Lord is good to all; he has compassion on all he has made.[42]

In making sense of the various biblical passages many scholars will conclude that while references to God or Yahweh may apply to a certain time and context, all of their relevance may not be universally meaningful today, especially if they refer to war, violence, and a "vengeful God" as is sometimes present within the Hebrew Scriptures. Some passages are more historical in nature and best understood as a depiction of God as perceived by

---

40. Wittgenstein, *Philosophical Investigations*, 132.
41. Deut 7:2–5 (NIV).
42. Ps 145:8–9. (NIV).

people at that time; other passages have a more spiritual, universal appeal. For example, despite the references to violence attributed to God, there are also claims of God as loving, evident most notably in Psalms.

Can you think of some other examples?

How do we explain these ambiguities or statements with more than one possible meaning? How is it possible to believe in a God who is depicted as both vengeful and compassionate?

Many mainstream scholars argue that you cannot believe in a God who is both loving and vengeful while attributing such references of vengeance to historical context. That is, an understanding of God emerged out of a situation and historical context of conflict with a particular cultural mindset or ideology. However, this view is not always consistent with other depictions of God in Hebrew writing or in the Bible. What scholars attempt to do is decipher the voice of God, so to speak, amongst the varying ideologies and cultures at the time of writing—not always a straightforward process.[43] This procedure is called the historical critical method by scholars since its focus is on historical influences on the Bible:

> There is a danger that we could think of the Bible as being dictated by God in such a way that the human limitations of the inspired writers and of the circumstances in which they wrote have no relevance to what we find in the text. We could read the Bible texts as though they came straight from God and share in God's transcendent truth, somehow unrelated to history or to human experience. We could read them as if they expressed some abstract and eternal truth that is equally relevant in every age and to every person, because it comes from God who is unchanging Truth, and whose words, therefore, transcend the limitations of time, place and language.
>
> The Bible is not like that. It is a record of limited human insights inspired by God that real people have expressed to other real people in limited human words and in specific cultural and historical circumstances. There is beauty and truth in the Bible texts. To find this beauty and this truth (as distinct from imposing on the text our own preconceived notions) we will need to explore the historically conditioned and

---

43. Fallon, *First & Second Kings*.

necessarily limited human experiences that gave rise to their inspired insights.[44]

1. What do you think the above passage means?
2. According to biblical scholar Michael Fallon, how do we understand the true meaning of passages in the Bible?

Student Activity: essay

Write an opposing view to the opinions expressed below:

> ". . . at the end of the Psalm we have 'Blessed be he who smashes the children's heads against the rocks.' You know, we tend to omit that Psalm, pretend it's not there, but we have to deal with those Psalms, those difficult texts. Otherwise those who want to use the texts for evil will succeed."[45] —Ed Kessler, Jewish academic

> "St Paul wrote in one of his letters, "Slaves obey your masters." Now for me as a Christian living in the 21 century, I think that's not acceptable . . . but I don't have any difficulty disagreeing with scripture in that way."[46] —Lucy Winkett, Christian Faith leader

Redaction criticism

Another technique used within literary criticism is called redaction criticism. When examining any passage from the text, scholars initially read it holistically and see if it is cohesive. Does the passage flow naturally from the previous line, paragraph, or whole text? The passage is inconsistent if the writing does not flow from the previous sentence, paragraph, or chapter. If these inconsistencies conflict with the author's previous ideas, scholars often suspect that the passage was edited or changed. The scholar then begins a process of reconstructing the text and looking for possible redactors. For example, the apostle Paul writes within the New Testament about women and prayer:

44. Ibid.
45. "Understanding Sacred Text," 3.
46. Ibid., 3.

> But every woman who prays or prophesies with her head uncovered dishonors her head—it is the same as having her head shaved.[47]

While Paul acknowledges the role of woman who do prophesy in this passage, he also states ambiguously in another verse the opposite message stating that,

> Women should remain silent in the churches. They are not allowed to speak but must be in submission . . . If they want to inquire about something, they should ask their own husbands . . . for it is disgraceful for a woman to speak in the church.[48]

This passage contradicts Paul's other writings as he discusses in Galatians the *equality of all* in the eyes of God, "There is neither Jew nor gentile, neither slave nor free, nor is there male and female, for you are all one in Christ Jesus" (Gal 3:28).[49] How then do we reconcile these obvious inconsistencies in Paul's writings? Some biblical scholars argue that these passages were not originally his work, while others state they are by Paul, but accepting the patriarchal attitudes present within that cultural context without necessarily applying them to modern times. Other scholars such as Murphy O'Connor argue that the passage about a woman covering her head is in reference to a symbolic gesture of dignity and authority and not pointing to inferiority, as has been interpreted.[50]

Biblical scholar Elizabeth Fiorenza applies an analysis of language in understanding Paul's writings. She argues that what is often forgotten within scholarship is the androcentric language used in the ancient world. This means that the word "man" was a generic term meant to apply to both men and women, like how "mankind" has been used in English. Hence, what is mentioned about men is also meant to apply to women. Therefore, what is presented about women is not comprehensive information, but rather submerged within gender-inclusive statements.[51] Fiorenza claims that ambiguity and inconsistency are especially evident in relation to leadership roles. While Paul appears in some phrases to disfavor female leaders within the early church, he also mentions women like Phoebe, Priscilla, and Aquila.

---

47. 1 Cor 11:5–15 (NIV).
48. 1 Cor 14:34–35 (NIV).
49. Gal 3:28.
50. Byrne, *Paul and the Christian Woman*, 1–2.
51. Ibid.

These ambiguities are strong indications of redaction, or replacements, made to the text:

> I commend to you our sister Phoebe, a deacon of the church in Cenchreae. (I ask you to receive her in the Lord) in a way worthy of his people and to give her any help she may need from you, for she has been the benefactor of many people, including me. Greet Priscilla and Aquila my co-workers in Christ Jesus. They risked their lives for me. Not only I but all the churches of the Gentiles are grateful to them.[52]

To what extent is the whole more important than its parts?

What is the message of the Bible as a whole? Is the Bible about peace and love? Reading the text holistically (not just individual verses or chapters), many scholars argue, will be necessary for an adequate understanding of its meaning. Throughout history, however, verses within the Bible have not been understood within the context of their literary writings, sometimes resulting in misplaced attitudes and even cruelty related to race and gender. For example, racial violence perpetrated by groups such as the Ku Klux Klan, who justify their actions from biblical verses, is an example of a serious misreading of the text.

As argued, when there are inconsistencies within the text, many scholars infer that the interpretations *are a reading into the text* and an imposition of assumptions, biases, and projections. The Bible's long history means inevitably there will be inconsistencies in its writings due to various translations, editions, and use over time. One could argue, therefore, that it is even more important for verses not to be taken literally. To interpret a text literally—that is, to read it without reference to genre, style, context, or the spirit of the *whole* text—is problematic. In doing so, we run the risk of reading the text inaccurately and falling into simplistic interpretations, which American scholar Carolyn Osiek argues has serious moral implications:

> Yet the Bible, precisely as the Word of God, cannot by nature be oppressive. If it is seen to be so, then the mistake lies with the interpreter and interpretative tradition, not with the text. It is the interpreter who is sinful, not the content . . . Biblical revelation is intended to foster the greater human happiness for all, but such happiness may not always conform to the

---

52. Rom 16:1–5 (NIV).

standards of contemporary culture. The Bible proclaims a message of true freedom and humanization, but according to a divine plan, not a human one. Men and women are intended to live in true happiness and mutual respect within that divine plan, not in oppressive patterns of domination and struggle against one another, which are sinful manifestations of the disorder of human nature without divine grace.

What do you think of Osiek's claims?[53] Is a theistic God one who favors men over women, black people over white? Is this consistent with the main themes of love and compassion mentioned within the text? Do these interpretations or messages contradict our natural intuition concerning morality?

These are questions which a fundamentalist approach to sacred texts will need to grapple with. Can you think of some responses?

Discussion questions

1. What are some advantages of biblical criticism? Give examples.
2. What ways of knowing are used when engaging in biblical criticism?
3. Can you think of some limitations to biblical criticism?
4. Drawing on your knowledge of epistemology, what are some factors that can hinder us from fully understanding the meaning of any sacred text?

Here are some ideas to consider:

1. The age of the text and distance in time from the text.
2. Limited understanding of the language and culture.
3. Epistemological limitations in gaining total objectivity as our current views—informed by our own culture—affect our understanding.[54]

---

53. Osiek, "Feminist and the Bible," 961–62.
54. Boadt, *Reading the Old Testament*, 13.

Despite these limitations in understanding the Bible in its fullest sense, we can still have knowledge of it that may serve us well. Many religious scholars propose that the importance of the Bible is not on what the author meant to say, but rather the personal meanings drawn from the text for people's lives today and the faith community at large:

> In this sense, the historical method has also given us many gifts. It has brought us back closer to the text and its originality, it has shown us more precisely how it grew, and much more besides. The historical-critical method will always remain one dimension of interpretation. Vatican II made this clear. On the one hand, it presents the essential elements of the historical method as a necessary part of access to the Bible. At the same time, though, it adds that the Bible has to be read in the same Spirit in which it was written. It has to be read in its wholeness, in its unity. And that can be done only when we approach it as a book of the People of God progressively advancing toward Christ.[55]

> ... cultural histories of scripture are "less interested in discovering meaning *in* biblical texts than [...] in how meaning is made *from* biblical texts in different cultural contexts, past and present."[56]

DISCUSSION QUESTIONS

1. What do you understand are the main ideas in these quotes?
2. What are some advantages of biblical criticism? Give examples.
3. What ways of knowing are used when engaging in biblical criticism?
4. Can you think of some limitations to biblical criticism?

---

55. Benedict XVI, *Light of the World*, 171.
56. Prickett, *Words and the Word*, 269.

Student activity—Teach a lesson on sacred texts

- You are a scholar and have to teach an introductory lesson on a sacred text.
- Choose one to two approaches discussed above, i.e., historical, textual, literary, narrative, traditional, form, or redaction criticism.
- Select one sacred text from a religious tradition. In a short, five-to-ten-minute talk, explain how this inquiry helps us understand the meaning of the text.
- Compare and contrast it to other ancient writings (optional).

STUDENT REFLECTIONS

WHAT ARE YOU NOW WONDERING ABOUT?

- What ideas, issues, and questions are you wondering about as a result of these lessons?
- Have these lessons made you think differently about certain ideas, issues, or questions? Why?
- What questions or ideas did you find interesting, challenging, or intriguing? Explain.

WHAT WAY OF KNOWING IS MOST APPROPRIATE WHEN READING SACRED TEXTS?

Hermeneutics is "The branch of knowledge that deals with interpretation, especially of the Bible or literary texts."[57]

> ... a rational dimension remains within the process of hermeneutical inquiry, the more creative dimensions of hermeneutics depends more fundamentally on the receptivity of the hearer or reader to *listen with openness* . . . [58]

---

57. *Oxford Dictionaries, s.v.* "Hermeneutics." http://www.oxforddictionaries.com/definition/hermeneutics.

58. Thiselton, *Hermeneutics,* 7 (emphasis in original).

This "listening" dimension is often described as part of the process of *"understanding"* in contrast to the more rational, cognitive or critical dimension of "explanation."[59]

> ... that both intensive training in methods and techniques and training in using imagination and creativity are required for reading the Bible ... [60]

Phenomenologists Paul Ricouer (1913–2005) and Hans-George Gadamer (1900–2002) present ideas that may provide effective ways of understanding sacred texts. Their approach to epistemology centers around the importance of standing back and becoming aware of our own assumptions that may influence what we read and perceive to be true. This is not an easy process, and begs the question: Is it possible to stand back from our own world view, as suggested by Ricouer and Gadamer?

Ricouer and Gadamer have explored in depth the assumptions made within Western thinking about the limitation of using reason alone in attaining knowledge (as discussed in chapter 1, which you may want to further investigate). However, in regard to understanding scared texts, what these philosophers suggest is a way of reading the text that embraces other ways of knowing in order to gain understanding. One way of achieving this, they claim, is through "active listening."[61] They argue this allows a text to speak to us subjectively, reaching beyond our assumptions and world views.[62] In doing so, we can learn something new rather than merely project our own ideas and views.[63] In relation to the sacred text, the task is for the reader to engage in "listening that is open and receptive" to its messages. Hence, tools beyond inductive and deductive logic are required, including a reliance on intuition, emotion, imagination, and open-ended reflective thinking, similar to the sense of wonder described in chapter 1. It belongs to the process of eisegesis. This approach also draws on Thiselton's distinction at the start, as an *understanding* as opposed to an *explanation* of text, the latter attributed to the critical process of exegesis.[64] As biblical scholar Samuel Tongue has noted:

---

59. Ibid., 8 (emphasis in original).
60. Carmody, *Reading the Bible*, ix.
61. Thiselton, *Hermeneutics*, 3–16.
62. Ibid., 3–16.
63. Ibid.
64. Ibid.

> [We] are left with the uncomfortable fact that a biblical narrative can . . . *neither* be treated as history *nor* as realistic ("fact-finding") fiction . . . meaning that we might have to turn again to the concept of the poetic.[65]

What does this quote mean? Explain how we can turn to the concept of the poetic in order to understand sacred texts.

Tongue argues that what is important is not the meaning of words within the text, but rather that which is derived *from the text* by the reader and the faith community.[66] It is what happens *between the reader and the text* which Tongue points out as significant. He continues to argue that the limitations of the critical approach leave us to look at the Bible as poetry.[67] When reading poetry, we don't just analyze the language structure or rhythm; we also *listen* to its deeper message. Many artists and philosophers have argued that the role of poetry (and art in general) is to open us up to a different level of experience and understanding.

While there are various interpretations from a range of philosophers and artists on what artworks mean, many point to their subjective and existential significance. Some argue that the role of art is to *transform the self.* For example, poetry (as can music, dance, or painting) allows the possibility of accessing emotions, intuition, and imagination, and therefore is able to speak to us subjectively through our experience. Perhaps poetry can help us become aware of emotions we otherwise were oblivious to, such as desires, hopes, sadness, or joys. From observation of our personal experiences (and those of others), our emotion, like our thinking, is what make us human and has the potential to speak to us meaningfully. The purpose of poetry, like parts of sacred texts, can therefore be used as an instrument that can potentially speak to us meaningfully, providing an existential purpose.

Many religious scholars would argue that the experiential aspect is the essence of religion. Although we use our minds in understanding various facets of faith, as we read in chapter 2, many religious writers such as Simone Weil and Søren Kierkegaard claim that religious faith is only fully understood through experience. We may study *about* religion, but what Weil and others have argued is that we must experience religion in order to really *know it.* This experience is essentially one that challenges us *beyond the mind.* However, it is not an irrational faith, as some have argued, but rather

---

65. Tongue, *Between Biblical Criticism,* 262.
66. Ibid.
67. Ibid.

it allows ourselves to draw on other ways of knowing, such as intuition, imagination, and emotions, in order to *understand*. Religious experience is a common feature within all the religious traditions. For Christians, it may involve what has been termed as an *encounter* with Jesus as the focus which allows a connection to the divine and transcendent.[68] Within Islam, the Sufi mystic Rumi describes God as likened to the experience of a lover.

STUDENT REFLECTION QUESTIONS:

1. To what extent can we listen to sacred texts when we read them? Is this approach appropriate in reading sacred texts?
2. Can you think of some limitations?

DISCUSSION QUESTIONS

In groups or pairs, discuss the following claims:

"... when you're holding something close to you it holds a deeper meaning... When you touch and feel something and it's messing with your senses, it plays on your emotions, I guess, and it has that effect of sacredness."[69]— Hamza (young Muslim)

"... in Judaism, you can use whatever version works for you... But the exception to that is where reading the text is the act in and of itself, reading the text is the act you're commanded to do. And that happens when we read the Torah during a prayer service... we're commanded to read off specially written scrolls, manuscripts that were written with the intention that they would be used for holy reading."[70]— Gila Sacks (Jewish educator)

68. Williams and Higton, *Wrestling with Angels*; Pope Francis, *Happiness in This Life*.
69. "Understanding Sacred Text," 4.
70. Ibid., 4.

Synthesis of the critical and subjective

The understanding of historical, literary, and redaction influences is important in shedding further light on ancient texts. Despite the problems which have been found in translations and interpretations over the years, sacred texts have endured in providing a source of spiritual and positive nourishment for many in a range of different cultures. As Tongue states, "The paradox of a Bible that can be deconstructed and yet still survive, still live on, is brought about by writers and critics who are 'bound to retell.'"[71] Perhaps what is important is to keep a balance of the critical method and a subjective listening to the text. This allows the Bible to be read not just as a historical text, but also as a spiritual one. We can then consider biblical scholar Milton Terry's synthesis below of the critical method and artistic way of reading the Bible as a necessary process. Keeping the tensions of both approaches, he argues, allows for a richer and more authentic reading of the text:[72]

> Hermeneutics, therefore, is both a science and an art. As a science, it enunciates principles . . . and classifies the facts and results. As an art, it teaches what application these principles should have . . . showing their practical value in the elucidation of more difficult scriptures.[73]

To what extent can we apply both the analytic and artistic approaches to the reading of scared texts? Discuss.

MAIN RESEARCH TASK: YOU MAY RESPOND TO ONE OR ALL OF THE TASKS LISTED BELOW.

STUDENT ACTIVITIES

1. Read the following verses from Psalms and respond:

   a. Choose a poem, myth, or parable that is not from a sacred text and compare it to one of the psalms below.

   b. What do you think the psalms mean?

   c. Is it a parable, story, or historical extract?

   d. What do you think is the author's purpose in writing this?

---

71. Tongue, *Between Biblical Criticism*, 1.
72. Terry, *Biblical Hermeneutics*, 17.
73. Ibid.

> I love you, Yahweh, my strength
> (my savior, you rescue me from violence.)
> Yahweh is my rock and my bastion,
> My deliverer is my God
>
> I take shelter in him, my rock,
> My shield, my horn of salvation,
> My stronghold and my refuge. (Ps 18:1–2)
>
> As a doe longs
> For running streams,
> so longs my soul
> for you, my God.
>
> My soul thirsts for God, the God of life;
> When shall I go to see
> the face of God?
> I have no food but tears,
> day and night;
> and all day men say to me,
> Where is your God?
>
> I remember, my soul
> Melts within me:
> I am on my way to the wonderful Tent,
> to the house of God,
> among cries of joy and praise
> and exultant throng. (Ps 42—43:1–4)

2. Select a relevant passage from a sacred text, preferably no more than ten lines long. Read the passage and, without too much thought, write down what *you think it means*. Now answer the following questions:

    a. What is the purpose of the writing?
    b. Can you identify its genre or style? Is it a poem, parable, story, or historical extract?

3. Choose a passage from a sacred text (approximately ten lines).

    a. Answer the following questions:

1. What is the verse about?
2. What message does it attempt to convey?
3. Can you identify its genre or style? Is it a poem, parable, story, or historical extract?

b. Analyze the text by applying biblical criticism. Select two approaches from below and explore the text. Refer to the earlier section on Biblical Criticism for guidance.

1. Historical criticism
2. Textual criticism
3. Narrative criticism
4. Tradition criticism
5. Form criticism
6. Redaction criticism

4. Read the following extract and write a response to the question below:

This Bible is one of the fundamental makers of the modern world. It has set free not only readers and its preachers but those who have used it as a springboard to achieve gains and enrichment in our world never before enjoyed by so many. This book walks with us in our life today.

Its impact on the English-speaking world is unparalleled. It can touch mysteries which seem beyond our reach yet at times we sense them to be there. It can teach us day-to-day morality. It gave us myths and stories which are as familiar to us as the histories of our families and communities. It stands still as a book of great language and beauty.

There has never been a book to match it. It has a fair claim to be most pivotal book ever written, a claim made by poets and statesmen and supported by tens of millions of readers and congregations.[74]

What claims does Melvyn Bragg make about the importance of the Bible? Do you agree/disagree?

74. Bragg, *Book of Books*, 5–6.

Some suggested resources:

- http://www.bl.uk/onlinegallery/features/sacred/homepage.html
- http://www.bbc.co.uk/schools/religion/
- http://www.bbc.co.uk/programmes/articles/1pYRg2f2o2rqWHrp3ywhTyX/religions-of-the-world
- http://www.reonline.org.uk
- http://mbfallon.com/new_testament.html

THE ROLE OF COMMUNITY IN INTERPRETING SACRED TEXTS AND RELIGIOUS FAITH

> Religion can be a very powerful force for bringing people together and a text can help to do that . . . However, there is a downside to the binding I think, which is that as we bind ourselves together with people whose views we share, it's very hard to avoid separating ourselves off from other groups of people who disagree with us.[75]—Julian Baggini

What do you think the above quote means?

Throughout history, theologians and religious scholars have always attempted to reinterpret the sacred text and religious tradition in a way that is meaningful to the times in which they lived. Within the community of scholars and theologians today, as has always existed, are debates and different views on exactly *how* the interpretation of a rich tradition is to be communicated. Some may find this difficult to understand and would rather have a more uniformed view of religion with neat black and white answers. However, this is not a true representation of religion. The differences of opinions and interpretations within religious traditions is what makes faith alive and rich; this richness can be found within its complexity and diversity.[76]

In forming religious beliefs, religious traditions draw on other sources, such as philosophy, literature, psychology, and the community of

---

75. "Understanding Sacred Text," 17.

76. The notion of diversity here does not point to relativism, but rather to the complexity of religious faith. For example, within the Christian tradition exists a range of literature derived from theologians, biblical scholars, philosophers of religion, and liberation and feminist theologians, all attempting to shed light in different ways on this ancient text and religious tradition. This points to the richness and complexity of religious faith.

believers—for example, the church, synagogue, mosque, sangha, and the religious leaders within those traditions. The community therefore has and still remains of importance in interpreting sacred texts for believers. The challenge faced by religion is always how it can speak in a language which is meaningful to a contemporary audience while maintaining its integrity and truthfulness to its traditions.

The community has functioned as a place for people to develop their spiritual and religious life. Community can be a place where people ask questions, share insight about their faith, and find support for daily living. It is a place where people engage in various rituals and in a sense practice an aspect of their religion. Within the Christian tradition, we see allusions to this in the writings of Paul, who set up the early Christian communities in Asia Minor, communities which initially existed within people's homes. The passages below must be read within the context of Paul's other writings, and in the spirit of his wider message of evangelization, also keeping in mind the ideas on biblical interpretation discussed earlier.

> In the church God has put all in place: in the first place, apostles, in the second place prophets, and in the third place teachers; then those who perform miracles, followed by those who are given the power to heal or to help others or to direct them or to speak in strange tongues.[77]

Discussion questions

1. What implications do these verses have on the nature and function of community within the Christian tradition?
2. What are some advantages and disadvantages of community for religious believers? Give examples.

---

77. 1 Cor 12:28 (NIV).

Can religious communities bind people together in a positive way?

Discussion questions

In groups/pairs discuss what the following statements might mean in regard to the importance of community:

> "I personally believe that the *shema*, the prayer for the morning and the evening, is very important . . . it makes me feel part of the greater Jewish community saying it at a service because everyone, every Jew, is taught it when they are very young."[78]—Harry, young Jew

> " . . . when God asks Abraham to sacrifice his long awaited son, Isaac. And Abraham binds his son Isaac . . . and although Abraham doesn't sacrifice Isaac, thank God, we Jews look at the binding as a significant story in our tradition."[79]—Ed Kessler, Jewish educator

> ". . . everything in the divinely revealed scriptures and texts is something that binds us, binds us to the Lord Almighty."[80]—Muhammad Yazdani, Muslim educator

> "a family which . . . all have a shared heritage of revelation and of communication with the one same, personal God of us all."—Muhammad Yusuf.[81]

Social researcher and psychologist Hugh Mackay has written about the importance of community for individual well-being and happiness.[82] He argues that Western societies have forgotten its importance and rather than focus on individual happiness solely, we should be putting our energies into creating communities. Although Mackay describes himself as a Christian agnostic, he argues that religion in the West can provide that sense of community which is often missing.

---

78. "Understanding Sacred Text," 6.
79. Ibid., 17.
80. Ibid.
81. Ibid.
82. Mackay, *Art of Belonging*.

Discussion questions

1. Muhammad Yazdani says that if a person doesn't agree with the Scripture, it's because he or she does not fully understand the words. Do you think Muslims or Jews would expect their texts to answer everyday problems?

2. Julian Baggini points out that many people disagree with elements of Scripture, and therefore reinterpret the words to fit their own arguments. There are different attitudes toward texts among religious people. What are these different attitudes? Can you think of any reasons for the differences? Is it okay that there are differences, and if so, how does this affect the idea of the Scripture as the word of God?[83]

Student activity—Discuss, present, debate, or write about one of the following:

1. Sacred texts are a valuable source of hope and spiritual nourishment.
2. Poetic truth is more important than historical truth.
3. It is possible that God acted throughout human history.
4. A positive aspect of religion is that it offers community.

STUDENT REFLECTIONS

What are you now wondering about?

- What ideas, issues, and questions are you wondering about as a result of these lessons?
- Have these lessons made you think differently about certain ideas, issues, or questions? Why?
- What questions or ideas did you find interesting, challenging, or intriguing? Explain.

83. "Understanding Sacred Text," 5.

FUNDAMENTALISM

> You can't escape your own responsibility to look at what's in the text and respond according to your own conscience. The minute you just say, 'Well it's in the text, I must do it,' in a way you're abdicating your own responsibility to try and interpret what's going on there and take responsibility for how you read it.[84]—Julian Baggini, atheist philosopher

What is your understanding of the above quote?

A definition of fundamentalism is, "Strict adherence to the basic principles of any subject or discipline."[85] It's also described as a set of beliefs or principles which is strongly adhered to and not open to criticism or question. Hence, by definition, we can say there exists both religious and nonreligious fundamentalism.

Can you think of examples?

Fundamentalism is a term we all hear frequently in world news, almost exclusively in a negative light, and often in association with an act of violence, hatred, or some other form of extremism. Discussed earlier in this chapter was fundamentalism as a perspective in sacred text interpretation, a different use of the word. Yet the two meanings are intertwined:

> . . . so words matter. And in fact, if people think that they can't—that blaming a whole religion is really the answer to the question [of] why those people are radicalized, then that's way too easy an answer. And it's not right. It's not true because, in fact, those guys—when I sit with them, when I sit with members of ISIS or al-Qaida, they don't talk to me about religion. They talk about politics first.[86]

Literal interpretation of sacred texts, which a fundamentalist approach claims to do, can create ideology that often fails to reasonably coexist with a modern society. All of the scholarly methods discussed earlier are usually disregarded while politics, culture, and economic disparity play major roles that can lead to violent extremism. However, it is also important to point out that the majority of fundamentalists are not violent:

---

84. Ibid.

85. *Oxford Dictionaries*, s.v. "fundamentalism." http://www.oxforddictionaries.com/definition/fundamentalism.

86. Mekhennet, in Davies, "Journalist Ventured 'Behind the Lines.'"

Every single fundamentalist movement that I have studied in Judaism, Christianity and Islam is rooted in profound fear... Rooted as a fundamentalism is in a fear of annihilation, its adherents see any such offensive as proof that the secular or liberal world is indeed bent on elimination of religion.[87]

In *The Case for God*, Karen Armstrong explores the issue of religious fundamentalism and claims its emergence is due to a fear of being attacked by a secular world.[88] She argues that often people who join these groups are disheartened and disappointed with society failing not only to provide economic and political stability, but also, for some groups, a meaningful spirituality. This failure she attributes to the excessive rational and scientific approach within the culture that leaves these people feeling alienated.[89] Armstrong argues that religious fundamentalism is a simplistic interpretation and distortion of religious faith. The more these groups are attacked, Armstrong claims, the stronger their aggressive responses, stating, "... history would show that when a fundamentalist movement is attacked, it almost invariably becomes more aggressive, bitter and excessive."[90]

Do you agree with Armstrong's claims? Explain. What other viable factors could lead to religious fundamentalism?

Characteristics of religious fundamentalism

The nature of fundamentalism is complex and many experts in the field have explored it. Below are some examples for you to consider and discuss:

Fundamentalism means uncritical, literal acceptance of what are supposed to be the founding doctrines or documents of a tradition. It demands a closed mind and the suspension of rational faculties; it is attractive only to the desperate and the dim. The huge allegiances it commands are proof of the strength of the reaction against relativism, evidence of the revulsion people feel from the prospect of a truthless universe. Its power to reassure is irresistible to its adherents, and repulsive to everyone else. For people who I recognize as religious, it is the very negation of religion, for doubt is a component of

---

87. Armstrong, *Case for God*, 263, 260.
88. Ibid.
89. Ibid.
90. Armstrong, *Battle for God*, 413.

faith and reason a divine gift which only devilish inducements can make you forego.[91]

It is relatively easy to convert the sinner, but the good are often completely unconvertible simply because they do not see any need for conversion . . . What matters then is to cultivate this quality of acceptance in a sociological milieu and then . . . even objectively unjust works can be counted virtuous and Christian, since they are approved by those who are locally certified as "good" . . . Truly the great problem is the salvation of those who being good, think they have no further need to be saved and imagine their task is to make others "good" like themselves.[92]

Fundamentalism is an emotional and intellectual way of looking at the world and a way of acting . . . Fundamentalists define themselves in large part by what they are *against*. They always have a very real and easily identifiable enemy. Quite often there are two enemies, the external enemy and the internal enemy . . . Only a minority of fundamentalists resort to violence, not to speak of terrorism. Fundamentalists pursue strategies of flight, radical separation, spatial separation, and institutional separation—none of which are violent—as well as confrontation. The great majority of confrontational acts are nonviolent: contesting elections, staging demonstrations, boycotting products, services, and entertainments . . . [93]

Christian fundamentalists seem to have little regard for the loving compassion of Christ. They are swift to condemn the people they see as the "enemies of God." Most would consider Jews and Muslims destined for hellfire and Urquhart has argued that all oriental religions are inspired by the devil.

There have been similar developments in the Muslim world which have been much publicized in the West. Muslim fundamentalists have toppled governments and either assassinated or threatened the enemies of Islam with the death

---

91. Fernandez-Armesto, in Vardy, *What Is Truth?*, 5.
92. Merton, in Vardy, *What Is Truth?*, 5.
93. Antoun, *Understanding Fundamentalism*, 164–65.

penalty. Similarly, Jewish fundamentalists have settled in the Occupied Territories of the West Bank and Gaza Strip with the avowed intention of driving out the Arab inhabitants, using force if necessary. Thus they believe that they are paving a way for the advent of the Messiah... In all its forms, fundamentalism is a fiercely reductive faith.

Rabbi Meir Kahane, the most extreme member of Israel's Far right [stated in 1990], "There are not several messages in Judaism. There is only one. And this message is to do with what God wants. Sometimes God wants us to go to war, sometimes he wants us to live in peace... But there is only one message: God wants us to come to this country to create a Jewish state."[94]

Reflection questions

1. What are some of the common characteristics of fundamentalism illustrated above? Discuss what these may mean.
2. What might be some implications or consequences of holding some of these attitudes and views?

Student activity: Research task

Choose one example of a religious fundamentalist movement from any of these religious traditions: Judaism, Christianity, Islam, Buddhism, Hinduism, or Sikhism.

1. Give a brief historical background of its development.
2. What is the population of this group (i.e., approximately how many people claim to be adherents)?
3. What are the characteristics that define it as a fundamentalist movement?
4. What can you identify as some of the *main causes* of its emergence? For example, is it political, economic, social, ideological, or a combination of these factors?

Record your findings and present them to your class.

---

94. Armstrong, *A History of God*, 447–48.

Nonreligious fundamentalism

While this discussion has focused on religious fundamentalism, there is also nonreligious fundamentalism. By definition, fundamentalism is a doctrine or view which is not open to question or critical discussion. Can you think of examples?

Karen Armstrong defines militant atheism as fundamentalism and makes a link to religious fundamentalism. To learn more, this source may be useful: "In Defence of the True God," by Alain de Botton.[95]

Do you think militant atheism is a type of fundamentalism? Explain.

STUDENT ACTIVITY—DEBATE, PRESENT, OR DISCUSS IN PAIRS OR GROUPS A RESPONSE ABOUT FUNDAMENTALISM FROM THE FOLLOWING:

> When one conception of God has ceased to have meaning or relevance, it has been quietly discarded and replaced by a new theology. A fundamentalist would deny this, since fundamentalism is anti-historical: it believes that Abraham, Moses and the later prophets all experienced their God in exactly the same way as people do today. Yet if we look at our three religions, it becomes clear that there is no objective view of "God": each generation has to create the image of God that works for them.[96]

STUDENT ACTIVITY

Read the extract below from "Praying the Psalms with Jesus," by Australian biblical scholar Father Michael Fallon, and answer the questions below.

> *The Psalms are Human Documents*
>
> We have the assurance of hundreds of years of believers in Ancient Israel that the psalms are inspired, and Jews and Christians continue to find them inspiring. We will fail to appreciate their meaning or their value if we don't read them in the spirit

---

95. https://www.theguardian.com/books/2009/jul/19/armstrong-case-god-alain-de-botton?CMP=share_btn_link.

96. Armstrong, *A History of God*, 5.

in which they were composed, cherished, copied, handed on, and prayed in the temple, the synagogue and the church. They continue to reveal aspects of God to us, and something of ourselves in relation to God, to the world and to each other . . .

We can hear Jesus praying because: "Jesus is able for all time to save those who approach God through him, since he always lives to make intercession for them" (Hebrews 7:25). Did he not say: "Where two or three are gathered in my name I will be there with them" (Matthew 18:20)?

It is precisely here that we encounter a serious problem. Before the psalms settled into a fixed form, they adapted, as one would expect of prayer, to changing circumstances. If, for example, a hymn was composed to celebrate a military victory of King Ahab in the ninth century BC, we should expect that those who were responsible for the liturgy at the time of King Josiah three centuries later would adapt the psalm to celebrate his victory.

Likewise, a hymn composed to lament the exile of the inhabitants of Israel in the eighth century BC would be adapted and sung to bemoan the exile of the inhabitants of Judah at the beginning of the sixth century. *It was typical of the writings of the Hebrew Bible to reshape the sacred text to give expression to the people's faith in the presence of the Living God in their present experience.*

Then comes Jesus. The religious authorities had him crucified because he contradicted many of their ideas about God and about how we should live in relation to God and to each other—ideas we find expressed in the psalms. The problem is that by the time of Jesus the psalms had settled into a fixed text. While the disciples of Jesus carried on the tradition of seeing new meaning in the psalms in the light of their experience of Jesus: "Everything written about me in the law of Moses, the prophets and the psalms must be fulfilled" (Luke 24:44), they left the text intact, but attempted to bypass the difficulty by interpreting offending texts in an "allegorical" sense. The problem with this is that it was done at the expense of the meaning intended by the psalmist and understood by those praying the psalms.

When, for example, the psalm speaks out against "enemies," those who composed the psalm, and those who prayed it, did not have in mind evil spirits who were warring against the soul. They were referring to identifiable enemies who, because they were Israel's enemies were assumed to be God's enemies. It was assumed that God hates them, and so should we. The psalms invite us to pray that God will destroy them. "Sinners" are often treated in a similar way. They are to be avoided. Jesus' attitude and behaviour is in stark contrast. He tells us to love our enemies, because God loves them (see Matthew 5:44–48). We are not to hate sinners, for that would mean hating ourselves. We are to love sinners with God's love.

God is frequently portrayed as being angry and vengeful, images that were at home in ancient religious literature but not in Jesus' experience or teaching. In Jesus' well-known parable of the Prodigal Son (Luke 15:11–31), the father is anything but angry with his wayward boy. He was longing for his return and when the boy did come home, the father welcomes him with love.

The psalmist looked forward to the coming of God's Messiah who would "break them with a rod of iron and dash them in pieces like a potter's vessel" (Psalm 2:9). This contradicts everything we know of Jesus.

Why put ourselves through the torture of praying in this way while having to contradict our prayer? Jesus said that he "came to seek and save what was lost" (Luke 19:10). He taught us not to condemn each other in our sin, but to embrace each other in love, and so attract each other out of our sin.

When we find sentiments in the psalms that do not reflect the spirit of Jesus, we need to recall the words of Jesus: "It was said to you of old, but I say to you" (Matthew 5:21–38). He was speaking in relation to the interpretation of the Ten Commandments, but his words apply just as importantly to the Psalms.

The point I am making here—that religious texts, even though inspired, are human documents— is fundamental to the study of any and every religious text.

God reveals God's Self to everyone. A person becomes aware of this when he or she has an insight into the Mystery, the Presence we call God. Whoever we are when we give expression to a religious insight, the expression comes from us. The words will be inspired to the extent that they come from a genuine communion with God and are sensitive to the movement of God's Spirit inspiring them. To the extent that this is true the words will reveal something of God and something of our relationship with God, with ourselves and with each other. We are assured by hundreds of years of praying the psalms that they are indeed inspired by God. At the same time they are still human expressions of religious insight, and they must be understood within the context of the situation in which the revelation was received.

The Pontifical Biblical Commission in a declaration entitled *The Interpretation of the Bible in the Church* (1993) states: "The exegete need not put absolute value in something which simply reflects limited human understanding" (page 94). "God has not given the historical conditioning of the message a value which is absolute" (page 113). "Addressing men and women, from the beginnings of the Old Testament onward, God made use of all the possibilities of human language, while at the same time accepting that his word be subject to the constraints caused by the limitations of this language. Proper respect for inspired Scripture requires undertaking all the labours necessary to gain a thorough grasp of its meaning" (page 133).

Any revelation is received by a human being, who grasps it and expresses it according to circumstances of time and place and situation. The history of religious thought reveals that there *are people of every religious persuasion who, rather than take the trouble to examine religious texts in their context, prefer, for reasons of security and power, to take the texts as coming directly from God. This seems to give the text a divine and unalterable aura. It might appear to offer more security, "knowing" what God is revealing without having to take the trouble to check our thinking. Security, ease, and power can be very tempting. We would do well to listen to Jesus as he tells us: "the truth will set you free" (John 8:43).*

Some religious texts are such that they speak directly to the culture of the time. Sometimes they continue to speak meaningfully to generation after generation. This is surely true of the psalms. This tells us a lot about the value of the religious insights expressed in them, *but we cannot simply ignore the historical context of the revelation,* or the fact that God's self-revelation necessarily transcends the words in which it is expressed.

This is necessarily true of the writings of the New Testament as well. The Gospels and the Letters of the New Testament are the responses to Jesus of Matthew, Mark, Luke, John, Paul, James and the others. Christians continue to treat Jesus' words and actions found in the Gospels with the greatest respect for they offer a privileged window into the way Jesus' disciples came to see him. However, we believe that it is Jesus himself who reveals God. The written words of the Christian New Testament were treasured by the early Christians because they judged them to point in an authentic way to Jesus, the revelation of God. *But nevertheless they were words written by people who, while in many ways transcending their culture, were still limited human beings with limited insight. God inspires limited human beings, for that is what we are.*

Christianity is not a "Religion of the Book." It is a Religion of a Person, Jesus. We believe that Jesus is the perfect human expression of God's Word, God's Self-revelation. Jesus' words and actions, recorded in the Gospels, take us into the heart of Jesus, into his prayer-communion with God. His words and his deeds are a precious gift, for they give expression to his person, and to his intimate communion with God whom he addressed as "Abba" ("My dear Father"; Mark 14:36). He encouraged his disciples to address God in the same intimate way (Matthew 6:9; Galatians 4:6; Romans 8:15).

In Jesus' day it was thought that the male was the sole source of human life. The role of the female was to receive that life and nourish it. With such an understanding, when Jesus addressed God as the source of his life and mission, it was natural to speak of God as "Father." Today, with our more accurate understanding of the mutual contribution of the male and the female to human life, we can follow Jesus' example, but address God as "Mother" as well as "Father."

Jesus experienced himself as God's "Son." Jesus felt that God knew him and that he knew God in an especially intimate way: "All things have been handed over to me by my Father; and no one knows the Son except the Father, and no one knows the Father except the Son and anyone to whom the Son chooses to reveal him" (Matthew 11:27). This intimacy bore fruit in an extraordinary capacity to love, and it was his love that gave authority to his teaching and healing power to his ministry. Jesus wanted to share this intimacy, this love, with everyone. In John's Gospel we hear Jesus say: "The Father and I are one" (John 10:30). He wanted his disciples to experience this communion: "May they be one, Father, as we are one" (John 17:11). "May they all be one. As you, Father, are in me and I am in you, may they also be in us, so that the world may believe that you have sent me" (John 17:21) . . .

The point I wish to establish in this introductory chapter is that if we are to pray the psalms as disciples of Jesus, if we are to pray the psalms with him, *we need to identify aspects of the psalms that do not fit with Jesus' prayer and ministry and edit them as best we can in the light of what we know of Jesus' mind and heart. Only then can the psalms be truly Christian prayer.*[97]

Student reflection questions

1. How are some themes in Psalms different than the teachings of Jesus?
2. What do you understand by the following:

    ". . . we need to identify aspects of the psalms that do not fit with Jesus' prayer and ministry and edit them as best we can in the light of what we know of Jesus' mind and heart. Only then can the psalms be truly Christian prayer."

3. What does Fallon mean by the phrase, "Christianity is not a 'Religion of the Book.' It is a Religion of a Person, Jesus?" Discuss.

---

97. Fallon, "Praying the Psalms With Jesus," 3–21 (emphasis added).

CONCLUSION

> In what sense is religion a kind of *binding* (from the Latin, *religāre*), a being bound to a web of principles, doctrines, certainties, and in what sense is it a *process of reading again*, as Cicero suggested (*relegĕre*, "to read over again [and again]"), a continuing engagement with texts, a way of articulating, by reading/writing, the most profound questions about life and death, identity and otherness? Is religion about asserting answers or crafting questions?[98]

As mentioned in chapter 1, American scholar Timothy Beal describes religion as an ongoing process of engaging with life, its questions, and its relationship to sacred texts. For him, the text becomes a continual reading over in order that new meanings emerge. The reader becomes engaged and inspired by the text as it *reveals* meanings about existence, the world, God, gods, or ultimate reality. In essence, it speaks to people's minds, spirits, and emotions. It has for centuries been a source of personal transformation. Sacred texts have inspired artists, philosophers, religious writers, and believers throughout history, as it still does today. How we read and interpret sacred texts is a delicate matter. It requires that we approach the text using our rational and analytic tools, our emotions, and imaginations, for each in its own way plays a significant part in helping us understand its relevance and possible transformative influence.

STUDENT REFLECTIONS

What are you now wondering about?

- Have any of the lessons in this chapter changed your thinking? Explain.
- What further questions do you have? Has this chapter opened your mind to further horizons? Explain.
- In years to come, what might you remember from these lessons? Explain.

---

98. Beal, "Opening," 1 (emphasis in original).

INDEPENDENT RESEARCH QUESTIONS

1. To what extent can the critical method be useful in understanding sacred texts?

2. To what extent can there be a synthesis between the critical and artistic approach in the interpretation of texts?

3. Liberation theology is an interpretation of the Bible focusing mostly on the power relationships and structures within the society of first-century Palestine and exploring how Jesus challenged these. Discuss this in general or select one main proponent of this approach and evaluate their approach—for example, Gustavo Gutierrez or Leonardo Boff. What are some ways liberation theology can be linked to the teachings of other religious traditions?

4. Feminist hermeneutics critique the patriarchal influences in sacred writings. Choose a sacred text and apply feminist hermeneutics. Discuss one main proponent of this approach and evaluate their position (for example, Elisabeth Schüssler Fiorenza, Osiek, or Pamela Sue Anderson).

5. Religious and nonreligious fundamentalism are a concern in our world today. Discuss one or two researchers of this issue and evaluate their response.

How Do We Act?: An Inquiry of Ethics

1. Introduction
2. What criteria do we apply for judging moral actions?
3. Moral relativism
4. Ethical egoism
5. Utilitarianism
6. Deontological ethics
7. Virtue ethics
8. Religious ethics
9. The effects of economic thinking on the good and moral life
10. Ethics of war
11. Scapegoating and racism
12. The importance of listening and empathy to the moral life
13. Main research task
14. Independent research questions

Objectives:

At the end of this chapter, students should demonstrate the ability to ask questions, wonder, and think critically about the following:

1. Secular and religious ethical theories which highlight different ways of thinking about moral issues.
2. Processes which underlie scapegoating and racism, as well as the moral implications which emerge in society.

3. The impact of an ideological framework such as economic rationalism (or neoliberalism) on the good and moral life.
4. Consider the importance of listening, empathy, and compassion to the moral life.

INTRODUCTION

> I cannot see how to refute the arguments for the subjectivity of ethical values, but I find myself incapable of believing that all that is wrong with wanton cruelty is that I don't like it.[1]

What does Russell's provocation say about the difficulties in assessing whether ethical values are right or wrong?

Humanity has achieved high levels of success in terms of development, most likely because of our ability to transfer knowledge and work together, along with sufficient autonomy that enables us to discover, create, and share information, knowledge, and beneficial breakthroughs. Yet we subjugate, enslave, and kill. In many of today's societies we often see gross inequality, exploitation, and harm. Humans span an extremely wide spectrum behaviourally, from being *creative* to *destructive*. Such behaviour leads to a clear need to think seriously about *what fosters good acts* while deterring bad ones.

However, when we examine how we ought or should act, we encounter conflicting situations and outcomes. Should a destitute father steal bread for his starving children? Should an individual escaping a concentration camp kill a guard? Should a society execute a murderer to deter others from doing the same? Along with these conundrums are questions of who decides what is right, whether rules should be based solely on outcome, and whether moral rules are invented by humans or discovered as universal or divinely revealed truths.

This chapter will include a brief introduction of the primary ethical theories and ways to explore them, along with a continued focus on epistemological inquiry. As with the rest of this book, chapter 4 moves beyond content and prompts questions, discussions, and further research. Students are encouraged to access further resources on ethics and there are some suggested links and resources included.

1. Russell, "Notes on Philosophy, January 1960," 146–47.

Student Activity—Terminology:

Working in student pairs, write down the definitions of the terms below and take turns explaining them to each other. Some of these concepts are still debated within philosophy and theology. However, familiarity with some common understandings of the terms will assist in engaging in the ideas presented. The Oxford and Webster dictionaries may be a good place to start:

relativistic argument, altruism, empathy, ethical egoism, ethics, secular ethics, criteria, utilitarianism, morals, moral relativism, consequentialism, deontological, ideological framework, religious ethics, veil of ignorance, virtue ethics, economic rationalism, eudaimonia, neoliberalism, Natural Law, scapegoating, normative values, mimetic theory

Main terms

Ethics: The branch of knowledge that studies moral principles.[2]

Morality: Principles concerning the distinction between right and wrong or good and bad behaviour.[3]

For the purpose of this chapter, ethics will be primarily understood as a *rational and systematic evaluation and examination of moral values and arguments.*[4]

WHAT CRITERIA DO WE APPLY FOR JUDGING MORAL ACTIONS?

Discussion questions

1. Do you think ethics and morals are important?

---

2. *Oxford Dictionaries*, s.v. "Ethics." https://en.oxforddictionaries.com/definition/ethics [slightly edited]

3. *Oxford Dictionaries*, s.v. "Morality." http://www.oxforddictionaries.com/definition/english/morality.

4. Thompson, *Ethical Theory*, 28.

2. What ways of knowing do you use when making moral decisions?
3. Do men make moral decisions differently than women do? Explain.
4. What criteria can be applied when assessing whether an act is moral?
5. Can a law be immoral?
6. Are there universal ethical theories or does ethics depend on culture, context, situation, or personal opinion?

Most people would probably claim there is a need for at least some morals within a society, and intuitively state that acts like murder are wrong. Morals and ethics may prevent social chaos and anarchy. This theme is developed in *The Lord of the Flies*, a novel by William Golding that depicts the trials of adolescent boys stranded on a remote island due to a plane crash. In their attempt to survive, they struggle with dilemmas and challenges of establishing and enforcing rules.[5]

With a global population of approximately 7.7 billion, is there a theory that can speak to people universally? How do we construct theories or principles which can provide a framework for assessing whether actions are right or wrong? It's a tough task as ethics cannot be easily identified as a basic set of rules to follow, nor be dependent on preferences or opinion.

The study of ethics requires an openness in thinking about various options presented in human dilemmas, while leaving aside, as much as possible, *personal views and beliefs*. Identifying immoral acts in films and stories as battles between good and evil unfold may often be simple. However, can we easily identify subtle types of immoral acts in everyday life? Identifying immoral behaviour will depend on the definition of morality and what is morally accepted.

If we are to assume that education provides people with the tools for thinking and good reasoning, and if reason is claimed to be the primary basis on which we make moral decisions, how then do we explain the *reasoning* of many educated and professional people who commit evil acts? Do we assume that educated people are better at reasoning and therefore making wiser moral decisions? This assumption maybe challenged, as throughout history highly educated people have been responsible for committing all kinds of atrocities.

People with the ability and knowledge to act morally can develop sophisticated and elaborate *rationalisations* and effective rhetoric in support of their immoral actions which are convincing to themselves and others. How do we challenge the legitimacy of their claims? Can we assess whether

---

5. Golding, *Lord of the Flies*.

their actions are immoral? You may argue that their actions are wrong due to the following:

1. They caused pain and suffering to themselves and other; or
2. They exploit people for an advantage at the expense of those people's happiness and well-being

To what extent are these adequate justifications? Are these valid criteria for judging whether actions are good or bad? Discuss.

Can you think of examples of these today?

MORAL RELATIVISM

> You are free, therefore choose—that is to say invent. No rule of general morality can show you what you ought to do: no signs are vouchsafed in this world.[6]

Do I follow my own moral code or universal laws?

Arguing that there are no universal laws or criteria which govern morality and ethics, and that they are dependent on culture, context, situation, or personal opinion, is adopting a relativistic argument. Moral relativism (also known as ethical relativism) can be defined as "the view that moral judgements are true or false only relative to some particular standpoint (for instance, that of a culture or a historical period) and that no standpoint is uniquely privileged over all others."[7] Cultural and situational context must be acknowledged when evaluating the moral rule in question, according to this view. When disparate cultures interact, cultural relativism accommodates the differences and often justifies results which some may argue are immoral. For example, arranged marriages are accepted in some cultures, but not others. There are those who support same-sex marriage, while others cite specific Bible passages to declare same-sex marriage unacceptable. Does one viewpoint invalidate another, or are they equally valid?

The Native American Makah tribe has been granted permission by the International Whaling Commission to hunt and kill grey whales because the hunt is an integral part of the tribe's cultural heritage. This allowance contrasts with the global prohibition on grey whale hunting, a practice deemed cruel and unnecessary by the international community.

---

6. Sartre, *Existentialism and Humanism*, 38.
7. Westacott, "Moral Relativism," para. 1.

The decision allowing the Makah tribe to hunt grey whales and affirm the tribe's cultural practice is an example of adopting a relativistic argument. Moral relativism claims that people cannot agree on universal ethics, since disagreement is more prevalent than agreement due to differences in attitudes, values, and beliefs among human cultures. This is the stance of metaethical theory, which proposes that there are no moral truths which we can apply universally. According to this theory, moral conflict is the result of cultural differences and must be understood with the context of each culture.[8]

Critics of Moral Relativism

Some have critiqued relativism as an easy option, an avoidance of engagement in a complex and vast field of ethical theory for a simple acceptance of any morality offered. Is it possible to live daily as a relativist without any objective references to ethics or truth? Are we able to discuss moral issues without at least implicitly making reference to agreed-upon concepts or truths?

If ethics is just a matter of opinion, or depends on the situation and culture—both of which are always changing—how can we make moral decisions? What adequate standards can we apply to ethical dilemmas? This position is in contrast with values inherent in the United Nations and the *UN Declarations of Human Rights* (which 33 countries are signatory to) that acknowledges a universal code of ethical conduct. The Golden Rule, an example of a moral tenet which advocates treating others as we would like to be treated, is found within all the major world religions' teachings, thus representing a universal moral code. These two examples contradict the basic concepts of moral relativism.

Opponents of relativism, called Objectivists (i.e., Kant, discussed below), argue that there are acts which are right or wrong independent of personal preference or culture. They argue that there are objective truths and morals to be discovered. American philosopher James Rachels (1941–2003) claims empirical evidence shows moral agreement across cultures. He proposed three examples: firstly, most cultures care for their young or infants; secondly, most cultures value truthful communication; and thirdly, most are against murder.[9] One could argue for pragmatic reasons that we need some objective reference point to work with when dealing with moral dilemmas.

---

8. Fieser, "Metaethics."
9. Rachels and Rachels, *Elements of Moral Philosophy*.

When confronted with issues involving murder, stealing, poverty, the environment, and all matters of justice pertaining to civil life, the importance of having an objective framework that allows us to access an approach to the issue is important—what many moral philosophers and theologians argue in favour of. As American professor Arthur Dobrin claims, despite the advantages of relativism in providing a tolerance for different perspectives, it cannot guarantee a standard of morals in judging behaviour beyond the interests of the self and group.[10] Relativism has the potential to allow all kinds of behaviour as part of social conventions or norms, which may not necessarily be moral or uphold the dignity and rights of people:[11]

> While relativism has its strengths (it is tolerant of different points of view), its primary weakness is that it reduces ethics either to social conventions or to personal preferences. Social conventions aren't identical to ethics. Sometimes the two may be at odds. If there were no distinction between convention and morality, anything done by a group would be ethical if that's how the group defined morality for itself. If social convention and morality were the same, long-standing discrimination against a group of people by the dominant group would be defined as ethical. Genocide would be moral because it was an expression of the values of those ordering the murders. But certainly those who risk their lives to save victims of oppression are moral heroes while the executioners are rightly condemned for having committed crimes against humanity. Asserting something is right doesn't make it right. Ethics is about how people get along with each other fairly. Without a standard that is beyond your own self or that of society, if things are fair then it is only a matter of luck.[12]

Discussion Questions

1. Do you agree/disagree with Arthur Dobrin's criticism of relativism? Explain.
2. Can relativism lead to a loss of standards for human rights and dignity as suggested?

10. Dobrin, "Moral Relativism," paras. 7–8.
11. Ibid., paras. 7–8.
12. Ibid.

3. How does Dobrin's opinion apply to the Makah tribe and its whale-hunting heritage?

4. Can you give examples of where relativist and objectivist approaches to ethics may be useful and also limiting?

EGOISM

Is ethics based on self-interests?

Egoism is the broad category of self-interest as a foundation for morals. Inititally, such a concept may seem contradictory—for many, morals intuitively appear to consider others before the self. However, is this really true, or do actions that look benevolent on the surface really just serve ourselves? A number of prominent thinkers have discussed this theory, including Thomas Hobbes (1588–1679), Friedrich Nietzsche (1844–1990), and Ayn Rand (1905–1982). There are two main types of egoism—psychological egoism and ethical egoism—the focus here being the former.

PSYCHOLOGICAL EGOISM

Psychological egoism maintains that humans are innately predisposed to act in their own self-interest. This view maintains that even when acting altruistically (an apparent demonstration of selfless concern for others), one is really engaging in an action that will also benefit themselves. When helping people, we are also satisfying our own needs, as we have assessed that there is some benefit for ourselves.

Thomas Hobbes argued that the emotion of pity, which may move us to help others, is really only an unconscious form of pity for ourselves. We pity others as we can imagine ourselves experiencing the same suffering. In an extreme example, if an individual risks their own life to rescue someone from drowning in a river, the act would still be in the rescuer's self-interest, satisfying an inherent desire to appease guilt or empathy. Although such an act appears as an extremely selfless act for another, it actually is for the self, according to psychological egoism.

Discussion Questions

1. Do you think that all of our actions are motivated by self-interests? If so, what are the advantages or limitations?
2. Is the emotion of pity described by Hobbes a sufficient explanation for altruism?
3. What is the difference between pity and empathy?
4. Can you think of examples in your own life when you acted purely out of self-interest or altruism? What were the results? Share your responses with another student.

Student Activity—Essay: Choose one of the following and write a response:

1. Research and summarize the similarities and differences between psychological egoism and ethical egoism.
2. Research the works of Thomas Hobbes, Friedrich Nietzsche, Ayn Rand, or other thinkers on ethical egoism.

Tragedy of the Commons

Acting in one's self-interest at the cost of others' interests has also been observed by economists. This phenomenon is known in economics as the Tragedy of the Commons. Examined by Garrett Hardin in his well-known 1968 essay of the same name, the concept describes a behaviour pattern often found in the abuse of the natural environment.[13] A typical scenario involves a renewable energy resource, available to many and yet neither owned nor regulated, that ends up being used to depletion levels. Hardin used the hypothetical scenario of a public grazing pasture, not owned by anyone and available for all herders to have their livestock graze without restrictions. In this situation, each herder could individually gain by adding

---

13. Hardin, "Tragedy of the Commons."

as many animals as possible to graze with the expense borne by the whole community. However, as each individual herder would understand and utilize this immediate advantage, the pasture would become overgrazed and, over time, permanently destroyed—the tragedy of the commons.[14] As professor Jonathan H. Adler explained in his article on this concept, "the pursuit of self-interest in an open-access common leads to ruin. Without controls on access and use of the underlying resource, the tragedy of the commons is inevitable."[15] Other environmental examples of the Tragedy of the Commons are depletion of the bluefin tuna population, degradation of the Great Barrier Reef from mining and pollution, overfishing of cod, and global warming from atmospheric carbon emissions.

STUDENT ACTIVITY—RESEARCH

Study an article that brings up the topic of the Tragedy of the Commons. Read and then write a summary.

UTILITARIANISM

John Stuart Mill

Jeremy Bentham

14. Ibid.
15. Adler, "Property Rights," para. 3.

Is an act wrong or right depending on the consequences or outcomes?

Consequentialism considers actions good or bad depending on their outcomes or consequences. This way of thinking includes a type of philosophy that is termed utilitarianism. The purpose is to achieve the greatest good for the greatest number of people. Utilitarianism claims that social and economic decisions should be made which result in the most beneficial results for the highest number of individuals. The concept utilizes a cost-benefit analysis of those affected, the utilitarian evaluating the usefulness of possible options and choosing the one benefiting the greatest number. English philosophers John Stuart Mill (1806–1873) and Jeremy Bentham (1748–1832) developed this approach. They drew on the previous ancient philosophical thinking found in hedonism and Epicureanism, which claimed that the main objective of life is achieving the greatest amount of well-being (pleasure) with the least amount of pain (suffering). Mill argued that all actions should be aimed at achieving the greatest amount of happiness and, unlike Bentham, made distinctions in the *quality* of pleasures. He argued that there are higher pleasures such as those found in the intellect, imagination, and spirituality, than those found when engaging in physical activities and our senses, which he identified as the lower pleasures. He writes:

> The creed which accepts as the foundations of morals "utility" or the "greatest happiness principle" holds that actions are right in proportion as they tend to promote happiness; wrong as they tend to produce the reverse of happiness. By happiness is intended pleasure and the absence of pain; by unhappiness, pain and the privation of pleasure. (II.2) If I am asked what I mean by difference of quality in pleasures, or what makes one pleasure more valuable than another, merely as a pleasure, except its being greater in amount, there is but one possible answer. If one of the two is, by those who are competently acquainted with both, placed so far above the other that they prefer it, even though knowing it to be attended with a greater amount of discontent, and would not resign it for any quantity of the other pleasure which their nature is capable of, we are justified in ascribing to the preferred enjoyment a superiority in quality so far outweighing quantity as to render it, in comparison, of small account. (II.5)[16]

---

16. Mill, *Utilitarianism*, II, 2, 5.

Discussion Questions

1. Do you agree with the distinctions made between higher and lower pleasures?
2. Think of a time when you engaged in both higher and lower pleasures; which do you think caused you greater pleasure and why?
3. Can you think of examples where the utilitarian approach is applied in decision making?
4. Are the utility and pleasure of an action the best criteria for judging whether an act is good or bad?
5. What are some advantages and disadvantages to the utilitarian approach to ethics?

For further research on utilitarianism, the following links may be useful:

Philosophy bites: Roger Crisp discussion on utilitarianism[17]
Video: PHILOSOPHY—Ethics: Utilitarianism, Part 1 [HD][18]

Discussion Questions

Work in pairs or groups. Construct your own ideal society. What would it look like? How would resources be allocated? What would be the rules? What privileges would people have? What obligations would they have? Would everyone be in agreement with this society?

The Veil of Ignorance

In his book *A Theory of Justice*, American philosopher John Rawls (1921–2002) approached issues of societal fairness and justice by proposing a hypothetical society in which rules are determined and agreed upon behind what he called a "veil of ignorance." Rawls meant that those establishing the rules would have no knowledge of their own social or economic positions

---

17. http://philosophybites.com/2007/07/roger-crisp-on-.html.
18. https://www.youtube.com/watch?v=uvmz5E75ZIA.

granted upon birth, and would not be able to choose; instead, their positions would be assigned randomly.

Rawls argued that with such a placement behind the veil, any individual, even one focused solely on self-interest, would greatly consider principles of fairness, as well as pay more attention to the most impoverished of a society. As the poorest of the poor might include them, the stakes would be too high for allowing extreme disparity and lack of opportunity. Rawls thought this hypothetical approach allowed for greater objectivity in thinking about issues of fairness and equity in society, removing people from personal agendas and interests which may cloud their own perspectives.

Student Activity—Video

After watching the video, "POLITICAL THEORY—John Rawls, The School of Life,"[19] answer the following questions:

1. Can Rawls' veil of ignorance provide an adequate approach in thinking about ethics? Explain.
2. How does the veil of ignorance affect egoism and utilitarian ethics?
3. Most legislators worldwide would likely claim they genuinely consider the well-being of all. If so, has the veil of ignorance already been applied? Does it work? Support your answer.

Utilitarian—Peter Singer

Australian philosopher Peter Singer warns of disastrous consequences from what he observes as the increase in actions based on self-interest in the world at large. He argues we run the risk of human self-destruction if we do not pay attention to this global trend.

Singer proposes that morals should not only focus on the interests of the individual, but also be linked to others in the wider community. He describes this proposal as exercising reason to detach oneself from one's own individual perspective and to look at the world from a *wider lens*—what English philosopher Henry Sidgwick (1838–1900) calls the "point of view of the universe."[20] Singer argues this wider lens can potentially allow us to understand the effects of our actions on others and the impact of groups and nations on the global scale. This approach can help focus our attention

19. https://www.youtube.com/watch?v=5-JQ17X6VNg.
20. Singer, *How are We to Live?*, 263.

to a greater understanding of others' suffering, and in doing so we may see that they are not very different from ourselves.[21] As mentioned earlier, an obvious consequence of self-interest, and with very high stakes, is the environmental crisis:

> One such moral truth could be Sidgwick's axiom of universal benevolence: "each one is morally bound to regard the good of any other individual as much as his own, except in so far as he judges it to be less, when impartially viewed, or less certainly knowable or attainable by him."[22]

Singer views current economic consumption, which results in the inequality between social classes and the cruelty of animals, as having negative and unethical consequences. These actions are immoral, according to Singer, because they lead to pain and suffering, and ultimately impinge on the quality of life. Singer, along with many other philosophers and theologians (i.e., Aristotle, Plato, and Aquinas) have argued that living an ethical life leads to our own happiness; the two are not necessarily diametrically opposed:[23]

> We must reinstate the idea of living an ethical life as a realistic and viable alternative to the present dominance of material self-interests. If, over the next decade, a critical mass of people with new priorities were to emerge, and if these people were seen to do very well, in every sense of the term—if their cooperation with each other brings reciprocal benefits, if they find joy and fulfillment in their lives—then the ethical attitudes will spread, and the conflict between ethics and self-interests will have been shown to be overcome, not by abstract reasoning alone, but by adopting the ethical life as a practical way of living, and showing that it works, psychologically, socially and ecologically.[24]

Singer extends his analysis to the personal benefits of living an ethical life which points beyond the material value we place in accomplishments based on self-interest. Existential philosophers also explore this connection

---

21. Ibid.
22. de Lazari-Radek and Singer, in Schultz, "Henry Sidgwick," 182–83.
23. Singer is making a point about happiness as a psychological state, whilst Aristotle and Plato are making a point about well-being/flourishing.
24. Singer, *How are We to Live?*, 279.

between morality and personal meaning. Singer highlights that living an ethical life can also bring a sense of fulfillment:

> You will not be bored or lack fulfillment in your life. Most important of all, you will know that you have not lived and died for nothing, because you will have become part of the great tradition of those who have responded to the amount of pain and suffering in the universe by trying to make the world a better place.[25]

Discussion questions

1. Do you agree/disagree with Singer's analysis of the prevailing material self-interest evident today? Does this have negative consequences, as Singer suggests?
2. What do you think of the solution proposed by Singer? Could it work? Explain.

DEONTOLOGICAL ETHICS

> Two things fill the mind with ever-increasing wonder and awe ... the starry heavens above me and the law within me.[26]

Are there any moral acts that are right or wrong regardless of the consequence?

Immanuel Kant (1724–1804) is a German philosopher who wrote extensive, rigorous, and complex work in many areas such as ethics, epistemology, metaphysics, and science. Kant believed that

25. Ibid., 280.
26. Kant, *Critique of Pure Reason*, 161.

morality depends on our *intention* and not the outcome. For example, if my intention is to help my sick friend and I bring her some medicine which turns out to make her even more ill, this, for Kant, would not be considered immoral as my intention is based on good motives. Kant wrote guidelines when making moral decisions, which are known as *categorical imperatives*. One common interpretation of these can be understood as the following:

1. I should only act if what I am going to do is feasible for everyone else to do as well. I should ask myself, would it be possible to *universalize* (apply equally everywhere) the action I am considering?
2. Following on from this, I should never use people merely *as means to an end, but as ends in themselves*.[27]

Discussion questions

1. What do you think of the categorical imperatives in guiding moral actions?
2. To what extent can they be useful today as a guide to moral decisions?
3. What are some of their limitations?

Kant goes beyond self-interest, culture, and personal experiences in order to come up with ethical rules which can be applied universally. For example, if killing, stealing, and lying are acceptable actions for an individual, that person would then need to accept that these actions would *be permissible as well for himself or herself*. Kant's second category, following from the first, is to avoid using people for means to a selfish end. He was opposed to using or exploiting others for one's own benefits and maintained that individuals should be treated with their own dignity and worth.

Kant believed in universal laws or principles. These laws pertain to moral codes that reveal what actions are right and wrong *in themselves and which are not dependent on consequences*. Kant stated we are capable of understanding these laws of morality through our *reasoning*. He was a rationalist philosopher proposing that reason should govern our actions and help us to discover objective principles. Kant argues that we are capable of thinking *beyond* our immediate experiences (which he argues are limited), such as personal likes and dislikes, in order to understand these universal

---

27. Kant and Paton, *Moral Law*, 27–30.

principles.[28] Moral actions should not be based purely on self-interest nor emotions, but rather on *duty to others*. Kant's moral philosophy fits into the category of what is called a deontological approach to ethics, which can be defined as "The study of the nature of duty and obligation."[29]

Discussion questions

1. What do you think of Kant's approach to ethics?
2. Are actions wrong in themselves regardless of the consequences?
3. Do we have a moral duty toward others which is beyond self-interest and how we feel?
4. To what extent can Kant's approach to ethics be useful today? Give examples.
5. Can you think of some its strengths and limitations?

Kant's rich, extensive, and complex work has engaged the minds of many philosophers and theologians for centuries. Some of the common criticisms directed toward his work include allowing no exceptions to the moral rule, and that he does not consider moral duties in conflict; for example, during World War II, we may have had to lie about the Jews we were hiding to the Nazis who were searching for Jews to kill. Kant also viewed emotions as a negative influence on moral actions.

David Hume—Emotions in moral actions

English empirical philosopher David Hume (1711–1776), on the other hand, acknowledged the presence of emotions in moral actions. He argued that humans are innately motivated by a "moral sense" or "sympathy," and that we are capable of experiencing the feelings of others.[30] It is this capacity to share others' feelings (what we might term as "empathy") that he argues is the *motivating factor* in moral actions, rather than reason or objective

---

28. Ibid.
29. *Oxford Dictionaries*, s.v. "Deontology." http://www.oxforddictionaries.com/definition/deontology.
30. Hume, *A Treatise of Human Nature*, 3:320–28.

universal principles.[31] Hume claimed that reason is a necessary tool in allowing us to reflect on the consequences of an action, but in and of itself cannot provide a motivation for moral action. He also viewed emotions as the driver of our reasoning capacities.[32]

ACTIVITY—CONVERSATION:

Research the moral dilemma below and in groups have a guided conversation about the following characters: Bentham, Mill, Kant, and Singer. Demonstrate how they would approach this situation.

The occurrence of Dudley and Stephens is a famous law case (named *Regina v. Dudley and Stephens*) as well as an ethical dilemma. Four people were forced to use a lifeboat at sea after their ship was damaged. They ran out of food and water, all close to impending death. Two of the group, Dudley and Stephens, decided to kill the weakest member closest to death, in their opinion, in order to eat his body and possibly survive. Research the case for the actual and legal outcome.[33] To start with a summary, watch "The Lifeboat Case," a short video of the event.[34]

ACTIVITY—ESSAY

Write a response to the following:

Actions are always right and wrong *in themselves* and we do not need to assess them according to their *consequences* or utility or our own *self-interest*. Discuss.

STUDENT REFLECTIONS

WHAT ARE YOU NOW WONDERING ABOUT?

- What ideas or questions are you wondering about as a result of these lessons?
- Have these lessons made you think differently? Explain.

31. Ibid.
32. Ibid.
33. *Regina v Dudley and Stephens*, 14 Q.B.D. 273 (Queen's Bench Division, 1884).
34. http://justiceharvard.org/lecture-2-the-case-for-cannibalism/

- What have you found challenging, provocative, or intriguing?

VIRTUE ETHICS

Can character traits be an important factor when considering ethical behavior?

As discussed in chapter 1, the ancient Greek philosophers often discussed the question of how to live and what constitutes the good life (i.e., the *flourishing life*). Their response was mostly connected to morality and ethics. Aristotle thought one of the main elements of a well-lived life included the development of character and virtues.

Virtue ethics is an interpretation of Aristotle's work taken from *Nicomachean Ethics*. Unlike debating the *criteria* of the action as good or bad, this approach explores the importance of *personal character*. People demonstrating the virtues of temperance, tolerance, long-suffering, courage, and other such qualities can be held up in society as exemplars of virtuous character. The focus here is on a person's virtue and character rather than what actions should be taken.

> Every art and every inquiry, and similarly every action and pursuit, is thought to aim at some good.[35]

Aristotle claimed that all human actions have an *end* to which they strive toward. That is, for humans, the end is to be the person they were made to be according to their *nature* or function.[36] We must explore what the function of humans is in order that we must understand their end or purpose.[37] Not all aims are the same and Aristotle claimed that the ultimate goal is to achieve "the good," termed *eudaimonia* in Greek, or human *flourishing*, meaning happiness:

> If, then, our activities have some end which we want for its own sake of which we want all the other ends—if we do not choose everything for the sake of something else (for this will involve an infinite progression, so that our aim will be

35. Aristotle, *Nicomachean Ethics*, 63.
36. Stumpf, *Socrates to Sartre*, 106.
37. Ibid.

pointless and ineffectual)—it is clear that this must be the Good, that is supreme good. Does it not follow then that a knowledge of the Good is of great importance to us for the conduct of our lives? Are we more likely to achieve our aim if we have a target?[38]

What are your thoughts so far? Do you agree or disagree with the ideas discussed?

Aristotle based ethics and happiness on the development of virtue. Virtue, he argued, was a quality of the soul developed through the application of right reasoning and action.[39] He believed we develop virtue though our actions and correct thinking in accordance to a well-lived life. We are not born with moral virtues, but *rather develop these through habits*.[40] He argued that all humans have the potential to attain these virtues, and that they emerge through our actions. "We become just by doing moral acts."[41] These moral virtues include: wisdom, courage, justice, temperance, self-respect, magnificence, liberality, and friendship.[42]

As mentioned in chapter 1, it is important to remember that Aristotle understood wisdom in two ways: one is *sophia,* which is a type of intellectual wisdom; the other is *phronesis,* which is practical wisdom.

Discussion questions

1. What do you understand by the virtues mentioned above? You may need to research their meanings.
2. Is it possible to develop these virtues today? Discuss.

---

38. Ibid., 63–64.
39. Ibid., 108.
40. Ibid., 108–10.
41. Ibid., 110.
42. Ibid.

How do I know when and how to apply these virtues?

Do I act courageously all of the time or is it wise to be cautious, and maybe even fearful, in some situations?

Aristotle argued that we need to act on these virtues in the right time, at the right place, and in the right way.[43] This is known as his teaching on the *mean*. He defines this concept as acting in ways that are appropriate to the situation, involving tempering or controlling our emotions and passions through the exercise of our reason. For example, if Tom yells unnecessarily at Fred on the playground, Fred's initial reaction might be to yell back. However, a wiser strategy could be for Fred to control his anger and talk to Tom at a more appropriate time when they are both calm.

Aristotle argued that in practicing these virtues in the *appropriate way* (that is, attending to our emotions), we develop what he termed *practical wisdom*. Whatever our emotions or temperance may be, Aristotle asserted that we can apply reason in choosing wisely the most appropriate action according to our situation.[44] In support of this approach, philosopher Julia Annas points out, "A virtue, or a vice, is the way I have *made myself* and chosen to be."[45] As Aristotle wrote:

> By virtue, I mean moral virtue since it is this that is concerned with feelings and actions, and these involve excess, deficiency and a mean. It is possible, for example, to feel fear, confidence, desire, anger, pity, and pleasure and pain generally, too much or too little; and both of these are wrong. But to have these feelings at the right times on the right grounds towards the right people for the right motive and in the right way is to feel them to an intermediate, that is the best, degree; and this is the mark of virtue.[46]

As we develop these virtues over time, we internalize them and are better placed at making the correct choices without too much internal conflict.[47] It is worth noting that the mean does not apply to actions which in themselves are evil, such as murder, stealing, and adultery. According to

---

43. Ibid., 108.
44. Annas, *The Morality of Happiness*.
45. Ibid., 4.
46. Aristotle, *Nicomachean Ethics*, 1106b9–1107a1.
47. Stumpf, *Socrates to Sartre*, 110.

Aristotle there is *no appropriateness* to these actions because they are *always immoral*.[48]

Discussion questions

1. What do you think the following phrase from Aristotle is telling us about feelings:

   "But to have these feelings at the right times on the right grounds towards the right people for the right motive and in the right way is to feel them to an intermediate, that is the best, degree; and this is the mark of virtue."

2. Do you agree with Aristotle on the importance of practicing virtues in the *appropriate way*? Is it useful?

3. Can you think of other situations where it is better to control your emotions in order to gain a better outcome? Explain.

Are the distinctions between the theories too narrow?

> Schools of ethics in Western philosophy can be divided, very roughly, into three sorts. The first, drawing on the work of Aristotle, holds that the virtues (such as justice, charity, and generosity) are dispositions to act in ways that benefit both the person possessing them and that person's society. The second, defended particularly by Kant, makes the concept of duty central to morality: humans are bound, from a knowledge of their duty as rational beings, to obey the categorical imperative to respect other rational beings. Thirdly, utilitarianism asserts that the guiding principle of conduct should be the greatest happiness or benefit of the greatest number.[49]

While there are distinctions presented above between approaches in virtue ethics, deontology, and consequentialism, not all scholars agree with the differences outlined. New Zealander philosopher Mary Rosalind Hursthouse

---

48. Ibid., 101.

49. *Oxford Dictionaries*, "Ethics." https://en.oxforddictionaries.com/definition/ethics.

argues that there are elements of consequentialism within virtue ethics.[50] For example, the person who has developed virtue thinks about the effects or consequences of their actions and behaves accordingly. Henry Sidgwick likewise argues for common-sense morality, which sees a connection between the approaches. He states that most of us can recognize the deontological weight of ethical rules, yet we can also see how they may be justified when they result in positive consequences.[51] He argues for a merging of theories; whilst deontological views provide a static presence, consequential thinking, if made explicit, can also lead to a greater flexibility and openness in thinking about moral issues.[52]

It is not in the scope of this chapter to explore all the ethical approaches and you are encouraged to research those omitted, such as metaethics, intuitivism, feminist ethics, and business ethics.

Student Activity—Discuss the following in groups:

Compare and contrast virtue ethics, deontology, and consequentialism. To what extent are there similarities and differences? Discuss in groups and record your responses.

Student Activity—Conversation:

Aristotle, Kant, Mill, and Singer are having a conversation about the current environmental crisis, world poverty, or modern democracy. You may either act this out or write a response.

STUDENT REFLECTIONS

What are you now wondering about?

- What ideas or questions are you wondering about as a result of these lessons?
- Have these lessons made you think differently? Explain.

---

50. Hursthouse, in Johnson and Reath, *Ethics*, 466.
51. Sidgwick, *The Methods of Ethics*, 497–509.
52. Ibid.

- What have you found challenging, provocative, or intriguing?

RELIGIOUS ETHICS

Discussion Questions

1. To what extent is the will of God or the gods an adequate justification for ethics?
2. How do we interpret divine will?

Socrates

In one of Plato's works about Socrates, a topic arises that applies to moral law deriving from religion. In a discussion with his acquaintance Euthyphro, Socrates asks if divine law is morally good because it comes from the Greek gods, or if it comes from the gods because it is morally good. In other words, are ethical rules only to be followed because they come from a deity the followers believe to be all knowing, and therefore correct, or are ethical rules correct independent of the gods? German philosopher Gottfried Leibniz summarized the problem: "But there remains the question whether it is good and just because God wills it or whether God wills it because it is good and just...."[53]

Student Activity—Excerpt

Read Euthyphro by Plato and answer the reflection question below.
    The following links may be useful:
    Euthyphro/Plato translated with an introduction by Benjamín Jowett.[54]
    The Internet Classic Archive, Euthyphro by Plato.[55]

Reflection question: How do you solve the Euthyphro dilemma? Two options are presented. Are there any others?

Religious ethics is the study of morality drawn from religious traditions. Although many scholars would place religious ethics within the deontological

---

53. Schneewind, *Moral Philosophy*, 322.
54. https://ebooks.adelaide.edu.au/p/plato/p71eup/complete.html.
55. http://classics.mit.edu/Plato/euthyfro.html

category of objective rules, there are some scholars who debate this. For example, some Christian scholars argue that the Bible resembles more virtue ethics than deontology.[56] Historically, religion has provided a way of living and ethical guidelines for generations. Today, religious ethics seems to face a complex and dynamic world. As we shall see, moral codes of religious traditions draw out fundamental attributes of humanity that are deemed to be important to many believers today.

You may already be familiar with the central themes and sources of religious ethics. In Christianity, ethics is informed by a number of sources such as the Bible, church community, Natural Law, the Holy Spirit, and personal conscience. The Beatitudes, the Commandment of Love, and the Ten Commandments are generally accepted as forming the basis of Christian teaching. In Buddhist ethics, the guidelines are drawn from teachings such as the Five Precepts, Eight-Fold Path, Three Jewels, and sacred writings which include the Tripitaka, Lotus of the Good Law, and Tibetan Book of the Dead.

Student activity—Research

Investigate one of the following questions, record your findings and present them to the class.

1. How does ethics emerge from religious traditions? Explore ONE religious tradition to answer this question.
2. To what extent can we avoid suffering as the Buddha taught? Discuss.
3. To what extent do the core principles found in the Five Precepts, Five Pillars of Islam, the Ten Commandments, or the Commandment of Love provide an adequate framework to live by?

This resource may be useful: "Education World—Lesson Planning Ideas: The World's Religions."[57]

Student activity—Excerpt

Read the following extracts given by contemporary religious leaders and answer the questions below.

---

56. Hursthouse, in Johnson and Reath, *Ethics*, 466.
57. http://www.educationworld.com/a_lesson/world-religions-multicultural-diversity.shtml.

VISIT TO THE JOINT SESSION OF THE UNITED STATES CONGRESS ADDRESS OF THE HOLY FATHER
United States Capitol, Washington, D.C. Thursday, 24 September 2015

Mr. Vice-President,

Mr. Speaker,

Honorable Members of Congress,

Dear Friends,

I am most grateful for your invitation to address this Joint Session of Congress in "the land of the free and the home of the brave." I would like to think that the reason for this is that I too am a son of this great continent, from which we have all received so much and toward which we share a common responsibility.

Each son or daughter of a given country has a mission, a personal and social responsibility. Your own responsibility as members of Congress is to enable this country, by your legislative activity, to grow as a nation. You are the face of its people, their representatives. You are called to defend and preserve the dignity of your fellow citizens in the tireless and demanding pursuit of the common good, for this is the chief aim of all politics. A political society endures when it seeks, as a vocation, to satisfy common needs by stimulating the growth of all its members, especially those in situations of greater vulnerability or risk. Legislative activity is always based on care for the people. To this you have been invited, called and convened by those who elected you.

Yours is a work which makes me reflect in two ways on the figure of Moses. On the one hand, the patriarch and lawgiver of the people of Israel symbolizes the need of peoples to keep alive their sense of unity by means of just legislation. On the other, the figure of Moses leads us directly to God and thus to the transcendent dignity of the human being. Moses provides us with a good synthesis of your work: you are asked to protect, by means of the law, the image and likeness fashioned by God on every human face.

Today I would like not only to address you, but through you the entire people of the United States. Here, together with their representatives, I would like to take this opportunity to dialogue with the many thousands of men and women who strive each day to do an honest day's work, to bring home their daily bread, to save money and—one step at a time—to build a better life for their families. These are men and women who are not concerned simply with paying their taxes, but in their own quiet way sustain the life of society. They generate solidarity by their actions, and they create organizations which offer a helping hand to those most in need.

. . . I would like to mention four of these Americans: Abraham Lincoln, Martin Luther King, Dorothy Day and Thomas Merton. This year marks the one hundred and fiftieth anniversary of the assassination of President Abraham Lincoln, the guardian of liberty, who labored tirelessly that "this nation, under God, [might] have a new birth of freedom." Building a future of freedom requires love of the common good and cooperation in a spirit of subsidiarity and solidarity.

All of us are quite aware of, and deeply worried by, the disturbing social and political situation of the world today. Our world is increasingly a place of violent conflict, hatred and brutal atrocities, committed even in the name of God and of religion. We know that no religion is immune from forms of individual delusion or ideological extremism. This means that we must be especially attentive to every type of fundamentalism, whether religious or of any other kind. A delicate balance is required to combat violence perpetrated in the name of a religion, an ideology or an economic system, while also safeguarding religious freedom, intellectual freedom and individual freedoms. But there is another temptation which we must especially guard against: the simplistic reductionism which sees only good or evil; or, if you will, the righteous and sinners. The contemporary world, with its open wounds which affect so many of our brothers and sisters, demands that we confront every form of polarization which would divide it into these two camps. We know that in the attempt to be freed of the enemy without, we can be tempted to feed the enemy within. To imitate the hatred and violence of tyrants and murderers is the best way to take their place. That is something which you, as a people, reject.

Our response must instead be one of hope and healing, of peace and justice. We are asked to summon the courage and the intelligence to resolve today's many geopolitical and economic crises. Even in the developed world, the effects of unjust structures and actions are all too apparent. Our efforts must aim at restoring hope, righting wrongs, maintaining commitments, and thus promoting the well-being of individuals and of peoples. We must move forward together, as one, in a renewed spirit of fraternity and solidarity, cooperating generously for the common good.

The challenges facing us today call for a renewal of that spirit of cooperation, which has accomplished so much good throughout the history of the United States. The complexity, the gravity and the urgency of these challenges demand that we pool our resources and talents, and resolve to support one another, with respect for our differences and our convictions of conscience.

In this land, the various religious denominations have greatly contributed to building and strengthening society. It is important that today, as in the past, the voice of faith continue to be heard, for it is a voice of fraternity and love, which tries to bring out the best in each person and in each society. Such cooperation is a powerful resource in the battle to eliminate new global forms of slavery, born of grave injustices which can be overcome only through new policies and new forms of social consensus.

Here I think of the political history of the United States, where democracy is deeply rooted in the mind of the American people. All political activity must serve and promote the good of the human person and be based on respect for his or her dignity. "We hold these truths to be self-evident, that all men are created equal, that they are endowed by their Creator with certain unalienable rights, that among these are life, liberty and the pursuit of happiness" (*Declaration of Independence*, 4 July 1776). If politics must truly be at the service of the human person, it follows that it cannot be a slave to the economy and finance. Politics is, instead, an expression of our compelling need to live as one, in order to build as one the greatest common good: that of a community which sacrifices particular interests in order to share, in justice and peace, its goods, its interests, its social life. I do not underestimate the difficulty that this involves, but I encourage you in this effort.

Here too I think of the march which Martin Luther King led from Selma to Montgomery fifty years ago as part of the campaign to fulfill his "dream" of full civil and political rights for African Americans. That dream continues to inspire us all. I am happy that America continues to be, for many, a land of "dreams." Dreams which lead to action, to participation, to commitment. Dreams which awaken what is deepest and truest in the life of a people.

In recent centuries, millions of people came to this land to pursue their dream of building a future in freedom. We, the people of this continent, are not fearful of foreigners, because most of us were once foreigners. I say this to you as the son of immigrants, knowing that so many of you are also descended from immigrants. Tragically, the rights of those who were here long before us were not always respected. For those peoples and their nations, from the heart of American democracy, I wish to reaffirm my highest esteem and appreciation. Those first contacts were often turbulent and violent, but it is difficult to judge the past by the criteria of the present. Nonetheless, when the stranger in our midst appeals to us, we must not repeat the sins and the errors of the past. We must resolve now to live as nobly and as justly as possible, as we educate new generations not to turn their back on our "neighbors" and everything around us. Building a nation calls us to recognize that we must constantly relate to others, rejecting a mindset of hostility in order to adopt one of reciprocal subsidiarity, in a constant effort to do our best. I am confident that we can do this.

Our world is facing a refugee crisis of a magnitude not seen since the Second World War. This presents us with great challenges and many hard decisions. On this continent, too, thousands of persons are led to travel north in search of a better life for themselves and for their loved ones, in search of greater opportunities. Is this not what we want for our own children? We must not be taken aback by their numbers, but rather view them as persons, seeing their faces and listening to their stories, trying to respond as best we can to their situation. To respond in a way which is always humane, just and fraternal. We need to avoid a common temptation nowadays: to discard whatever proves troublesome. Let us remember the Golden Rule: "Do unto others as you would have them do unto you" (Mt 7:12).

This Rule points us in a clear direction. Let us treat others with the same passion and compassion with which we want to be treated. Let us seek for others the same possibilities which we seek for ourselves. Let us help others to grow, as we would like to be helped ourselves. In a word, if we want security, let us give security; if we want life, let us give life; if we want opportunities, let us provide opportunities. The yardstick we use for others will be the yardstick which time will use for us. The Golden Rule also reminds us of our responsibility to protect and defend human life at every stage of its development.

. . . How much progress has been made in this area in so many parts of the world! How much has been done in these first years of the third millennium to raise people out of extreme poverty! I know that you share my conviction that much more still needs to be done, and that in times of crisis and economic hardship a spirit of global solidarity must not be lost. At the same time I would encourage you to keep in mind all those people around us who are trapped in a cycle of poverty. They too need to be given hope. The fight against poverty and hunger must be fought constantly and, on many fronts, especially in its causes. I know that many Americans today, as in the past, are working to deal with this problem.

It goes without saying that part of this great effort is the creation and distribution of wealth. The right use of natural resources, the proper application of technology and the harnessing of the spirit of enterprise are essential elements of an economy which seeks to be modern, inclusive and sustainable. "Business is a noble vocation, directed to producing wealth and improving the world. It can be a fruitful source of prosperity for the area in which it operates, especially if it sees the creation of jobs as an essential part of its service to the common good" (*Laudato Si*, 129). This common good also includes the earth, a central theme of the encyclical which I recently wrote in order to "enter into dialogue with all people about our common home" (ibid., 3). "We need a conversation which includes everyone, since the environmental challenge we are undergoing, and its human roots, concern and affect us all" (ibid., 14).

In *Laudato Si*, I call for a courageous and responsible effort to "redirect our steps" (ibid., 61), and to avert the most serious effects of the environmental deterioration caused by human activity. I am convinced that we can make a difference and I have no doubt that the United States—and this Congress—have an important role to play. Now is the time for courageous actions and strategies, aimed at implementing a "culture of care" (ibid., 231) and "an integrated approach to combating poverty, restoring dignity to the excluded, and at the same time protecting nature" (ibid., 139). "We have the freedom needed to limit and direct technology" (ibid., 112); "to devise intelligent ways of . . . developing and limiting our power" (ibid., 78); and to put technology "at the service of another type of progress, one which is healthier, more human, more social, more integral" (ibid., 112). In this regard, I am confident that America's outstanding academic and research institutions can make a vital contribution in the years ahead.

. . . When countries which have been at odds resume the path of dialogue—a dialogue which may have been interrupted for the most legitimate of reasons—new opportunities open up for all. This has required, and requires, courage and daring, which is not the same as irresponsibility. A good political leader is one who, with the interests of all in mind, seizes the moment in a spirit of openness and pragmatism. A good political leader always opts to initiate processes rather than possessing spaces (cf. *Evangelii Gaudium*, 222–223).

Being at the service of dialogue and peace also means being truly determined to minimize and, in the long term, to end the many armed conflicts throughout our world. Here we have to ask ourselves: Why are deadly weapons being sold to those who plan to inflict untold suffering on individuals and society? Sadly, the answer, as we all know, is simply for money: money that is drenched in blood, often innocent blood. In the face of this shameful and culpable silence, it is our duty to confront the problem and to stop the arms trade.

Three sons and a daughter of this land, four individuals and four dreams: Lincoln, liberty; Martin Luther King, liberty in plurality and non-exclusion; Dorothy Day, social justice and the rights of persons; and Thomas Merton, the capacity for dialogue and openness to God.

Four representatives of the American people.

. . . A nation can be considered great when it defends liberty as Lincoln did, when it fosters a culture which enables people to "dream" of full rights for all their brothers and sisters, as Martin Luther King sought to do; when it strives for justice and the cause of the oppressed, as Dorothy Day did by her tireless work, the fruit of a faith which becomes dialogue and sows peace in the contemplative style of Thomas Merton.

In these remarks I have sought to present some of the richness of your cultural heritage, of the spirit of the American people. It is my desire that this spirit continue to develop and grow, so that as many young people as possible can inherit and dwell in a land which has inspired so many people to dream.[58]

How to Be a Buddhist in Today's World by the Dalai Lama

Once people adopt a religion, they should practice it sincerely. Truly believing in God, Buddha, Allah or Shiva should inspire one to be an honest human being. Some people claim to have faith in their religion but act counter to its ethical injunctions.

58. https://w2.vatican.va/content/francesco/en/speeches/2015/september/documents/papa-francesco_20150924_usa-us-congress.html.

They pray for the success of their dishonest and corrupt actions, asking God or Buddha for help in covering up their wrongdoings. There is no point in such people describing themselves as religious.

Today the world faces a crisis related to lack of respect for spiritual principles and ethical values. Such virtues cannot be forced on society by legislation or by science, nor can fear inspire ethical conduct. Rather, people must have conviction in the worth of ethical principles so that they want to live ethically.

The U.S. and India, for example, have solid governmental institutions, but many of the people involved lack ethical principles. Self-discipline and self-restraint of all citizens—from CEOs to lawmakers to teachers—are needed to create a good society. But these virtues cannot be imposed from the outside. They require inner cultivation. This is why spirituality and religion are relevant in the modern world.

India, where I now live, has been home to the ideas of secularism, inclusiveness and diversity for some 3,000 years. One philosophical tradition asserts that only what we know through our five senses exists. Other Indian philosophical schools criticize this nihilistic view but still regard the people who hold it as rishis, or sages. I promote this type of secularism: to be a kind person who does not harm others regardless of profound religious differences.

In previous centuries, Tibetans knew little about the rest of the world. We lived on a high and broad plateau surrounded by the world's tallest mountains. Almost everyone, except for a small community of Muslims, was Buddhist. Very few foreigners came to our land. Since we went into exile in 1959, Tibetans have been in contact with the rest of the world. We relate with religions, ethnic groups and cultures that hold a broad spectrum of views.

Further, Tibetan youth now receive a modern education in which they are exposed to opinions not traditionally found in their community. It is now imperative that Tibetan Buddhists be able to explain clearly their tenets and beliefs to others using reason. Simply quoting from Buddhist scriptures does not convince people who did not grow up as Buddhists of the validity of the Buddha's doctrine. If we try to prove points only by quoting scripture, these people may respond: "Everyone has a book to quote from!"

Religion faces three principal challenges today: communism, modern science and the combination of consumerism and materialism. Although the Cold War ended decades ago, communist beliefs and governments still strongly affect life in Buddhist countries. In Tibet, the communist government controls the ordination of monks and nuns while also regulating life in the monasteries and nunneries. It controls the education system, teaching children that Buddhism is old-fashioned.

Modern science, up until now, has confined itself to studying phenomena that are material in nature. Scientists largely examine only what can be measured with scientific instruments, limiting the scope of their investigations and their understanding of the universe. Phenomena such as rebirth and the existence of the mind as separate from the brain are beyond the scope of scientific investigation. Some scientists, although they have no proof that these phenomena do not exist, consider them unworthy of consideration. But there is reason for optimism. In recent years, I have met with many open-minded scientists, and we have had mutually beneficial discussions that have highlighted our common points as well as our diverging ideas—expanding the world views of scientists and Buddhists in the process.

Then there is materialism and consumerism. Religion values ethical conduct, which may involve delayed gratification, whereas consumerism directs us toward immediate happiness. Faith traditions stress inner satisfaction and a peaceful mind, while materialism says that happiness comes from external objects. Religious values such as kindness, generosity and honesty get lost in the rush to make more money and have more and "better" possessions. Many people's minds are confused about what happiness is and how to create its causes.

If you study the Buddha's teachings, you may find that some of them are in harmony with your views on societal values, science and consumerism—and some of them are not. That is fine. Continue to investigate and reflect on what you discover. In this way, whatever conclusion you reach will be based on reason, not simply on tradition, peer pressure or blind faith.[59]

Reflection questions: write a response to the following:

1. What are the main points in each of the articles?
2. How does Pope Francis' speech reflect Christian ethical teaching and perspectives? Give examples.
3. To what extent do the words of the Dalai Lama reflect Buddhist ethical teaching and perspectives? Give examples.

Alternative task:

You may select a different significant speech from another religious leader and discuss how it relates to ethics.

Student Activity—Moral dilemma

Create a table containing those from religious and nonreligious perspectives on ethics: Aristotle, Kant, the Dalai Lama, the Pope, Singer, and two others of your choice. How would they respond to the moral dilemmas below?

Moral dilemma number one:
You are a single parent with three children. The past month has been difficult because your hours at the grocery store have been unexpectedly reduced and, after paying the bills you owe, you will not have enough money to feed your kids and yourself. However, a co-worker tells you how to take food supplies from a delivery truck at work without getting caught.

Moral dilemma number two:
An executive at a nationwide bank decides to surreptitiously add small fees to common transactions, unbeknownst to the customers. These fees add

---

59. Gyatso, "Approaching the Buddhist Path." https://www.dalailama.com/messages/religious-harmony-1/how-to-be-a-buddhist-in-todays-world.

up, over time, to millions of dollars for the bank and a healthy bonus for the executive, all the while affecting each customer so slightly that no one complains.

Moral dilemma number three:
A corporation dumps waste in the water, thus contaminating ground water. This has a negative effect on the drinking water of people in town. Some people have reported some illnesses, which they have attributed to the water they are drinking. The action of dumping waste is not illegal.

How would those in your table respond to the above dilemmas? How would you answer? Why?

Comparing the three dilemmas, if the person in the first dilemma chooses to steal, is that person more justified than the banker? What about the corporation?

Are religious ethics about following a strict code of law?

Our discussion on religious ethics leads us to then ask if religious ethics ought to be followed to the letter of the law—sometimes referred to as a legalistic approach—or whether moral behavior should be better understood as emerging from a deep spiritual experience. Does religious ethics need its focus on the experience of love with the divine, rather than a strict code of law?
What do you think?

Some have argued that ethical guidelines, while they are useful and necessary, cannot be the focus of religious faith. Psychologist and priest Dr. Michael Whelan argues that moralism is not the focus of Christianity.[60] What he means is that a strict adherence to rules, regulations, and righteous judgements are not the essence of Christian faith. Whelan explains that this approach to faith only leads people to unhealthy psychological conflicts as they "strive with egos willfully to do good" rather than good acts emerging naturally from a positive experience with God.[61]

Christian monk and writer Thomas Merton (1915–1968) illustrated that Christian faith is essentially *more than an ethical system*—its central focus is on a deep religious and spiritual experience with God. Merton

60. Whelan, "Sexual Abuse."
61. Ibid., para. 19.

believed that living a spiritual life is able to *transform* the person. These changes result in a spiritual life that leads to inner joy and peace, which naturally leads a person to good actions. The focus of religious faith, he argued, was a love of God which was experienced at the deepest core of the person, rather than a strict adherence to ethical codes.

Thomas Merton

> By focusing on the human person primarily as moral agent rather than the recipient of God's love, Moralism makes of the Christian life an ego project; in this way it tends to promote the image of God as primarily judge, someone to be feared therefore. It places rules and regulations and laws at the center of the Christian life, usurping the primacy of Covenant and relationships and the freedom and dignity of the person as one made lovingly in the image of God. It tends to develop a radical conflict in the human psyche that prompts dysfunctional and even destructive behaviors. It is a travesty of the Good News. When we who claim to be Christian are dominated by Moralism, we in fact cease to be Christian. "Christianity is more than an ethical system . . . Jesus not only teaches us the Christian life, He creates it in our souls by the action of the Spirit."[62]

Lawrence Kohlberg—Moral Development

In attempting to shed some light on the challenging questions posed at the start of this section, the work of American psychologist Lawrence Kohlberg (1927–1987) might be useful. Kohlberg does not address religious faith or ethics directly, but does suggest that moral development does not occur instantly, but rather in *stages*.[63] A person develops their sense of what is right and wrong over time and there are stages in acquiring certain ways of thinking about morals. Kohlberg proposes that there are three stages, what he termed as: preconventional, conventional, and postconventional.[64] The first stage is linked to obedience and authority; here moral behavior is

---

62. Merton, *The New Man*, 116.
63. Porter, "Kohlberg and Moral Development," 123–28.
64. Ibid., 123–28.

motivated by self-interest and avoiding punishment. The conventional phase is characterized by adherence and observances to social norms, customs, and laws. The importance of relationships and approval from social classes is the focus. In the postconventional stage, the person is able to move beyond social norms, customs, and laws to understand abstract and universal principles which govern morality. If we accept Kohlberg's theory and apply it to religious ethics, adherence to rules and a strict code of laws may be required in at least some stages of religious faith development.

Can you think of examples for each of these three stages?

Do women and men think the same way about morals and ethics?

Søren Kierkegaard

> Let us now compare an ethical and an esthetic individual. The primary difference, the crux of the matter, is that the ethical individual is transparent to himself and does not live *ins Blaue hinein* [in the wild blue yonder], as does the esthetic individual. This difference encompasses everything. The person who lives ethically has seen himself, knows himself, penetrates his whole concretion with his consciousness, does not allow vague thoughts to rustle around inside him or let tempting possibilities distract him with their juggling; he is not like a "magic" picture that shifts from one thing to another, all depending on how one shifts and turns it. He knows himself. The phrase [know yourself] is a stock phrase, and in it has been perceived the goal of all a person's striving. And this is entirely proper, but yet it is just as certain that it cannot be the goal if it is not also the beginning. The ethical individual knows himself, but this knowing is not simply contemplation, for then the individual comes to be defined according to his necessity. It is a collecting of oneself, which itself is an action, and this is why I have with aforethought used the expression "to choose oneself " instead of "to know oneself."[65]

What do you think the above quote means?

Christian existentialist philosopher Søren Kierkegaard (1813–1855) observed that the individual experience of religious faith occurs in stages. He describes these stages as the *aesthetic, ethical,* and *religious.* The aesthetic

---

65. Kierkegaard et al., *Essential Kierkegaard*, 81.

stage is the initial stage. Here the focus of life is organized around pleasure and hedonistic endeavors. We might see a person organize activities solely around the purpose of pleasure.[66] Kierkegaard describes this stage as ultimately leading a person to despair and loss of oneself. The ethical stage is an awareness of a hierarchy in the moral life. The person here becomes aware of the importance of choosing and living a moral life. The person becomes increasingly aware of their moral duties, choices, and responsibilities which they attempt to fulfill.[67] However, Kierkegaard argues that many in this stage come to realize their inability to fully live up to their moral responsibilities alone, which leads to a sense of despair. The last stage, as Kierkegaard shows in his famous work *Fear and Trembling*, is the religious phase. Here the individual is aware of the human limitation to live up to their moral responsibilities on their own, and thus becomes aware of the human need for God.

The introspective journey toward God which Kierkegaard describes is directed by a strong invitation of divine love. The individual is always free to resist and reject this or submit to the process which, in the end, Kierkegaard states is an act of pure faith.

What do you think of Kierkegaard's three stages of religious faith?

Discussion Questions

1. Can religion maintain the tension between adherence to its laws and divine love? Can a religion exist without at least some guidelines, laws, or codes? Discuss.
2. What is your understanding of moralism?
3. How useful are the ideas of Whelan, Merton, Kierkegaard, and Kohlberg in understanding religious faith and/or moral behavior?
4. How would you explain the immoral actions of some religious people?

---

66. Ibid., 38–63.
67. Ibid., 66–83.

STUDENT ACTIVITY 1—ESSAY

Write an appraisal of Kohlberg on the stages of moral development, or Kierkegaard on the stages of religious experience and faith.
The following resources may be useful:

Encyclopedia Britannica: Lawrence Kohlberg's Stages of Moral Development[68]
Schoolwork Helper: Kierkegaard and Johannes de Silentio's Religious Stages[69]

STUDENT ACTIVITY—ESSAY

To what extent can we apply any of the theories discussed above to our understanding of religious ethical beliefs? Write a response or discuss in class.

STUDENT REFLECTIONS

WHAT ARE YOU NOW WONDERING ABOUT?

- What ideas or questions are you wondering about as a result of these lessons?
- Have these lessons made you think differently? Explain.
- What have you found challenging, provocative, or intriguing?

ETHICS OF WAR

STUDENT ACTIVITY: VIDEO

Watch the film trailer for *Eye in the Sky*, "Eye in the Sky Official North

---

68. https://www.britannica.com/topic/Lawrence-Kohlbergs-stages-of-moral-development
69. https://schoolworkhelper.net/kierkegaard-and-johannes-de-silentios-religious-stages/

American Trailer (2015)—Aaron Paul, Helen Mirren HD,"[70] and answer the following questions:

Should the allied forces attack? What about the civilian child? What ethical theories are relevant here?

Perhaps the most vexing ethical dilemma humans face is the pervasive and ongoing spectre of warfare. Mass conflict within and between nations, cultures, ethnicities, and religions brings forth staggering atrocities, yet remains a fixture in our world. There have been solutions to specific wars which is why the wars have ended, but what has not been found is an alternative to warfare as a way of resolving civil and international conflict or disagreement.

Are, therefore, wars necessary in some instances? Do they serve a function in some very complex way? While every war can be questioned, some conflicts have persuasive elements of the lesser of two evils, the other option being inaction leading to atrocity. The Allied Forces of WWII discovered the appalling policy of genocide methodically implemented by Nazi Germany against Jews—as well as Gypsies, homosexuals, and others deemed inferior—that killed millions. The American Civil War was ultimately caused by the institution of slavery, a system now almost universally declared unacceptable. A lesser-known invasion of Cambodia by Vietnam in the 1970s was in response to the cruel dictator, Pol Pot, who was engaging in mass extermination of his own Cambodian population. Extreme situations such as these require extreme solutions, according to some, and war is viewed as the necessary last resort.

Student Activity—Research

Investigate a war that occurred within the last 200 years and address the following questions. Write your response and present the findings to the class:

1. What was the nature of the conflict and what were the reasons for the war?
2. From the information gathered, what appear to be the political and ideological reasons for engaging in the war?
3. Was there an attempt for peaceful resolution prior to the conflict? What were the roadblocks?
4. Did the war result in displacing people from the war zone? What happened to these people? Who looked after them?

70. https://www.youtube.com/watch?v=hOqeoj669xg.

5. In your opinion, whose interests did the war serve?
6. Could the war have been prevented? Explain.
7. Some historians have stated that war is often written by the winners. In your example, did the accounts of the war reveal a bias? Would the historical accounts look different if they were written by the defeated group or by women? Explain.
8. What have been the lessons of Ghandi (India), Mandela (South Africa), and Martin Luther King (America) in dealing with conflict? To what extent did their approach work in providing a resolution?

Just War Theory

Do you think it is ever justified to go to war? Explain.

Thoughts on war and its moral and pragmatic value have existed for thousands of years, going back to the ancient Greeks.[71] These concepts are currently written and applied via the Hague and Geneva Conventions, which govern the rules of war, including use of warfare and the humane treatment of combatants and noncombatants. These international legal frameworks currently govern all wars, although unfortunately not all parties to a conflict adhere to them.

The Just War Theory, as it is known today, was first developed by St. Thomas Aquinas. He developed two main concepts: first, the right conditions in which war is permissible, stipulating that under some circumstances war can be justified; and second, how to conduct a war in an ethical manner once it has commenced.[72] In this section, we will only focus on the first component, the justification of engaging in war, known as *jus ad bellum* in the Latin, or "right to war."

Jus ad bellum requires six elements:

1. having a just cause

---

71. Moseley, "Just War Theory."
72. Ibid.

2. war as a last resort
3. the war declared by a proper authority
4. a justified intention
5. having a reasonable chance of success
6. the end result in proportion to the means

Not only is there debate about this list being complete, but each one of these elements is rife with complexities in itself.

1. *Just cause*—A nation must have a justifiable reason, or just cause, to enter into war. The most understandable reason to engage in conflict is self-defence. If a nation is being attacked by another, most agree there is necessity to retaliate for protection or self-preservation. But what is an attack by another nation? Throughout history there have been constant struggles in which two nations repeatedly attack one another, blurring the definition of who attacked and who responded in defence. If a nation was attacked five years ago and lost a portion of its land to its adversary, can the nation defend itself and get its land back through war? What about ten years ago? One hundred years ago?

    Sometimes nations claim that preemption, or a first attack prior to an inevitable invasion, is just cause. Terrible occurrences taking place in another nation have also been used as just cause to invade and stop the abuse. Nearly every conflict in history has claims of just cause and those who disagree.

2. *War as a last resort*—A nation must exhaust every other option first before declaring war. Negotiations, treaties, and economic sanctions are all devices used to change a problematic situation between nations and can often negate the need for extreme destruction and suffering through war. However, they often don't work. So, when does a nation know there are no other options? This question usually is the contentious issue with last-resort policies.

3. *War declared by a proper authority*—What if part of a country declares it no longer belongs to that country? Can it defend itself through war if it is "invaded" to bring it back to its former homeland? Such confusing situations happen when nations split apart or collapse entirely. A group may claim it is its own nation, but *jus ad bellum* requires an actual, recognized nation to declare war, not simply a group in dispute with its own government.

4. *A justified intention*—This requirement seems very similar to the first requirement, and it is. However, intention rests in the reasons why the nation itself believes it is going to war, regardless of whether a just cause exists. For example, if a nation declares war on a neighbour who is regularly abusing its own citizens, other nations may view this as just cause for starting a war. However, if evidence is discovered proving that, for example, the invasion is solely to take valuable natural resources, then there would not be a justified intention.

5. *A reasonable chance of success*—This requirement is straightforward and pragmatic; a war is not worth the extreme cost if it will accomplish very little, regardless of justification. However, can this ever be calculated accurately? The United States has examples of both extremes: it's War of Independence was won by a small group of colonists who persisted and eventually defeated the mighty world power of Great Britain. At the outset, a reasonable analysis would determine the rebelling colonists had little chance of success. Conversely, America in the twentieth century, a world power with elite weapons and finances which required military service of its enormous population, lost a long, hard-fought war to the small, undeveloped nation of Vietnam.

6. *The end result in proportion to the means*—This requirement is one of degree. The war effort must reasonably match the result to be achieved. If a nation at war meets all of the other five criteria, but the results are an extremely high casualty rate to liberate just a few oppressed people, then this criterion has not been met.

STUDENT ACTIVITY—REFLECTION QUESTION:

Give examples of war and conflicts relating to the *jus ad bellum* for the six elements described above.

Pacifism

Not all agree with the Just War theory. Pacifists, for example, argue that it is never justified to engage in war under *any* circumstances. Pacifism is defined as "The belief that war and violence are unjustifiable and that all disputes should be settled by peaceful means."[73] There are religious and nonreligious pacifists. Can you think of some well-known pacifists?

Student activity—Research

Investigate the topic of pacifism:

a. Summarise the main ideas of pacifism.

b. What are some distinctions made between different types of pacifists?

c. Select one pacifist and summarise his/her life. What were the main arguments in their stance on war and conflict.

For further research on this issue, the following link may be a useful—BBC Ethics Guide: War.[74]

Student Activity: Extension—*Jus ad bello*, right conduct of war

Dr. Jeff McMahan is an American moral philosopher who claims that the Just War Theory advocated by earlier thinkers such as Aquinas is manipulated in contemporary times to suit political pragmatic purposes. He argues this trend has negative moral implications. McMahan suggests a need for transparency and in-depth discussion on the morality and conduct in war as opposed to following current conventions. He makes a distinction between the law and morality, arguing that many of the recent wars are actually immoral and unjustified.

---

73. *Oxford Dictionaries*, s.v. "Pacifism." http://www.oxforddictionaries.com/definition/pacificism.

74. http://www.bbc.co.uk/ethics/war/.

STUDENT ACTIVITY

Listen to the following podcast with Dr. Mchahan and answer the following questions: "Philosophy Bites: Jeff McMahan on Killing in War."[75]

1. According to McMahan, how has the current Just War Theory changed from its original notion proposed by Aquinas? How is this theory misused for pragmatic purposes? What could this mean?
2. What is the difference between morality and convention?
3. What is the distinction McMahan makes between the law and morality of war?
4. Do you agree with McMahan that open discussions and a sound ethical framework need to guide the actions related to war? Explain.
5. Should morality or politics guide the decision to engage in war? Discuss.

For further research the following resources could be useful:

Video: Michael Walzer, "Just and Unjust Wars, Updated."[76]
Video: Noam Chomsky, "The Limitation and Problems With 'Just War' Theory."[77]
Documentary: John Pilger, *War on Democracy*.[78]
Book: Sun Tzu, *The Art of War*.[79]

EXTENSION STUDENT ACTIVITY

Research the works of Noam Chomsky and Michael Walzer and summarise or have a conversation between the two people concerning Just War Theory. Include the following:

1. What do Chomsky and Walzer state are the advantages and disadvantages of the Just War Theory?
2. How are they similar to and different from the claims made by McMahan?

---

75. http://philosophybites.com/2009/11/jeff-mcmahan-on-killing-in-war.html.
76. https://www.youtube.com/watch?v=Xqmnx5hESrM.
77. https://www.youtube.com/watch?v=e1pNz8A5vMAandt=328s.
78. Pilger, *The War on Democracy*.
79. Tzu, *The Art of War*.

Draw a table and include the advantages and disadvantages of each of the points raised.

Characteristics of war

Often, the call to war brings strong emotions of patriotism. In his recent work, *War: An Inquiry,* English philosopher Anthony Grayling describes some common characteristics of war:

    a. Often romanticised and viewed as heroic, which gives misleading notions of the reality and horrors of war

    b. Institutionalised within our society and heavily resourced

    c. Planned and/organised with increased sophisticated technology

    d. The enemy is often dehumanized (perceived as *not human*)

    e. In the nuclear age, it can potentially destroy us[80]

Do you agree/disagree with the claims made? Can you give examples for these claims?

Are there some exceptions? For example, do these characteristics include cyberwarfare? Cold warfare? Drone warfare? Discuss.

STUDENT ACTIVITY: EXPECT

Read the following stimulus and answer the questions below:

EMOTIONS AND WAR

> "When" and "how" are not the only morally important questions to ask about waging war. Just war theory also raises challenging questions about the emotions and their place in ethics. One of these regards what, if anything, we ought to feel about doing the right thing in different circumstances. Most of us think that you usually ought to feel good about doing the right thing. You ought to feel *proud*, not ashamed, about donating to charity; you ought to take *pleasure* in the fact that you returned a lost wallet; and so on. But this is not the case when it comes to warfare. Pride and other sorts of "positive"

80. Grayling, *War*, 122–23, 160–84.

emotions seem to be unfitting or inappropriate in the face of unimaginable suffering and destruction, even if the war in question was waged rightly. How are we to explain this discrepancy? How do we know whether to feel good or bad about doing the right thing?

One way to begin solving this puzzle is to distinguish between a *right* action and an unqualifiedly *good* action. A right action, of course, is what you ought to do in the circumstances, but an unqualifiedly good action is one that is not bad in *any way*. The two come apart when we notice that circumstances themselves bear upon our evaluations of actions. Consider what philosophers have called *tragic lemmas*. A tragic lemma is a scenario where an agent is forced to choose one course of action from a set of two or more, but all of the choices available are in some way evil or tainted. Suppose you are forced to decide whether or not to tell your friend a hurtful but important truth. Both of your options are "stained" in some way. Either you tell the truth and hurt your friend's feelings, or you withhold something that they ought to know. Even if you know that one course of action or the other is morally *right*, this does not mean that it was unqualifiedly *good*, because something other than your action was amiss—your lemma was a tragic one.

Most of us will agree that there is something similar going on in the case of just wars. In order to wage war justly, you must have a good reason for that decision (a humanitarian crisis, an imminent threat, etc). But there will always be countervailing reasons not to go to war—reasons, that is, to say that waging war was not unequivocally good. The fact that one has a good reason to wage war has not somehow erased or negated the displacement, the suffering, the massive death tolls, and whatever other evils the war will bring about. Just wars, according to the just war theorist, are always going to take place in the context of a tragic lemma, and the act of waging a just war will always be marred by the circumstances that action takes place in.

This makes space for the thought that an action can be *right* yet still in some way evil or wrong, but a question remains: why should this make us feel bad? Here is one possible answer. Philosophers of emotion have sometimes argued that emotions track or detect *value* and *disvalue*. Suppose you discover that a close friend has divulged a secret of yours to someone else. Most of us, of course, will feel angry or upset about this, and importantly, most of think that this is how you *ought* to feel. If a close friend betrays you and you are apathetic about this, something has gone wrong. Some philosophers of emotion will explain this by claiming that you ought to be angry and upset because there is *disvalue* in betraying a close friend. There is something valuable or important about being able to trust your friends with your secrets, and your emotions are a response to the loss of this. Your anger, in this way, is like a kind of perception, in the same way that your eyes perceive colour. The reason your anger/upset is *justified* or *fitting*, then, is that you are perceiving or have perceived *genuine* disvalue. Something bad has *actually* happened. Compare this with a case where your partner becomes mad at you for something you did in his or her dream. There is no *actual* disvalue here, because dreams are not real. So your partner's emotions are *unjustified* because they have responded to disvalue that isn't actually there. Thus, we might say that a particular emotion is fitting when it constitutes an appropriate or proportionate response to a perception of true value or disvalue in the world.

If we accept this picture of emotion, then we can make sense of the idea that you should abhor war, regardless of whether it was the right thing to do. War, to the just war theorist, is always going to be the outcome of a tragic lemma. But by admitting that the lemma is tragic, the just war theorist has built disvalue into the concept of a just war. Every option in a tragic lemma is in some way evil, and this is just to say that there is disvalue in every option. So, the argument will conclude, you should always feel some type of negative emotion—regret or guilt, most likely—in response to war because that is the only fitting emotional response to such extreme disvalue.[81]

---

81. Steyl, "Emotion and Peacebuilding," 1–3 (emphasis in original).

Discussion Questions

1. Can consequentialism and deontology make sense of emotions?
2. Are regret and guilt practical in any way?
3. Are emotions always value-trackers? Can you think of any examples where an emotion doesn't track or respond to value or disvalue?

Casualties of War

There are many causalities in war. Those on the battlefield, if not killed, will suffer trauma from the war for the rest of their lives. There are many war veterans all over the world who testify to the post-traumatic experience of war. Not only are these people psychologically affected by the war for the rest of their lives, but their families are as well.

Another casualty of war is asylum seekers and refugees. The United Nations High Commissioner for Refugees (UNHCR) claims we are now witnessing the highest rate of displacement on record with 65 million people forced from their homes.[82] Amongst these, 22.5 million are under 18.[83] According to the terms of the UN convention, countries outside the conflict are expected to protect war civilians and people escaping from political persecution—these people are known as asylum seek-

---

82. UNHCR, "Figures at a Glance," paras. 1–3.
83. Ibid.

ers. The reality, however, is that many end up living under extremely harsh conditions until governments or other organizations arrange more permanent settlements, some for many years. UNHCR statistics reveal that approximately 10 million displaced people are denied access to basic services such as adequate health care, education, or freedoms, with some countries such as Australia imposing long mandatory detentions. The engagement of war has catastrophic effects on human lives beyond immediate casualties, and affects many for years after the conflict has ended.

Student activity—Group work:

- Research a past or present conflict.
- In groups, work on presenting this conflict to the class.
- Each member represents one of the following people below.
- Group members have about five to eight minutes to present their findings to the class.
- Once the group is finished, the class asks questions.

Each person is to research the conflict through the lens of one of the following people:

1. an academic specializing in international affairs or warfare. You may study Anthony Grayling, Noam Chomsky, Michael Walzer, or Jeff McMahan.
2. an aid worker.
3. a journalist working on international affairs.
4. a representative of an international organization.
5. an NGO that provides assistance to war-affected communities.
6. a religious leader.
7. a politician involved in international affairs.

How have your findings added to or changed your perceptions on war?

Extension student Activity—Research

Study Machiavelli's *The Prince* or Thucydides' *History of the Peloponnesian War*.

HOW DO WE ACT?: AN INQUIRY OF ETHICS

Outline their perspectives on the ethics of war.

Write up your findings present these to your class.

Student activity—Watch a film or documentary

View a story on the human impact of war for asylum seekers and refugees. Record the experiences of people who have had to flee as a result of war and conflict. Present your findings to the class.
The following resources maybe useful:

UNHCR—"Figures at a Glance."[84]
New York Times—"Australia's Refugee Policy of Cruelty."[85]
Films on war: *Waltz with Bashir, My Lia, Guantanamo, Causalities of War.*
Strengthing Asylum—"Future Worlds Center: 13 Powerful Films about Refugees You Need to See."[86]

---

84. UNHCR "Figures at a Glance."

85. https://www.nytimes.com/2017/11/16/opinion/australia-refugees-manus-island.html

86. https://strengtheningasylum.wordpress.com/2015/10/21/13-powerful-films-about-refugees-you-need-to-see/

SCAPEGOATING AND BULLYING

When examining issues of how we ought to act, we cannot ignore scapegoating and bullying. Blaming others for our own problems and mistakes is a common ploy known as scapegoating. A scapegoat can be defined as "A person who is blamed for the wrongdoings, mistakes, or faults of others, especially for reasons of expediency."[87] The unusual word goes back to a ritual of symbolically placing sins of a society onto a goat and sending the goat away into the desert, a practice even mentioned in the Hebrew Scriptures. The strategy eases guilt by falsely shifting responsibility to another person, group, or even concept, and is a problem in society worth identifying. Psychiatrist Dr. Neel Burton describes the process in the following ways:

> The scapegoated target is then persecuted, providing the person doing the scapegoating not only with a conduit for his uncomfortable feelings, but also with pleasurable feelings of piety and self-righteous indignation. The creation of a villain necessarily implies that of a hero, even if both are purely fictional.[88]

Student activity

Discuss the process of scapegoating and bullying described in both *The Hunger Games* and *The Lord of the Flies*, or even another account. Write down names of films, books, television shows, or other stories which demonstrate scapegoating.

Discussion questions

1. What do you think of Burton's definition of scapegoating?
2. Can you give examples, in history or today, of groups or individuals who have been scapegoated?

---

87. *Oxford Dictionaries, s.v.* "Scapegoat." http://www.oxforddictionaries.com/definition/scapegoat.

88. Burton, "Psychology of Scapegoating," para. 1.

3. Have you experienced scapegoating or bullying, or do you know anyone who has? What impact did this have emotionally and psychologically?

What Is Scapegoating? By Dr. Arthur D. Colman

Understanding why scapegoating exists in group life is an important step in aiding both the victim and perpetrator. Scapegoating is above all a group process. Anthropologists tell us that scapegoating is one of humanity's most ancient rituals. Its origins are in child and animal sacrifice; it is manifested through genocide and mass slaughters, such as the Holocaust, but also through traumatic abuse within distressed families, in schoolyards and work settings.

We commonly experience scapegoating as bullying, hazing, sexism, racism, and ageism. Scapegoating is as old as humankind, and it can be at the root of great social evils, but it also has the potential for helping individuals and groups transform in new and creative ways. Many of our most renowned prophets and leaders are the product of extreme scapegoating—Nelson Mandela, for example—just as subgroups who are victimized may become the source of great creativity and inspiration, such as America's native population. By definition, the scapegoat is a person or people "made to bear the anxious blame for others." The scapegoated individual or subgroup is seen as a threat to the comfort and the successful functioning of the group as a whole and therefore must be eliminated. Whether the perceived threat is true or not is incidental: scapegoating is more about feelings than truth. As far as the group is concerned, the scapegoat is the sacrifice needed to ensure survival.

Group Survival
Scapegoating relies on the natural insecurities of both the group and its individual members, but it is not intrinsically negative. All groups, all people want to survive and thrive. Scapegoating is about the grouping of like-minded people

guarding against what they believe is the intrusion of rogue elements that will be a detriment, not a contribution. Simply put, what they can't accept, they scapegoat

"The search for a scapegoat is the easiest of all hunting expeditions."
—Dwight D. Eisenhower

Bullying, hazing, sexism, racism, and ageism are classic examples of scapegoating gone awry. Wars are fought and won and ideologies cemented by the creation of stereotypical scapegoats.
—Dr. Arthur D. Colman[89]

Discussion questions

After reading the above article and watching the video, "Beyond Scapegoating: Arthur Colman at TEDxPrinceAlbert,"[90] answer the following questions:

1. What are the examples of scapegoating mentioned?
2. What do you think Coleman means by the following, "Whether the perceived threat is true or not is incidental: scapegoating is more about feelings than truth. As far as the group is concerned, the scapegoat is the sacrifice needed to ensure survival?"
3. How do scapegoats generally deal with their experiences and work through them?
4. What does Colman propose is the role of the artist, and why is it important?
5. Do you agree or disagree with Dr. Colman's descriptions about scapegoating? Explain.
6. What wider social and moral implications does scapegoating pose?
7. How can individuals and the community address scapegoating?

---

89. Colman, "What Is Scapegoating?," paras. 1–6, 17–18.
90. https://www.youtube.com/watch?v=cjBBhYCpLko.

STUDENT ACTIVITY—EXPERT

Read the following extract on racism and answer the questions below:

Thinking About Racism by Dr. Christopher Chaves

> Racism can be defined as "prejudice, discrimination, or antagonism directed against someone of a different race based on the belief that one's own race is superior" (Google, 2017). Racism is rearing its ugly head again in many parts of the world. Much of racism in the history of human civilizations has been based on skin colour, cranial head shape, cultural background, civilizational level, technological progress, perceived superior intellectual endowment, religious affiliation, and for other unfounded reasons. While racism has existed since the dawn of mankind, a brief exploration of its manifestations during recent centuries is instructive.
>
> During the 19th and 20th centuries, racial and ethnic groups from mainly western and northern Europe, whose civilizations no longer existed mainly on hunter-gatherer and agricultural subsistence, began to advance in many ways using knowledge and technology developed within their own societies; but, also from those that had earlier been developed within Chinese, Arabic, Indian, Hebrew, and Slavic civilizations. However, it became increasingly evident that western European civilization failed, or refused, to credit non-white civilizations for knowledge and technologies they now benefitted from. Moreover, European ethnic mythologies—that roaming Aryan groups were responsible for developing high culture and civilization in many parts of the eastern and western worlds—also went unquestioned and eventually contributed to the creation of the ideology of white supremacy. Majority groups in current day India, South Korea, Japan, Mexico, sub-saharan Africa, or Iran still justify their discrimination toward minority groups based different skin color, shape of eyes, or perceived race. Unfortunately, unfounded or biased racist ideas often lead to what is called scapegoating.

"Scapegoating is a psychological and social process in which the mechanisms of projection or displacement are utilized in focusing feelings of aggression, hostility, and frustration upon another individual or group; the amount of blame being unwarranted" (Mondofacto, 2018); for instance, when a majority group member loses his job, he will then decide to blame the new immigrants in the country for taking his job without providing the evidence for his claim. According to the Dictionary of Psychology (2019) scapegoating is also defined as the "Practice wherein an undeserving party is singled out for unmerited negative treatment, generally by someone or something more powerful than themselves." Scapegoating can be employed against both minority and majority groups; for example, the larger population of German Gentiles against the small population of Semitic Jews in Germany or the Dutch Afrikaners against the larger Black groups in South Africa; the Jews were blamed for social and economic ills and black South Africans were blamed for high crime rates. How is scapegoating usually justified against others?

This kind of eugenic junk science would be exported from the United States to Germany during the early 20th century, where eventually the Nazi party would use junk sciences to extend unfounded tenets of white Aryan supremacy to unreasonable and criminal conclusions; that is, exterminating those they considered to be of lesser racial stock. Nazi German thinking concluded that those of non-Germanic stock were to be viewed as the "other" and as threats to the survival of the German civilization. Thus, scapegoating many groups in German society became a part of social, economic, and political policy during 1930s and 1940s Germany. Germany would be militarily defeated during World War Two along with their ideas of racial supremacy; ultimately, German territory would be parcelled by the Allies into many pieces to be managed by other nation-states, as the former could not be trusted to conduct itself as a civilized democratic society.

The phenomena of racism is vast and complicated; it represents fear of others, a lack of knowledge about those who are different, the ability to act with evil intentions, and important human lessons. Used appropriately, knowledge about racism can inform and improve the racial experiences of increasingly pluralistic societies around the globe. Racism can be reduced by enabling young people, as well as older, to engage in cross-cultural experiences and open dialogues about what they do not know of each other. Moreover, enabling diverse individuals to work on common human challenges around the world can produce closer relationships between different cultures and religions. Today we have a similar opportunity to engage the human challenge of racism with more light than heat. But we need more than simply reminding the world about the evils of the past; we also need laws and societal cultures which enforce the rule of law that prevents most of those evils of racism.[91]

REFLECTION QUESTIONS

1. How is racism defined in the article?
2. List the examples of racism mentioned. What are the reasons for racism?
3. What solutions are proposed in addressing racism?
4. What do you think of the claims made? Do you agree? Discuss.
5. To what extent is it justifiable to adopt racist attitudes and actions and still be religious?
6. How are scapegoating and racism related?

---

91. Chaves, "Thinking about Racism," 1–3.

It doesn't seem rational to be racist, so why do we do it?

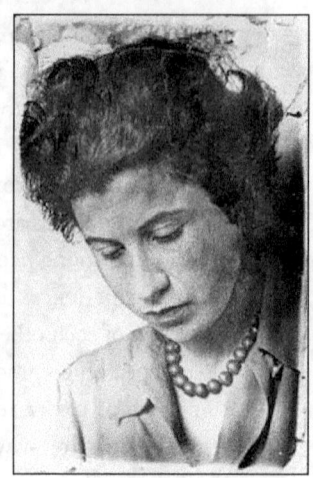

Etty Hilesum

> It is the only thing we can do... Each of us must turn inward and destroy in himself all that he thinks he ought to destroy in others. And remember that every atom of hate we add to this world makes it still more inhospitable. I no longer believe that we can change anything in the world until we have first changed ourselves. And that seems to me the only lesson to be learned from this war.[92]

> For [Hannah] Arendt the Nazi regime... created a terror... of being superfluous and provided a people—Jews, Gypsies, Homosexuals, etc.—who came to embody that superfluousness. "It is them who are superfluous—not me." The discourse on immigrants and asylum seekers follows a similar logic. We are all anxious about our place in the world, increasingly fear being surplus to requirements, an unhappy state of affairs. Asylum seekers serve as a perfect projective object and through them we can dispose of this unhappy insight.[93]

What do the extracts from Hilesum and Morgan say are the causes of racism?

The resistance to people who we find different from us often tells us more about ourselves than them. Since the influences of Sigmund Freud's work that explored the notion of unconscious emotions, we are able to better understand the process of scapegoating and racism as related to internal conflicts. Similar to the ideas of Dr. Colman mentioned earlier, psychoanalyst and writer M. Fakhry Davids states that people who seem very different from us can cause personal and group anxiety. Some find it difficult to resolve within themselves the differences other people present and they then project these unresolved feelings toward the outside group.[94] According to this theory, when strong negative emotions are directed at minorities

---

92. Hilesum, *Interrupted Life*, 40–41.
93. Morgan, "Psychoanalysis and Perversion," 4.
94. Davids, *Internal Racism*.

or vulnerable groups, it usually indicates a person's inability to *process their own inner vulnerabilities and fears,* so they project this onto a group or individual who are perceived a threat—often resulting in hatred and violence. We see this process play out in the elimination of the Jews in WWII and the Tutsi referred to as cockroaches by the opposing Hutu people during the Rwandan genocide in the 1990s, along with virtually every other historical instance of racial and ethnic hatred.

American psychologist Abraham Maslow (1908–1970) describes below Freud's understanding of unconscious fears, which Freud argues humans often fail to face and therefore project them onto the outside world. In other words, our greatest fear is the unknown parts within ourselves.

> Freud's great discovery, the one which lies at the root of psychodynamics, is that the great cause of much psychological illness is the fear of knowledge of oneself—of one's emotions, impulses, memories, capacities, potentialities, of one's destiny. We have discovered that fear of knowledge of oneself is very often isomorphic with, and parallel with, fear of the outside world.[95]

Discussion questions

1. In the context discussed above, what does the word "project" mean?
2. Do you agree/disagree that racism is due to a projection of unconscious emotional conflicts?
3. What do you think the following phrase means: "We have discovered that fear of knowledge of oneself is very often isomorphic with, and parallel with, fear of the outside world"?
4. To what extent are the ideas above able to explain racism adequately?

Student activity – Research

Rene Girard—Religion and violence

95. Maslow, "The Need to Know," 119.

Investigate the work of Rene Girard's mimetic theory and answer the following questions:

1. What are the main ideas in Girard's theory?
2. How does he explore the notion of mimesis?
3. Explain how mimetic desires lead to violence and scapegoating.
4. Can you think of events, past or current, where this theory is relevant or applicable?
5. According to Girard, how does Christian belief (although not always in practice) offer a positive contribution to the process of scapegoating? This is discussed (in the video below) by Bishop Barron.

Some useful links include:

- Internet Encyclopedia of Philosophy: René Girard (1923—2015)[96]
- The philosopher's Zone: Scapegoats and sacrifices—Rene Girard[97]
- Bishop Barron On Rene Girard.[98]

STUDENT REFLECTIONS

WHAT ARE YOU NOW WONDERING ABOUT?

- What ideas, issues, and questions are you wondering about as a result of these lessons?
- Have these lessons made you think differently about certain ideas, issues, or questions? Why?
- What questions or ideas did you find interesting, challenging, or intriguing? Explain.

---

96. http://www.iep.utm.edu/girard/.
97. http://www.abc.net.au/radionational/programs/philosopherszone/scapegoats-and-sacrifices—rene-girard/3167092.
98. https://www.youtube.com/watch?v=LSzF2OG2ejI.

THE EFFECTS OF ECONOMIC THINKING ON THE ETHICAL AND MORAL LIFE

> [W]hile making use of [material possessions], man has to be careful to protect himself from [their] tyranny. If he is weak enough to grow smaller to fit himself to his covering, then it becomes a process of gradual suicide by shrinkage of the soul.[99]

What does Rabindranath Tagore (1861–1941) mean by the tyranny of material possessions? To what extent can this tyranny affect our souls?

Is the focus on money eroding the good life?

Harvard University philosophy professor Dr. Michael Sandel is a critic of the focus on money and economics in governing society. He argues that the emphasis on money and economic thinking in *all areas* of society are eroding civil liberties and "the good life."[100] Sandel's notion of the good life is closely linked to the ancient Greek philosophers' concept mentioned earlier, understood as one that leads a person to *flourish* and live according to their potential. Sandel argues it is imperative that good quality health care, education, and the civil and political life be accessible to all members of a society in order to allow citizens to flourish and experience the good life.

Dr Michael Sandel

Sandel identifies what he views as an increasing trend within Western countries to measure *all* facets of society in purely *economic* terms (known as neoliberalism, or a policy of allowing free markets to generally determine most systems in a society). Sandel argues that this dominant economic paradigm used in accessing the nature of services in education, health, justice, politics, and national security, for example, has enormous moral implications to individuals and societies at large, and is often ignored in contemporary political debate. In his recent book, *What Money Can't Buy*, Sandel writes:

99. Tagore, in Nussbaum, *Not for Profit*, 1.
100. Sandel, *What Money Can't Buy*.

If the only advantage to affluence were the ability to buy yachts... inequalities of income and wealth would not matter very much. But as money comes to buy more and more—political influence, good medical care... elite schools... the distribution of income and wealth looms larger and larger. Where all good things are bought and sold, having money makes all the difference in the world... So to decide where the market belongs, and where it should be kept at a distance, we have to decide how to value the goods in question–health, education, family life, nature, art, civic duties and so on. These are moral and political questions, not merely economic ones. To resolve them, we have to debate, case by case, the moral meaning of these goods and the proper way of valuing them.

This debate we didn't have during the era of market triumphalism. As a result, without quite realizing it, without ever deciding to do so, we drifted from *having* a market economy to *being* a market society.

The difference is this: A market economy is a tool—a valuable and effective tool—for organising productive activity. A market society is a way of life in which market values seep into every aspect of human endeavour. It's a place where social relations are made over in the image of the market.[101]

Discussion questions

1. What are your thoughts about the claims made in this extract? Do you agree/disagree?

2. Should all citizens in a society be entitled to the good life—quality health care, education, civic and political life? Why?

3. Do you agree that discussions related to health, education, family life, nature, art, civic duties, etc., have focused on economic debates while avoiding moral and political ones? Why might this be the case?

---

101. Ibid., 8, 10–11.

4. Why might it be wrong to buy political influence? Explain.
5. What do you think Sandel means by the following phrase, "A market society is a way of life in which market values seep into every aspect of human endeavour. It's a place where social relations are made over in the image of the market?"
6. Who benefits from neoliberalism?
7. How do some of Sandel's ideas link to religious ethics?

Sandel views economics as an effective tool in organising productivity within a society. However, what he is critical of is the dominance of economics in *all* facets of society, which he argues changes its nature radically. He argues that in the West, and particularly in America, there has been an evolution in recent decades from a *market economy* (which has a specific role) to what he defines as a *market society* that "governs our way of life."[102] Economic principles applied to material goods such as cars and homes may work efficiently, but evaluating aspects of society like education, health care, and civic and political life in this way results in social and moral problems. When these domains become monetized, their nature is affected and inequality emerges in a way that goes far beyond what type of car a person drives. As money governs access to quality education, health care, and political influence, the gap between the rich and poor widens while the nature of these institutions is affected.[103]

What has resulted in many instances is that institutions like prisons, rather than being a public responsibility, are now outsourced to private companies whose main goal is to make a profit. The problem presented is that these companies do not have an incentive to uphold civil human rights, and there are many examples of corruption emerging. A *Washington Post* article questions whether commodifying the justice system leads to results based on profitability instead of justice:

> Still, several reports have documented instances when private-prison companies have indirectly supported policies that put more Americans and immigrants behind bars—such as California's three-strikes rule and Arizona's highly controversial anti-illegal immigration law—by donating to politicians who support them, attending meetings with officials who back

---

102. Ibid., 10.
103. Ibid.

them, and lobbying for funding for Immigration and Customs Enforcement.[104]

Sandel claims a market society is a way of life where market values filter into the social fabric as "social relation is made in the framework of the market."[105] For example, Sandel discusses the impact of paying to enter universities and points out that, while this may result in a raise in revenue, it also diminishes the integrity and quality of the educational standards. Another example is the initiative of paying children to read. Can this diminish or enhance the quality of their learning? What do you think?

Watch the online video, "Michael Sandel: Should We Pay Children to Read? IQ2 Talks."[106]

How would you answer the question Dr. Sandel proposes and why?

Sandel, like Tagore, claims that looking through the sole lens of money limits our human freedom. In a democracy, concepts of freedom should be enlarged beyond the consumer and extend to a *notion of a citizen*. Western democracies, by definition, view people as citizens with inalienable human rights and liberties (as reflected, for example, in the UN Declaration of Human Rights) rather than as *consumers* competing to purchase their way to freedom and civil liberties through paying for education, health and a political voice. Importantly, debates about moral and political concerns should stand outside the economic paradigm which often dominates.

Do you agree with Sandel's claims? Discuss.

For further discussion on these issues, the following may be useful:

Video: Michael Sandel—"Why We Shouldn't Trust Markets with Our Civic Life."[107]

"The Lost Art of Democratic Debate."[108]
Podcast: Michael Sandel—"Michael Sandel on What Shouldn't Be Sold."[109]

---

104. Cohen, "How For-Profit Prisons," para. 3.
105. Sandel, *What Money Can't Buy*, 10–11.
106. https://www.youtube.com/watch?v=wiMMqV91U2g.
107. https://www.ted.com/talks/michael_sandel_why_we_shouldn_t_trust_markets_with_our_civic_life?language=en#t-590134.
108. https://www.ted.com/talks/michael_sandel_the_lost_art_of_democratic_debate/transcript.
109. http://philosophybites.com/2009/05/michael-sandel-on-what-shouldnt-be-sold.html.

Student activity—Debate or present one of the following claims made above:

1. Why we shouldn't trust markets with our civic life.
2. Have we lost the art of democratic debate?

Student activity—Essay

Write a response to one of the following:

1. The principles of neoliberalism are contrary to the ethical teachings of Judaism, Christianity, Islam, Buddhism, Hinduism, and Sikhism.
2. Compare and contract Sandel's ideas to the ethics of Singer, Aristotle, or Kant.

STUDENT REFLECTIONS

What are you now wondering about?

- What ideas or questions are you wondering about as a result of these lessons?
- Have these lessons made you think differently? Explain.
- What have you found challenging, provocative, or intriguing?

THE IMPORTANCE OF LISTENING AND EMPATHY TO THE MORAL LIFE

Can we really know other people?

> ... That may seem trivial but I think it is profound all the same. We never look beyond our assumptions and what's worse, we have given up trying to meet others; we just meet ourselves. We don't recognize each other because other people have become our permanent mirrors. If we actually realized

this, if we were to become aware of the fact that we are only ever looking at ourselves in the other person, that we are alone in the wilderness, we would go crazy . . . As for me, I implore fate to give me the chance to see beyond myself and truly meet someone.[110]

Discussion questions

1. Do you agree with the following claim, "We never look beyond our assumptions and what's worse, we have given up trying to meet others; we just meet ourselves?"
2. How can our assumptions get in the way of getting to know people?
3. Is it possible that we never really see the other person and that we only see ourselves?
4. What personal qualities do you think are needed in order to go "beyond the self" and truly *know another person*? Why do you think this may be important?
5. To what extent is it even possible to really know ourselves?

Why are listening and empathy important?

There are skills and dispositions (or ways of being) that can help us better understand other people. Some have argued that effective listening and empathy can increase our ability to gain a greater understanding of other people. The Oxford Dictionary defines listening as "The ability to pay attention to and effectively interpret what other people are saying."[111] Similarly, empathy can be understood as an ability to understand what the other person is feeling and experiencing. When we really hear others, we are able to empathise and are better placed to give them what they need. For example, if a mother listens attentively to her child's distress she may gradually be able to understand what is causing it and address the concern. Her ability to listen and empathise with her child will be important in providing what

---

110. Barbery, *The Elegance of the Hedgehog*, 141.
111. *Oxford Dictionaries*, s.v. "Listening." https://en.oxforddictionaries.com/definition/listening_skills.

the child needs. This ability to respond to people when we listen well applies not only to our immediate family, friends, and co-workers, but also to those in our wider community. Effective listening and empathy can have moral implications as they facilitate our ability to respond appropriately to others with greater care and compassion.

Listening for understanding

There are many philosophers who have argued that listening is necessary to gain knowledge and understanding. For example, German philosopher Martin Heidegger (1889–1976) explored the importance of listening as having a vital *epistemic role*. What this means is that our attentive listening is an important tool for understanding. Heidegger linked listening with *understanding*, claiming that "one cannot understand unless one is listening."[112]

Do you agree? Is it possible to understand *without listening*? Give examples.

Within the literature of psychology and counselling, it is widely accepted that the use of listening skills is important in developing effective interpersonal skills. Contemporary French feminist and psychoanalyst Luce Irigaray, like Heidegger, viewed listening as not only necessary for thinking, but also important as a tool in *connecting us to others*. She argues that we relate to others deeply, not just with our thinking, but also through our listening and bodily senses.[113]

> This listening amounts to "a fundamental dimension of thinking" (Irigary 2002: 162), a dimension that receives without being passive. It involves a bodily dimension of perception that connects us with the other and with what the other is able to say. Listening helps to keep "alive the astonishment, the questioning, the movement of thinking and saying" (Irigary 2002: 164)...[114]

---

112. Heidegger, *Poetry, Language, Thought*, xv.
113. Irigaray, in Walker, *Slow Philosophy*, 119.
114. Walker, *Slow Philosophy*, 119.

How well do you listen to others?

Can you remember a time when you felt someone really listened to you? What did that feel like?

> The practice of mindfulness will help you to love properly ... the most precious gift you can give to your loved one is your true presence, with mind and body...[115]

What does the passage from Thich Nhat Hanh mean?

Listening and hearing are not the same. You may hear sounds, but true listening requires more than hearing—it demands *attentiveness*. This type of skill requires an ability to be *present* and *still*. When our minds are busy and preoccupied with worries about our individual concerns, we may not have the necessary internal space to be attentive to others and really listen. This is a common experience. Many people have tried various practices to help with busy and worried thoughts, such as meditation, prayer, mindfulness practice, exercise, and talking to either friends, a family member, or a counsellor. Learning to be aware of our thoughts and feelings, cultivating attentiveness, and living in the present moment will be important skills for effective listening. Like any skills, we can learn how to improve our attentiveness, listening skills, and empathy. When we listen effectively, we are better able to empathise and understand the other person's experiences and feelings.

Religious contemplation and listening

The emergence of mindfulness in recent years has been a reminder to people of the importance of stillness, meditation, and attention—qualities and practices which for centuries have been part of religious contemplative life. Contemplation, in a religious context, means, "the act of thinking about spiritual things: meditation, the act of looking at or thinking about something for some time."[116] Listening, from this context, is not only directed toward others, but also to ourselves and God. This notion of listening in

---

115. Hạnh and McLeod, *You are Here*, 91.

116. *Oxford Dictionaries*, s.v. "Contemplation." https://en.oxforddictionaries.com/definition/listening_skills. It is important to note contemplation is also understood outside of a religious context.

the broader sense can help us, as religious scholar Max Picard (1888–1965) points out, listen to the "silence of God."[117] Likewise, religious mystic and philosopher Simone Weil (1909–1943) understood listening to music as a way of experiencing and connecting with the divine. Deep listening within this religious context is a way that leads to *transformation*, opening the individual to new experiences of the self and their world, which will be explored further in chapter 5.

> When one listens to Bach or a Gregorian melody, all faculties of the soul fall silent and strain to apprehend this perfectly beautiful thing, each in its own way. The intellect among others finds nothing in it to affirm or deny, but it feeds on it. Must not faith be an adherence of this kind?[118]

To what extent can listening help us experience something beyond ourselves, such as the divine or God?

Listening and empathy

Broadly speaking, empathy can be defined as a deep understanding of what another person is feeling, thinking, and experiencing. Empathy requires not only reason, but also the use of imagination as we attempt to *imagine or feel* what the other person may be experiencing. American philosopher Mathura Nussbaum explores the cognitive aspects of empathy. As we shall discuss further in chapter 5, she argues that empathy as an emotion can reveal reasons that embody values and truths. She argues that literature is able to expand our empathy. For example, stories can allow access to the experiences of others that open us up to feeling empathy.

Psychologist Carl Rogers (1902–1987) claimed that when we listen deeply to another, we are able to offer empathy. This ability to listen and be empathetic, he argued, is a powerful factor that heals and helps people psychologically. He claimed that what essentially most people need is to be heard in the "presence of other people."[119] Rogers worked with many people experiencing sadness,

Carl Rogers

117. Picard, *World of Silence*, 229.
118. Weil, *Cahiers*, 139.
119. Ibid., 41.

grief, and depression, and was able to see how deep listening resulted in profound positive change in people's lives.[120]

Student activity—Excerpt

Read the following extract and answer the questions below.

The following excerpt on the importance of empathic listening is taken from the book, *The 7 Habits of Highly Effective People* by Stephen R. Covey:

> "Seek first to understand" involves a very deep shift in paradigm. We typically seek first to be understood. Most people do not listen with the intent to understand; they listen with the intent to reply. They're either speaking or preparing to speak. They're filtering everything through their own paradigms, reading their autobiography into other people's lives. When I say empathic listening, I mean listening with intent to *understand*. I mean *seeking first* to understand, to really understand. It's an entirely different paradigm. Empathic (*from empathy*) listening gets inside another person's frame of reference. You look out through it, you see the world the way they see the world, you understand their paradigm, you understand how they feel . . . Empathic listening involves much more than registering, reflecting, or even understanding the words that are said. Communications experts estimate, in fact, that only 10 percent of our communication is represented by the words we say. Another 30 percent is represented by our sounds, and 60 percent by our body language. In empathic listening, you listen with your ears, but you also, and more importantly, listen with your eyes and with your heart. You listen for feeling, for meaning. You listen for behavior. You use your right brain as well as your left. You sense, you intuit, you feel. Empathic listening is so powerful because it gives you accurate data to work with. Instead of projecting your own autobiography and assuming thought, feelings, motives, and interpretation, you're dealing with the reality inside another person's head

---

120. Ibid.

and heart. You're listening to understand. You're focused on receiving the deep communication of another human soul.[121]

Discussion questions

1. How does Covey define empathic listening?
2. What benefits are gained from empathic listening?
3. When was the last time you experienced empathetic listening? How did this make you feel?
4. Can empathy be a limitation in effectively helping someone? How?

Student activity — Active listening

Some skills we can develop and practice to improve our ability to listen effectively:

1. When listening to another person, first stop and become *aware of your own thoughts*. Try and let go of these thoughts and worries, relax your body, acknowledge any physical tensions, and set them aside for a while.
2. Notice the other person's body language as an indication of what they may be feeling. For example, they might be fidgeting, which may indicate feelings of anxiety.
3. Try not to interrupt what is said and value the silence. If the person is upset or confused, you may at some stage say something like "It must be hard for you." Always maintain focus on the other person.
4. Refrain from giving advice unless the person has asked for it. Some conversations may not have conclusive resolutions. Do not worry about this, as your listening and presence will have a positive impact on the person..
5. At the end of the conservation, you may want to summarize what has been said and the feelings expressed and thank the person for sharing. Try to keep what is said in confidence.

121. Covey, *7 Habits*, 152–54.

Remember that to *be present* and listen effectively *is a great gift to another person*. Even if the problem or concern remains unresolved, your *presence and attentiveness* will be valuable for the other person.

Please note: if the situation or problem disclosed involves a serious matter such as a person engaging in self-harm, involved in abuse, contemplating suicide, or experiencing serious depression, it is important to report this to a teacher, parent, or professional for further assistance.

Student activity—Practice your listening skills further

Organize into groups of three. Each person is allocated a number: one, two, or three.

Everyone thinks about a personal situation to share with the group.

Some suggestions include: being undecided about a decision (i.e., whether to attend a party), feeling lonely, isolated or misunderstood, or experiences on a holiday.

1. Person One talks for about three minutes to Person Two while Person Three listens attentively and observes the conversion carefully, noting what has been said, including body language.
2. Person Two then communicates to Person One what they heard and felt the person was saying.
3. When Person Two has finished, Person Three then comments on Person Two's ability to be empathetic to Person One and how well they showed sensitivity and awareness to all they said, including verbal and nonverbal communication.
4. In conclusion, Person One discusses whether what was said was accurate and what may have been missed.
5. After this process is completed, exchange roles and start again.
6. Respond to the reflection questions below.
7. This activity can take approximately forty to fifty minutes.

Discussion Questions

1. Was I attentive and still while listening? If not, why?
2. Was I able to listen effectively? If not, why?
3. Did I show empathy? If not, why?
4. Did I feel I was heard by others? Did they show me understanding? What did that feel like?
5. Do you think or feel differently about listening as a result of this exercise? Explain.
6. What did you learn about yourself or others from this exercise?
7. What new questions arose from this lesson? What did you find interesting?

Can effective listening and empathy be connected to living a moral life?

As discussed earlier, living a life of virtue and morality was of great importance to both the ancient philosophers and religious thinkers. However, it is difficult to develop virtues and do good acts without relating to other people. In other words, living a moral life necessarily involves our ability to relate to people well. Therefore, skills such as effective listening and empathy can be considered important tools in fostering better relationships with other people. It can be argued that relationships create the groundwork for an ethical and moral life. Treating other people justly with respect and dignity is a central theme in both secular and religious ethics. Not only can empathy be considered important, but some philosophers and religious scholars argue compassion also plays a significant role in morality.

Are there limitations to empathy?

American psychologist Dr. Paul Bloom argues that while empathy is a useful tool in many ways, including developing and deepening our relationships with other people, it also has its limitations.[122] He claims that we can also use empathy for negative purposes such as manipulating and exploiting people, as is the case with psychopaths and con artists. It also can lead to

---

122. Bloom, *Against Empathy*.

bias in moral reasoning, as we tend to feel only empathy toward people who are like us.[123] Bloom claims politicians can exploit empathy for their own purposes, from describing stories of suffering by certain groups in society to justifying war.[124] Bloom argues that compassion is more important than empathy. Empathy might allow us to understand other people's feelings and plights, but compassion includes our kind action toward others. Compassion allows us to care for people without necessarily *feeling empathy*. Bloom states that, according to neurological research, empathy and compassion show up in different parts of the brain.[125] He cites studies even suggesting that people are better at helping others when they are not necessarily feeling empathy.[126] Bloom claims that when making moral decisions we should draw on moral principles and consider a cost-benefit analysis when helping people rather than relying solely on empathy.

What are your thoughts about the above passage? Do you agree?

STUDENT ACTIVITY—WATCH AND READ THE FOLLOWING:

View the following video and read the article, then answer the questions below.

Video: Paul Bloom—Against Empathy: The Case for Rational Compassion.[127]

Article: "Why Paul Bloom Is Wrong about Empathy and Morality."[128]

1. Can empathy make us ineffective when helping others?
2. Are moral principles and the analysis of costs and benefits more reliable in moral decisions than empathy?
3. Can empathy and the appeal to moral rational principles work together?
4. Is the act of compassion more effective in helping others than empathy? How?

---

123. Ibid.
124. Bloom, "Empathy and Its Discontents," 24–31.
125. Ibid.
126. Ibid.
127. https://www.youtube.com/watch?v=Si1YSUAEH4w.
128. https://www.psychologytoday.com/blog/good-thinking/201310/why-paul-bloom-is-wrong-about-empathy-and-morality.

Compassion

Compassion is defined by the Oxford Dictionary as a "sympathetic pity and concern for the sufferings or misfortunes of others."[129] The notion of compassion is discussed by both secular and religious writers.

Philosopher Martha Nussbaum writes the following:

Dr. Martha Nussbaum

> Compassion is an emotion directed at another person's suffering or lack of well-being. It requires the thought that the other person is in a bad way, and a pretty seriously bad way. (Thus we don't feel compassion for people's loss of trivial items like toothbrushes and paper clips.) It contains within itself an appraisal of the seriousness of various predicaments. Let us call this the judgement of seriousness.[130]

> ... at the start of judgement of similar possibilities: Aristotle, Rousseau, and others suggest that we have compassion only insofar as we believe that the suffering person shares vulnerabilities and possibilities with us. I think we can clearly see that this judgement is not strictly necessary for the emotion, as the other two seem to be. We have compassion for nonhuman animals, without basing it on any imagined similarity—although, of course, we need somehow to make sense of their predicament as serious and bad.[131]

> Indeed, the events of September 11 make vivid a philosophical problem that has been debated from the time of Euripides through much of the history of the Western philosophical tradition. This is the question of what to do about compassion, given its obvious importance in shaping the civic imagination, but given, too, its obvious propensity for self-serving

---

129. *Oxford Dictionaries*, s.v. "Compassion." https://en.oxforddictionaries.com/definition/compassion.

130. Nussbaum, "Compassion and Terror," 15.

131. Ibid., 15.

narrowness. Is compassion, with all its limits, our best hope as we try to educate citizens to think well about human relations both inside the nation and across national boundaries?[132]

Discussion Questions

1. What are your thoughts about these passages above?
2. What does it mean to be compassionate?
3. According to Nussbaum, can we extend compassion to others who are different from ourselves? Explain.
4. Why might compassion be important?

The core of religion is compassion

In religious ethics, the feeling of empathy is extended to compassion. There are many examples of religious teachings pointing to compassion: Jesus' commandment of love; Zakat, one of the Five Pillars of Islam which states that followers are required to give charity to the poor; and Buddhism's compassion as a central component to enlightenment. All of these religious teachings demonstrate the importance of compassion as part of their traditions.

Karen Armstrong

Religious scholar Karen Armstrong argues that the principle of compassion is the focus and connection that unites the three Abrahamic religions of Judaism, Christianity, and Islam. She defines compassion as the "ability to feel with the other" and states that religion is about *practicing* compassion.[133] Armstrong proposes that the concept of the Golden Rule, which is to treat others as you would like to be treated, is also central within Abrahamic traditions. A religion can only be understood when it is "put into practice," referring to the word "creed," which translates to the Greek word *credo*, meaning "I commit and engage

---

132. Ibid., 12.
133. Armstrong, "My Wish."

myself."[134] Armstrong suggests that compassion is the test of any true religiosity. Through the act of compassion, we are brought into the presence of God and the divine.

Compassion, Armstrong suggests, is not confined to a person's group, but extends to a concern for everyone, a "universal outreach."[135] Causes of the world's problems that are often associated with religion are not caused by religion, but politics, as humans seek to misread and distort religion for their own ego and gain. She claims that often what causes conflict is the desire for people to be right rather than compassionate.[136] Armstrong challenges the assumptions that religious faith is just about prescribing or adopting a set of claims. Concepts like "I believe in God, Jesus, the Trinity, Muhammed etc." on their own do not necessarily mean a person is religious. What does count is a person's actions. It is not, therefore, in just making claims of accepting a religion, but rather it is in the *doing that one becomes religious*. Armstrong proposes that the concept of common values, such as compassion and the Golden Rule within Abrahamic traditions, can be used as a tool for dialogue and interfaith understanding.[137]

Armstrong justifies her claim through references to the Bible, the Quran, and the Hebrew Scriptures. She specifically refers to the words of Jewish Rabbi Hallal, who states, "That which is hateful to you do not do onto your neighbor. That is the Torah, the rest is commentary—go and study it" and Rabbi Meir, who states, "Any interpretation of scripture which leads to hatred and disdain, or contempt of other people is illegitimate."[138] Christian theologian St. Augustine (AD 354–430) wrote, "Scripture teaches nothing but charity" and further claims that any interpretation which is not in line with this concept must be rejected.[139]

For further information, see the video by Karen Armstrong, "My Wish: The Charter for Compassion."[140]

---

134. Ibid.
135. Ibid.
136. Ibid.
137. Ibid.
138. Ibid.
139. Ibid.
140. https://www.ted.com/talks/karen_armstrong_makes_her_ted_prize_wish_the_charter_for_compassion.

STUDENT REFLECTIONS

WHAT ARE YOU NOW WONDERING ABOUT?

- What ideas or questions are you wondering about as a result of these lessons?
- Have these lessons made you think differently? Explain.
- What have you found challenging, provocative, or intriguing?

STUDENT ACTIVITY—RESEARCH:

Explore ONE of the following: The Golden Rule or The UN Declaration of Human Rights resolution and discuss:

1. its origins and historical developments.
2. the significance it holds today. Give examples.
3. to what extent your country upholds the principles espoused. Give two to three examples. Compare and contrast with two to three countries.
4. how these core principles are similar to or different from religious ethics. Give examples.

Present your findings to the class or write a response.

STUDENT ACTIVITY—ROLE-PLAY:

You are a government minister who is going to present to your parliament the extent to which your nation is upholding the guidelines stated by the Human Rights Commission.

Choose two guidelines from the list below and discuss to what extent your country abides by these.

Commission of Human Rights resolution 2000/64 identified good governance as including the following:

- Transparency
- Responsibility
- Accountability

- Participation
- Responsiveness (needs of the people).[141]

Student Activity—Debate:

The UN Declaration of Human Rights, the Golden Rule, or the Commission of Human Rights resolution provide an adequate framework for ensuring justice in a democracy. Choose one.

Student activity—Debate, present, or write about one of the following:

1. Moral relativism upholds human rights and dignity.
2. Kant's categorical imperatives provide an adequate guide to morality.
3. The development of virtue is important to living a moral life.
4. Men and women make moral decisions differently.
5. Economics should guide all decisions within a society.
6. The actions of self-interest as a global trend are not sustainable in the future.
7. Racism and scapegoating exist today.
8. Listening and empathy are crucial skills for leadership.
9. Compassion is a core component to religious ethics.
10. Leaders should be wise and uphold moral virtue.

MAIN RESEARCH TASK

Investigate one of the moral issues below and apply one listed ethical theory. Record your findings and present these to the class.

Some suggested moral issues:

1. Poverty: its causes and solutions
2. The ethics of war

141. OHCHR, "Good Governance and Human Rights," paras. 1–10.

3. Torture
4. Child trafficking
5. Violence against women
6. Child abuse
7. The weapons industry
8. Animal cruelty
9. Scapegoating and racism
10. Euthanasia
11. Stem cell research
12. Abortion
13. Environmental issues
14. Genetic modification of foods
15. Media influence—ownership and ethical accountability
16. The ethical implications of neoliberalism or economic rationalism
17. Accountability in corporations and business

Ethical theories

1. Utilitarianism
2. Ethical egoism
3. Deontological ethics
4. Religious ethics
5. Situational ethics
6. Virtue ethics
7. Ethical intuitionism
8. Feminist ethics
9. Metaethics
10. Business ethics

Some guidelines for the presentation:

1. Present the moral issue you have selected from a range of perspectives, including crosscultural studies. For example, if you are

exploring the topic of torture, compare statistics from at least three to four countries.
2. Be aware of identifying Western and non-Western perspectives to the moral issue.
3. Present both sides of the argument.
4. Generate relevant questions.

Student Activity 4—Extension task:
Ethics conference

Imagine you are attending an ethics conference and the topic is *Ethics for the Modern World*. Working in groups, select an individual as your representative to summarise the group's main ideas in a speech. The speech will need to include the following:

1. an outline of an ethical theory for the modern world
2. a description of what this would *look like* and *why* they think it will work
3. some possible limitations foreseen in its application
4. a demonstration of how the theory will address one to two moral issues (i.e., war, refugees, poverty)
5. a question-and-answer period in which the audience may ask anything about the topic

CONCLUSION

The ancient Greek philosophers understood that in order to live a good life and allow human flourishing and happiness, ethics was fundamental. It was the duty of the individual to not only live in harmony within oneself, but to act justly toward their community. Wisdom was the ability to live a moral life. In other words, according to the ancient Greeks, it was not possible to cause harm and commit evil toward others and still be considered *wise*.

Likewise, moral behaviour has crucial implications within a religious context. All of the religious traditions have understood a connection with belief and living a moral life. Broadly speaking, the practices of compassion and loving thy neighbour are central themes within all religious teachings. How do we ensure that ethics informs and guides important global, national, and international decisions? What about scientific research, laws, and education? To what extent do we need to ensure that decisions move beyond self-interest and the immediate group to work toward the interests of the common good?

Many believe the ethics of self-interest, as Singer points out, is no longer tenable.[142] The environmental crisis, world poverty, nuclear weapons, mass refugees emerging due to conflict, and increasing economic disparity point to the seriousness of ethics for our world today.

Student reflection questions

WHAT ARE YOU NOW WONDERING ABOUT?

- What ideas, issues, and questions do have as a result of these lessons?
- Do you now think differently about certain ideas, issues, or questions? Explain.
- What ideas did you find interesting, challenging, or intriguing? Explain why.
- In years to come, what might you remember from these lessons?

INDEPENDENT RESEARCH QUESTIONS

1. How does a person know if a type of behaviour is right or wrong? To what extent does it depend on the outcomes or consequences of actions?
2. Can the development of character be an important part of living a moral or good life?
3. How does ethics emerge from religious traditions? Why do practitioners of the same faith tradition often disagree on what the right thing to do actually is?
4. Are empathy and compassion not as reliable in guiding moral actions as the appeal to rational principles and analysis?
5. What implications does neoliberalism pose for religious or secular ethics?

142. Singer, *How are We to Live?*, 64, 26. See also, Younis, *On the Ethical Life*, 100–1.

6. Does the success of a society depend on its ability to look after its most vulnerable?
7. If the goal of corporations and businesses is to make a profit, do they still have a moral responsibility to their staff welfare, the environment, and the community?

How Do We Find Meaning and Happiness?

Outline

1. Introduction
2. Philosophy on happiness
3. Pleasure: Hedonism and Epicurus
4. The "flourishing life"—eudaimonia—Socrates/Plato/Aristotle, and Stoicism
5. Religion on happiness: Buddhism, Christianity, and Cults
6. Philosophy of emotions
7. Psychology on happiness and well-being
8. Existentialism and the arts as a response to the search for meaning
9. Religious experience and mysticism as a response to meaning and happiness
10. Main research task
11. Independent research questions

Objectives

At the end of this chapter, students should demonstrate the ability to ask questions, wonder, and think critically about the following:

1. How happiness is understood by philosophers, religious writers, and psychologists

2. How the nature of subjective experiences can provide a justification for truth
3. The arts as a response to the search for personal meaning and happiness
4. Mysticism providing a response to the search for personal meaning and happiness
5. How life skills can be developed through the discussion on therapy, mindfulness, existentialism, and mysticism

What does the following passage say about what humans are seeking?

> People say that what we're all seeking is a meaning for life. I don't think that's what we're really seeking. I think that what we're seeking is an experience of being alive, so that our life experiences on the purely physical plane will have resonances with our own innermost being and reality, so that we actually feel the rapture of being alive.[1]

INTRODUCTION

Happiness, at first glance, seems to be a simple concept universally understood by all. From content children having fun at a friend's birthday party to an elderly couple enjoying their morning coffee on the porch during a beautiful sunrise, we know and recognize the concept of happiness. We all have clear memories of being happy—earning an award at school, watching our favourite team win a championship, spending time with good friends—and whatever the occurrence, we all could list something special to us.

Equally memorable is when we are not happy. Misery also comes in many forms—an embarrassing mistake witnessed by others, an excruciating injury, the end of a relationship, the death of someone close, just to name a few. So, does a concept as obvious, basic, and universal as happiness warrant an in-depth analysis? As we shall discover, happiness, sought by all, is elusive at its most fundamental level. What is happiness? Is it an emotion such as contentment, pleasure, or euphoria? Or does happiness consist of

1. Campbell, *The Power of Myth*, 1.

personal meaning, peace, well-being, virtue, and spirituality? Does it require success? If so, what kind of success? How can we know and find it? Through our senses, emotions, intuition, or reason? How can we then maintain it? How can religion provide happiness? The search for these answers is as old as humankind and still continues. What will be presented in this chapter is the importance of personal meaning as a response to happiness.

This chapter will introduce secular and religious perspectives on this issue, while stimulating material will be drawn from philosophers, religious writers, and psychologists. Epistemological questions will continue to guide the inquiry. It is not in the scope of this chapter to provide an in-depth comprehensive discussion on what is a broad and highly debated area, but rather to identify key elements of the topic and pose questions for discussion and further inquiry.

Student Activity: Terminology

Some of the terms below are still debated amongst scholars; however, familiarity with common understandings of the these will assist with engaging in the ideas presented. The Oxford and Webster dictionaries may be a good place to start.

Working in student pairs, write down the definitions of the terms below and take turns explaining them to each other:

hedonism, well-being, cognitive behavioural therapy, positive psychology, existential counselling, mindfulness, existentialism, religious experience, mysticism, virtue, utilitarian, indifference, theologian, equilibrium, disproportionate, aesthetics, technology, epistemic, authentic, altruism, contemplation, resilience, transcendence, spirituality, flourishing

DISCUSSION QUESTIONS

1. Think of when you last felt happy. What activity were you engaged in? Was it solitary, or were you with other people? Do you remember what you were thinking and feeling? Can you describe this?
2. What is your understanding of happiness? Can you define it?

3. Do family and friends make you happy? What other factors contribute to your happiness?
4. Is pleasure happiness? How do we define it? Is pleasure a justification in itself for happiness?
5. Is happiness an emotion?
6. Are finding meaning in life and happiness the same thing?
7. What are some common assumptions about what makes people happy?

Student Activity: Interviews

Ask three to four people you know (i.e., a teacher, friend, parent, aunt, uncle, or grandparent) the following questions:

1. Are pleasure and happiness the same thing?
2. What do you think makes up a meaningful life? Is it the same as a happy life?
3. Are feelings or moods a measure of happiness?

Student Activity: Excerpt

Read the following extract from *Psychology Today*:

> ... Tom always enjoys his job as a janitor at a local community college. What he likes most about his job is how it gives him a chance to meet the young female students who are attending the community college. Almost every single day Tom feels good and generally experiences a lot of pleasant emotions. In fact, it is very rare that he would ever feel negative emotions like sadness or loneliness. When Tom thinks about his life, he always comes to the same conclusion: he feels highly satisfied with the way he lives.

The reason Tom feels this way is that every day he goes from locker to locker and steals belongings from the students and re-sells these belongings to buy himself alcohol. Each night as he's going to sleep, he thinks about the things he will steal the next day.

Are Tom's good feelings and happiness a good thing? Explain.[2]

PHILOSOPHY ON MEANING AND HAPPINESS

Philosophers have reflected on the issue of happiness for centuries. Many Greek philosophers believed happiness to be the ultimate goal in life. Religious thinkers have also written about happiness in relation to the internal experience of peace and liberation resulting from a connection to God, ultimate reality, the divine, or enlightenment. Many, but not all, of these thinkers believed happiness was connected to living a moral life.

Dionysius

What is the role of pleasure in the happy life?

Hedonism

Hedonism is the belief that the central goal for human happiness is the pursuit of pleasure. The movement emerged in the fourth century BC from the Cyrenaic school of philosophy and asserted that physical pleasure and immediate satisfaction were to be sought before intellectual pursuits or long-term gains.[3] The nature of the pleasure was sensual and self-indulgent.

   2. Phillips, "What Does it Take?," para. 1.
   3. Shields, *Ancient Philosophy*, 229–30.

Hedonism advocated a life that sought to reduce pain and attain the greatest amount of pleasure possible. It believed that the human psyche is constructed to seek pleasure. Similar to the utilitarian approach discussed in the Ethics chapter, it seeks to maximize the greatest amount of pleasure possible. Hedonism is connected to ethical egoism, where decisions are based solely on self-interests, as depicted in the example above with Tom the janitor focusing on his own happiness at the expense of others.

What are your thoughts on hedonism?

Epicurus (341–270 BC)

It is said by Cicero, concerning Epicurus:

Epicurus

> ... We are investigating what is the final and ultimate good, which all philosophers agree must be of such a kind that it is the end to which everything is the means, but it is not itself the means to anything. Epicurus situates this in pleasure, which he wants to be the greatest good, whilst pain is the greatest bad. His doctrine begins this way: as soon as every animal is born, it seeks after pleasure and rejoices in it as the greatest good, while it rejects pain as the greatest bad and avoids it as far as possible.[4]

At first glance, it would seem Epicurus advocated a gluttonous lifestyle of extravagance, but he perceived a flaw in attempting to satisfy an extensive amount of desires. He developed the idea of seeking pleasure with a moderate approach. Epicurus agreed that pleasure was important, but viewed it as that which, in the end, results in a tranquil state. He acknowledged that pleasure was found within the bodily sensations yet also discussed the pleasures of the mind.[5] The body was not independent, however, but closely connected to the mind. Philosopher Christopher Shields argues, "according

---

4. Cicero, *De Finibus*, 29 (= LS 21 A) in Shields, *Ancient Philosophy*, 229.
5. Shields, *Ancient Philosophy*, 229–30.

to Epicurus, the mind is itself bodily, because composed of atoms in the void, this perception is equally an awareness of bodily well-being."[6] Hedonism is sometimes associated with indulgence in excessive consumption of food, wealth, or sensual pleasures, but Epicurus did not propose such a lifestyle. For him, pleasure was mostly about an absence of both bodily pain and an unsettled mind (or soul).[7]

> ... So, when we say that pleasure is the goal, we do not mean that pleasure of the profligate or the pleasure of consumption ... but rather the lack of pain in the body and disturbance in the soul.[8]

Epicurus understood that the state of the mind was important for happiness. Engaging in activities which resulted in only short pleasure was not good for us; rather, we need to find pleasures which are long lasting. For example, consuming sweets in excess may bring short-term pleasures, but might in the end cause physical discomfort and even pain. In support of his view, Epicurus lived a communal life that was simple and self-sufficient. He often wrote about eating simple foods with good friends and thought that friendships produced great long-lasting pleasure. There were also intellectual pleasures to be experienced. This kind of pleasure was found in his contemplation of nature.[9]

As discussed in the Ethics chapter, utilitarian English philosophers Jeremey Bentham (1748–1832) and John Stuart Mill (1806–1873) developed Epicurus' idea of maximizing the most pleasure for the most number of people and even sought to discuss how we could measure or quantify pleasure, with Mill distinguishing between higher and lower pleasures.

Student Activity: Research

Investigate further how Epicurus develops the importance of friendship, freedom, and the analyzed life as key components to happiness.

The following resources may be useful:

1. Alain de Botton, "02 - Epicurus on Happiness—Philosophy: A Guide to Happiness."[10]

6. Ibid.
7. Ibid., 147.
8. Long and Sedley, *Hellenistic Philosophers*, 21.
9. Hadot, *Philosophy as a Way*, 88.
10. https://www.youtube.com/watch?v=irornIAQzQY.

HOW DO WE FIND MEANING AND HAPPINESS?

2. Epicurus, *Letters, Principal Doctrines, and Vatican Sayings*.[11]

Student Activity: Presentation

In groups, choose one of the following—psychological hedonism, ethical hedonism, or utilitarianism—and present the main ideas to your class.

Discussion Questions

1. Do some pleasures have positive and negative consequences? Explain.
2. Are there pleasures found only in the body and others in the mind? To what extent are they connected?
3. Is it possible to quantify pleasure?
4. To what extent is the discussion on pleasure adequate? Can you think of some counterarguments?

Pleasure Machine—Thought Experiment

> Suppose there was an experience machine that would give you any experience you desired. Super-duper neuropsychologists could stimulate your brain so that you would think and feel you were writing a great novel, or making a friend, or reading an interesting book. All the time you would be floating in a tank, with electrodes attached to your brain. Should you plug into this machine for life, reprogramming your life experiences? [. . .] Of course, while in the tank you won't know that you're there; you'll think that it's all actually happening [. . .] Would you plug in?[12]

How would you respond?

American philosopher Robert Nozick (1938–2002) conducted a thought experiment on subjects by presenting them with the hypothetical situation illustrated above. What is interesting is that most of the people

---

11. Epicurus, *Letters, Principal Doctrines*.
12. Nozick and Nagel, *Anarchy, State, and Utopia*, 42–45.

responded that they would not enter the machine. Nozick's analysis of the experiment's outcome indicates that feelings of pleasure may not be the most important driver, but rather a *connection with reality*.[13] His findings suggest that people generally want their feelings to be real and not illusory. Most also want the power to choose, change, and craft for themselves the lives they want rather than have it dictated to them.

STUDENT ACTIVITY: QUESTION

For more on the thought experiment, read the following article: BBC News—Would you plug into a machine that makes you happy?[14]

STUDENT ACTIVITY: DEBATE

Read Book Two of Plato's *Republic*. Would you use the ring at the expense of compromising morality and the law? Present your reasons to the class.

EUDAIMONIA—HUMAN FLOURISHING

Parthenon in Greece

> The word eudaimonia derives etymologically from eu (good) and daimon (god, demigod), and thus suggests a state of blessedness; literally, having a good god within one. The gods were thought to be supremely happy, and philosophers in the Socratic tradition held that human beings are happiest when they devote their lives to the exercise of the most divine element in themselves, namely their intellect, in accordance with the highest virtue, namely sophia or contemplative wisdom.[15]

Ancient Greek philosophers Socrates, Plato, and Aristotle argued that happiness was linked to the cultivation of wisdom from a life lived according to the highest ideals of virtue. The term for happiness was *eudaimonia*, sometimes translated as "human flourishing," and was viewed as the highest

13. Nozick, *Examined Life*, 106–7.
14. http://www.bbc.com/news/magazine-14789249.
15. Collins and O'Brien, *Greenwood Dictionary of Education*, 171.

good in life. This term pointed to more than pleasure or positive feelings (although it could include these), but ultimately a life which was lived well in its *totality*. It was a life of reflection in accordance with the highest ideals of knowledge which, for these thinkers, was virtue and wisdom that culminated in what they termed "the good life."

Socrates

Socrates (469–399 BC) argued that the greatest pleasures came from the attention to our soul. He understood the soul as the structure of a person's character which holds its intelligence and morality, "... that within us in virtue of which we are pronounced wise or foolish."[16] In attaining knowledge of what is good, just, and virtuous, we would take care of our souls and live in harmony. As we saw in chapter 1, Socrates proposed a dialectic method which included the process of examining and cross-examining in order to arrive at truth. This process of examination leads a person to arrive at the understanding of what it means to live a good life. A good life meant one lived by virtue and wisdom. Socrates stated, "I sought to persuade every man that he must look to himself and seek virtue and wisdom."[17]

Socrates claimed that learning to skillfully apply our reason in controlling unhealthy desires and harmonizing our souls were the routes to happiness that resulted in tranquillity. A person who discerned which desires to pursue that led to a wholesome and meaningful life, according to Socrates, was wise.

Socrates argued that living a virtuous life brought greater pleasure than an unvirtuous one and was more desirable than physical pleasures. He claimed that a virtuous person is happier simply because their good deeds result in a greater sense of equanimity than those of a person who is not virtuous. The unvirtuous life results in an unhealthy mind characterised by inner chaos, guilt, and anxiety. Socrates stated that when we harm another knowingly, we also harm ourselves.[18]

What the just person also gains is not only inner tranquillity, Socrates argued, but also the pleasure of seeking knowledge which can allow access to a higher realm that is almost godlike. Here, the mind is able to understand that there is an order in the universe which the mind can discover.[19] For example, the beauty of a rose exists and despite it passing away the idea

16. Stumpf, *Socrates to Sartre*, 39.
17. Plato, "Apology," 418.
18. Stumpf, *Socrates to Sartre*, 39.
19. Ibid., 43.

of beauty nevertheless remains. The rose is beautiful as it partakes in the idea of beauty. The idea is part of the general or universal, which remains and is unchanging, providing an intelligible order. In discovering this order, we are able to understand notions of justice and truth and therefore act accordingly. To Socrates, virtue was considered the highest form of knowledge, and one could not find happiness unless they acted virtuously.

The Wise Person

Socrates claimed that humans desire happiness, the underlying drive of all actions. The attainment of wealth or possessing inborn traits like talents or good looks doesn't bring happiness in themselves, but is dependent on *how* they are used.[20] For example, wealth can be spent frivolously with no real benefits or value, and good looks or talents may be used for manipulation or evil acts. For Socrates, the key was developing into a wise person who was able to use all external attributes toward a wholesome and good life, leading to happiness.

Discussion Questions

1. According to Socrates, how does a person live the good life?
2. How is virtue connected to happiness?
3. How does a person live in harmony with their souls?
4. Can you think of counterarguments to the claims made?

---

20. Ibid., 44–45.

Plato's Academy mosaic —from the *Villa of T. Siminius Stephanus in Pompeii.*

Plato—Contemplation

Plato also investigated the concept of happiness by focusing on the mind and introspection. In *The Republic,* Plato argued that the mind is made up of three components: reasoning, courage, and the appetites, or passions. He described virtue as accomplished when each part of the soul fulfilled its function. For example, the soul keeps appetites within the limits of reason and avoids excesses, resulting in a moderation that leads to the virtue of *temperance.*[21] Plato argued that appetites and passions must be controlled by reason in order to find harmony between different parts of the soul. The equilibrium achieved is equated to a divine state similar to that of Greek gods.

In Plato's dialogue *The Symposium,* the power of desire is represented by Eros. Eros seeks physical pleasures in the world and initially finds satisfaction. However, he is trained to then seek higher pleasures that exist within universal concepts. Plato challenges us to move beyond the appreciation of beauty in the world, such as an appreciation of a beautiful woman or

21. Ibid., 72.

a sunset, to an awareness of beauty in general—existing as a concept, greater than just certain things around us. These universal concepts for Plato are the Ideal Forms, which include beauty, justice, and truth:

> For he who would proceed aright in this matter should begin in youth to visit beautiful forms; and first, if he be guided by his instructor aright, to love one such form only—out of that he should create fair thoughts; and soon he will of himself perceive that the beauty of one form is akin to the beauty of another; and then if beauty of form in general is his pursuit, how foolish would he be not to recognize that the beauty in every form is one and the same![22]

The Oxford Dictionary defines contemplation as "The action of looking thoughtfully at something for a long time. Deep reflective thought."[23] For Plato, contemplation was a path that arose out of temporal, human love, leading to the eternal love.[24] This path started with the desire or love for earthly things or people, moving to a consummation with the vision and experience of the divine which was the good and beauty itself. Plato argued that beauty is the eternal universal objective reality. An understanding of this reality allowed a heightening of the soul as it ascended to a high awareness. Plato understood that the intention of contemplation is for union with unchanging beauty.[25]

Plato thought contemplation was a step-by-step process specific to each soul and guided by reason, moving away from the illusions of this world to a connection with the truth which was the divine.[26] The recognition of beauty moved from the external to the internal beauty of the soul and in doing so developed virtue and a union with the divine. *Contemplation started with the recognition of beauty in the world to the realization of the divine beauty of the Ideal Form*:

> . . . suddenly perceive a nature of wondrous beauty . . . which in the first place is everlasting. . . secondly, not fair in one point of view and foul in another, or at one time or in one relation or at one place fair, at another time or in another relation or at

---

22. Plato, *Symposium*, 210.

23. *Oxford Dictionaries*, "Contemplation." http://www.oxforddictionaries.com/definition/contemplation.

24. Caranfa, "Contemplative Instruction," 566.

25. Ibid.

26. Ibid., 567.

another place foul, as if fair to some and foul to others ... but beauty absolute, separate, simple, and everlasting, which ... is imparted to the ever-growing and perishing beauties of all other things.[27]

Contemplation led to mystical experiences which, for Plato, could only be achieved by philosophers. However, there are many interpreters of Plato's work who have taken this theme to a religious context. Christian writers such as Plotinus (204–270) and St. Augustine (354–430), known as Neoplatonists, understood Plato's reference to the divine as a union with the Christian God.

Discussion questions

1. What do you think of Plato's concept of beauty and how we come to understand it?
2. Can contemplation described by Plato lead us toward a type of pleasure? Can it help us to find truth? Explain.

Aristotle

Student Activity

> Every rational activity aims at some end or good. One end (like one activity) may be subordinate to another.[28]

> But what is happiness? If we consider what the function of man is, we find that happiness is a virtuous activity of the soul.[29]

What do the above quotes mean?

Aristotle

---

27. Plato, *Symposium*, 211.
28. Aristotle, *Nicomachean Ethics*, 1094a1–22.
29. Ibid., 1097b22–1098a8.

Aristotle developed the idea of happiness in his well-known book *Nicomachean Ethics*. He argued happiness was the ultimate goal of all human life. Like Socrates, Aristotle believed humans seek pleasure, money, and honor in order to attain happiness.

As we read in chapter 3, Aristotle, like Socrates, understood happiness as connected to the application of virtue. A good life is one based on virtue which leads to *eudaimonia* (*flourishing*) or living well. For Aristotle, eudaimonia was not the result of momentary pleasures, but emerged from a successful life lived well. The judgement of life as a whole and how it was lived to its human potential was happiness, and best measured toward the end of life.

As a logician, Aristotle believed we develop virtue though correct thinking and actions in accordance to living a good life. The use of reason distinguishes us from the animal, allowing us to control our pleasurable physical urges. Reason allows us to make decisions which enhance our potential to flourish. As it was for Socrates, intellectual contemplation was important to Aristotle; it included the cultivation of wonder and curiosity about the world, which he felt should be part of education.

Can wonder be understood as a way of knowing? Should it be taught in schools? How can it help us to be happy? What could be its purpose?

Aristotle, like Socrates, believed that pleasures on their own did not result in happiness. Some pleasures may result in momentary satisfactions, but result in greater unhappiness or even distress. For example, we may consume alcohol in order to relieve our feelings of stress and while this may relieve some pressure momentarily and make us feel good in the short term, we will most likely feel worse the next day. This may propel us to drink more, which could result in an addiction. Addictions in whatever form (i.e., drinking, drugs, gambling, food, shopping) only bring momentary relief from distress while burdening budgets, friends, and family. Aristotle would argue here that what the person needs is to apply virtues so they become part of one's character, preventing addictions from forming in the first place.

Virtue, Aristotle argued, was a quality of the soul developed through the application of right reason and action.[30] Aristotle proposed that virtues were to be understood in terms of means, dispositions, and robust habits or characteristics.[31] We are not born with moral virtues, he argued, but rather develop these through *habits of correct thinking and action*.[32] Our virtues are

---

30. Stumpf, *Socrates to Sartre*, 108.
31. Younis, "Neuroscience, Virtues, Ethics, Compassion," 108–10.
32. Ibid.

important in building moral character. Aristotle believed that these virtues should be taught as part of a holistic education, focusing on the development of moral character.

A virtue is a character trait needed for *eudaimonia* to develop.[33] Moral virtues emerge through our actions as "we become just by doing moral acts."[34] These moral virtues include wisdom, courage, justice, temperance, self-respect, magnificence, liberality, and friendship. Broadly speaking, a virtue is understood as a disposition to act in a certain way between two means. As discussed in the Ethics chapter, Aristotle believed that virtues were found in the golden mean, a middle ground existing between two extreme emotions. For example, the virtuous act of courage would neither be one of unreasonable risk, or foolhardiness, nor an act of cowardice; it would exist between the two extremes. Moral education therefore should teach us how to act and feel *appropriate emotions*. Each should aim to become a balanced personality. Aristotle claimed that not only were our actions important in living a virtuous life, but he also considered external goods important. He argued that health, friends, and money, for example, provided a function that allowed us to exercise virtue and human flourishing. These were factors which helped contribute to a happy life, according to Aristotle:

> He is happy who lives in accordance with complete virtue and is sufficiently equipped with external goods, not for some chance period, but throughout a complete life.[35]

Student Activity: Video

1. Watch the following videos and take notes on Aristotle's views of happiness.

Video—Aristotle: Ethics Book 1—The Meaning of Life: Summary and Analysis[36]

Aristotle on "Flourishing." BBC[37]

---

33. Johnson and Reath, *Ethics*, 458.
34. Ibid., 110.
35. Aristotle, *Nicomachean Ethics*, 1100b27–1101a20.
36. https://www.youtube.com/watch?time_continue=5andv=fY3qNYFUaWM.
37. https://www.youtube.com/watch?v=j_7deRoidvs.

Philosophy—Aristotle. The School of life[38]

2. Outline the differences between hedonism and eudaimonia. These links may be useful: "What is Eudaimonia?"[39] and "Why happiness is an illusion and you should seek contentment instead."[40]
3. How do the ideas of Socrates and Aristotle on happiness compare?
4. Do you think virtue is a necessary component of happiness? Explain.

Friendship—what qualities make a good friend?

> ... The most salient characteristics shared by the 10% of students with the highest levels of happiness and the fewest signs of depression were their strong ties to friends and family and commitment to spending time with them....[41]

Aristotle emphasized friendship as an important component to a happy life. He thought we should dedicate time and energy to developing good friendships and believed that we are attracted to friends who have similar virtues or values. Friendship ensured a communal life as it connected us to others, according to Aristotle.[42] He distinguished three types of friendships: the first was based on utility or gain; the second, a short-term friendship based on pleasure; and the third being a deep, long-lasting friendship of mutual love and respect for one another.[43] The company of good friendships with similar values allowed one to experience both pleasure and develop virtue. The cultivation of good

---

38. https://www.youtube.com/watch?v=csIW4W_DYX4.
39. http://positivepsychology.org.uk/the-concept-of-eudaimonic-well-being/.
40. https://theconversation.com/happiness-is-an-illusion-heres-why-you-should-seek-contentment-instead-43709.
41. Hasson, *Happiness*, 171. See also Diener and Seligman, "Very Happy People," 81–84.
42. Vardy, *The Puzzle of Ethics*, 31.
43. Ibid., 261–65.

friendships was an important aspect that fostered a higher form of pleasure and the development of virtue, which led to a happy and fulfilling life.

Student Activity: Podcast

Listen to the following talk and take notes on Aristotle's view of friendship.

Mark Vernon—"Mark Vernon on Friendship."[44]

Student Activity: Excerpt

Read the extracts on friendship below and examine their main ideas. Compare and contrast the two accounts. Record your ideas and discuss them in pairs or in a group.

1. Aristotle on Friendship

   ... After what we have said, a discussion of friendship would naturally follow, since it is a virtue or implies virtue, and is besides most necessary with a view to living. For without friends no one would choose to live, though he had all other goods; even rich men and those in possession of office and of dominating power are thought to need friends most of all; for what is the use of such prosperity without the opportunity of beneficence, which is exercised chiefly and in its most laudable form towards friends?[45]

   The perfect form of friendship is that between the good, and those who resemble each other in virtue. For these friends wish each alike the other's good in respect of their goodness, and they are good in themselves; but it is those who wish the good of their friends for their friends' sake who are friends in the fullest sense, since they love each other for themselves and not accidentally. Hence the friendship of these lasts as long as they continue to be good; and virtue is a permanent quality...[46]

---

44. http://philosophybites.com/2007/12/mark-vernon-on.html.
45. Aristotle, *Nicomachean Ethics*, 1155a3–24.
46. Ibid., 1156b.

2. Anthony Grayling on *Friendship*

... And yet: like love, friendship is a matter far more of emotion than rational calculation. Indeed, if it is wholly or even largely the latter, we scarcely think that it merits the name.

Of course, there are considerations of mutual benefit, help, advantage and support implicit in the idea of friendship, but generally these are the sequelae of the engagement of emotion which constitutes friendship, rather than the motivations for it. For when these are indeed the motivations for one person to seek friendship with another we are instinctively suspicious; we talk of a person so befriended as "being used," of insincerity, untrustworthiness; we talk of false friendship, in which the seeming-relationship, and we can be cheered by the reflection that since we are very clear about when it is lacking, we should be somewhat clear about what it is. It cannot be hard to find the focus of the concept, even if what ranges away on all sides into variety and particularity covers much territory.

Nor is it too hard. Essential and fundamental to friendship is that it is a natural, spontaneous, freely given and entered into relationship promised as much on subliminal cues that prompt liking as on anything that the parties could specify as a reason for engaging in it. Such reasons would *ex post facto* doubtless abound: shared interests, attitudes, views, taste, style, appearance, behaviour, similarity in sense of humour, will figure largely. But we are reliably informed by students of human interaction that much, perhaps most, of the basis for our judgements about others is unconscious, and it might be that there are aspects of the complex network of factors underlying our choices of friends that we are never aware of—even so unexpected a thing as smell of the unrecognised similarity of appearance, tone of voice, or gesture, of people previously liked or admired. . . .[47]

Further resources on friendship:
Nicomachean Ethics by Aristotle

---

47. Grayling, *Friendship*, 3–4.

How do we find meaning and happiness? 295

Psychology Today: Aristotle on Friendship.[48]

STUDENT ACTIVITY—DEBATE, PRESENT,
OR WRITE ON ONE OF THE FOLLOWING:

1. Living a moral life makes people happy all the time, sometimes, or always.
2. Friendship is an important factor in a happy life.
3. Learning to be comfortable with solitude is vital for well-being and happiness.
4. Wealth, good looks, and talent are important for happiness.
5. The contemplation of ideas is the highest form of pleasure or happiness.

Stoicism

The Stoics not only think of virtue as the human good, but also have a highly distinctive view of that in which virtue consists: virtue is living in accordance with nature. Living in accordance with nature, in turn, requires coming to terms with what nature requires: nature itself is pervaded with *right reason* (*orthos logos*), which we must ascertain if we are to mould ourselves to nature's direction. This we wish to do, say the Stoics, because it is good for us; and they take it as beyond controversy that we all want what is good for us.[49]

Marcus Aurelius

What do you think this quote means?

48. https://www.psychologytoday.com/blog/hide-and-seek/201210/aristotle-friendship-0.

49. Shields, *The Ancient Philosophy*, 184 (emphasis in original).

The philosophical movement called Stoicism, founded by Zeno of Citium (334–262 BC) in Athens, did not agree with Epicurus that pleasure was the goal of happiness, for the Stoics thought, like Aristotle, that virtue led to a happy life.[50] To the Stoics, one could endure hardship and pain when living harmoniously with nature. Nature was understood as an unchanging condition directed by rational principles. The role of humans, they claimed, was to apply this universal reason to everyday life. The use of reason was important in achieving inner tranquility. The Stoics encouraged people to accept circumstances and their fate rationally.[51] Examples of Stoic thinkers include Epictetus (AD 50–130), Seneca (1 BC—AD 65), Marcus Aurelius (AD 129–201), and Cicero (106–43 BC).

Christopher Shields describes the main beliefs of the Stoics in the following ways:

1. Living according to virtue means living with the experience accorded by nature
2. The world is deterministic as cause and effect govern the universe
3. Fate determines that things will eventuate as they are intended
4. The universe is ordered by supreme rationality and individuals should model themselves by it
5. Reason should be used by individuals to control desires and passions in accordance with supreme reason[52]

Discussion questions

a. Analyze and discuss the five points described by Shields.
b. How did the Stoics understand virtue?
c. Is the world governed by cause and effect?
d. Do you think the universe is ordered by "supreme rationality?" If so, how can humans model themselves by it?

---

50. Ibid., 182–95.
51. Ibid.
52. Ibid.

To what extent is our attitude important for happiness?

> People are not troubled by things, but by their judgements *about* things.[53]

The Stoics often wrote about the importance of developing an attitude of indifference or nonattachment to the world. The Oxford Dictionary defines Stoicism as "The endurance of pain or hardship without the display of feelings and without complaint."[54] Epictetus illustrates that we must become indifferent to the external events that happen and not allow them to disturb or distress us.[55] Our attitude, or "convictions about things," can help us prevent especially unfavorable events from upsetting or disturbing us.[56] If we can change our thinking about unfavorable events and view them as part of fate, or the will of the gods, we may be better about accepting these situations and not suffer their effects:

> The school taught that virtue, the highest good, is based on knowledge; the wise live in harmony with the divine reason (also identified with fate and providence) that governs nature and are indifferent to the vicissitudes of fortune and to pleasure and pain.[57]

Individuals were encouraged to live a life of equanimity, developing a tranquil mind and resistance to the futility of negative emotions such as anxiety and fear. Destructive emotions were considered a disorder within reasoning. For the Stoics, living a life of virtue meant living in harmony with reason which was believed to be the divine order of the universe:

> Since all occurs by fate . . . if there were some human being who could see with his mind the interconnection of all causes, he would certainly never be deceived. For whoever grasps the causes of future things must necessarily grasp what the future will be. But since no one other than god can do this, it is left to

---

53. Epictetus, *Epictetus*, I, 1 (emphasis in original).
54. *Oxford Dictionaries*, s.v. "Stoicism." http://www.oxforddictionaries.com/definition/stoicism.
55. Epictetus, *Epictetus*, I, 1.
56. Ibid.
57. *Oxford Dictionaries*, s.v. "Stoicism." http://www.oxforddictionaries.com/definition/stoicism.

man he comes to know what will be by means of various signs which indicate what will occur in the future . . .[58]

To find out more about the Stoics, the following video may be a useful start: The School of Life, Philosophy—Plato[59]

Discussion questions

1. "It is not things themselves that disturb men, but their convictions about things." Do you agree? Explain.
2. Can a tranquil mind help us to be happy? Explain.
3. If events happen according to fate, what about free will?
4. Is focusing on the present moment good for us? Are there problems with this approach?
5. Do you think that nature is governed by rational principles? Discuss.
6. Are Stoic ideas relevant today? Give examples.
7. How possible is it in our modern world, with instant communication, immediate access to entertainment, and other distractions of technology available, to have a tranquil mind and reach equilibrium? Is it more difficult than in the past?

Student activity—Organize a philosophy conference: What is the understanding of happiness from some of our great thinkers of the past?

Organise a panel of important speakers who will discuss the nature of happiness. The panel includes the following figures: Socrates, Confucius, Aristotle, Epicurus, Menicus, al-Ghazali, Epictetus, or another relevant thinker.

- Form groups and research the works of these figures
- Select one or two people to represent your group on the panel.

---

58. Cicero, in Shields, *Ancient Philosophy*, 194.
59. https://www.youtube.com/watch?v=VDiyQub6vpw.

- Each of the chosen speakers will present to the class a summary of the main ideas in an eight-to-ten-minute presentation
- The class will then ask questions
- The group that responds most accurately to the questions wins
- The teacher and two to three students will adjudicate the presentations

The class will take notes as the speakers present their research on each of the figures above.

STUDENT REFLECTIONS

What are you now wondering about?

- What ideas, issues, and questions are you wondering about as a result of these lessons?
- Have these lessons made you think differently about certain ideas, issues, or questions? Why?
- What questions or ideas did you find interesting, challenging, or intriguing? Explain.

RELIGION ON MEANING AND HAPPINESS

Discussion questions

In pairs or groups discuss the following:

- How do each of the writings below define happiness? Compare and contrast the different claims.
- Do you agree with the claims about happiness? Give your reasons.

> ... we call pleasure the beginning and end of the blessed life.[60]

---

60. Epicurus, in Annas, *The Morality of Happiness*, 188.

Do not seek to have everything that happens as you wish but wish for everything to happen as it actually does happen, and your life will be serene.[61]

Our hearts are restless until they rest in thee.[62]

Blessed are the poor in spirit,
for theirs is the kingdom of heaven.
Blessed are those who mourn,
for they will be comforted.
Blessed are the meek,
for they will inherit the earth.
Blessed are those who hunger and thirst for righteousness,
for they will be filled.
Blessed are the merciful,
for they will be shown mercy.
Blessed are the pure in heart
for they will see God.
Blessed are the peacemakers,
for they will be called children of God.
Blessed are those who are persecuted because of righteousness,
for theirs is the kingdom of heaven.

Blessed are you when people insult you, persecute you and falsely say all kinds of evil against you because of me. Rejoice and be glad, because great is your reward in heaven, for in the same way they persecuted the prophets who were before you.[63]

Therefore, the Buddhist moral evaluation in terms of "skillful" and "un-skillful" is based on psychology, on a distinction made between positive mental dispositions which promote our happiness, on the one hand, and negative mental dispositions which lead to our suffering, on the other ... According to the Buddha: It is only when we have a mind under our own

---

61. Epictetus, *Epictetus*, 367.
62. Augustine, *Confessions of Saint Augustine*, 3.
63. Matt 5:3–12 (NIV).

control that we can be truly happy, not when we come under the control of our own mind.[64]

Does religion make us happy?

It's interesting to note though, that following *any* religion is one of the factors correlated with happiness. And studies show if you're religious you're less likely to be depressed, anxious and suicidal than nonreligious people. Chances are you also cope better with life crises such as illness and bereavement.[65]

Does religion provide happiness? There have been studies suggesting that religious people are generally happier than nonreligious people.[66] Brain scans of Buddhist monks, for example, have shown high levels of positive emotions and general well-being.[67] Social scientist Dr. Jeffery Martin has found that people who have spiritual experiences have a higher level of overall well-being.[68]

If the studies are even partially true, that religious people are happier than nonreligious people, what factors can we attribute to this? While the studies are not conclusive on this issue, some researchers have suggested that religious people often have a high level of social support networks which contribute to their well-being.[69] Others claim that the sense of meaning and purpose offered by religion is also a contributing factor.[70]

Buddhism and happiness

Buddhism is a religion originating in India and founded by Siddhartha Gautama (6th–4th century BC), a nobleman who was unsatisfied with his privileged life and abandoned it to find the source of happiness, according to many historical sources. He journeyed to

64. Karunadasa, "Pursuit of Happiness," 7, 9.
65. Graham, "Buddhism and Happiness," para. 36.
66. Cohen-Zada and Sander, "Religious Participation Versus Shopping."
67. Graham, "Buddhism and Happiness," para. 36.
68. Martin, *The God Formula*.
69. Cohen-Zada and Sander, "Religious Participation Versus Shopping," 890.
70. Graham, "Buddhism and Happiness."

numerous places in order to discover the truth about life and witnessed a significant amount of suffering. He concluded that the reason for suffering was due to an attachment and desire for wealth, power, pleasure, and prestige. Siddhartha thought that attachment to these life goals were problematic since they would either not be attained or eventually disappear, resulting in unhappiness. He believed attachment to earthly things, all of which are transient and temporary, as a source of happiness, leads to suffering once they are gone. For example, we can get sick, lose money or friends, and grow tired of possessions we once prized. While these used to bring us pleasure, they eventually leave us with only suffering in their absence. Even with earthly possessions, we live with the possibility of losing them in the future. Buddhist teachings state that a way of dealing with these attachments is through following the Five Precepts, Three Jewels, and the Eightfold Path, which includes a process of detachment to worldly desires through introspection that includes the training of the mind and meditation. With practice, the Buddhist learns to live in the world without attachment to it, by transforming suffering which leads to happiness. Such an attainment is described as enlightenment. Buddhism asserts that an enlightened follower will subsequently live a moral life and abstain from causing harm.

There are over 500 million Buddhists worldwide as Buddhism has grown significantly in Western countries. Also, there are many prominent authorities who continue to draw on this ancient tradition in order to explore happiness, including Thich Nhat Hanh, Matthieu Ricard, and the Dalai Lama.

Broadly speaking, most scholars would state that in Buddhism happiness has an immanent dimension, compared to a transcendent dimension like that evident in Christianity, as discussed in chapter 2.

The 14th Dalai Lama Tenzin Gyatso

The word "immanent" is understood as "remaining within."[71] In contrast, the term "transcendent," within religious writings, is a broad concept that points to the divine as beyond the world, rather than within it:

> Whatever living beings there may be—feeble or strong, long, stout, or of medium size, short, small, large, those seen or those

---

71. *Oxford Dictionaries*, s.v. "immanent," http://www.oxforddictionaries.com/definition/immanent.

unseen, those dwelling far or near, those who are born as well as those yet to be born—may all beings have happy minds."[72]

Student activity: Research

1. Read the following article, ABC Health Features: Buddhism and Happiness.[73] Summarise the research related on Buddhist meditation and its positive effects on happiness and well-being.
2. Watch the following video about a Buddhist monk's view on happiness and summarise the main ideas: Matthieu Ricard—"The Habits of Happiness."[74]
3. Review two of the key teachings in Buddhism—the Five Precepts, Three Jewels, and the Eightfold Path—and summarise the main ideas. How can these teachings help a person find happiness?

Christianity and happiness

... Man's ultimate happiness consists solely in the contemplation of God ... [75]

Christianity has allowed many to find meaning and happiness within its tradition. Its focus is derived essentially from the teachings of Jesus Christ (4 BC—AD 30) who often told stories and parables in order to convey his central ideas. However, unlike Buddhism, where the reliance is on the individual to find enlightenment by following its teachings and practices, Christianity places emphasis on a reliance of belief in God for happiness. Christian belief proposes that in order to be happy, one must ultimately find peace and connection with God. The understanding of God is both transcendent (beyond the world) and immanent (within the world):

> Happiness can't be bought. And when you buy happiness you realise that the happiness has gone ... The happiness that is

---

72. Keown, *Contemporary Buddhist Ethics*, 119.
73. http://www.abc.net.au/health/features/stories/2007/10/11/2054844.htm.
74. http://www.ted.com/talks/matthieu_ricard_on_the_habits_of_happiness.html.
75. Aquinas and Pegis, *Basic Writings*, 60.

bought does not last. Only the happiness of love is the one that lasts. And the path of love is simple: love God and love your neighbour, your brother, the one who is close to you, the one who needs love and needs so many things. "But father, how do I know if I love God?" Simply, if you love your neighbour, if you don't hate, if you don't have hatred in your heart, you love God. That is the certain proof.[76]

How does Pope Francis describe happiness?

As with Buddhism, Aristotle, and the Stoics, Christianity makes a connection between happiness and living a moral life. As we saw in the Beatitudes, the idea of living a moral life is synonymous with happiness. Although scholars debate the meaning of certain words within the Beatitudes, broadly speaking, these passages are understood as pointing to a connection between happiness, morality, and justice. Causing harm and living immorally would not bring the notion of Christian happiness or joy depicted in the text. Jesus, like Aristotle, understood that happiness was connected to morality and how we treat people. This is best exemplified through the commandment of love illustrated in the Gospels: "Love the Lord your God with all your heart and with all your soul and with all your mind and with all your strength. The second is this: love your neighbor as yourself. There is no commandment greater than these."[77] These pivotal biblical verses make a strong connection between the love of God and one's neighbor. As alluded to by Francis, if you claim that you are a Christian who loves God, you would equally need to also act lovingly and with compassion toward your neighbor. Likewise, in the Beatitudes we see Jesus offering comfort and happiness to those who do good acts. In doing so, they are comforted and receive mercy. Treating others with compassion leads to a connection with God, resulting in the Christian concept of happiness.

It is important to note that the term "neighbor" is not used necessarily to mean those we know within our immediate community, as Jesus indicates in other verses, such as his encounter with the Samaritan woman, who is a non-Jew. The challenge he poses is to extend our good acts to those beyond our own group:

> Jesus sought to broaden the definition of neighbor. Neighbors included your enemies. Love meant doing good for them (Matthew 5:44). His most comprehensive definition of

76. Francis, *Happiness in This Life*, 19.
77. Mark: 2:30–31 (NIV).

neighbor came in response to a lawyer's question, "Who is my neighbor?" (Luke 10:29). Jesus replied with the story of a man who had been beaten, robbed, and left to die. First, a priest went by and did nothing. Then, a Levite went by and did nothing. Finally, a foreigner (Samaritan) came and compassionately assisted the dying man, saving his life and making provisions for his immediate future (Luke 10:30–35). Two truths are found from the parable. First, a neighbor is any person we encounter who has any need. Since every person we encounter has a need of some kind, we can understand the term to include every person we encounter. Second, we are to *be* a neighbor. The question is not just "Who is my neighbor?" but also, "Am I being a neighbor?" Neighboring is done as we show mercy (Luke 10:37). Loving our neighbor is second in importance only to loving God (Matthew 25:35–39) and means more than all the offerings and sacrifices we could ever give (Mark 12:33).[78]

Can you think of the examples today of people who would be considered neighbors?

As we shall see further in the section on mysticism, many Christians also found happiness within a religious experience, which is an encounter with God in this life. St. Thomas Aquinas (1224–1274) argued that true happiness was found when he contemplated God. St. Augustine (354–430) claimed that the human heart is restless until it finds union with God. These mystical experiences were *transformative* and often resulted in a profound sense of joy. Examples of Christian mystics include Therese of Lisieux, Meister Eckhart, C. S. Lewis, Julian of Norwich, St. John of the Cross, St. Ignatius, and St. Benedict. There are many who continue to write about the Christian message as bringing good news and hope to the modern world. Some examples include Pope Francis, Rowan Williams, and Rob Bell.

Rowan Williams

---

78. Lain, "Neighbor," paras. 4–5 (emphasis in original).

Discussion Questions

1. What are your thought about what you have read above?

2. From the above readings, what are the components for happiness in Christianity? Are they feasible? Explain.

3. Do Christians and Buddhists have an obligation to accept asylum seekers and refugees into their communities? Explain.

Extension Question: Discuss the Following:

Christianity and Buddhism make distinctions between *immanent* and *transcendent* happiness. To what extent is happiness the same or different under these concepts?

Some dangers of seeking happiness in religion

The search for happiness in religion, ironically, can also lead to despair. Along with the multitude of religious believers worldwide who have found happiness in myriad religions and spiritual beliefs, some have travelled down fruitless—and sometimes sinister—paths with leaders, groups, and organizations that have promised some form of happiness, but have ultimately failed to deliver. Individuals have tried and rejected different religions, while some have become members of organizations others would consider cults.

A "cult" is defined as "A relatively small group of people having religious beliefs or practices regarded by others as strange or as imposing excessive control over members."[79] Groups with such tendencies usually offer a belief or lifestyle that appears as a form of happiness or salvation in order to attract members, and then engage in extreme practices of coercion to maintain power and control without fulfilling their promise.

Many cults have come and gone throughout history, but some have become infamous because of tragic endings. The Manson family of late-1960s Los Angeles consisted of many young teenage converts to the leader, Charles Manson, who convinced them to engage in brutal acts of murder.

---

79. *Oxford Dictionaries*, s.v. "cult," http://www.oxforddictionaries.com/definition/cult.

The People's Temple, an allegedly Christian sect, formed in San Francisco and eventually moved to the small South American country of Guyana to establish founder Jim Jones' vision of Utopia, but ended with the mass suicide of nearly 1,000 members. A current controversial group recognized as a religion by the US Government, Scientology, has been accused by many former members as having practices that fit the definition of a cult.

What personal needs do you think would drive a person to join a cult? If someone believes in a movement based on intuition and the experience turns bad, has intuition failed that person?

Student Activity: Written response

Research a cult and describe why people joined. Find testimony of those who survived and describe their experiences of how they ended up in dangerous situations.

Student Activity: Presentation

Choose either a philosopher or religious thinker and explore their ideas on happiness.

Include the following:

1. How do these thinkers view happiness?
2. Summarize their main ideas on happines.
3. Briefly describe their social and historical context
4. What is their particular or unique understanding of happiness?
5. To what extent are the ideas of happiness connected to living a moral life?
6. What are the strengths and limitations of their ideas?

Some suggestions include: The Buddha, Socrates, Confucius, Aristotle, Epicurus, Mencius, al-Ghazali, the Stoics (i.e., Epictetus, Cicero), Lao Tsu, Jesus, St. Thomas Aquinas, St. Augustine, Teresa of Avila, Thich Nhat Hanh, Matthieu Ricard, Dalai Lama, Thomas Merton, Pope Francis, Rowan Williams, and Rob Bell.

Record your findings and present them to the class.

PHILOSOPHY OF EMOTIONS: WHAT CAN THEY TELL US?

Discussion questions

1. To what extent can emotions reveal truths about ourselves and the world?
2. Are emotions a barrier to knowledge?
3. Do women experience emotions more than men? If so, what does this mean?
4. To what extent can emotions make us happy?

The Scream by Edward Munch

Student activity: role-play

An alien from another planet arrives on Earth. The alien does not possess emotions. One student plays the role of the alien and must ask questions of another student about emotions, who then has to explain.

How can we understand emotions?

Excitement, grief, contentment, frustration, sadness, loneliness, euphoria—the exhaustive list of words describing human emotions barely represents the complexity of this critical human trait. We know from our own experiences and observing others that emotions are an integral part of human experience. Emotions can be positive, leading us to enjoy life, experience pleasure, and have passion for our work. Through the emotion of empathy, we are better equipped to relate with others.

As discussed in the critical thinking section, emotions can also cloud our judgement and at times lead to prejudices and false assumptions. Emotions arise in response to external events such as death, disappointment, and selfishness. Such negative emotions are seemingly natural responses to certain events. There are also emotions, classified as moods, which do not always have an obvious cause. However, counsellors generally agree that negative emotions become problematic and can detract from happiness when their frequency and duration is excessive and disproportionate. In this case, help to release them can be sought.

Psychologists have pointed out some primary emotions, such as happiness, sadness, fear, anger, surprise, and disgust.[80] The term "emotions" here will be used in the broad sense to include feelings, passions, and moods. Intuition can also be understood as a type of feeling, but will not be explored here as it is discussed in chapter 1.

So, what role do emotions play in achieving happiness? Are emotions an opportunity for revealing insights into how we achieve this goal or are they a hindrance? How do emotions connect with reason, beliefs, morals, and our physical bodies? Are our emotions a reliable indicator of happiness? Answering these complex and broad questions definitively is a difficult task; however, below are some responses.

Do our emotions reside in our bodies?

> Our natural way of thinking... is that the mental perception of some fact excites the mental affection called the emotion, and that this latter state of mind gives rise to the bodily expression. My thesis, on the contrary, is that the bodily changes follow directly the perception of the exciting fact, and that our feeling of the same changes as they occur IS the emotion.... We feel sorry because we cry, angry because we strike, afraid because we tremble.[81]

What do you think the above is saying about emotions?

---

80. de Sousa, *Emotion*, 3.
81. Solomon and Higgins, *Big Questions*, 192.

There are studies that suggest emotions are connected to bodily functions.[82] The James-Lange Theory proposes that emotions are caused by physical sensations.[83] This theory claims that there is a close relationship between our primary emotions and our bodies.[84] It argues that emotions are feelings which are caused by a physiological reaction.[85] For example, stress can be evident in physical symptoms such as aches and pains. Bodily changes may cause certain emotions, such as stomach cramps, leading to feelings of irritability or anxiousness. Dr. Esther Sternberg also claims there is a strong connection between our emotions and bodies that is not fully resolved and needs further research:

> Every minute of the day and night we feel thousands of sensations that might trigger a positive emotion such as happiness, or a negative emotion such as sadness, or no emotion at all: a trace of perfume, a light touch, a fleeting shadow, a strain of music. And there are thousands of physiological responses, such as palpitations or sweating, that can equally accompany positive emotions such as love, or negative emotions such as fear, or can happen without any emotional tinge at all. What makes these sensory inputs and physiological outputs emotions is the charge that gets added to them somehow, somewhere in our brains. Emotions in their fullest sense comprise all of these components. Each can lead into the black box and produce an emotional experience, or something in the black box can lead out to an emotional response that seems to come from nowhere . . .[86]

> Rather than seeing the psyche as the source of such illnesses, we are discovering that while feelings don't directly cause or cure disease, the biological mechanisms underlying them may cause or contribute to disease . . . The questions need to be rephrased, therefore, to ask which of the many components that work together to create emotions also affect that other constellation of biological events, immune responses, which come together to fight or to cause disease. Rather than asking

---

82. de Sousa, *Emotion*, 3, 5, 10, 12, 27.
83. Colman, *Dictionary of Psychology*, 396.
84. Ibid., 7.
85. Ibid.
86. Sternberg, *The Balance Within*, 32.

if depressing thoughts can cause an illness of the body, we need to ask what the molecules and nerve pathways are that cause depressing thoughts. And then we need to ask whether these affect the cells and molecules that cause disease.[87]

What are Sternberg's claims?

Similarly, American philosopher Robert Nozick (1938–2002) describes emotions as not only containing cognitive, but also physiological dimensions. He argues that emotions are very present in our bodies and proposes that they can provide a point of integration between our minds and physical selves.[88]

Discussion questions

1. What is the relationship between our feelings and our body? Do some emotions emerge in bodily symptoms?
2. Do our emotions affect the body or does the body create emotions?
3. Was there a time when you felt happy or unhappy when you were hugged? Or you were ill and felt miserable? Does this tell you something about how emotions are connected to the mind and body?

Are emotions and thoughts connected?

"The heart has its reasons of which reason knows nothing."[89]

What does Pascal mean in this quote? Do you agree?

There has been neurological research to suggest links between emotions and cognition. Antonio Damasio found that victims of accidents that impaired their emotional responses through their brain cortices were

---

87. Ibid., 13–14.
88. Nozick, *Examined life*, 91.
89. Pascal, *Pensées*, 78.

hindered in their ability to show adequate rational thought processes.[90] Their intellectual abilities were affected by the lack of emotional responses. There is also neurological research pointing to connections in the brain between affective and cognitive parts mediated by empathy.[91] These studies have suggested the importance of empathy and compassion in our cognitive and thinking processes. Howard Gardner, for example, talks about "empathic intelligence"[92] linking empathy to a range of thinking skills such as logic.

Read the passage and answer the questions below.

> ... Empathy has a primary role in brain function and thus survival, involving extensive interplay between affective and cognitive regions of the brain ... If nature and nurture work in concert, innate precipitators are likely to be present to activate the nurturing desire for an empathic response (Gerdes and Segal, 2011). Motivation, drive, creativity, imagination, and reflective/reflexive processes act to prod the subject to move into empathy and would be activated in certain activity (Erez and Isen, 2002; Gerdes and Segal, 2011; Kasapi and Mihiotis, 2014; Lachmann, 2008; Yaniv, 2012). Affirming the nature/nurture connection, studies have shown significance for increased perspective—taking and empathic concern (altruistic compassion) when watching films (Gerdes, Segal, Jackson, and Mullins, 2011; Martin et al., 2015). Additionally, reading fiction has resulted in significant transformation in empathic fantasy development (Bal and Veltkamp, 2013). Empathy, as more than simply promoting compassion, aids in increasing intelligence (Dearing and Steadman, 2009; Gardner, 2006). Gardner (2006) connected empathic intelligence/wisdom to interpersonal, intrapersonal, logic, kinetic, linguistic, spatial, and naturalistic experience. As an example, Gardner (2006) identified musical intelligence as a valuable empathy outcome.[93]

---

90. de Sousa, *Emotion*, 32–33.
91. Van Cleave, "Contributions of Neuroscience," 369–89.
92. Ibid.
93. Ibid., 369–70.

HOW DO WE FIND MEANING AND HAPPINESS?

DISCUSSION QUESTIONS

1. What does the following mean: "Empathy, as more than simply promoting compassion, aids in increasing intelligence?"
2. According to the study, how can empathy increase intelligence?

Philosophers on emotions and reason

Some philosophers like Plato, Aristotle, and Kant thought our emotions needed to be in check with our reason. That is, we must not allow emotions to have autonomy over reason. Plato did not exclude emotions, instead claiming that in order to gain harmony, reason must rule over courage and passion.[94] Aristotle described emotions as the irrational appetites and desires that needed to be controlled by reason. The Stoic philosophers believed that we should become indifferent toward emotions in order to live a life of equilibrium.[95] A tranquil mind, free of emotional attachments, to Stoics, leads to happiness and attaining the good life.[96] British philosopher David Hume recognized the power of our emotions, claiming that they directed our reasoning.

The influence of emotions on beliefs

> ... the emotions ... are *about* something ... they have an object ...
>
> Emotions are not *about* their objects merely in the sense of being pointed at them and let go, the way an arrow is let go against its target. Their aboutness is more internal, and embodies a way of seeing ... these emotions, embody not simply ways of seeing an object, but beliefs—often very complex—about the object.[97]

What do you think the above quote means?

---

94. Nozick, *Examined Life*, 18.
95. de Sousa, "Emotion," 32–33.
96. Aurelius, *Meditations*.
97. Nussbaum, *Upheavals of Thought*, 27–28 (emphasis in original).

American philosopher Martha Nussbaum argues that emotions have a cognitive dimension that includes thinking as part of a complex belief system, describing them as "ways of seeing."[98] She argues emotions can inform us of important truths, signifying what is of value and important to us.[99] Robert Nozick describes emotions as having a structure composed of three parts: a belief, an evaluation, and a feeling.[100] Nozick states that emotions are an internal psychological response to values, describing them as providing a representation of values.[101] For example, when we grieve over the loss of someone, this emotion can tell us how much we valued that person. Alternatively, our anger toward an issue or person can also indicate the underlying value which caused our reaction; if you are angry at someone for lying, cheating, or acting unfairly, this indicates *your values* for honesty and fairness. From Nussbaum's and Nozick's descriptions, emotions can help us understand and make sense of our values and beliefs.

Beliefs about the world can generate emotion. For example, a person may feel disappointment when a friend fails to show up at an arranged outing, concluding that the friend does not like them or is unreliable, only to find out later the friend was in an accident. When finding out the friend had a legitimate reason for not showing up, the person should no longer feel disappointed since his or her understanding of the situation has changed. This example suggests our emotions are connected to beliefs about events and people. We may also say that an emotion which more *correctly reflects* a situation is *more rational* than one which does not. In the previous example, to feel upset and disappointed with the friend for not showing up to the planned event is a reasonable emotional response, but to continue feeling disappointed when knowing she had been in a car accident would be considered irrational. In other words, the feeling cannot be justified. There are many instances of emotions which are *disproportionate* to events, such as the fear of harmless spiders, cockroaches, or flying in an airplane; while people may feel great anxiety and fear toward these, the risk of actual harm is minimal and therefore disproportionate to the actual event.

Discussion questions

1. Has there been a time when you felt angry toward someone for doing something you

98. Ibid., 27–28.
99. Ibid.
100. Nozick, *Examined life*, 91.
101. Ibid., 53.

thought was unjust? What was unjust about it? What personal value did it violate? For example, was it about honesty, justice, or integrity?

2. Can you think of a time when you or someone you know reacted to an event in which the emotions were *disproportionate* to the event? Explain.

3. Do you agree with Nussbaum and Nozick that emotions reveal values?

STUDENT ACTIVITY—PODCAST: LISTEN TO SABINE DÖRING, "SABINE DÖRING ON EMOTION,"[102] AND ANSWER THE FOLLOWING QUESTIONS:

1. How does Sabine Döring define emotions?
2. What are the differences between emotions and moods?
3. What role do emotions have in our understanding of the world (e.g., evaluative, morals, learning)?
4. To what extent can we understand the world without emotions? Discuss.
5. What questions does this discussion raise?

Emotions and attachments

Many researchers have observed the various ways in which emotions emerge from life's circumstances. Emotions emerge due to an attachment and interaction with an object outside oneself, including a person or situation. For example, I may feel a sense of gratitude when a friend helps me find my lost keys. It is this situation and the relationship with my friend from which my feeling of gratitude emerges. However, this then leads us to the question about emotions which do not seem related to an obvious object or circumstance, such as melancholy or sadness. How do we describe these emotions? Many researchers have classified these as moods that are different from feelings and are not always directly attached to an object outside oneself.

Did you have a time when you were sad or felt low, but didn't really know why?

102. http://philosophybites.com/2009/08/sabine-d%C3%B6ring-on-emotion.html.

Emotions—cultural and social influences

Many scholars studying emotions suggest that culture and society have an influencing factor.[103] How we react and feel about certain issues such as love, morality, and grief, for example, are largely affected by our society and culture.[104] To illustrate, we see various expressions of grief and mourning in different cultures, from strictly sombre occasions to celebrations. Arranged marriages in some countries are acceptable yet Western societies look down on them, suggesting differing values and beliefs about love and commitment.

Can you think of other examples? How much of our beliefs and emotions are the by-product of social and cultural factors?

Moral decisions and emotions

Emotions can influence moral decisions. We can often make moral decisions based on our emotions. The Stoics argued that emotional maturity which involved an equanimity of the mind was conducive to living a moral life. Martha Nussbaum argues that emotions can educate us about certain moral decisions.[105] She, like many others, including Iris Murdoch (1919–1999) and Azar Nafisi, argues that the arts—and, particularly, good literature—provide tools for "educating our emotions."[106]

The arts can also allow us to understand and view life from an outlook other than our own. In presenting to us a broader perspective, it may allow us to better understand a range of human issues and dilemmas. The arts can engage our emotions, for example, through good stories in which we are able to "feel with" characters and understand their situations and dilemmas. In doing so, we are potentially more capable of treating others with greater insight, compassion, and fairness:

> I would include the arising of emotion in the definition of art, although not every occasion of experiencing art is an emotional occasion . . .[107]

---

103. de Sousa, "Emotion," 14.
104. Ibid., 19, 34–35.
105. Ibid., 38.
106. Ibid. See also Murdock, *Existentialists and Mystics,* and Nafisi, *Republic of Imagination.*
107. Murdoch, *Existentialists and Mystics,* 10.

Of course, good literature does not look like "analysis" because what the imagination produces is sensuous, fused, reified, mysterious, ambiguous, particular. Art is cognition in another mode. Think how much thought, how much truth, a Shakespeare play contains, or a great novel.[108]

A poem, play or novel usually appears as a closed pattern. But it is also open in so far as it refers to a reality beyond itself, and such a reference raises the questions about truth . . . [109]

Discussion questions

1. What do you think Murdoch means by the following claim, "Art is cognition in another mode?"[110]

2. According to Murdoch, how does art raise questions about truth? Can you think of examples?

3. Nussbaum suggests that good literature develops empathy. Do you agree? If so, can you think of examples?

4. To what extent do you think we make moral decisions based on emotions? Provide examples from your own experiences.

Student activity — Research

1. Select a culture and research how grief, love, or morality related to a certain issue is understood.

2. Choose a piece of art (i.e., book, poem, painting, song). Did it engage your emotions? What did it teach you? Did it help you develop a sense of empathy? If so, how?

Record your findings and present these ideas to the class.

---

108. Ibid., 11.
109. Ibid., 25.
110. Ibid., 11.

To what extent do unconscious emotions influence thought?

Sigmund Freud

Sigmund Freud (1856–1939) is known as the founder of psychoanalysis. This is a type of therapy which works in uncovering unconscious memories and emotions directly with patients. As discussed in chapter 3, what Freud introduced to the modern world was the idea that our thoughts may not be totally independent and free from emotions and traumas.

Building on philosophical explorations of the unconscious by German philosophers such as Franz Brentano (1838–1917), Arthur Schopenhauer (1788–1860), and Friedrich Nietzsche (1844–1900), Freud argued that there are emotions of which we are not fully aware in our consciousness influencing our ideas and actions. He observed many people who were highly distressed and understood their conditions to be the result of traumatic experiences in their childhoods. He attempted, with therapy, to make clients aware of these experiences by bringing them to the conscious mind. Freud viewed the unconscious as holding childhood memories which could influence our desires, emotions, and attitudes during the present, resulting in internal conflicts. Many argue that Freud's work was a breakthrough in understanding the underlying cause of severe mental illnesses. He also raised our awareness of the possibility that *nonrational factors can influence our thinking.* Many modern theorists such as John Bowlby (1907–1990), a researcher on attachment theory, have drawn on Freud's initial insights about the influence of the unconscious to mental life.[111]

---

111. de Sousa, "Emotion," 23.

What can emotions tell us?

In this brief discussion, emotion's connection to our bodies, thoughts, beliefs, culture, morals, and the unconscious has shown to be a complex issue, leaving us with more questions than answers. However, we can relate to situations when our emotions have deceived us or let us down. We might have lost our temper, or have become irritated or angry at a friend and later regretted it. Conversely, emotions can also bring us joy and happiness, a fundamental part of human experience. The provocative film *Equilibrium* depicts a society which prohibits the expression of emotions and all forms of art. The film shows a bleak world as the characters struggle to keep their emotions at bay. What the characters learn in the end is that the expression of emotions is a vital component to their humanity and happiness. Samuel Coleridge (1772–1821) wrote, "Deep thinking is attainable only by a man of deep feeling,"[112] suggesting that our emotions, despite their complexities and ambivalences, remain an influential way of knowing.

Student activity—Videos

Watch the following videos and answer the questions below:

1. Alain de Botton: What is Emotional Intelligence?[113]

    How does de Botton describe emotions?

    What is emotional education?

2. Watch "Daniel Coleman Introduces Emotional Intelligence"[114]

    How does Coleman define emotional intelligence?

    According to Coleman, what are the advantages of emotional intelligence?

3. Kris Girrell "How We've Been Misled by 'Emotional Intelligence.'"[115]

    How does Kris describe grief as emotional intelligence that allows us to develop empathy and compassion?

---

112. Coleridge, *Letters*, 2:709.
113. https://www.youtube.com/watch?v=LgUCyWhJf6s.
114. https://www.youtube.com/watch?v=Y7m9eNoB3NU.
115. https://www.youtube.com/watch?v=6l8yPt8S2gE.

Extension activity—Research

Research an Eastern or Western philosopher, artist, psychologist, neuroscientist, or feminist—for example, Sigmund Freud, Martha Nussbaum, or Daniel Coleman.

1. What is their definition of emotions? You may focus on the topic of emotions in general or select an emotion such as love, desire, grief, anger, wonder, or empathy.
2. How is emotion (or type of emotion) understood and described by this thinker?
3. To what extent are emotions connected or separate from reasoning? Discuss.

Record your findings and/or present them to the class.

Student activity—Debate:

Emotions provide an important tool in understanding the world and gaining knowledge.

STUDENT REFLECTIONS

What are you now wondering about?

1. What ideas, issues, and questions are you wondering about as a result of these lessons?
2. Have these lessons made you think differently about certain ideas, issues, or questions? Why?
3. What questions or ideas did you find interesting, challenging, or intriguing? Explain.

PSYCHOLOGY AND COUNSELLING ON HAPPINESS AND MEANING

DISCUSSION QUESTIONS

Which way of knowing is best able to make us happy?

Is it reason, logic, emotions, intuition, imagination, faith, or a combination of these? Explain.

This brings us to the next topic: How do we understand the nature of happiness and well-being? What are some obstacles? Philosophers, artists, theologians, and psychologists have attempted to address these questions. In response, we will briefly touch on counselling, existentialism, art, and religious mysticism as various approaches in responding to meaning and happiness.

Are happy people less reflective and generous?

Dr. June Gruber's research on happiness has revealed interesting insights. Her studies suggest that happy people are not always the most generous—nor are they necessarily the deepest thinkers.

Watch the following presentation and answer the questions below: Video Lecture on Happiness—Dr. June Gruber.[116]

What do you think of Dr. Gruber's suggestions? To what extent are happy people not always the most generous or reflective thinkers? Do you think this could be true?

REFLECTION QUESTIONS

1. Is it possible to be happy all of the time? To what extent can *expecting* to be happy be counterproductive?
2. Can we know real joy or happiness without feeling its opposite, i.e., sadness? Give examples.

---

116. https://www.youtube.com/watch?v=eB3cwLtO9UQ

3. How can we approach uncomfortable, difficult, and negative emotions such as sadness, grief, depression, anger, and frustration?

4. Have there been times in your own life (or in the life of someone you know) where you experienced negative emotions and were able to move past them? *How* did you do this? Did you learn something useful? Write about this time.

DEPRESSION AS AN OPPORTUNITY FOR GROWTH

Dr. Neel Burton is a psychiatrist, philosopher, and writer who argues that some of our negative moods, such as depression, should not be viewed as limitations, but rather opportunities for reflection, self-knowledge, and personal growth.

For more on Dr. Neel Burton you may watch the following video: The Anatomy of Melancholy—can depression be good for you?[117]

Or read the following article: "What Is Depression?" In *Psychology Today*.[118]

Existential counselling—Finding meaning

> ... man's main concern is not to gain pleasure or to avoid pain but rather to see a meaning in his life ... [119]

Victor Frankl (1905–1997), a professor of neurology and psychiatry, as well as a holocaust survivor who spent three years in Auschwitz and Dachau, offers some wisdom in how to deal with suffering. Frankl argues that we should eliminate suffering if we can because in itself, suffering is not desirable. However, he states that sometimes suffering is inevitable. Frankl argues that we can transform and endure suffering when we have a meaning for it, stating that he who has a meaning to live for *can tolerate almost any suffering*.[120]

Frankl observed, both in his work as a therapist and in his reflections on his own experience in concentration camps, that the main ingredients for finding happiness are found in directing our lives to someone or

---

117. https://www.youtube.com/watch?v=ndsB37KUAs0.
118. https://www.psychologytoday.com/blog/hide-and-seek/201701/what-is-depression.
119. Frankl, *Man's Search for Ultimate Meaning*, 117.
120. Ibid., 109.

something *other than oneself*.[121] In giving ourselves in this way, he argues, we are actualizing our human potential.[122] Frankl attributes the reasons for crime, depression, and addiction to a lack of meaning and purpose in life. He states that there are three components in attaining meaning:

1. creating meaningful work
2. experiencing someone or something outside oneself (e.g., beauty, goodness, nature, culture) or the experience of another person through loving them
3. attitude adopted toward unavoidable suffering[123]

> For success, like happiness, cannot be pursued; it must ensure, and it only does so as the unintended side effects of one's dedication to a cause greater than oneself or as the by-product of one's surrender to a person other than oneself. Happiness must happen, and the same holds for success; you have to let it happen by not caring about it.[124]

STUDENT ACTIVITY—DEBATE THE FOLLOWING:

Happiness is a by-product of one's surrender to another person or to a cause greater than themselves.

Psychology on well-being

Psychologists today often talk about well-being in reference to happiness. Well-being is generally understood as pertaining to that which is essentially good for a person.[125] The research on factors leading to well-being, broadly speaking, is often attributed to the following factors:

a. Good relationships
b. Positive self-esteem and self-regard
c. Optimistic thinking

121. Ibid., 115.
122. Ibid.
123. Ibid.
124. Ibid., 12.
125. Haybron, "Happiness," 1–3.

d. Setting goals

e. A meaningful purpose in life[126]

What do you understand by these terms? Explain.
Can you add something else?
Is "well-being" an adequate term for happiness? Explain.

Counselling

Counselling (also referred to as therapy) includes a range of strategies and approaches that deal with negative thoughts and emotions which can cause unhappiness. One common therapeutic approach is called Cognitive Behavioral Therapy (CBT), a technique that challenges our counterproductive thinking. The aim is to foster positive changes in how we feel and subsequently affect our behavior in a more positive manner. For example, the fact that you did not get selected by a particular soccer team is not necessarily a reflection on your skills; there could be a range of factors which prevented you from being selected, such as the number of new players needed or the inexperience of the coach. To *assume* that because you did not get chosen for the team you are a failure at soccer, or in life generally, is a *false assumption and generalization*.

These types of thought processes are an example of generalizations and negative thinking. The way CBT could help is by challenging thoughts and assumptions about such situations. For example, CBT may assist in creating counterclaims, like identifying the range of skills and hidden talents such as writing, music, or chess, which may challenge the claim of "being a failure."

How is the example above evidence of a generalization or negative thinking? Explain. Can you think of another similar example?

CBT can help us become aware of our unhelpful thoughts which may cause anxiety and sadness if not addressed, leading to depression. Empirical research has shown CBT to be effective in dealing with difficult psychological states, such as depression, and is now commonly used in counselling.

STUDENT ACTIVITY: VIDEO

Watch the following videos on CBT and answer the following questions:

---

126. Seligman, *Flourish*, 24. Daniel Haybron's research on happiness has identified the above factors as significant, and has also added the importance of security and autonomy. See Haybron, *Happiness*, 54.

1. CBT: Cognitive Therapy and The Thinking/Feeling Connection[127]

   Describe the ABC model which discusses the connections between our thoughts and feelings and how they affect our moods.

2. Cognitive Behavioral Therapy (CBT) Simply Explained.[128]

   What are some of the similarities between CBT and Stoic philosophy. For more information on CBT, you may watch the following:

   a. What is CBT? | Making Sense of Cognitive Behavioural Therapy.[129]

   b. Case study clinical example CBT: First session with a client with symptoms of depression (CBT model).[130]

   c. Accoding to Stoicism, how does one approach obstacles? How is this a similar approach to CBT?

3. Can you think of examples in your own life when you use one or more of the following thought processes such as "catastrophizing," generalizations, "mindreading" and "should" statements?

How did this make you feel? Were you able to become aware of these negative thoughts?

Did you talk to someone about these?

Perhaps explore these ideas in a journal. Writing down thoughts and emotions can be an effective way of resolving difficult and challenging feelings and worries.

---

127. https://www.youtube.com/watch?v=c2yFVdfs_88.
128. https://www.youtube.com/watch?v=WhMmZJ3H1E8.
129. https://www.youtube.com/watch?v=7LD8iC4NqXM.
130. https://www.youtube.com/watch?v=7LD8iC4NqXM.

Positive Psychology

Years of research on the psychology of well-being have demonstrated that human beings are often happiest when they are engaged in meaningful pursuits and virtuous activities.[131]

In recent years, well-being researchers have distinguished between eudaimonic happiness (e.g., meaning and purpose; taking part in activities that allow for the actualization of one's skills, talents, and potential) and hedonic happiness (e.g., high frequencies of positive affect, low frequencies of negative affect, and evaluating life as satisfying).[132]

What does the above quote say about factors which lead to happiness?

American psychologist Martin Seligman has completed a significant amount of research on positive psychology, which has become a popular approach in the West. He defines positive psychology as not just about hedonistic pleasures, but—similar to Aristotle and the existential approach mentioned—about a life that is meaningful and develops human flourishing. He claims that by focusing on individual strengths, virtues, and meaning, people can learn to be happy. Similar to the ancient Greeks, Seligman understood that the concept of human flourishing goes beyond the fleeting pleasures of life to one aimed at purpose and utilizing personal strengths for the greater good. It also includes a life of developing virtues.

Positive psychology not only challenges negative thoughts, as CBT also does, but directly uses a strength-based approach through optimistic and positive reinforcement. It claims that by applying these diligently and over time, people can see positive changes in their lives. Positive psychology attempts to identify individual strengths, set goals, and focus on the future. In *Authentic Happiness*, Seligman identifies three main components to happiness: The Pleasant Life, The Good Life, and The Meaningful Life.[133]

The Pleasant Life is one that increases the most amount of pleasures. Seligman's research shows that fleeting pleasures are a significant factor for gaining happiness, yet on their own do not give people lasting satisfaction.[134] For example, he identifies spending time with friends as more satisfying than the fleeting pleasures of buying new clothes or eating lots of

---

131. Kashdan et al., "Reconsidering Happiness," 230.
132. Ibid., 1.
133. Seligman, *Authentic Happiness*.
134. Ibid., 61.

sweets. Seligman argues that meaning and engagement in a person's life are factors which result in more lasting gratification and a sense of fulfilment than just pleasure.

Can you think of a time you were so engaged and absorbed in an activity that you lost track of time and place? What does the experience tell you?

> Use your signature strengths and virtues in the service of something much larger than you are.[135]

Seligman defines an engaged life as one not just of pleasure, but rather absorption. It is absorption in an activity (i.e., work or a hobby) where a person is in what he terms "the flow," so engaged that time stops and is similar to the state of eudaimonia discussed by Aristotle. This level of engagement facilitates living the good life. Seligman proposes that people need to know their personal or, what he termed, "signature strength" in order to commit to something or someone outside oneself in creating "The Meaningful Life."[136]

Seligman's Meaningful Life

> The meaningful life has one additional feature: using your signature strengths in the service of something larger than you are. To live all three lives is to lead a full life.[137]

Seligman defines the meaningful life as one which focuses on the person's strengths and uses these to the benefit of the wider community. He argues that someone living a meaningful life may still experience feelings of depression yet manage to function and continue their meaningful life.[138] He also argues that while positive emotions are important for happiness, they are not always a reliable factor in evaluating fulfillment. As an example, Abraham Lincoln's positive contribution to others and society (which is a focus on something greater and outside himself), for Seligman, would be defined as a meaningful and fulfilled life despite the presence of negative moods he experienced.[139]

The development of positive relationships and the achievement of goals are also significant factors leading to well-being. Seligman, like Aristotle, understands happiness in the broad sense, encompassing a whole life.

135. Ibid., 263.
136. Kashdan et al., "Reconsidering Happiness," 61.
137. Seligman, *Authentic Happiness*, 249.
138. Seligman, *Flourish*, 51–55.
139. Ibid.

It is a life that is meaningful, not just because it is pleasurable or feels good, but rather because a person engages in activities that use their gifts and strengths, makes a commitment to something or someone outside oneself, sets goals, and develops positive relationships with people.[140]

> [Positive Psychology] takes you through the countryside of pleasure and gratification, up into the high country of strength and virtue, and finally to the peaks of lasting fulfillment: meaning and purpose.[141]

Student Activity—Habits of happy people

1. Researchers in Positive Psychology have found that apart from living a meaningful life, absorption in an activity, and harnessing our personal strengths, people who are happiest generally demonstrate the following factors: gratitude, optimistic thinking, enthusiasm toward life, curiosity, and an ability to love and be loved.[142]

What do you understand by the terms above? Explain each of the terms in one to two sentences.

2. Complete the happiness quiz at the Pursuit of Happiness.[143] You may discuss the results with your partner. What did you find interesting and why?

Student activity—Personal strengths

Complete this survey at www.authentichappiness.org.

Discuss the findings of the survey with your partner. Think about ways that you may incorporate your strengths in your life, such as at home or school.

---

140. Seligman, *Authentic Happiness*, 61.
141. Ibid.
142. Kashdan et al., "Reconsidering Happiness."
143. http://www.pursuit-of-happiness.org/science-of-happiness/happiness-quiz/.

How do we find meaning and happiness? 329

Student activity—Gratitude and positive thinking

In the book *Flourishing*, Seligman describes the process of asking his students and clients at the end of each day to write down three events that went well and *why* they think they went well.[144]

The aim, he argues, is that people move away from focusing on what is *not working* in their lives to *what is* working. Seligman found this simple exercise of gratitude resulted in positive changes in thinking and reported levels of well-being and happiness.[145]

You may want to try this yourself:

1. Each evening, write down three things that went well and the reasons why. For example, perhaps you enjoyed a friend's birthday party as you danced most of the night or spent time with a close friend who was a good listener—even more simply, activities such as a nice meal or completing tasks.

   Do this exercise for at least four weeks and see if there is a change in your feelings, mood, or outlook on life. If there is, you could continue this practice of gratitude each evening.

2. Ask another family member or friend to also do this exercise and compare your experiences.

Nations in the West may be wealthier, but are they happier?

Research has shown that an increase in money for those already living above the poverty line does not result in an increase in their level of happiness.[146] Psychologists have also found that lottery winners may experience a surge of initial pleasure and yet, within a year, return to their "base level" of happiness before their win.[147] Martin Seligman claims that despite the increase in wealth (which is measured by a term called Gross Domestic Product [GDP]) in Western countries, these nations are not happier. Seligman states that nations like the US have seen dramatic increases in depression over the last fifty years, with the levels of life satisfaction failing to increase with the rise of wealth. What Seligman proposes is that policy makers should find ways of increasing people's well-being—a measurable indicator, according

---

144. Seligman, *Authentic Happiness*, 33.
145. Ibid., 33–35.
146. Brickman et al., "Lottery Winners and Accident Victims."
147. Ibid.

to Seligman—within a society so that all may flourish. Ways of increasing people's happiness, meaning, relationships, and goals, he argues, fosters a more democratic nation as they provide opportunities for *all* citizens to flourish and live to their potential.

> Gross domestic product measures the volume of goods and services which are produced and consumed, and any events that increase that volume increase the GDP. It does not matter if those events happen to decrease the quality of life. Every time there is a divorce, the GDP goes up. Every time two automobiles collide the GDP goes up . . . GDP is blind when it comes to whether it is human suffering or human thriving that increases the volume of goods and services . . . Life satisfaction in the United States has been flat for fifty years even though GDP has tripled.
>
> Even scarier, measures of ill-being have not declined as gross domestic product has increased; they have gotten much worse. Depression rates have increased tenfold over the last fifty years in the United States. This is true of every wealthy nation, and, importantly, it is not true of poor nations. Rates of anxiety have also risen. Social connectedness in our nation has dropped, with declining levels of trust in other people and in governmental institutions, and trust is a major predictor of well-being.[148]

For further research on Martin Seligman, this video may be a useful start: "The New Era of Positive Psychology."[149]

Discussion questions

1. What are some similarities between Victor Frankl's existentialism and positive psychology?
2. Do you agree with Seligman that judging feelings on their own in assessing happiness is limited? Can you give examples?

---

148. Seligman, *Flourish*, 223.
149. https://www.ted.com/talks/martin_seligman_on_the_state_of_psychology.

3. To what extent do you think that developing positive emotions, engagement, healthy relationships, personal meaning, and achievement lead to improved well-being?
4. Is a nation's increase in wealth (or GDP) necessarily an accurate measure of its success? Explain.
5. If Seligman's beliefs on happiness are true, what implications does this have on government policies and religious responses? Should government and religious leaders be concerned about improving people's level of well-being and happiness? Why?
6. Can you think of counterarguments to Seligman's claims?

Student Extension: Role-play an interview

Set up an interview between Martin Seligman and Aristotle. Your questions will aim to find out what each person thinks are ingredients to a happy life, identifying similarities and differences.

Is happiness in the mind or does it depend on social and economic factors?

English psychoanalyst David Morgan, in counselling a range of clients over many years, came to the conclusion that the causes of unhappiness are mostly linked to economic factors. The focus on financial success and the neoliberal approach to governance, he argues, is making people sick. Morgan states that the economic pressures placed on many are leading to mental health issues.[150] He claims money and economic thinking often take priority over the quality of life, alienating people from core human value systems.[151] Morgan states that rather than creating a caring society, we have instead created a consumer one in which everything is based on financial security.[152] As a result, we have a growing gap between rich and poor. The wealthy, Morgan claims, are also riddled with anxiety, since they rely on unstable economic market forces.[153] Society structured purely around economics, he argues, provides a weak foundation for a healthy community.

150. Morgan, "Is Neo-Liberalism Making Us Sick?"
151. Ibid.
152. Ibid.
153. Ibid.

STUDENT ACTIVITY: RESEARCH

For further research on David Morgan, you may listen to this link:

"Is Neo-liberalism Making Us Sick?"[154]

1. Can economic pressures make people unhappy? How?
2. What other claims does Morgan make about whistle-blowers or truth tellers?
3. Can unstable market forces lead to a sense of anxiety within society? If so, what are some ways to address this problem?

Technology and well-being

1. Define technology and give examples.
2. What are some positive and negative influences of technology in modern life today?
3. How has technology influenced the way we live today?

Technology, the practical application of scientific knowledge, has existed well before our current advent of global positioning, cell phones, and Google searches, all of which keep the world instantly interconnected. However, new devices and processes that affect our everyday lives are continuing to change at an unprecedented rate, outpacing our ability to sufficiently study and reflect on their effects on us as humans. We have the ability to make interpersonal connections worldwide, access art and entertainment by previously unknown creators, as well as purchase goods and services once controlled by only a handful of corporations. Yet we are now more vulnerable to con artists and predators, face an increase in questionable sources of information and news, and are engaging in less face-to-face interaction. Is our ability to invent and improve through technology a short-term gain of brief satisfaction at the cost of long-term discontent? Does technology make us happy?

---

154. http://www.abc.net.au/radionational/programs/breakfast/is-neo-liberalism-making-us-sick/7993190.

Increased distraction diminishes quality of work

An article in the Association for Psychological Science reviews a study identifying the constant interruptions by smartphones and their effects on work production.[155]

> Plenty of research has shown that distractions cause people to take longer to complete a task, but now a team of psychological scientists from George Mason University has found that interruptions don't just take up time, they also degrade the overall quality of people's work. "No participant scored higher when interrupted compared to the no-interruption condition, in either experiment. Nearly everyone who was interrupted did worse. In fact, 96 percent of the participants performed worse, and 4 percent stayed the same.[156]

Interruptions are just one negative result of constant connection through technology, but they directly affect everyday life for just about everyone in societies where smartphones are prevalent. Another negative result is overuse of the internet, which some researchers are suggesting is resulting in mental health issues such as depression, anxiety, and addiction.[157]

Student Activity

Read the following quotes and answer the questions below:

Exploring Internet Addiction

> . . . As the Internet continues to become an integral aspect of daily life, and as people devote increasing amounts of time to Internet use, there is potential for overuse and misuse. Suggested negative outcomes of Internet overuse include addiction, social isolation, poor interpersonal relations, family instability, and low academic performance (Flisher, 2010; Kelleci and Inal, 2010; Liberatore, Rosario, Colon-De Marti, and

---

155. Association for Psychological Science, "Even Small Distractions Derail Productivity."
156. Ibid., paras. 2, 12.
157. Snyder et al., "There's A New Addiction."

Martinez, 2011). Furthermore, excessive Internet use has been linked to psychiatric symptoms such as insomnia (Cheung and Wong, 2011), depression (Cheung and Wong, 2011; Jang, Hwang, and Choi, 2008; van Rooij, Schoenmakers, Vermulst, van den Eijnden, and Van De Mheen, 2011), obsessive-compulsiveness (Jang et al., 2008; Kelleci and Inal, 2010), anxiety and interpersonal sensitivity (Kelleci and Inal, 2010).[158]

Social media and well-being

THE INTERNET PROVIDES a new communication medium that enables access to unlimited resources of information across various topics. On the other hand, heavy Internet use has been associated with potential detrimental side-effects. In general, adolescents have been found to spend more time on the Internet than adults, predisposing themselves to Internet addiction. Serious problems associated with Internet addiction among adolescents include refusal to attend school and mental health problems, such as loneliness, low self-esteem, insufficient sleep, anxiety and depression. Students who spend more time playing computer games and using the Internet spend less time sleeping and experience higher levels of tiredness. Like other addictions, Internet addiction disrupts studies, school life, and other aspects in the daily life of an individual adolescent.[159]

DISCUSSION QUESTIONS

1. According to the studies above, what are some factors which contribute to the negative psychological consequences of internet use?

2. Can you think of counterarguments to the claims above?

---

158. Carlisle et al., "Exploring Internet Addiction," 171.
159. Kawabe et al., "Internet Addiction," 405.

3. If it is true that social media is affecting our well-being, what could be some measures to address this problem?

Student Activity: Role-Play

Role-play an addict of technology and an older person whose use of technology is limited. How might their actions and interactions differ?

Reflection after the role-play: What does this reveal about the patterns that play out in addiction?

If we take the claims made earlier in the chapter that healthy relationships with family and friends are a major factor contributing to our well-being and happiness, we must then ask whether technology has helped or hindered us in developing our relationships with other people. Despite it providing us with new methods of connecting socially, some researchers suggest that, ironically, technology has led to feelings of loneliness and isolation.[160] If the studies above are even partly true, demonstrating worldwide the negative effects of social media on well-being, how do we make sense of this and *who* is responsible for addressing this issue?

On the positive side of technology, we live in a world with opportunities and ways of connecting never before afforded us. Positive psychologist Amy Blankson states, "I encourage you to avoid the road of the tech doomsday-sayers, because I don't see that it is truly possible for us to eliminate technology and I don't think we should have to eliminate technology to find happiness."[161] According to Blankson, studies indicate over half of email users have better relationships with both friends and family members. Over 22 percent of individuals are married to, engaged to, or living with someone they initially met through an internet-based platform, with equivalent success as those who meet through more traditional methods.[162]

> . . . Tech is not a toxin that we need to flush out of our systems—it's a tool. And it's a tool that we must learn to wield effectively.[163]

So, while social media provides us the ability to connect with people, perhaps a more important question to ask is what is the *quality of these connections?* Can the *physical presence* of the other ever be replaced by social media? The successful relationships mentioned above were only through

---

160. Kormas et al., "Risk Factors and Psychosocial Characteristics".
161. Blankson, *The Future of Happiness*, 123.
162. Ibid., 45.
163. Ibid., 144.

digital connections for the initial contact that led to face-to-face, real-world relationships.

Are we expecting social media to do more than it is capable of? As discussed in the Ethics chapter, many have argued that effective listening and empathy are important in forming quality relationships leading to well-being. Should we expect social media to fulfill this role? The rapid growth of social media is perhaps telling us more about *our own needs* as individuals and as a community collectively. What is it that *we are seeking* from technology (or social media) and has it fulfilled those needs? Do we ask these important questions individually or collectively? Are we informed consumers?

> Today's media do enable us to communicate and to share our knowledge and affections. Yet at times they also shield us from direct contact with the pain, the fears and the joys of others and the complexity of their personal experiences. For this reason, we should be concerned that, alongside the exciting possibilities offered by these media, a deep and melancholic dissatisfaction with interpersonal relations, or a harmful sense of isolation, can also arise.[164]

What does Pope Francis say about the effects of social media? Do you agree?

> ... technology has become a field of ultimate and thus of religious concern: to know or not to know in the manner promoted by technology, to be or not to be the being that technology is making of us: this now is a real and urgent question for thinking as well as for political, economic, and environmental policy-making. Yet if one asks, how then can these questions *not* demand the most serious attention of Christian thinkers...[165]

What do you understand by the above quote?

---

164. Francis, "Laudato Si," para. 47.
165. Pattison, *Thinking about God*, 4 (emphasis in original).

Martin Heidegger

German philosopher Martin Heidegger (1889–1976), as seen in chapter 2, wrote extensively about a range of topics, including epistemology, science, art, and technology. He critiqued technology, which he predicted would dominate Western culture:

> The power concealed in modern technology determines the relation of man to that which exists. It rules the whole earth.[166]

Although Heidegger never experienced the mobile phone or laptop the premise of his logic remains the same. He argued that we must be in control of technology rather than *it in control of us*.[167] Heidegger was not completely opposed to technology and thought that it had its practical uses and benefits. However, what concerned him was the areas of influences it would pervade, which he found problematic. He thought that technology would affect our mental and emotional landscapes, which would have negative consequences. He argued it could potentially impact our way of thinking and being in the world if we were not aware it. Heidegger claimed technology could have the capacity to estrange us from our deepest self or *essence*.[168] In other words, Heidegger thought that the unquestioning use of technology actually hindered us from being fully human:

---

166. Heidegger, *Discourse on Thinking*, 50.
167. Ibid., 53–54.
168. Wheeler, *Martin Heidegger*.

> In truth, however, precisely nowhere does man today any longer encounter himself, i.e., his essence.[169]

> It would be foolish to attack technology blindly ... We depend on technical devices; they even challenge us to greater advances. But suddenly and unaware we find ourselves so firmly shackled to these technical devices that we fall bondage to them ... We can use technical devices as they ought to be used, and also let them alone as something which does not affect our inner and real core.[170]

Heidegger's claims about technology are connected to his understanding of thinking (or epistemology). As discussed in chapter 2, Heidegger distinguishes between two types of thinking: *meditative* and *calculative*. Meditative thinking, he argued, is one which is more closely linked to our being or essence.[171] Calculative thinking is evident in the domain of quantitative measurement, logic, and research, and is used mostly within the sciences. This type of thinking does not help us understand our deepest selves or essence; only meditative thinking does. On the other hand, meditative thinking is slow, reflective, and open-ended, encompassing not just our thinking, but our whole being—a type of thinking that is primarily compatible toward the arts, our intuition, and emotions. Heidegger argued that while calculative thinking has its place in the world of research and serves practical applications in a range of areas, it should not dominate our way of being in the world, nor should it replace meditative thinking:

> Thinking is not so much an act as a way of living or dwelling ... It is a gathering and focusing of our *whole selves* on what lies before us and a taking to heart and mind these particular things before us in order to discover in them their essential nature and truth.[172]

Discussion questions

1. Does the increased use of technology hinder meditative thinking? How?

169. Heidegger, *Basic Writings*, 332.
170. Heidegger, *Discourse on Thinking*, 53–54
171. Heidegger, *What Is Called Thinking?*
172. Gray, "Preface," xi (emphasis added).

2. Can a scientist use meditative thinking, as described by Heidegger?
3. What do you think of Heidegger's critique of technology? Are his ideas relevant today?

Student Activity: Essay

Write an appraisal of Heidegger's critique of technology.

Student Activity: Debate

The increased growth of technology in modern society has contributed to the good life.

STUDENT REFLECTIONS

What are you now wondering about?

1. What ideas, issues, and questions are you wondering about as a result of these lessons?
2. Have these lessons made you think differently about certain ideas, issues, or questions? Why?
3. What questions or ideas did you find interesting, challenging, or intriguing? Explain.

EXISTENTIALISM AND THE ARTS— A PATH TO MEANING

> ... man first of all exists, encounters himself, surges up in the world—and defines himself afterwards. If man as the existentialist sees him is not definable, it is because to begin with he is nothing. He will not be anything until later, and then he will be what he makes of himself.[173]

---

173. Sartre, *Existentialism and Humanism*, 28.

What do you think this passage means? Do you agree with the French philosopher Jean-Paul Sartre's claims?

Existentialists discussed the importance of living courageously and making decisions which reflect a person's authenticity or *true self*. To be authentic can be understood as being true to oneself. It can be defined in the following terms: "true to one's own personality, spirit, or character,"[174] or "relating to or denoting an emotionally appropriate, significant, purposive, and responsible mode of human life."[175]

What do you think it means to be authentic or true to yourself? Can you give examples?

Existentialists claim that what gives meaning to people's lives is their freedom and choice. Social and political factors which hinder human freedoms and choice are often criticised by existentialists. They reject the traditional philosophical and systematic approach to knowledge, proposing an alternative that considers a more spontaneous expression focusing on the importance of subjective knowledge.[176] For existentialists, "truth" is not just an objective reality found in abstract concepts, but rather a *lived one*. Many existentialists also view the arts as significant in revealing truth. As discussed in chapter 1, there were existentialists who sought to find meaning and authenticity within a religious framework, such as Kierkegaard and Jaspers. There were also existentialists who rejected religion, claiming that it was an impediment to personal freedom and authenticity; they included Nietzsche, Sartre, and Simone De Beauvoir (1908–1986). As discussed in chapter 2, the philosophical movement of existentialism attempts to examine the conditions related to human existence.

---

174. "Authentic," https://www.merriam-webster.com/dictionary/authentic.

175. *Oxford Dictionaries*, s.v. "authentic," http://www.oxforddictionaries.com/definition/authentic.

176. Stumpf, *Socrates to Sartre*, 455.

Student Activity: Excerpt

Read the following, summarize, and answer the questions below. This article from the Philosophy Now website may be useful: "A Student's Guide to Jean-Paul Sartre's Existentialism and Humanism."[177]

Existentialism and Human Nature by Dr Lewis R. Gordon

Existentialists, including this author, reject the notion of "human nature." We reject it on the grounds that human beings live in a world of possibility. This means whatever human beings claim to be, what we will become is always in the making. Whatever we "are" belongs to the dried up ground or ashes of the dead.

Nature, when applied to human beings, is an essentialist notion. By "essentialist," it means what we are and will be are closed and determined. To know a human being would then mean to know his or her essence. The essence is that which makes something what it is no matter what else is introduced. Knowing human essence would be enough to know what human beings—*any human being*—will do by virtue of what they *are*. Studying human beings would then be no different than studying any other animal, plant, or material object of nature.

The classic objection, formulated by the French existential philosopher Jean-Paul Sartre, is that in the human world exists *prior* to its essence. For each human being, essence is *in the making*. Such a task does not mean that human beings are not placed. It doesn't mean we lack biographies, families, communities, and, biologically speaking, are not made of flesh, blood, and bone. Everyone has to start from somewhere, and that or those are conditions of possibility for a human world.

Existentialists often prefer to speak or write of human condition or *conditions* for these reasons. What human beings produce from these conditions are ways of life in and through which human beings emerge *as human*. Responsible for producing ourselves, human beings are "free."

---

177. https://philosophynow.org/issues/15/A_students_guide_to_Jean-Paul_Sartres_Existentialism_and_Humanism.

Human beings produce human worlds, whether good or bad. Such worlds offer a network of relationships through which many other things are produced. The most significant of these "things" is meaning. The question thus becomes not what human beings are but what does "human being" *mean*.

Some existentialists are critical of this line of reasoning. Ironically, Martin Heidegger, the most famous German existentialist, objected to the *human* element of this argument. In his "Letter on Humanism," he criticized Sartre for what he claimed was subordinating "Being" or Absolute Reality to human being. There are ways of being or living other than being human.

Although Heidegger has a point, other existentialists such as I have argued Sartre's argument is not that meaning *can only emerge* from human beings. We just know that we live in a world of meaning, and each response we make to that is saturated with meaning.

The world human beings live in is one of meaning that produces culture, which is a source of producing more meanings. Though cultural production is, as far as we know, a human activity, a more radical understanding of culture raises the question of the human being as the producer of *an open reality*.

Another name for culture is "human reality." It is the condition in which thought for human beings takes place. Where the human being is the subject of the thought, there is the paradox of a subject that reaches beyond its subjection. We human beings transcend—that is, go beyond—ourselves when we pose ourselves as an object of study.

What does this mean if not that human beings are open instead of closed subjects?

The etymology—that is, the history or origins—of the word *existence* already points to these elements. From the Latin *ex* ("out") *sistere* ("to stand"), it means to stand out, to emerge, or to appear.

Existence, then, stands out and against invisibility or submergence. In the stream of effects through which the human world appears, much is brought into being through the creative and at times alchemic force of human thought and deed. To stand out, emerge, or appear brings with it a profound realization, since we do so to ourselves. Doing so raises the question of how each of our actions is a form of appearance pointing back to us as the source.

We arrive, then, at an important element of existential thought. Existentialism is a philosophy of freedom because in producing the human world, human beings are responsible for it.

How much are we responsible? The "we" is crucial here. It means the human world. If we bring into appearance our responsibility, it means we are also responsible for that. In existential thought, responsibility is a radical idea. It frightens many people to the point of their attempting to flee it.

We come now to an important insight in existential philosophy. If human beings are free—*really free*—then we are free to attempt to evade our freedom. If we couldn't do so, we would not be free. Thus, whenever we meet people trying to lie to themselves, trying to deny responsibility for their actions, claiming they are not free, we are in fact encountering manifestations of freedom. We are equally responsible for attempting to flee our freedom as we are for embracing it.[178]

Questions:

1. Why do many existentialists reject the notion of human nature? Explain.
2. What do existentialists mean by "essence?" What does it mean that a human being's existence precedes her or his essence?
3. Why is existentialism described as a philosophy of freedom?
4. What does it mean to live a free and authentic life?
5. To what extent are existential ideas relevant today?
6. What could be some limitations of existentialism?[179]

---

178. Gordon, "Existentialists and Human Nature," 1–3 (emphasis in original).
179. Ibid.

How can art help us understand ourselves and the world?

DISCUSSION QUESTIONS

1. Aristotle viewed the arts as having an important role in conveying knowledge and, in particular, pointing to the truth. Truth for Aristotle was termed and understood as the highest Good or Universal. Can art tell us the truth? If so, what kind of truth? Explain.

2. Does art make you happy? Why? Give examples.

3. Engage in some art form; listen to a song or composition, read an excerpt from a book or play, watch a film or dance. How did it make you feel? Did you learn something from it?

The benefits of the arts in education

Researchers have shown there are positive outcomes for students who engage in the arts (e.g. drama, dance, drawing, etc.). These benefits include developing a range of skills where students demonstrate engagement in learning, a greater level of communication and thinking skills, and overall self-esteem.[180]

For further information on this research, watch the following video and read the following article:

Video: "ACARA—Arts Participation and Students' Academic Outcomes."[181]

"The Benefits of Music Education" by Laura Lewis Brown.[182]

Perspectives on art and its connection to personal meaning

Many of the existential philosophers considered the arts as significant in creating a meaningful and authentic life as well as a vehicle for truth. Art

---

180. Martin et al., "Role of Arts Participation," 709–27. See also Liem et al., "Role of Arts-related Information," 348–63.
181. https://www.youtube.com/watch?v=9ebEQpRJK14andfeature=youtu.be.
182. http://www.pbs.org/parents/education/music-Arts/the-benefits-of-music-education/.

not only could be appreciated by others, but allowed artists to also *develop themselves*. Hence, it is in the creation of the artwork that personal meaning emerges. Artists also challenge societal norms and values which do not help individuals live an authentic life. Some have argued that art facilitates the development of moral character by educating us in moral issues. Art can also engage us in multiple ways of knowing, such as emotion, intuition, imagination, and reason from both secular and religious perspectives. As discussed in chapter 1, religious existentialists such as Jaspers and Weil viewed the arts as significant in understanding God.

Plato and Darwin on the arts

As we saw in chapter 1, Plato believed in the importance of reason. Yet Plato wrote about the significance of music and thought that this was an important part of an education for a young person. He gave the following reasons:

> Musical training is a more potent instrument than any other, because rhythm and harmony find their way into the inward places of the soul, on which they mightily fasten, imparting grace, and making the soul of him who is rightly educated graceful ... and also because he who has received this true education of the inner being will most shrewdly perceive omissions or faults in art and nature, and with a true taste, while he praises and rejoices over and receives into his soul the good, and becomes noble and good, will justly blame and hate the bad, now in the days of his youth, even before he is able to know the reason why; and when reason comes he will recognize and salute the friend with whom his education has made him long familiar.[183]

Likewise, the famous naturalist Charles Darwin (1809–1882), during his last years of life, identified an emotional part of our nature which, he

183. Plato, *Republic* (1937), 401–2.

argued, needed to be developed through music and poetry. He stated that neglecting our emotions is detrimental to the mind:

> My mind seems to have become a kind of machine for grinding general laws out of large collections of facts, but why this should have caused the atrophy of that part of the brain alone, on which the higher tastes depend, I cannot conceive . . . If I had to live my life again, I would have made a rule to read some poetry and listen to some music at least once every week; for perhaps the parts of my brain now atrophied would thus have been kept active through use. The loss of these tastes is a loss of happiness, and may possibly be injurious to the intellect, and more probably to the moral character, by enfeebling the emotional part of our nature.[184]

According to Plato and Darwin, why are the arts and emotions important?

The arts and self-knowledge

Many artists and existentialists understood the arts as provoking self-knowledge. The arts in their various forms can reveal the processes within our interior lives, such as our inner thoughts, feelings, and imagination, what we term our subjective experiences. David Malouf, a contemporary Australian author, writes the following:

> What else should our lives be but a continual series of beginnings, of painful settings out into the unknown, pushing off from the edges of consciousness into the mystery of what we have not yet become, except in dreams that blow in from out there, bearing the fragrance of islands we have not yet sighted in our waking hours, as in voyaging sometimes the first blossoming branches of our next landfall come bumping against the keel, even in the dark, whole days before the real land rises to meet us. . . . It is that that drives us on to what we must finally become. We have only to conceive of the possibilities and somehow the spirit works in us to make it actual. This is the true meaning of transformation. This is the real

---

184. Darwin, *Life and Letters*, 81–82.

metamorphosis. Our further selves are contained within us, as the leaves and blossoms are in the tree. We only have to find the spring and release it. Such changes are slow beyond imagination. They take generations. But it works, this process.[185]

How does Malouf describe the process of transformation that can occur within a person's life?

Iris Murdoch (1919-1999), a British moral philosopher and novelist, says the following about art, and, in particular, literature:

> I think good art is good for people precisely because it is not fantasy but imagination. It breaks the grip of our own dull fantasy life and stirs us to the effort of true vision. Most of the time we fail to see the the big wide real world at all because we are blinded by obsession, anxiety, envy, resentment, fear. We make a small personal world in which we remain closed. Great art is liberating, it enables us to see and take pleasure in what is not ourselves. Literature stirs and satisfies our curiosity, it interests us in other people and other scenes, and helps us be tolerant and generous. Art is informative and even mediocre art can tell us something, for instance about how other people live. But to say this is not to hold a utilitarian or didactic view of art. Art is larger than such narrow ideas. Plato at least saw how tremendously important art is and he raised interesting questions about it. Philosophers on the whole have not written very well about art, partly because they have regarded it as a minor matter which must be fitted in with their general theory of metaphysics or morals.[186]

Iranian-born writer professor Azar Nafisi comments on the inner self and its relation to the arts:

> That inner self is what makes it possible for private individuals to become responsible citizens . . . linking their own good to that of their society . . . For this they need to know, to pause, to think, to question . . . how can we protect ourselves from a culture of manipulation, where tastes and flavors are re-created

---

185. Malouf, *Imaginary Life*, 135-36, 64.
186. Murdoch, *Existentialists and Mystics*, 14-15.

chemically in laboratories . . . we need the pristine beauty of truth as revealed to us in fiction, poetry, music and the arts: we need to retrieve the third eye of the imagination.[187]

1. According to Murdock and Nafisi, why are the arts important? Explain.
2. Compare and contrast the two accounts above.
3. What do you think of Murdock's claim that "Literature stirs and satisfies our curiosity, it interests us in other people and other scenes..."[188] Give examples.
4. Can you think of counterclaims?

The arts and moral development

As mentioned earlier, some philosophers have understood the arts as important to moral development. The arts can allow us to view and understand life from a different perspective than our own. In presenting to us a viewpoint in a medium separate from everyday experience, it may allow us to better understand a range of human issues, dilemmas, and emotions. Through quality stories and films, for example, we can empathize with the situations and dilemmas of their characters:

> By literature, I mean literature in the normative sense, the sense in which literature incarnates and defends high standards. By society, I mean society in the normative sense, too—which suggests that a great writer of fiction, by writing truthfully about the society in which she or he lives, cannot help but evoke (if only by their absence) the better standards of justice and of truthfulness that we have the right (some would say the duty) to militate for in the necessarily imperfect societies in which we live. Obviously, I think of the writer of novels and stories and plays as a moral agent . . . This doesn't entail moralizing in any direct or crude sense. Serious fiction writers think about moral problems practically. They tell stories. They narrate. They evoke our common humanity in narratives with which we can identify, even though the lives may

---

187. Nafisi, *Republic of Imagination*, 17.
188. Murdoch, *Existentialists and Mystics*, 14–15.

be remote from our own. They stimulate our imagination. The stories they tell enlarge and complicate—and, therefore, improve—our sympathies. They educate our capacity for moral judgement.[189]

According to Susan Sontag's statement above, what does it mean to "educate our capacity for moral judgement?"

What are some counterarguments to Sontag's claim?

Art and the divine

Algerian-French philosopher Albert Camus (1913–1960) discussed the importance of the arts. He explored the existential drive which motivates people in seeking out the arts:

> Thus I draw from the absurd three consequences which are my revolt, my freedom and my passion. . . . When Nietzsche writes: "It clearly seems that the chief thing in heaven and on earth is to *obey* at length and in a single direction: in the long run there results something for which it is worth the trouble of living on this earth as for example, virtue, art, music, the dance, reason, the mind—something that transfigures, something delicate, mad or divine."[190]

What do you think of Camus' intense passion for meaning sought through "virtue, art, music, the dance, reason, the mind—something that transfigures, something delicate, mad or divine?"

American historian and philosopher John Herman Randall (1899–1980) argued that religious symbols are useful in helping us understand our own experiences and the world around us. He stated that these symbols are likened to the way the arts also help us make sense of and find meaning in the world and to find the divine:

> The work of the painter, the musician, the poet, teaches us how to use our eyes, our ears, our minds, and our feelings with greater power and skill . . . It shows us how to discern unsuspected qualities in the world encountered, latent powers and possibilities there resident. Still more, it makes us see the new

---

189. Sontag, "Truth of Fiction," paras. 12–14.
190. Camus, in MacDonald, *Existentialist Reader*, 181.

qualities with which the world in cooperation with the spirit of man, can clothe itself . . . Is it otherwise with the prophet and the saint? They too can do something to us, they too can effect changes in us and in our world . . . They teach us how to see what man's life in the world is, and what it might be. They teach us how to discern what human nature can make out of its natural conditions and materials . . . They make us receptive to qualities of the world encountered; and they open our hearts to the new qualities with which that world, in co-operation with the spirit of man, can clothe itself. They enable us to see and feel the religious dimension of our world better, the "order of splendour" and of man's experience in and with it. They teach us how to find the Divine; they show us visions of God.[191]

Do you agree with the comparison made by Randall between the arts and religion? What does he mean by the arts showing us "how to find the Divine?" Explain.

Throughout human history, the arts have inspired humans in a number of ways. They do this by not only engaging our reason, but also our emotion and imagination. The arts provide self-knowledge through introspection (i.e., access to inner thoughts and feelings) and can potentially help us in our moral development. Good literature and stories, for example, can allow us to develop empathy. The arts, as Murdock points out, open up a world beyond our own and in doing so *broaden our perspectives and views.*

Student activity:

1. Why do the arts appear among thinkers from different backgrounds and perspectives, as shown above?
2. What are some differences and similarities between the role of arts to religion.

Student Activity—Research:

Select a well-known artwork. It can be one from below or a well-known verse from literature, a painting, or a piece of music. Your teacher may guide you here.

---

191. Randall, *Role of Knowledge*, 114.

In groups, research and answer the questions below.

Pablo Picasso's *Guernica*.

For an in-depth discussion about Guernica's social impact, listen to BBC: In Our Time—Picasso's Guernica.[192]

Michelangelo's *The Creation of Adam*

---

192. http://www.bbc.co.uk/programmes/b09bxkdm.

352 INQUIRY INTO PHILOSOPHICAL AND RELIGIOUS ISSUES

An Experiment on a Bird in the Air Pump by Joseph Wright "of Derby"

STUDENT REFLECTION QUESTIONS:

1. What messages or themes does the work convey?
2. To what extent are these significant messages or themes? Explain.
3. How does the artwork help us understand another person's experiences, historical events, or the divine? How does it achieve this?
4. Does the artist's intent in how the art is perceived by the viewer matter?
5. Are there cultural issues raised?
6. What are some implications of the artwork to the wider community?
7. To what extent is the theme or message of the artwork universal and relevant to all cultures?
8. What did the artwork teach you?
9. How did this work engage your emotions, senses, imagination, and thinking?

10. Did the artwork help you develop a sense of empathy? If so, how? Explain.

Deliver your presentation to class and record your findings.

Student Activity—Research Task

Explore existentialist ideas through the work of either a philosopher or an artist. Research their main ideas in relation to one or two of the following issues:

- Human nature
- Human freedom, choice, and responsibility
- Anxiety
- Death

Some suggested questions to follow include:

1. What are the social and cultural contexts of the writings?
2. How are the main terms defined?
3. How did the philosopher and artist explore the main ideas?
4. To what extent are the arguments convincing?
5. Are there wider implications to their work? Are they relevant today?
6. What are some limitations to their work?
7. How did this work engage your emotions, senses, imagination, and thinking?
8. What did the artwork teach you?
9. Did the artwork help you develop a sense of empathy? If so, how?
10. What did you find most interesting or intriguing about their work? Explain.

Some examples

Michelangelo, Leonardo Da Vinci, William Shakespeare, William James, Fyodor Dostoevsky, Søren Kierkegaard, Friedrich Nietzsche, Karl Jaspers, Martin Heidegger, Maurice Merleau-Ponty, Paul Tillich, Martin Buber, Gabriel Marcel, Jean-Paul Sartre, Albert Camus, Simone De Beauvoir, Simone

Weil, W. H. Auden, Victor Frankl, Henri Bergson, Jacob Bohme, Blaise Pascal, John Keats, Marcel Proust, Samuel Beckett, J. D. Salinger.

Record your findings and present them to the class.

STUDENT ACTIVITY—DEBATE

The arts play an important role in a happy society.

PERSONAL EXPERIENCES AND MYSTICISM AS A WAY TO FIND MEANING AND HAPPINESS

Can our senses tell us the truth? An inquiry into mindfulness

How many of us can actually claim to be present right now? Are you really focused on what you are reading or is your mind distracted with other thoughts? Maybe you are thinking about what you will be doing the next hour or next week. Perhaps your phone is distracting you. These are important questions to ask since we know attention is important for learning and relating meaningfully to others, as we discussed in chapter 3.

How can we become more present?

> A typical meditation consists of focusing your full attention on your breath as it flows in and out of your body ... Focusing on each breath in this way allows you to observe your thoughts as they arise in your mind and, little by little, to let go of struggling with them. You come to realise that thoughts come and go of their own accord; that *you* are not your thoughts. You can watch as they appear in your mind, seemingly from thin air, and watch again as they disappear, like a soap bubble busting. You come to the profound understanding that thoughts and feelings (including negative ones) are transient. They

come and go, and ultimately, you have a choice about whether to act on them or not.

Mindfulness is about observation without criticism; being compassionate with yourself. When unhappiness or stress hover overhead, rather than taking it all personally, you learn to treat them as if they were black clouds in the sky and you observe them with a friendly curiosity as they drift past. In essence, mindfulness allows you to catch negative thought patterns before they tip you into a downward spiral. It begins the process of putting you back in control of your life.[193]

As illustrated above, the practice of mindfulness teaches people the skill of how to *be in the present moment*. It does this by teaching practices which aim to encourage an awareness of breathing, thinking, emotions, and bodily sensations. The aim of these practices is to move away from preoccupations and from overthinking, particularly thoughts related to worry and anxieties. Mindfulness encourages a movement away from the emphasis of analysis within the mind, to an embodying of the *senses* and our physical body. Its practices encourage the skills of *awareness of the mind* and its thought process. The aim is a greater control over thinking, especially negative thoughts and worries:

> Over time, mindfulness brings long term changes in mood and levels of happiness and well-being. Scientific studies show that mindfulness not only prevents depression, but that it also positively affects the brain patterns underlying day-to-day anxiety, stress, depression and irritability so that when they arise, they dissolve away again more easily.[194]

The practices of meditation and mindfulness allow us to connect with the body and sense experiences. It acknowledges that to ignore awareness of the breath and bodily sensations is to deny important personal knowledge. In this sense, mindfulness has shown us the importance of our senses and body. Mindfulness has become an important practice today in many Western countries within a range of settings such as education, counselling, and daily personal life.[195] It reminds us of the importance of an awareness of the present moment, including not only our thoughts, but also our bodies and

---

193. Williams and Penman, *Mindfulness*, 4–5.
194. Ibid.
195. See https://www.conted.ox.ac.uk/about/mst-in-mindfulness-based-cognitive-therapy.

emotions. It can be argued that mindfulness challenges us in understanding the *senses as a way of knowing*.

You may be familiar with prayer and meditation in your school. Contemplative practices of meditation and mindfulness in some form exist within all religious traditions. For example, Vipassana meditation within Buddhism and Christian meditation encompasses practices which many engage in today. St. Ignatius of Loyola, Thomas a Kempis, Thich Nhat Hanh, and Rumi are examples of religious writers who explore ways of attending to thoughts and feelings. These spiritual writers also explore methods of how to approach anxious thoughts and disturbing emotions. However, unlike mindfulness, as mentioned earlier, these methods are discussed within a religious and spiritual context.

Student activity—Meditation and mindfulness practice:

1. Read the following article by Buddhist monk Thich Nhat Hanh. How does he define mindfulness? What are some practices suggested?

    "Thich Nhat Hanh on The Practice of Mindfulness"[196]

2. You may try meditation and mindfulness practice for yourself. Play one of the meditations below over eight weeks, twice per day, and notice any changes to your feelings and thoughts.

    The *Mindfulness In Schools* website has some material which may be useful at https://mindfulnessinschools.org:

    - Meditation by MiSP[197]
    - Playing Attention by MiSP[198]

    The following article explains the benefits of mindfulness: "Everyday Mindfulness. Actualise Daily."[199]

3. You may also be interested in religious approaches to mindfulness and meditation. The following links are a good start. Read one of the following (or other resource) and summarise the main ideas related to the practice of mindfulness and meditation within a religious context.

196. https://www.lionsroar.com/mindful-living-thich-nhat-hanh-on-the-practice-of-mindfulness-march-2010/.
197. https://www.youtube.com/watch?v=T5ut2NYdAEQ.
198. https://www.youtube.com/watch?v=LgXZW6Xqokw.
199. https://actualisedaily.com/wellbeing/everyday-mindfulness/.

1. Vipassana Meditation. Suggested website: dhamma.org
2. The World Community for Christian Meditation. Suggested website: wccm.org
3. Ignatian Spirituality. Suggested website: ignatianspirituality.com/ignatian-prayer/the-spiritual-exercises.

STUDENT REFLECTIONS

What are you now wondering about?

1. What ideas, issues, and questions are you wondering about as a result of these lessons?
2. Have these lessons made you think differently about certain ideas, issues, or questions? Why?
3. What questions or ideas did you find interesting, challenging, or intriguing? Explain.

Buddha and Muhammad:
From subjective experiences to religious beliefs

In this section you will explore the subjective experiences of Siddhartha Gautama (known also as the Buddha) and Muhammad that led to the formation of Buddhism and Islam.

Student Activity: Film

Watch the film *The Buddha* and summarise the experience of enlightenment.

Student Activity—Research

Investigate the nature of spiritual or religious experiences through the life stories of Siddhartha Gautama and Muhammad.

Research the experiences of both religious leaders and summarise your findings by focusing on the following questions:

1. How did the life of Siddhartha Gautama lead to his discoveries of enlightenment?
2. How did the life of Muhammad lead to his spiritual and religious experiences?

These sources may be useful:
BBC, "The life of Buddha: A spiritual journey."[200]
BBC, "The life of Muhammad—The Seeker."[201]

Discussion questions

1. What are some common themes or processes in the spiritual and religious experience of both leaders?
2. What are the differences between these significant leaders?
3. To what extent are these the same or different to spiritual experiences of indigenous religious traditions? Give examples.

Mysticism

What do you understand by the terms "mysticism" and "personal transformation?"

Student activity—Video

Watch either of the following:

1. "Life of Pi—Island scene."[202]
2. "Star Wars—Do. Or do not. There is no try."[203]

What do you think are the mystical or spiritual elements in these scenes? Explain.

---

200. http://www.bbc.co.uk/timelines/zg8c9j6.
201. Three-part series hosted on various video websites.
202. https://www.youtube.com/watch?v=c—6ZAfWR9Q.
203. https://www.youtube.com/watch?v=BQ4yd2W5oNo.

How do we find meaning and happiness? 359

The Oxford Dictionary defines mysticism as "Belief that union with or absorption into the Deity or the absolute, or the spiritual apprehension of knowledge inaccessible to the intellect, may be attained through contemplation and self-surrender."[204] As seen in the previous chapters, scholars Rudolf Otto (1869-1937) and Mircea Eliade (1907-1986) moved away from abstract philosophical arguments and focused on religious experience as a justification for religious belief. Otto's research describes such experiences as powerful and numinous—*mysterium tremendumet fascinas* in Latin—causing a sense of fear, awe, and ecstasy.[205] There are written accounts of mysticism within all religious traditions which show similar features. In the Western tradition they are often described in the form of a union with God—in Eastern traditions, as ultimate or absolute reality. There is also mysticism within pantheism expressed as a union with nature. Pantheism is found within indigenous and ancient religions such as Shamanism.

Many scholars claim that mysticism (part of religious experience) is at the very core of religion. Without the experience of mysticism, they argue, one cannot *know* or *truly understand* the *essence of religion*. As we read in previous chapters, philosophers such as Karl Jaspers, Simone Weil, and Abu Hamid Al-Ghazâlî had profound mystical experiences which they claimed were difficult to explain in words. Most describe this as a way of knowing attained through intuition or a "unitive" experience.[206] There are many artists, scientists, philosophers, and theologians throughout history who have written about this experience of the mystical. For these people, such experiences brought happiness and a sense of meaning. Some examples are Gabriel Marcel, Jacque Maritain, William James, Alfred North Whitehead, Albert Einstein, Teresa of Avila, Jacob Bohme, Thomas a Kempis, Lao Tsu, Liu Yiming, and Dōgen Zenji. The word "spiritual" will be used in the broad sense, pointing to a reality beyond the material world and intertwined with religious and mystical experiences.

---

204. *Oxford Dictionaries*, s.v. "mysticism," http://www.oxforddictionaries.com/definition/mysticism.
205. Otto, *The Idea of the Holy*.
206. Gellman, "Mysticism," 6.

Contemplation

Rembrandt—*The Philosopher in Meditation*

The experience of mysticism is often associated with "contemplation," a broad term applicable both within and outside a religious framework. Contemplation can be defined as "The action of looking thoughtfully at something for a long time. Deep reflective thought; or religious meditation."[207] It may also be described as a concentration on spiritual things as a form of private devotion or "a state of mystical awareness of God's being."[208]

The religious contemplative looks at the whole from a broader context—or what we might term "the bigger picture." It is unlike many scientific investigations that may examine sections of data and analyze samples, dissect parts, and organize classifications, but rather seeing the world as a whole. Contemplatives see the interconnectedness of all things from their whole being. This means they not only use reason, but also their emotions, intuition, and imaginations to aid in their understanding of the world. Religious contemplatives view the world as sacred or holy ("holy" being defined as "Dedicated or consecrated to God or a religious purpose; sacred."[209]). The term "holy," as discussed in previous chapters, is connected to the awareness of mystery, which induces a sense of *wonder* about the world.

207. *Oxford Dictionaries*, s.v. "contemplation," http://www.oxforddictionaries.com/definition/contemplation.

208. "Contemplation," https://www.merriam-webster.com/dictionary/contemplation.

209. *Oxford Dictionaries*, s.v. "holy," http://www.oxforddictionaries.com/definition/holy.

Student Activity: Podcast

Listen to the following podcast with scholar and priest Father Francis Rohr, who describes contemplation, and answer the following questions: Dr. Rachael Kohn, podcast, *20/20 Series Part 5: Remember, Regret and Rejoice*.[210]

1. What do you think the phrase "the soul just wants to live in the now" means?
2. How does Rohr describe contemplation?
3. According to Rohr, how is scripture read from a contemplative mindset?

William James (1842–1910)

> With such relations between religion and happiness, it is perhaps not surprising that men come to regard the happiness which a religious belief affords as a proof of its truth. If a creed makes a man feel happy, he almost inevitably adopts it. Such a belief ought to be true; therefore it is true—such, rightly or wrongly, is one of the "immediate inferences" of the religious logic used by ordinary men.
>
> Nevertheless, in the interests of intellectual clearness, I feel bound to say that religious experience, as we have studied it, cannot be cited as unequivocally supporting the infinitist belief. The only thing that it unequivocally testifies to is that we can experience union with SOMETHING larger than ourselves and in that union find our greatest peace. Philosophy, with its passion for unity, and mysticism with its monoideistic bent, both "pass to the limit" and identify the something with a unique God who is the all-inclusive soul of the world. Popular opinion, respectful to their authority, follows the example which they set.
>
> Meanwhile the practical needs and experiences of religion seem to me sufficiently met by the belief that beyond each man and in a fashion continuous with him there exists a larger power which is friendly to him and to his ideals. All that the facts require is that the power should be both other

---

210. http://www.abc.net.au/radionational/programs/spiritofthings/20-20-series-part-5-anniversaries-regrets-and-fusion/9255034.

and larger than our conscious selves. Anything larger will do, if only it be large enough to trust for the next step. It need not be infinite, it need not be solitary. It might conceivably even be only a larger and more godlike self. [211]

As we saw in chapter 2, William James, American philosopher, psychologist, and founder of pragmatism, claimed that religious experience can be a justification for religious belief. James believed that religious experience could help people deal with the normal challenges of everyday life and therefore provide a practical purpose. It can do this effectively, he stated, as the experience allows a person to expand to a greater consciousness *beyond the self*. This consciousness, as described above, can take many different forms; however, the main goal is the sense of unity it creates within the individual psyche. James stated, "The only thing that it unequivocally testifies to is that we can experience union with something larger than ourselves and in that union find our greatest peace."[212] James acknowledged that while there are different features of mysticism, he identified some common characteristics, including a new zest for living, peace, moral transformation, and a loving attitude toward others. James has significantly influenced the modern understanding of how experiential dimensions of religion can have significant practical benefits for people's happiness.

Discussion questions

1. What do you think of James' understanding of mysticism as providing practical benefits for daily living?
2. To what extent could the characteristics of mysticism described by James, such as a "new zest for living, peace, moral transformation and a loving attitude toward others," be considered an adequate standard in judging the authenticity of mystical experiences?

According to James, can someone claim to have a mystical experience and act unkindly and immorally?

---

211. James, *Varieties of Religious Experience*, 62.
212. Ibid., 62.

Christian Mysticism: Teresa of Avila (1515–1582)

> What more do you want o soul! And what else do you search for outside, when within yourself you possess your riches, delights, satisfaction and kingdom—your beloved whom you desire and seek?[213]

There are many examples of mystical writing within the Christian tradition. These writings have emerged throughout the whole of Christian history. Those who have written about their experiences include St. Gregory of Nyssa, John Cassian, Hildegard of Begin, Meister Eckhart, St. Benedict, St. Ignatius and C. S. Lewis. These mystics described their experiences with God as powerful and transformative, ranging from a sense of awe to visions, a deep feeling of love, and radical personal change. Teresa of Avila and John of the Cross lived in monastic communities and wrote about their experiences with the divine.

Teresa of Avila was a Spanish Carmelite nun and is recognized as the first female doctor of the Catholic Church. She was known to have visions and ecstatic experiences. In her famous book, *Interior Castle,* she writes about the process of religious experience, using imagery of light signifying God as a presence within the soul. This light can be obstructed by sin, hindering true seeing or insight:[214]

Saint Teresa of Avila

> You must note that hardly any of the light coming from the King's royal chamber reaches these first dwelling places. Even though they are not dark and black, as when the soul is in sin, they nevertheless are in some way darkened so that the soul cannot see the light. The darkness is not caused by the flaw in the room ... but so many bad things like snakes and vipers ... that enter with the soul and don't allow it to be aware of the light. It's as if a

---

213. John of the Cross, *Collected Works,* 480.
214. Teresa of Avila, *Collected Works,* 295.

person were to enter a place where the sun is shining but be hardly able to open his eyes because of the mud in them.[215]

> ... a genuine heavenly vision yields to her a harvest of ineffable spiritual riches, and an admirable renewal of bodily strength. I alleged these reasons to those who so often accused my visions of being the work of the enemy of mankind and the sport of my imagination ... I showed them the jewels which the divine hand had left with me—they were my actual dispositions. All those who knew me saw that I was changed; my confessor bore witness to the fact; this improvement, palpable in all respects, far from being hidden, was brilliantly evident to all men. As for myself, it was impossible to believe that if the demon were its author, he could have used, in order to lose me and lead me to hell, an expedient so contrary to his own interests as that of uprooting my vices, and filling me with masculine courage and other virtues instead, for I saw clearly that a single one of these visions was enough to enrich me with all that wealth."[216]

1. Comment on and explain the following: "For I saw clearly that a single one of these visions was enough to enrich me with all that wealth." How does this explain Teresa of Avila's transformation?
2. What do you think of Teresa of Avila's image of the soul? Explain.
3. Are there any similarities to the images of Plato's Cave discussed in chapter 1? Explain.

Islamic mysticism: Abû Hamid al-Ghazâlî (c. 1056–1111)

As mentioned in chapter 2, Abû Hamid al-Ghazâlî was a well-known philosopher and mystic within the Islamic golden age, a period of scholasticism and great discoveries in a range of areas. Al-Ghazâlî used reason in exploring metaphysical questions about God, existence, meaning, and happiness. However, Al-Ghazâlî had a mystical experience which led him to question his prior ideas about God. What he came to realize is that philosophy and

215. Ibid.
216. Ibid.

reason in themselves were limited in fully understanding God. He claimed that the only way to *know God* was through the heart versus the intellect. Al-Ghazâlî abandoned his scholarly life as a teacher and became a Sufi. Sufism is the mystical branch within Islam which teaches about God through the medium of poetry and fables, with the purpose of individual transformation.

Rumi (Mewlana Jalaluddin Rumi, also known as Jalal-ad-Din Muhammad [1207–1273])

Rumi is a thirteenth-century Sufi mystic and poet born in Afghanistan, whose works have been widely translated in the West. His evocative and emotional writings depict an understanding of the divine which parallels human interaction and is often depicted as a lover. His writings use imagery in order to entice the reader to a union with God. Rumi often compares the religious experience to falling in love. He employs images which depict an experience of deep divine inner joy, ecstasy, and personal transformation. Love of the divine becomes a way of seeing and understanding the world, which can lead us to a higher or different form of knowledge. Love is a power not easily expressed in language, but its presence is known intuitively through personal experience and change:[217]

> By love bitter things become sweet; by love pieces of copper become golden; By love dregs become clear; by love pain becomes healing; By love the dead is made living; by love the king is made slave.[218]

> According to Rumi, how is the power of love transformative?

---

217. D'Souza, "What can Activist Scholars Learn?," 13.
218. Rumi, in D'Souza, 13.

One of the themes in Rumi's work, and Sufism in general, is its appeal to another way of knowing rather than reason. It seeks to teach through poetry rather than philosophy or dogma. This approach attempts to convey truths in a way that can connect with people emotionally rather than purely through their intellect. Rumi's poetry sought to ignite change and personal transformation.

Jewish Mysticism: Isaac Luria (1534–1572)

Judaism has a tradition of mysticism known as the Kabbalah. This school of thought is purported to originate in Moses' contact with God while on Mt. Sinai, a transformative event in Judaism and Western religion in general. The Kabbalah includes what is perceived as religious knowledge deeper and more reflective of knowing God than mainstream Judaism—although opinions within Jewish culture vary widely regarding its value.

A prominent figure in the Kabbalah's history is mystic Isaac Luria (1534–1572). Luria grew up in Cairo, Egypt, in a traditional Jewish family, but became interested in mystical thought during his twenties. He eventually moved to the city of Safed in Palestine, then an active center of Jewish religion at the time. He gathered with other thinkers to discuss and reflect on their beliefs while writing poetry and religious concepts that eventually became influential in the Kabbalah's body of knowledge.[219]

Student Activity: Research

Study opinions on mystics within a particular religion.

219. Fine, *Physician of the Soul*.

The Kabbalah and Hasidism, a sect of Judaism focusing on tradition and spirituality, have been viewed with various opinions about their value within Jewish society. Research these opinions and discuss why there would be critical views of mystics or mystical practices.

Thomas Merton (1915–1968)

A door opens in the center of our being and we seem to fall through it into immense depths that, although they are infinite, are all accessible to us; all eternity seems to have become ours in this one placid and breathless contact. God touches us with a touch that is emptiness and empties us. He moves us with a simplicity that simplifies us. All variety, all complexity, all paradox, all multiplicity cease . . . For already a supernatural instinct teaches us that the function of this abyss of freedom that has opened out within our own midst is to draw us utterly out of our own selfhood and into its own immensity of liberty and joy.

You seem to be the same person and are the same person that you have always been: in fact, you are more yourself than you have ever been before. You have only just begun to exist. You feel as if you were at last fully born. All that went before was a mistake, a fumbling preparation for birth. Now you have come into your element. And yet now you have become nothing. You have sunk to the center of your own poverty, and there you have felt the doors fly open into infinite freedom, into a wealth that is perfect because none of it is yours and yet it all belongs to you. And now you are free to go in and out of infinity.

> For me to be a saint means to be myself. Therefore, the problem of sanctity and salvation is in fact the problem of finding out who I am and of discovering my true self.[220]

How does Merton describe mystical experience?

Thomas Merton was an American theologian, writer, and Trappist monk. His exploration of mysticism was a lifelong journey to what he describes as "discovering my true self."[221] His description of the mystical experience was akin to a "homecoming," an experience which allowed him to be *more of himself*, stating, "You are more yourself than you have ever been before . . ."[222] It is a space where he encountered God and through this experience claimed that a new identity emerged and expanded, leading to feelings of joy and a sense of freedom. His description of this new identity, or sense of self encompassing something greater—in this case, the Christian God—is a common feature within many accounts of mystical writings:

> In Christianity the inner self is simply a stepping stone to an awareness of God. Man [sic] is the image of God, and his inner self is a kind of mirror in which God not only sees Himself, but reveals Himself to the "mirror" in which He is reflected. Thus, through the dark, transparent mystery of our own inner being we can, as it were, see God "through a glass." All this is of course pure metaphor. It is a way of saying that our being somehow communicates directly with the Being of God, Who is "in us." If we enter into ourselves, find our true self, and then pass "beyond" the inner "I," we sail forth into the immense darkness in which we confront the "I AM" of the Almighty. [223]

Some of us may find it a surprise to hear of freedom in a life spent within a monastic community of silence and prayer. However, despite his physical seclusion from the modern world, Merton not only experienced freedom, but engaged in politics and was a known pacifist. He advocated for positive social and political change, promoting interreligious dialogue.

For more on mysticism, this article by Elizabeth Alvilda Petroff—"The Mystics"[224]—could be useful.

220. Merton, *Seeds of Contemplation*, 31, 151.
221. Ibid., 31.
222. Ibid.,151.
223. Merton, *Inner Experience*, 11.
224. http://www.christianitytoday.com/history/issues/issue-30/mystics.html.

It is important to note that the mystics discussed here wrote from a particular time and culture, drawing on relevant metaphor and figurative language to describe what they experienced internally. This experience of introspection included thoughts, feelings, intuitions, imaginations, and the senses. The mystical experience is often associated with a shedding of the ego, or false self, and a detachment from the world. Mystics often testified to being "born again or anew" and "seeing reality" for what it is without illusions.[225] Generally speaking, most mystics did not concern themselves with the accumulation of wealth, status, societal norms, or values.[226] Their focus was mostly on a life based in spiritual and religious truths. Some lived in solitude or religious communities. Mystics, in many cases, not only focused on their interior lives, but also demonstrated a concern for and compassion toward others, often advocating for social change. Mysticism, however, is not only a reality of the past, but remains alive and well in various forms today.

Student Activity—Indigenous religions

1. Research one indigenous religion such as that of the Maori, Native Americans, Celts, Aboriginal culture, or Ryukyuan people.
2. Compare with the approach to mysticism described within the traditional religions.

Student Activity—How do people today describe religious and spiritual experiences?

1. Research one contemporary example of an individual or group of people testifying to religious or mystical experience. Present your findings to the class and/or write a response.
2. The following programmes may be useful:

BBC—*Heart and Soul*[227]
ABC—*Spirit of things*[228]

---

225. Oliver, *Mysticism*, 129–58.
226. Ibid., 129.
227. http://www.bbc.co.uk/programmes/p002vsn4.
228. http://www.abc.net.au/radionational/programs/spiritofthings/.

On Being[229]

Mysticism Today

One of the common characteristics of the mystical experience, as mentioned earlier, is the transformative power on the individual. People today continue to have mystical experiences. Catholic Benediction monk and scholar Brother David Steindl-Rast illustrates below the power of mysticism and the awareness of mystery in a person's life as a core component of religion:

> All religious doctrine can be traced to its roots in mystical experience... Every religion has its mystical core. The challenge is to find access to it and to live in its power.[230]

> But when you realize it, every moment you are confronted with that great mystery that is life. I've often said when I use that term mystery I don't mean something vague. I mean something very specific; that reality—that actuality—that we cannot grasp. We cannot get it in our grip. We cannot intellectually conceive of it with concepts, but we can understand it and we understand it by standing in it and by letting it do something to us, and that is the great difference. Are you living moment by moment trying to grasp something and take hold of it and having your plans and your own ideas and concepts? Or are you going into every moment and allowing life to move you deeply, to touch you? And that takes a lot more courage because we always want to have everything under control. If we are in the moment and open ourselves to life and keep our eyes and ears and all our senses open to "what is life giving me at this present moment? What is life saying to me? What is life expecting from me?" That is living the spiritual life. That means being really in touch with mystery.[231]

---

229. http://onbeing.org.
230. Steindl-Rast, "The Mystical Core of Organized Religion," 35–36.
231. Steindl-Rast, in Olson, "Everyday Mysticism," para. 9.

Discussion Questions

1. According to Steindl-Rast, what does the term "mysticism" mean?
2. What are the common characteristics of mystical experiences described?
3. Have you experienced this or something similar? Or, do you know someone who has?
4. To what extent is it possible to be a mystic today?

Student Activity: Video

Faith and mystery: David Steindl-Rast

Watch the following clip and answer the questions below: Brother David Steindl-Rast: Faith, Mysticism, and Prayer.[232]

1. What is Steindl-Rast's definition of religious faith?
2. How is God defined?
3. What are Thomas Merton's ideas about religious faith?
4. According to psychiatrist Abraham Maslow, what contributes to people's humanity? What examples does he use?
5. What differences does Steindl-Rast claim exist between the religious traditions?
6. How does prayer work? What connections are made to the Lord's Prayer?

Watch the following videos and answer this question: What is prayer? How to be Grateful—Brother David Steindl-Rast[233]

---

232. https://www.youtube.com/watch?v=IqoIxrQq9r0.
233. https://www.youtube.com/watch?v=ap2SNCNN_Fw.

Student Activity—Video

Mystical experiences in Judaism, Christianity, and Islam
Watch the discussions on mysticism drawn from the three main religious traditions.
Video title: *1 of 4—The Mystical Experience*
The panel includes Brother David Steindl-Rast (Christian), Maata Lynn Barron (Sufi), and Rabbi Jonathan Omer-Man (Jewish).[234]

Recommended—watch Parts 2, 3 and 4 of the series on mystical experiences.

Summarise the main ideas

Write words or images describing mystical experiences. Identify some of the processes involved with the mystical experiences found in the Christian, Jewish, and Islamic traditions.

1. What similarities exist? What are the differences?
2. Can you think of some differences between theistic and indigenous religious traditions?
3. What are the ways of knowing used mostly within the mystical experience?
4. According to these speakers, what hinders the mystical experience from developing or having a voice in the modern world? Do you agree? Explain.
5. What could be some limitations to the experience of mysticism? Explain.

MAIN RESEARCH TASK

Select one religious writer or spiritual text that explores a religious or mystical experience. Become the authority and give a lecture to your class either individually, in pairs, or in groups. Remember, your challenge will be to unpack the meanings of the language, some written within a particular historical context and for an intended audience. Make sure you define key terms.

---

234. https://www.youtube.com/watch?v=TRGJ1vuPiM8.

Included below is a suggested list to choose from; you may select other relevant figures. Each student or group must investigate and present a different individual or writing.

Hindu and Buddhist traditions

Shankara
Anandamayi Ma
Huineng
Kyabjé Bokar Rinpoché
Lao Tsu
Liu I-ming
Dōgen
D. T. Suzuki
Thich Nhat Hanh
Dalai Lama

Theistic traditions

Abraham Abulafia
R. Shnuer Zalman of Liadi
Menahem Nahum
Abd al-Wahab al-Sha" rani
Husayn Mansur al-Hallaj
Avicenna (Ibn Sina)
Rumi
Ibn Arabi
Ibn Abbad of Ronda
St. Gregory of Nyssa
John Cassian
Jacob Boehme
St. Teresa of Avila
Julian of Norwich
St. Ignatius of Loyola
St. John of the Cross
Cloud of Unknowing (anonymous author)
Hildegard von Bingen
Søren Kierkegaard
Karl Jaspers
Jacque Maritain
Gabriel Marcel
C. S. Lewis
Meister Eckhart
Dietrich Bonhoeffer
Thomas Merton
Simone Weil
Evelyn Underhill
George Fox
William Black
John O'Donohue
Bede Griffiths
Brother David Steindl-Rast

Indigenous religions

Ryukyuan
Celts
Native American
Maori
Aboriginal religion
Aztecs
Inuit of the Arctic
Maasai

OTHERS

William James
Rudolf Otto
Mircea Eliade
Ninian Smart

Ken Wilber
Kahlil Gibran
Henry David Thoreau
Leo Tolstoy
Herman Hesse

Some guiding questions:

1. Identify significant social, cultural, and political factors which may have influenced the author.
2. Who was the intended audience?
3. What are some of the main characteristics in the mystical experience described?
4. What ways of knowing did the experience draw on? Was it intuition, emotions, or reason?
5. Was the mystical experience positive or negative for the individual?
6. What did you think of the experience? Was it authentic? What criteria did you use to make this judgement? Did this experience lead to happiness or a sense of meaning? If so, how?

SOME SUGGESTED RESOURCES:

BBC—*Heart and Soul* and *In Our time*
ABC—*Spirit of things*
On Being
School of life

STUDENT ACTIVITY: DEBATE, PRESENT, OR WRITE A RESPONSE TO THE FOLLOWING QUESTION.

To what extent can religious or mystical experiences contribute to personal meaning and happiness?

INDEPENDENT RESEARCH QUESTIONS

1. Does pleasure or eudaimonia equate with a happy life?
2. Does living a moral life make us happy?
3. To what extent is it important to understand the influences of emotions on knowledge?
4. To what extent do friendships make us happy?
5. Can cultivating solitude lead to well-being and happiness?
6. To what extent has technology helped make us happier and contributed to our well-being?
7. Is the focus on economic prosperity taking a priority over having a caring and healthy society?
8. To what extent is a nation increasing its wealth (or GDP) an accurate measure of its success?
9. What does neuroscience have to say about happiness and well-being? Is it convincing?
10. To what extent are the arts important in a society?
11. What are some connections between art and religion?
12. Which discipline can best teach us about happiness and/or meaning, religion, psychology, or philosophy?
13. What does it mean to be a contemplative person today?

CONCLUSION

The search for meaning and happiness is still as prevalent today as it was for our ancestors. How we attain it is complex, yet remains a significant human goal. Does pleasure or eudaimonia equate with a happy life? What does it mean to live the good life? What does a meaningful life look like? These questions have engaged theologians, philosophers, artists, and scientists for millennia. Religious writers and believers answer these questions from the framework of religion. The happy and meaningful life is in reference to a contemplative approach, one which sees the world as sacred, filled with meaning, and potentially personally transformative. The religious contemplative person views the world not only through the lens of reason, but also from their whole being and endeavors to understand it holistically, drawing on intuition, faith, imagination, and emotions. Atheists, scientists, and humanists may argue that life can still be contemplative, meaningful, and happy without necessarily resorting to religion. They claim there is inadequate justification for religious faith as it cannot be rationally or empirically verified.

In whatever view adopted, it will be important in the search for truth, meaning, and happiness to remain open to *all ways of knowing*. The empirical approach may be a useful way of understanding the world, yet it does not answer *all* our questions. The challenge will be to maintain a sense of wonder, awe, and humility about a universe which largely remains *mysterious*.

STUDENT REFLECTION

What are you now wondering about?

- Have any of the lessons in this chapter changed your thinking? Explain.
- What further questions do you have? Has this chapter opened your mind to further horizons? Explain.
- In years to come, what might you remember from these lessons? Explain.

Bibliography

Academy of Ideas. "The Limits Of Science—A Critique Of Scientism." https://academyofideas.com/2013/04/the-limits-of-science-a-critique-of-scientism/.

Adler, Jonathan H. "Property Rights and the Tragedy of the Commons." *The Atlantic* (May 2012). https://www.theatlantic.com/business/archive/2012/05/property-rights-and-the-tragedy-of-the-commons/257549/.

Adorno, Theodor. *Metaphysics: Concepts and Problems*. Edited by Rolf Tiedemann. Translated by Edmund F. N. Jephcott. Stanford: Stanford University Press, 2001.

Adorno, Theodor, and Max Horkheimer. *Dialectic of Enlightenment*. London: Verso, 2016.

Alston, William. *Perceiving God: The Epistemology of Religious Experience*, Ithaca, NY: Cornell University Press, 1991.

Anderson, Pamela Sue. *New Topics in Feminist Philosophy of Religion: Contestations and Transcendence Incarnate*. New York: Springer, 2010.

Annas, Julia. *The Morality of Happiness*. 1st ed. New York: Oxford University Press, 1995.

Anscombe, G. E. M. "Modern Moral Philosophy." *Philosophy* 33.124 (1958) 1–19.

Anselm, Saint. *Proslogion: With the Replies of Gaunilo and Anselm*. Translated by Thomas Williams. Indianapolis: Hackett, 2001.

Anselm, Saint. *Proslogium: Monologium; An Appendix in Behalf of the Fool By Gaunilo; And Cur Deus Homo*. Translated by Sidney Norton Deane. Chicago: The Open Court, 1903.

Antoun, Richard T. *Understanding Fundamentalism*. Lanham, MD: Rowman & Littlefield, 2008.

Aquinas, Thomas. "Summa Theologiae." In *Aquinas, Selected Philosophical Writings*, translated by Timothy McDermott, 4:200–1. 6 vols. Oxford University Press, 1993.

Aquinas, Thomas, and Anton C. Pegis. *Basic Writings of St. Thomas Aquinas.* Indianapolis: Hackett, 1997.
Arendt, Hannah. *Eichmann in Jerusalem: A Report of the Banality of Evil.* New York: Penguin, 1977.
———. *The Human Condition.* Chicago: University of Chicago Press, 1998.
———. *The Origins of Totalitarianism.* London: George Allen and Unwin, 1961.
———. "Thinking and Moral Considerations." *Social Research* 38.3 (1971) 417.
Aristotle. *Aristotle's Metaphysics: A Revised Text.* Translated by W. D. Ross. Oxfordshire, UK: Clarendon, 1924.
———. *The Nicomachean Ethics.* Translated by James Alexander Kerr Thomson. Harmondsworth, UK: Penguin, 1976.
———. *Posterior Analytics.* 2nd ed. Translated by Jonathan Barnes. Oxford: Oxford University Press, 1956.
"Aristotle, Nicomachean Ethics, Bekker Page 1156B." *Perseus.Tufts.Edu*, 2018. http://www.perseus.tufts.edu/hopper/text?doc=Perseus%3Atext%3A1999.01.0054%3Abekker+page%3D1156b.
Armstrong, Karen. *The Case for God: What Religion Really Means.* London: Vintage Digital, 2011.
———. *A History of God.* London: Vintage, 1999.
———. *Islam.* London: Phoenix, 2009.
———. "My Wish: The Charter for Compassion." Filmed in February 2008 in Monterey, CA. TED video, 21:24. https://www.ted.com/talks/karen_armstrong_makes_her_ted_prize_wish_the_charter_for_compassion.
———. *Twelve Steps to a Compassionate Life.* New York: Alfred A. Knopf, 2010.
Association for Psychological Science. "Even Small Distractions Derail Productivity." https://www.psychologicalscience.org/news/minds-business/even-small-distractions-derail-productivity.html.
Augustine. *The Confessions of Saint Augustine.* Translated by F. J. Sheed. New York: Sheed & Ward, 1943.
Aurelius, Marcus. *Meditations.* Translated by George Long. New York: Clydesdale, 2018.
Australian Psychological Society. "Psychology Week." http://www.psychology.org.au/psychologyweek/.
Barbery, Muriel. *The Elegance of the Hedgehog.* Translated by Alison Anderson. New York: Europa Editions, 2014.
Barnes, L. Philip. "Ninian Smart and the Phenomenological Approach to Religious Education," *Religion* 30.4 (2000) 315–32.
Barnett, Lincoln. *The Universe and Dr. Einstein.* New York: Dover, 1985.

Beal, Timothy K. "Opening: Cracking the Binding." In *Reading Bibles, Writing Bodies: Identity and the Book*, edited by Timothy K. Beal and David M. Gunn, 1–12. New York: Routledge, 1997.

Bell, Rob. *What is the Bible?* San Francisco: Harper One, 2018.

Benedict XVI, Pope. *Light of the World: The Pope, the Church, and Signs of the Times*. San Francisco: Ignatius, 2011.

Benedictus. *Biblical Interpretation in Crisis: The Ratzinger Conference on Bible and Church*. Grand Rapids: Eerdmans, 1989.

Bennett, Jonathan. *An Essay Concerning Human Understanding Book IV: Knowledge John Locke*. 2017. http://www.earlymoderntexts.com/assets/pdfs/locke1690book4.pdf.

Bergson, Henri. *An Introduction to Metaphysics*. Translated by T. E. Hulme, et al. Basingstoke, UK: Palgrave Macmillan, 2007.

Bhargava, Rajeev. "Facts Matter Even More in the Post-Truth Age." *The Hindu*, (2017). https://www.thehindu.com/opinion/columns/facts-matter-even-more-in-the-post-truth-age/article19862606.ece.

Bird, Michael. "Why We Need to Teach Historical Criticism." *Euangelion* (blog) *Patheos*, April 29, 2013. http://www.patheos.com/blogs/euangelion/2013/04/why-we-need-to-teach-historical-criticism/.

Blankson, Amy. *The Future of Happiness*. Dallas: BenBella, 2017.

Bloom, Paul. *Against Empathy: The Case for Rational Compassion*. New York: Harper Collins, 2016.

———. "Empathy and Its Discontents." *Trends in Cognitive Sciences* 21.1 (2017) 24–31.

Boadt, Lawrence. *Reading the Old Testament*. 1st ed. New York: Paulist, 1984.

Boniwell, Ilona. "What is Eudaimonia? The Concept of Eudaimonic Well-Being and Happiness." http://positivepsychology.org.uk/the-concept-of-eudaimonic-well-being/.

Bowie, Robert. "Review of *Engaging Religious Education: Liverpool Hope University Studies In Ethics Series. Volume One: Ethics and Religious Education*," *British Journal of Religious Education* 341 (2012) 111–13.

Bowker, John. *The Oxford Dictionary of World Religions*. Norwalk, CT: Easton, 2006.

Boyer, Ernest. "Teaching Religion In the Public Schools and Elsewhere." *Journal of the American Academy of Religion* 60.3 (1992) 515–24.

———. "Why Study Religion? – UCR | Department Of Religious Studies." https://religiousstudies.ucr.edu/about-the-department/why-study-religion/.

Bragg, Melvyn. *The Book of Books: The Radical Impact of the King James Bible, 1611–2011*. London: Hodder & Stoughton, 2011.

Branch, Jennifer, and Dianne Oberg. *Focus on Inquiry*. Edmonton: Alberta Learning, 2004. https://www.teachingbooks.net/content/FocusOnInquiry.pdf

Brandhorst, Kurt. *Descartes' Meditations on First Philosophy*. Edinburgh: Edinburgh University Press, 2010.

Breed, Brennan. "How Was the Bible Written and Transmitted?" http://www.bibleodyssey.org/tools/bible-basics/how-was-the-bible-written-and-transmitted.

Brickman, Philip, et al. "Lottery Winners and Accident Victims: Is Happiness Relative?" *Journal of Personality And Social Psychology* 36.8 (1978) 917–27.

Brown, Laura Lewis. "The Benefits of Music Education." http://www.pbs.org/parents/education/music-Arts/the-benefits-of-music-education/.

Brown, Raymond E. *The Critical Meaning of the Bible*. New York: Paulist, 1981.

Buber, Martin. *I and Thou*. Translated by Ronald Gregor Smith. London: Bloomsbury, 2013.

Bultmann, Rudolf. *New Testament and Mythology and Other Basic Writings*. Edited and translated by Schubert Miles Ogden. Philadelphia: Fortress, 1984.

Burton, Neel. "Aristotle on Friendship." *Psychology Today* (October 18, 2012). https://www.psychologytoday.com/blog/hide-and-seek/201210/aristotle-friendship-0.

———. "The Psychology of Scapegoating." *Psychology Today* (December 21, 2013). https://www.psychologytoday.com/blog/hide-and-seek/201312/the-psychology-scapegoating.

Byrne, Brendan. *Paul and the Christian Woman*. Homebush, NSW: St. Paul, 1988.

Cam, Philip. *Teaching Ethics in Schools: A New Approach to Moral Education*. Camberwell, VIC: ACER, 2012.

———. *Thinking Together: Philosophical Inquiry for the Classroom*. Sydney: Hale and Iremonger, 1995.

Campbell, Joseph, et al. *The Power of Myth*. New York: Anchor, 1991.

Caranfa, Angelo "Contemplative instruction and the gifts of beauty, love and silence" *Educational Theory* 60, no. 5 (2010) 561-585.

Carlisle, Kristy L., et al. "Exploring Internet Addiction as a Process Addiction." *Journal of Mental Health Counseling* 38.2 (2016) 170–82.

Carmody, Timothy R. *Reading the Bible: A Study Guide*. New York: Paulist, 2004.

Chapman, Carole, et al. "Strong Community, Deep Learning: Exploring the Link." *Innovations in Education and Teaching International* 42.3 (2005) 217–30.

Chapman, Judith, et al. *International Handbook of Learning, Teaching and Leading in Faith-Based Schools*. London: Springer, 2014.

Chapman, William E. "IX A Theoretical Proposal Regarding Church-State Relations in Education." *Religious Education* 64.2 (1969) 122–28.

Chappell, Sophie Grace. "Plato on Knowledge in the Theaetetus." In *The Stanford Encyclopedia of Philosophy* (Winter 2013 Edition), edited by Edward N. Zalta. https://plato.stanford.edu/archives/win2013/entries/plato-theaetetus/.

Chaves, Christopher. "Thinking about Racism." Unpublished manuscript, last modified 19 March, 2017. Microsoft Word file.

Chesters, Sarah Davey. *The Socratic Classroom: Reflective Thinking through Collaborative Inquiry*. Boston: Sense, 2012.

Chomsky, Noam. "The Limitation and Problems with 'Just War' Theory.'" Filmed on April 20, 2006, at the United States West Point Military Academy, in West Point, New York. Video, 45:43. https://www.youtube.com/watch?v=e1pNz8A5vMA&t=328s.

Cicero, Marcus Tullius, and Charles Duke Yonge. *On the Nature of the Gods, on Divination, on Fate, on the Republic, on the Laws and on Standing for the Consulship*. London: G. Bell & Sons, 1911.

Cohen, Michael. "How For-Profit Prisons have Become the Biggest Lobby No One is Talking about." *Washington Post*, April 28, 2015. https://www.washingtonpost.com/posteverything/wp/2015/04/28/how-for-profit-prisons-have-become-the-biggest-lobby-no-one-is-talking-about/?utm_term=.9e741303c08b.

Cohen-Zada, Danny, and William Sander. "Religious Participation Versus Shopping: What Makes People Happier?" *The Journal of Law and Economics* 54.4 (November 2011) 889–906.

Cohn, Leisegang, et al., eds. *De Specialibus legibus (On the Special Laws)*. Vol. 5. Berlin: Reimerus, 1926.

Coleman, Daniel. *Emotional Intelligence, Working with EQ*. London: Bloomsbury, 2004.

Coleridge, Samuel Taylor. *Letters*. Edited by E.L. Griggs. 6 vols. London: Clarendon, 1956–1971.

Collins, John W., and Nancy P. O'Brien. *Greenwood Dictionary of Education*. Westport, CT: Greenwood, 2011.

Colman, Andrew M. *A Dictionary of Psychology*, Oxford: Oxford University Press, 2009.

Colman, Arthur. "What Is Scapegoating?" https://drscapegoat.com/what-is-scapegoating/.

Conroy, James C. *Does Religious Education Work?: A Multi-Dimensional Investigation*. London: Bloomsbury Academic, 2013.

Conroy, James C., et al. "Failures of Meaning In Religious Education." *Journal of Beliefs & Values* 33.3 (2012) 309–23.
Conway, Daniel. *Kierkegaard's Fear and Trembling: A Critical Guide*. Cambridge: Cambridge University Press, 2015.
Copleston, Frederick. *A History of Philosophy: Vol. II*. New York: Image, 1994.
Covey, Stephen R. *The 7 Habits of Highly Effective People*. New York: Free Press, 2004.
Craig, William Lane. *The Kalam Cosmological Argument*. London: Macmillan, 1979.
Crane, Rebecca S., and Willem Kuyken. "The Implementation of Mindfulness-Based Cognitive Therapy: Learning from the UK Health Service Experience." *Mindfulness* 4.3 (2012) 246–54.
Crisp, Roger. "Well-Being." In *The Stanford Encyclopedia of Philosophy* (Fall 2017 Edition), edited by Edward N. Zalta. https://plato.stanford.edu/archives/fall2017/entries/well-being/.
Crossman, Ashley. "What's the Difference between Deductive and Inductive Reasoning?" https://www.thoughtco.com/deductive-vs-inductive-reasoning-3026549.
Curie, Marie. "Marie Curie Quotes." http://www.azquotes.com/author/3506-Marie_Curie.
Dalai Lama, The. "How to be a Buddhist in Today's World." *Wall Street Journal*, July 6, 2017. https://www.wsj.com/articles/how-to-be-a-buddhist-in-todays-world-1499381040.
Darwin, Charles. *The Life and Letters of Charles Darwin*. Edited by Francis Darwin. New York: Basic, 1959.
Davids, M. Fakhry. *Internal Racism: A Psychoanalytic Approach to Race and Difference*. Basingstoke, UK: Macmillan Education, 2011
Davies, Dave. "Journalist Ventured 'Behind the Lines of Jihad' to Interview the World's Most Wanted." *Fresh Air*. Radio program. National Public Radio. 2017. https://www.npr.org/2017/06/13/532594281/journalist-ventured-behind-the-lines-of-jihad-to-interview-the-worlds-most-wante.
Dawkins, Richard. *The God Delusion*. London: Transworld, 2006.
De Botton, Alain. "In Defence of the True God." *The Guardian*, July 18, 2009. https://www.theguardian.com/books/2009/jul/19/armstrong-case-god-alain-de-botton?CMP=share_btn_link.
———. "02—Epicurus on Happiness—Philosophy: A Guide to Happiness." Filmed in 2012. Video, 23:58. https://www.youtube.com/watch?v=irornIAQzQY.
de Sousa, Ronald. "Emotion." *Stanford Encyclopedia of Philosophy* (Fall 2018 Edition), edited by Edward N. Zalta. http://plato.stanford.edu/archives/fall2018/entries/emotion/.

Del Nevo, Matthew. *The Continental Community of Inquiry*. Sydney: Self-published, 2002. https://philosophypathways.com/download/Continental_Community.pdf

Descartes, Rene. *Descartes: Selected Philosophical Writings*, Translated by John Cottingham, et al. Cambridge: Cambridge University Press, 1988.

———. *The Philosophical Works of Descartes*. Translated by Elizabeth S. Haldane. London: Cambridge University Press, 1973.

Descartes, René, et al. *Meditations on First Philosophy*. New Haven, CT: Yale University Press, 1996.

Diener, Ed, and Martin E. P. Seligman. "Very Happy People." *Psychological Science* 13.1 (2002) 81–84.

Dobrin, Arthur. "Moral Relativism: Its Limit." *Psychology Today* (blog) April 27, 2012. https://www.psychologytoday.com/blog/am-i-right/201204/moral-relativism-its-limit.

D'Souza, Radha. "What can Activist Scholars Learn from Rumi?" *Philosophy East And West* 64.1 (2014) 1–24.

Eliade, Mircea. *The Sacred and the Profane: The Nature of Religion*. New York: Harcourt, Brace & World, 1959.

Eliot, T. S. *T. S. Eliot: Selected Poems*. London: Faber & Faber, 1975.

Elliot, Mark. "Inquiry Learning in the Religion Classroom." *Curriculum Matters* 3.1 (2004) 3–4.

Endō, Shusakō, and William Johnston. *Silence*. New York: Taplinger, 1979.

Epictetus. *Epictetus: The Discourses as Reported by Arrian, the Manual and Fragments*. Edited and translated by William Abbott Oldfather. 2 vols. London: Harvard University Press, 1928.

Epicurus. *Letters, Principal Doctrines, and Vatican Sayings*. Translated by Russel M. Geer. New York: Macmillan, 1985.

Erickson, H. Lynn. *Concept-Based Curriculum and Instruction: Teaching Beyond the Facts*. Thousand Oaks, CA: Corwin, 2002.

Erricker, Clive. *Religious Education: A Conceptual and Interdisciplinary Approach for Secondary Level*. Abingdon, UK: Routledge, 2010.

Erricker, Clive, et al. *Primary Religious Education, a New Approach: Conceptual Enquiry in Primary RE*. 1st ed. London: Routledge, 2011.

Fallon, Michael. *First & Second Kings Second Chronicles: Introductory Commentary*. Kensington, UK: Chevalier, 2018.

———. *Praying the Psalms with Jesus*. Kensington, UK: Chevalier, 2018.

———. "Praying the Psalms with Jesus." http://mbfallon.com/psalms_1-150/praying_psalms_with_jesus.pdf.

Farb, Norman A. S., et al. "Attending to the Present: Mindfulness Meditation Reveals Distinct Neural Modes of Self-Reference." *Social Cognitive And Affective Neuroscience* 2.4 (2007) 313–22.

Feuerbach, Ludwig. *The Essence of Christianity.* Dinslaken, Germany: Anboco, 2016.
Fieser, James. "Metaethics." http://www.iep.utm.edu/ethics/#H1.
Fine, Lawrence. *Physician of the Soul, Healer of the Cosmos: Isaac Luria and His Kabbalistic Fellowship.* Stanford: Stanford University Press, 2003.
"First Cause." *New World Encyclopedia.* http://www.newworldencyclopedia.org/entry/First_Cause.
Flavell, John H. "Metacognitive Aspects of Problem Solving." In *The Nature of Intelligence,* edited by L. B. Resnick 231–36. Hillsdale, NJ: Erlbaum, 1976.
Foroughi, C. K., et al. "Do Interruptions Affect Quality of Work?" *Human Factors* 56.7 (2014) 1262–71.
Forrest, Peter. "The Epistemology of Religion." In *The Stanford Encyclopedia of Philosophy* (Summer 2017 Edition), edited by Edward N. Zalta. https://plato.stanford.edu/archives/sum2017/entries/religion-epistemology/.
Fox, Emily, and Michelle Riconscente. "Metacognition and Self-Regulation in James, Piaget, and Vygotsky." *Educational Psychology Review* 20.4 (2008) 373–89.
Francis, Pope. *Happiness in This Life: A Passionate Meditation on Earthly Existence.* New York: Random House, 2017.
———. "Laudato Si" http://w2.vatican.va/content/francesco/en/encyclicals/documents/papa-francesco_20150524_enciclica-laudato-si.html.
———. "Visit to the Joint Session of the United States Congress Address of the Holy Father." https://w2.vatican.va/content/francesco/en/speeches/2015/september/documents/papa-francesco_20150924_usa-us-congress.html.
Frankl, Viktor. *Man's Search for Ultimate Meaning.* London: Rider, 2011.
Freud, Sigmund. *The Unconscious.* London: Penguin, 2005.
Gaarder, Jostein. *Sophie's World.* London: Phoenix, 1995.
Gadamer, Hans-Georg. *The Relevance of the Beautiful and Other Essays.* Edited by Robert Bernasconi. Translated by Nicholas Walker. Cambridge: Cambridge University Press, 1996.
Gallagher, Brian. "Bernard Williams against Utilitarianism." *From The Notebook of Brian Gallagher,* January 5, 2012. https://briansgallagher.wordpress.com/2012/01/05/bernard-williams-against-utilitarianism.
Gellman, Jerome. "Mysticism." *The Stanford Encyclopedia of Philosophy* (Spring 2017 Edition), edited by Edward N. Zalta. https://plato.stanford.edu/archives/spr2017/entries/mysticism/.
Gibbs, John C. *Moral Development and Reality.* Oxford: Oxford University Press, 2014.

Girrell, Kris. "How We've Been Misled by 'Emotional Intelligence.'" Filmed in January 2016, in Natick, MA. TED video, 14:34. https://www.youtube.com/watch?v=6l8yPt8S2gE.

"The Global Religious Landscape." Pew Research Center's Religion & Public Life Project. https://www.pewforum.org/2012/12/18/global-religious-landscape-exec/.

Goldberg, "How is Inquiry Viewed In Religious Education?" https:/bertstlstudy.wordpress.com/how-is-inquiry-viewed-in-religious.

Golding, William. *Lord of the Flies*. New York: Penguin, 1999.

Gordon, Lewis R. "Existentialists and Human Nature." Unpublished article, last modified 13 Feburary, 2018. Microsoft Word file.

Graham, Kathy. "Buddhism and Happiness." http://www.abc.net.au/health/features/stories/2007/10/11/2054844.htm.

Grayling, Anthony C. *Friendship*. New Haven: Yale University Press, 2014.

———. *The God Argument: The Case against Religion and for Humanism*. New York: Bloomsbury, 2014.

———. *War – An Enquiry*. New Haven: Yale University Press, 2017.

Gary, J. Glen. "Preface." In *What Is Called Thinking?*, written by Martin Heidegger, xi. New York: Perennial Library, 1976.

Groome, Thomas. *Sharing Faith: A Comprehensive Approach to Religious Education and Pastoral Ministry*. San Francisco: Harper Collins,1991.

Hadot, Pierre. *Philosophy as a Way of Life*. Edited by Arnold Ira Davidson. Oxford: Blackwell, 2011.

Hanh,Thich Nhat, *Be Still and Know: Reflections from Living Buddha, Living Christ*. New York: Riverhead, 1996.

Hanh, Thich Nhat, and Melvin McLeod. *You are Here: Discovering the Magic of the Present Moment*. Boston: Shambhala, 2010.

Hardin, Garrett. "The Tragedy of the Commons." *Science* 162.3859 (1968) 1243–48.

Harper, Jennifer. "84 Percent of the World Population has Faith: A Third are Christian." *The Washington Times*, December, 23, 2012. https://www.washingtontimes.com/blog/watercooler/2012/dec/23/84-percent-world-population-has-faith-third-are-ch/.

Harris, Sam. *The End of Faith: Religion, Terror, and the Future of Reason*. New York: W. W. Norton, 2004.

Hasan, Ali, and Richard Fumerton. "Foundationalist Theories of Epistemic Justification." In *Stanford Encyclopedia of Philosophy*, (2016), edited by Edward N. Zalta. https://plato.stanford.edu/archives/win2016/entries/justep-foundational/.

Hasson, Gill. *Happiness: How to Get into the Habit of Being Happy*. Chichester, UK: Capstone, 2018.

Hattie, John. *Visible Learning*. London: Routledge, 2009.

Haught, John F. *What is Religion?* New York: Paulist, 1990.

Haybron, Dan. "Happiness." *The Stanford Encyclopedia of Philosophy* (Fall 2011 Edition), edited by Edward N. Zalta. https://plato.stanford.edu/archives/fall2011/entries/happiness/.

———. *Happiness: A Very Short Introduction.* Oxford: Oxford University Press, 2013.

Hayden, Mary, and Thompson, Jeff. "International Schools: Antecedents, Current Issues and Metaphors for the Future." In *International Education and Schools: Moving Beyond the First 40 Years*, edited by Richard Pearce, 3–24. London: Bloomsbury Academic, 2013.

Hayden, Mary, and Thompson, Jeff, eds. *International Education: Principles and Practice.* London: Kogan Page, 1998.

Hayes, John H., and Carl R. Holladay. *Biblical Exegesis.* 1st ed. Atlanta: Jon Knox, 1987.

Heidegger, Martin. *Basic Writings.* Edited by David Farrell Krell. New New York: HarperCollins, 1997.

———. *Being and Time.* Translated by John Macquarie and Edward Robinson. Oxford: Basil Blackwell, 1962.

———. *Discourse on Thinking.* Translated by John M. Anderson & E. Hans Freund. New York: Harper & Row, 1966.

———. *Poetry, Language, Thought.* Translated by Albert Hofstadter. New York: Harper & Row, 1975.

———. *Philosophical and Political Writings.* Translated by John M. Anderson and E. Hans Freund. New York: The Continuum International, 2003.

———. *What Is Called Thinking?* Translated by J. Glenn Gray. New York: Perennial Library, 1976.

Heidegger, Martin, and John M. Anderson. *Discourse on Thinking.* New York: Harper Perennial, 2000.

Heidegger, Martin, et al. *Basic Writings*, 1st ed. London: Routledge Classics, 2011.

Hicks, John. *Faith and Knowledge*, 2nd ed. Ithaca, NY: Cornell University Press, 1966.

———. *An Interpretation of Religion: Human Response to the Transcendent.* 2nd ed. New Haven: Yale University Press, 2004.

Hilesum, Etty. *An Interrupted Life.* London: Persephone, 1999.

Hobbes, Thomas, and Noel Malcolm. *Leviathan.* Oxford: Clarendon, 2012.

Hume, David. *An Enquiry Concerning Human Understanding*, Indianapolis: Bobbs-Merrill, 1955.

———. *A Treatise of Human Nature.* Edited by Lewis Amherst Selby-Bigge, Oxford: Oxford University Press, 1978.

Hursthouse, Rosaland. *On Virtue Ethics.* Oxford: Oxford University Press, 1999.

Husserl, Edmund. *The Crisis of the European Sciences*. Translated by David Carr. Evanston, IL: Northwestern University Press, 1970.
Irigaray, Luce. *The Way of Love*. London: Continuum, 2008.
James, William. *The Varieties of Religious Experience*. London: Collier Macmillan, 1961.
Janssens, Jules, and Daniel De Smet. *The Heritage of Avicenna: The Golden Age of Arabic Philosophy, 1000 ca. 1350*. Leuven: Leuven University Press, 2002.
Jaspers, Karl. *Way to Wisdom*. New Haven: Yale University Press, 2003.
John of the Cross, Saint. *The Collected Works of Saint John of The Cross*. Washington: ICS, 1991.
John of the Cross, Saint, and E. Allison Peers. *Dark Night of the Soul*. 3rd rev. ed. London: Burns & Oates, 1976.
Johnson, Oliver A., and Andrews Reath, eds. *Ethics: Selections from Classical and Contemporary Writers*. 9th ed. Belmont, CA: Thomson/Wadsworth, 2004.
Jones, Alexander. *The Jerusalem Bible*. London: Longman & Todd, 1966.
Joy, Morny. *Continental Philosophy and Philosophy of Religion*, Dordrecht, Netherlands: Springer, 2011.
———. "Paul Ricoeur, Solicitude, Love and the Gift." In *Phenomenology and Religion: New Frontiers*, edited by Jonna Bornemark and Hans Ruin, 83–105. Södertörn Philosophical Studies 8. Södertörn, Sweden: Södertörn University Press, 2010.
Kahneman, Daniel. *Thinking, Fast and Slow*. New York: Random House, 2011.
Kanigel, Robert. *The Man Who Knew Infinity*. New York: Washington Square, 2016.
Kant, Immanuel. *Critique of Pure Reason*. Translated by Norman Kemp Smith. New York: Humanity, 1950.
———. *Grounding for the Metaphysics of Morals*. Translated by James W. Ellington. 3rd ed. Cambridge: Hackett, 1993.
———. *Prolegomena to Any Future Metaphysics*. New York: Bobbs-Merrill, 1950.
Kant, Immanuel, and H. J. Paton. *The Moral Law: Groundwork of the Metaphysic of Morals*. London: Routledge, 2005.
Kant, Immanuel, and John Richardson. *Prolegomena to any Future Metaphysic Which Can Appear as a Science*. London: Printed for W. Simpkin and R. Marshall, 1819.
Kant, Immanuel, et al. *Groundwork of the Metaphysics of Morals*. Cambridge: Cambridge University Press, 2012.
Karunadasa, Yakupitiyage. "Pursuit Of Happiness: The Buddhist Way." Presentation given at the University of Hong Kong, April 13, 2013.

Kashdan, Todd B. "Does Being Religious Make Us Happy?" https://www.psychologytoday.com/us/blog/curious/201510/does-being-religious-make-us-happy.

Kashdan, Todd B., et al. "Reconsidering Happiness: The Costs of Distinguishing between Hedonics and Eudaimonia." *The Journal of Positive Psychology* 3.4 (2008) 219–33.

Kawabe, Kentaro, et al. "Internet Addiction: Prevalence and Relation with Mental States In Adolescents." *Psychiatry And Clinical Neurosciences* 70.9 (2016) 405–12.

Keown, Damien. *Contemporary Buddhist Ethics*. London: Routledge, 2000.

Kierkegaard, Søren. *Concluding Unscientific Postscript*. Translated by David F. Swenson and Walter Lowie, Princeton: Princeton University Press, 1941.

Kierkegaard, Søren, et al. *The Essential Kierkegaard*. Princeton: Princeton University Press, 2013.

Kirkwood, Robert, and Edward McLachlan. *God Knows Who I Am*. London: Hodder & Stoughton, 1997.

———. *Looking for Proof of God*. London: Longman, 1990.

Kohlberg, Lawrence. *The Philosophy of Moral Development*. New York: Harper & Row, 1981.

Kormas, Georgios, et al. "Risk Factors and Psychosocial Characteristics of Potential and Problematic Internet Use among Adolescents: A Cross-Sectional Study." *BMC Public Health* 11.1 (2011) 1–8.

Kristeva, Julia. *New Maladies of the Soul*. Translated by Ross Guberman. New York: Columbia University Press, 1995.

Kuhn, Thomas. *Conjectures and Refutations: The Growth of Scientific Knowledge*. 2nd ed. London: Routledge. 1963.

———. *The Structure of Scientific Revolutions*. Chicago: University of Chicago Press, 1970.

Lain, Gil. "Neighbor." *Holman Bible Dictionary* (1991), edited by Trent C. Butler. https://www.studylight.org/dictionaries/hbd/n/neighbor.html.

Law, Stephen. *The Great Philosophers*. 1st ed. New York: Quercus, 2014.

———. "Why Study Philosophy?" *Think* 12.33 (Spring 2013) 5–8.

Leibniz, Gottfried Wilhelm. *Leibniz: Philosophical Writings*. Edited by G. H. R. Parkinson. Translated by Mary Morris. London: J. M. Dent & Sons, 1973.

———. *New Essays on Human Understanding*. Edited by G. H. R. Parkinson. Translated by Mary Morris. London: J. M. Dent & Sons, 1973.

Liem, Gregory, et al. "The Role of Arts-related Information and Communication Technology Use In Problem Solving and Achievement: Findings from the Programme for International Student Assessment." *Journal of Educational Psychology* 106.2. (2014) 348–63.

Lipman, Matthew. *Thinking for Education*. New York: Cambridge University Press, 1991.
Locke, John. *An Essay on Human Understanding*. Edited by Roger Woolhouse. London: Penguin, 1997.
Long, Tony, and David Sedley. *The Hellenistic Philosophers*. Cambridge: Cambridge University Press, 1987.
Lovat, Terence. "Action Research and the Praxis Model of Religious Education." *British Journal of Religious Education* 11.1 (1988) 30–36.
———. *What is this Thing Called Religious Education?* Wentworth Falls, NSW: Social Science, 1989.
Lugo, Luis. "The Global Religious Landscape: A Report on the Size and Distribution of the World's Major Religious Groups as of 2010." http://www.pewforum.org/2012/12/18/global-religious-landscape-exec/#.
MacDonald, Paul S. *The Existentialist Reader: An Anthology of Key Texts*. New York: Routledge, 2001.
MacInerney, Peter K. *Introduction to Philosophy*. New York: Harper Perennial, 1993.
Mackay, Hugh. *The Art of Belonging*. Sydney: Pan Macmillian, 2014.
———. *Beyond Belief*. Sydney: Pan Macmillian, 2016.
Magee, Bryan. *Ultimate Questions*. Princeton: Princeton University Press, 2017.
Malone, Patricia, and Maurice Ryan. *Sound the Trumpet: Planning and Teaching Religion in the Catholic Primary School*. Wentworth Falls, NSW: Social Science, 1994.
Malouf, David. *An Imaginary Life*. London: Vintage, 1999.
Marar, Ziyad. "Why Does Social Science Have Such a Hard Job Explaining Itself?" *The Guardian*, 8 April 2013. https://www.theguardian.com/higher-education-network/blog/2013/apr/08/social-science-funding-us-senate.
Markie, Peter. "Rationalism vs. Empiricism." *The Stanford Encyclopedia of Philosophy* (2015 Edition), edited by Edward N. Zalta. http:/plato.stanford.edu/archives/sum2015/entries/rationalism-empiricism/.
Marshall, Joey. "Are Religious People Happier, Healthier? Our New Global Study Explores This Question." Pew Research Center, 2019. https://www.pewresearch.org/fact-tank/2019/01/31/are-religious-people-happier-healthier-our-new-global-study-explores-this-question/.
Martin, Andrew J., et al. "The Role of Arts Participation in Students' Academic and Nonacademic Outcomes: A Longitudinal Study of School, Home, and Community Factors." *Journal of Educational Psychology* 105.3 (2013) 709–27.
Martin, Jeffery A. *The God Formula: A Simple Scientifically Proven Blueprint that has Transformed Millions of Lives*. Charleston, SC: Integration, 2011.

Maslow, A. H. "The Need to Know and the Fear of Knowing." *The Journal of General Psychology* 68.1 (1963) 111–25.

McCain, Kevin. "The Epistemic Regress Problem." *Wiphi*, October 2017, video, 10:55. http://www.wi-phi.com/video/epistemic-regress-problem.

McDonald, William. "Søren Kierkegaard." *The Stanford Encyclopedia of Philosophy* (Fall 2016 Edition), edited by Edward N. Zalta. https://plato.stanford.edu/archives/fall2016/entries/kierkegaard/.

McGrath, Alister, and Joanna Collicutt McGrath. *The Dawkins Delusion*. London: SPCK, 2007.

McInerney, Peter, K. *Introduction to Philosophy*. New York: Harper Resources, 1992.

McMahan, Jeff. "The Ethics of Killing in War," November 2009, in *Philosophy Bites*, podcast, 18:43. http://philosophybites.com/2009/11/jeff-mcmahan-on-killing-in-war.html.

Medawar, Peter. B. *The Limits of Science*. Oxford: Oxford University Press, 1987.

Meister, Chad. *Introducing Philosophy of Religion*. London: Routledge, 2009.

Merton, Thomas. *The Inner Experience: Notes on Contemplation*. San Francisco: Harper Collins, 2004.

———. *New Man*. London: Bloomsbury, 2003.

———. *Seeds of Contemplation*. New York: New Directions, 1986.

Mill, John Stuart. *Utilitarianism*. Auckland: Floating, 1879.

Moran, Dermot. *Introduction to Phenomenology*. London: Routledge, 2008.

Morgan, David. "Psychoanalysis and Perversion." Presentation, Guildford Psychotherapy Centre. London, 2017.

Morgan, David. "Is Neo-liberalism Making Us Sick?" *RN Breakfast*, podcast audio, December 28, 2016. http://www.abc.net.au/radionational/programs/breakfast/is-neo-liberalism-making-us-sick/7993190.

Morison, Benjamin. "Sextus Empiricus." *The Stanford Encyclopedia of Philosophy* (Spring 2014 Edition), edited by Edward N. Zalta. https://plato.stanford.edu/archives/spr2014/entries/sextus-empiricus/.

Morrison, Karin, et al. *Making Thinking Visible*. San Francisco: Jossey-Bass, 2013.

Moseley, Alexander. "Just War Theory." http://www.iep.utm.edu/justwar/.

Murdoch, Iris. *Existentialists and Mystics*. New York: Penguin, 1999.

Murdock, Kath, and Jeni Wilson. *Learning for Themselves: Pathways for Thinking and Independent Learning in the Primary Classroom*. London: Routledge, 2009.

Nafisi, Azar. *The Republic of Imagination*. New York: Penguin, 2015.

Newell, Ben. "Explainer: What is Intuition?" *The Conversation*. (May 2013). http://theconversation.com/explainer-what-is-intuition-13238.

Newell, J. Philip. *Shakespeare and the Human Mystery*. New York: Paulist, 2003.

Ngamaba, Kayonda Hubert. "Are Religious People Happier than Non-Religious People?" http://www.atimes.com/article/religious-people-happier-non-religious-people/.

Nozick, Robert. *The Examined Life*. New York: Simon & Schuster, 2006.

Nozick, Robert, and Thomas Nagel. *Anarchy, State, and Utopia*. New York: Penguin, 2013.

Nussbaum, Martha. "Compassion and Terror." *Daedalus* 132.1 (Winter 2003) 10–26.

———. *Not for Profit: Why Democracy Needs the Humanities*. Princeton, NJ: Princeton University Press, 2010.

———. *Upheavals of Thought: The Intelligence of Emotions*. New York: Cambridge University Press, 2001.

Ogden, Steven G. *I Met God in Bermuda*. Winchester, UK: O, 2009.

OHCHR. "Good Governance and Human Rights." http://www.ohchr.org/EN/Issues/Development/GoodGovernance/Pages/GoodGovernanceIndex.aspx.

Oliver, Paul. *Mysticism: A Guide for the Perplexed*. Guides for the Perplexed. London: Continuum, 2009.

Olson, Kate. "Everyday Mysticism: A Report." http://gratefulness.org/resource/everyday-mysticism-life-legacy-br-david-steindl-rast-report/.

Osiek, Carolyn. "The Feminist and the Bible: Hermeneutical Alternatives." *HTS Teologiese Studies / Theological Studies* 53.4 (1997) 961–62.

———. "Perspective on Biblical Scholarship." Lecture presented at the Sydney College of Divinity, in Sydney, Australia, in 1995.

Osiek, Carolyn A., et al. *A Woman's Place*. Minneapolis: Fortress, 2006.

Otto, Rudolf. *The Idea of The Holy*. Translated by John W. Harvey. 2nd ed. London: Oxford University, 1950.

Paley, William. *Natural Theology*. Indianapolis: Bobbs–Merrill, 1963.

———. *Natural Theology: Or Evidences of the Existence and Attributes of the Deity Collected from the Appearances of Nature*. Boston: Gould and Lincoln, 1867.

Pascal, Blaise. *Pascal's Pensees*. Lanham, MD: Dancing Unicorn, 2016.

———. *Pensées*. Rev. ed. Translated by A. J. Krailsheimer. New York: Penguin, 1995.

Pattison, George. *Thinking about God in an Age of Technology*. 1st ed. Oxford: Oxford University Press, 2007.

Petroff, Elizabeth Alvilda. "The Mystics." *Christianity Today*. February 2, 2018. http://www.christianitytoday.com/history/issues/issue-30/mystics.html.

Phillips, Jonathan. "What Does it Take to be Truly Happy?" *Psychology Today* (blog), February 13, 2017, https://www.psychologytoday.com/blog/experiments-in-philosophy/201702/what-does-it-take-be-truly-happy.

"Philosophy—Plato." *The School of Life,* October 20, 2014. Video, 6:29. https://www.youtube.com/watch?v=VDiyQub6vpw.

Picard, Max. *The World of Silence*. Wichita: Eighth Day, 1952.

Pirsig, Robert, M. *Zen and the Art of Motorcycle Maintenance*. London: Vintage, 2004.

Plantinga, Alvin, and Nicholas Wolterstorff, eds. *Faith and Rationality*. Notre Dame: University of Notre Dame Press, 1983.

Plato. *The Collected Dialogues of Plato: Including the Letters*. Edited by Edith Hamilton, and Huntington Cairns. Princeton: Princeton University Press, 1973.

———. *The Dialogues of Plato*, vol. 1. 5 vols. Translated by Benjamin Jowett. New York: Random House, 1937.

———. *Euthyphro*. Translated by Benjamin Jowett. 2018. http://classics.mit.edu/Plato/euthyfro.html.

———. *Plato in Twelve Volumes, Vol. 3*. Translated by Walter Rangeley Maitland Lamb. Cambridge: Harvard University Press, 1967.

———. "The Republic." In *The Dialogues of Plato*, vol. 1, translated by Benjamin Jewett, 401–2. 5 vols. New York: Random House, 1937.

———. *The Republic*, Ebook. The Project Gutenberg, 2008. http://www.gutenberg.org/cache/epub/150/pg150-images.html.

———. *Symposium*. Translated by Tom Griffith. New York: Knopf, 2001.

Popova, Maria. "How Our Minds Mislead Us: The Marvels and Flaws of Our Intuition." https://www.brainpickings.org/2013/10/30/daniel-kahneman-intuition/.

Popper, Karl. *Conjectures and Refutations: The Growth of Scientific Knowledge*. London: Routledge, 1963.

———. "Natural Selection and the Emergence of Mind." *Dialectica* 32 (1978) 339–55.

Porter, Nancy. "Kohlberg and Moral Development." *Journal of Moral Education* 1.2 (1972) 123–28.

Prickett, Stephen. *Words and the Word*. Cambridge: Cambridge University Press, 1986.

Putnam, Ruth A. *The Cambridge Companion to William James*. Cambridge: Cambridge University Press, 2006.

Rachels, Stuart, and James Rachels. *The Elements of Moral Philosophy*. Boston: McGraw–Hill College, 1999.

Randall, John Herman. *The Role of Knowledge In Western Religion*. Boston: Starr King, 1958.

Raynova, Yvanka. "All that Give Us to Think: Conversations with Paul Ricoeur." In *Between Suspicion and Sympathy: Paul Ricoeur's Unstable Equilibrium*, edited by Andrzej Wiercinski, 670–96. Toronto: Hermeneutic, 2003.

Regina v Dudley and Stephens, 14 Q.B.D. 273. Queen's Bench Division. 1884. https://la.utexas.edu/users/jmciver/357L/QueenvDS.PDF.

Reid, George. "Biblical Criticism (Higher)." http://www.newadvent.org/cathen/04491c.htm.

Reindal, Solveig M. "*Bildung*, The Bologna Process and Kierkegaard's Concept of Subjective Thinking." *Studies in Philosophy and Education* 32.5 (2012) 533–49.

Ricoeur, Paul. *The Course of Recognition*. Translated by David Pellauer. Cambridge: Harvard UP, 2005.

———. *Oneself as Another*. Chicago: University of Chicago Press, 1995.

Ricard, Matthieu. "The Habits of Happiness." Filmed in February 2004, in Monterey, CA. TED video, 20:51. http://www.ted.com/talks/matthieu_ricard_on_the_habits_of_happiness.html

Rilke, Rainer Moira, and M. D. Herter Norton. *Letters to a Young Poet*. New York: W. W. Norton, 1934.

Ritchhard, Ron et.al. *Making Thinking Visible: How to Promote Engagement, Understanding and Independence for All Learners*. San Francisco: Jossey-Bassy Wiley, 2011.

Rogers, Carl R. *A Way of Being*. New York: Houghton Mifflin, 1995.

Rūmī, Jalāl al-Dīn, and Coleman Barks. *The Essential Rumi*. San Francisco: Harper San Francisco, 2004.

Russell, Bertrand. "Notes On Philosophy, January 1960." *Philosophy* 35.133 (1960) 146–47.

———. *The Problems of Philosophy*. New York: Oxford University Press, 1959.

———. *Unpopular Essays*. London: George Allen and Unwin, 1950.

Ryan, Sharon. "Wisdom." *The Stanford Encyclopedia of Philosophy* (Winter 2014 Edition), edited by Edward N. Zalta. https://plato.stanford.edu/archives/win2014/entries/wisdom/.

Sandel, Michael. "Justice: The Lifeboat Case (Lecture 1 & 2)." September 30, 2016. Video, 2:23. https://www.youtube.com/watch?v=GeZEvSMMRoo.

———. *What Money Can't Buy: The Moral Limits of Markets*. London: Penguin, 2013.

———. "Why We Shouldn't Trust Markets With Our Civic Life." Filmed in June 2013, in Edinburgh, Scotland. TED video, 14:34. https://www.ted.com/talks/michael_sandel_why_we_shouldn_t_trust_markets_with_our_civic_life?language=en#t-590134.

Sartre, Jean-Paul. *Existentialism and Humanism*. London: Methuen, 1973.

Schneewind, J. B. *Moral Philosophy from Montaigne to Kant*. Cambridge: Cambridge University Press, 2003.

Schultz, Barton. "Henry Sidgwick." *The Stanford Encyclopedia of Philosophy* (Summer 2015 Edition), edited by Edward N. Zalta. https://plato.stanford.edu/archives/sum2015/entries/sidgwick/,

Seligman, Martin E. P. *Authentic Happiness: Using the New Positive Psychology to Realize Your Potential for Lasting Fulfilment*. New York: Free Press, 2002.

———. *Flourish*. Sydney: Random House Australia, 2012.

———. "The New Era of Positive Psychology." Filmed in February 2004 in Monterey, CA. TED video, 23:38. https://www.ted.com/talks/martin_seligman_on_the_state_of_psychology.

Shields, Christopher. *Ancient Philosophy: A Contemporary Introduction*. Florence: Taylor and Francis, 2014.

Shields, Christopher J. *The Blackwell Guide to Ancient Philosophy*. Malden, MA: Blackwell, 2003.

Sidgwick, Henry. *Henry Sidgwick: The Methods of Ethics*. Charlottesville, VA: InteLex, 1995.

Siegel, Harvey. "Why Teach Epistemology in Schools?" In *Philosophy in Schools*, edited by Michael Hand and Carrie Winstanley, 78–84. London: Continuum, 2008.

Singer, Peter. *How are We to Live?: Ethics in an Age of Self-Interest*. Port Melbourne, VIC: Mandarin, 1995.

Skilton, Andrew. "The Life of Buddha: A Spiritual Journey." http://www.bbc.co.uk/timelines/zg8c9j6.

Snyder, Susan M., et al. "There's A New Addiction on Campus: Problematic Internet Use (PIU)." *The Conversation*, February 15, 2016. https://theconversation.com/theres-a-new-addiction-on-campus-problematic-internet-use-piu-54226.

"Socrates." *Internet Encyclopedia of Philosophy*. http://www.iep.utm.edu/socrates/.

Solomon, Robert C., and Kathleen M. Higgins. *The Big Questions: A Short Introduction to Philosophy*. Belmont, CA: Wadsworth, 2010.

Sontag, Susan. "The Truth of Fiction Evokes Our Common Humanity." *The Los Angeles Times*, December 28, 2004. http://www.latimes.com/local/obituaries/la-122804sontag_archives-story.html.

Sprod, Tim, and Montclair State University. "Philosophy in Schools." *Thinking* 19.2 (2009) 97–99.

Steindl-Rast, David. "The Mystical Core of Organized Religion." *New Realities* 10.4 (March/April 1990) 35–37.

Sternberg, Esther M. *The Balance Within: The Science Connecting Health and Emotions*. New York: Henry Holt, 2013.

Steyl, Steven. "Emotion and Peacebuilding." Presentation at the Conference of the International Society for Military Ethics: Asia-Pacific Chapter, UNSW Canberra, November 7–8, 2017.
Stumpf, Samuel E. *Socrates to Sartre.* New York: McGraw-Hill, 2000.
Swinburne, Richard. *The Existence of God.* New York: Oxford University Press, 2004.
———. *Faith and Reason.* 2nd ed. Oxford: Clarendon, 2005.
Tarnas, Richard. *The Passion of the Western Mind.* New York: Ballantine, 2011.
Taylor, C. C. W. and Mi-Kyoung Lee. "The Sophists." *The Stanford Encyclopedia of Philosophy* (Winter 2016 Edition), edited by Edward N. Zalta. https://plato.stanford.edu/archives/win2016/entries/sophists/.
Teresa of Avila. *The Collected Works of Saint Teresa of Avila*, vol 2, Translated by Kieran Kavanaugh and Otilio Rodriguez. Washington: ICS, 1980.
———. *The Interior Castle.* New York: Paulist, 1979.
Terry, Milton S. *Biblical Hermeneutics: A Treatise on the Interpretation of the Old and New Testaments.* Grand Rapids: Zondervan, 1974.
Thera, Piyadassi, trans. "Karaniya Metta Sutta: The Discourse on Loving-kindness." http://www.accesstoinsight.org/tipitaka/kn/snp/snp.1.08.piya.html.
Thiselton, Anthony C. *Hermeneutics.* 1st ed. Grand Rapids: Eerdmans, 2009.
Thompson, Mel. *Ethical Theory.* London: Hodder Murray, 2008.
Tongue, Samuel. *Between Biblical Criticism and Poetic Rewriting: Interpretative Struggles over Genesis 32:22–32.* Leiden: BRILL, 2014.
"Understanding Sacred Texts." https://www.bl.uk/learning/resources/pdf/sacredactandquest.pdf.
UNESCO. *Philosophy: A School of Freedom: Teaching Philosophy and Learning to Philosophize: Status and Prospects.* Paris: UNESCO, 2007. http://www.scribd.com/doc/7120613/Philosophy-A-School-of-Freedom.
UNHCR. "Figures at a Glance." http://www.unhcr.org/en-au/figures-at-a-glance.html.
United Nations. *Universal Declaration of Human Rights.* http://www.un.org/en/universal-declaration-human-rights/.
Van Cleave, Diane S. "Contributions of Neuroscience to a New Empathy Epistemology: Implications for Developmental Training." *Advances in Social Work* 17.2 (2017) 369–89.
van de Lagemaat, Richard. *Theory of Knowledge for the IB Diploma.* Cambridge: Cambridge University Press, 2005.
Van Deurzen, Emmy. *Everyday Mysteries.* London: Routledge, 2009.
Vardy, Peter. *What Is Truth?* 1st ed. Sydney: UNSW, 1996.
Vardy, Peter, and Paul Grosch. *The Puzzle of Ethics.* London: Fount, 1999.
Vardy, Peter, and Charlotte Vardy. *Ethics Matters.* London: SCM, 2012.

Walker, Michelle Boulous. *Slow Philosophy*. London: Bloomsbury Academic, 2016.
Walzer, Michael. "Just and Unjust Wars, Updated." October 20, 2016. Video, 13:10. https://www.youtube.com/watch?v=Xqmnx5hESrM.
Weil, Simone. *Cahiers*, vol. 1. Paris: Plon, 1972
———. *Gravity and Grace*. Translated by Emma Craufurd. New York: Routledge, 2002.
———. *Waiting for God*. New York: G. P. Putman's Sons, 1951.
Westacott, Emrys. "Moral Relativism." *The Internet Encyclopedia of Philosophy*. 2018. https://www.iep.utm.edu/moral-re/.
Wheeler, Michael. "Martin Heidegger." *The Stanford Encyclopedia of Philosophy* (Winter 2016 Edition), edited by Edward N. Zalta. https://plato.stanford.edu/archives/win2016/entries/heidegger/.
Whelan, Michael. *The Call to be: Reflections on Christian Life Formation*. Sydney: St. Paul's, 2000.
———. "Sexual Abuse in the Catholic System - Moralism." http://www.aquinas-academy.com/2014-01-15-23-49-43/essays/michael-whelan-sm/370-sexual-abuse-in-the-catholic-system-moralism.
White, Michael, and John Gribbin. *Einstein: A Life in Science*. New York: Penguin, 1994.
Whittle, Sean. "Philosophy in Schools: A Catholic School Perspective." *Journal of Philosophy of Education* 49.4 (2015) 590–606.
Raynova, Yvanka. "All that Gives Us to Think: Conversations With Paul Ricoeur." In *Between Suspicion and Sympathy*: Paul Ricoeur's Unstable Equilibrium, edited by Andrzej Wierciński, 670–96. Toronto: Hermeneutic, 2003.
Williams, Mark, and Daniel Penman. *Mindfulness: Finding Peace in a Frantic World*. London, Piatus: 2011.
Williams, Rowan, and Mike Higton. *Wrestling with Angels*. Grand Rapids: Eerdmans, 2007.
"Wisdom." https://www.psychologytoday.com/us/basics/wisdom.
Wittgenstein, Ludwig. *Philosophical Investigations*. 2nd ed. Oxford: Blackwell, 1958
———. *Tractatus Logico-Philosophicus*. New York: Humanities, 1961.
Wivestad, Stein M. Review of *Critical Religious Education, Multiculturalism and the Pursuit of Truth*, by Andrew Wright. *Journal of Philosophy of Education* 45.1 (2011) 157–61.
"Word of the Year 2016 Is . . ." https://en.oxforddictionaries.com/word-of-the-year/word-of-the-year-2016.
Wright, Andrew. "The Contours of Critical Religious Education: Knowledge, Wisdom, Truth." *British Journal of Religious Education* 25.4 (2003) 279–91.

Wrong, Dennis H. "The Oversocialized Conception of Man in Modern Sociology." *American Sociological Review* 26.2 (1961) 183–93.
Younis, Raymond Aaron. "Neuroscience, Virtues, Ethics, Compassion, and the Question of Character." Presentation given at the Philosophy of Education Society of Australasia Conference, Melbourne, VIC, December 2015. http://pesa.org.au/conference-2015/papers.
———. *On the Ethical Life*. 1st ed. Newcastle-upon-Tyne, UK: Cambridge Scholars, 2009.
———. "These Ultimate Springs and Principles." *Forum Philosophicum* 15.2 (2010) 317–34.
Zalta, Edward N., ed. "Teleological Arguments for God's Existence." *The Stanford Encyclopedia of Philosophy* (Winter 2016 Edition). https://plato.stanford.edu/archives/win2016/entries/teleological-arguments/.

Index

A

Adorno, Theodore, 56
Alston, William, 125–26
Annas, Julia, 212
Anselm, 96–97
Aquinas, Thomas, 56, 94–95, 101, 233, 303
Arendt, Hannah, 76, 79–80, 250
Aristotle, xix, 9, 34, 94–95, 210–13, 293, 313, 327, 344
see also *Nicomachean Ethics*
Armstrong, Karen, 181–84, 268–69
art, 316, 344–54
    and moral development 348–49, 316–17
    and science, 345–46
    and the divine, 349–50
    and truth, 340, 344, 346
    in education, 344–45
asylum seekers, 241

B

Baggini, Julian, 145, 148, 176, 180
Beal, Timothy, 16–17, 190
Bentham, Jeremy, 201–3
Bhargava, Rajeev, 50–53
biblical hermeneutics, 156–69, 173
    and biblical criticism, 156–58, 168
    and redaction criticism, 164–68
Bragg, Melvyn, 175
Buber, Martin, 136–37

Buddhism
    and ethics, 223–26
    and happiness, 301–3
Burton, Neel, 244, 322

C

Caranfa, Angelo, 288
Carl, Rogers, 261–62
categorical imperatives, 207
CBT (cognitive behavioral therapy), 324–25
Chaves, Christopher, 247–49
Christianity
    and ethics, 217–23
    and happiness, 303–5
    see also mystical experience
Cicero, 281, 296
Colman, D Arthur., 245–46
compassion, 266–69
confirmation bias, 72–73
contemplation, 260, 282, 287–89, 290, 303, 359, 360–61
cosmological argument, 92–96
counselling, 324–25
critical thinking, 41–54
    see also logic
cults, 306–7

D

Darwin, Charles, 345–46
D'Souza, Radha, 365

Dalai Lama, The, 223–26,
Davids, Fakhry, 250
Dawkins, Richards, 106–8
Descartes, Rene, 21, 25–27, 34, 37, 78–79
Dobrin, Arthur, 198

E

Einstein, Albert, 109–111, 123
Eliade, Mircea, 111
Ethics, definition, 194–96
    and deontology, 206–208
    and economics, 253–57
    and egoism, 199–200
    and emotions, 208–9
    and empathy/listening, 258–66
    and intuition, 65
    and relativism, 196–99
    and religion, 215–26
    and scapegoating/racism, 244–52
    and utilitarianism, 201–6
    and virtue ethics, 210–13
    and war, 231–24
    see also, Plato, *The Euthyphro*;
    tragedy of the commons;
    veil of ignorance;
    Pope Francis; The Dalai Lama
empathy, 258–65
    and its limitations, 265–66
    and listening, 258–65
    and morality, 265
    compassion, 267–69
empiricism, 34–38, 78–79
emotions, philosophy of, 308–9, 319
    and art, 316–17
    and culture, 316
    and empathy, 257–66
    and ethics 316–17, 208–9
    and reason, 311–15
    and the body, 309–311
    and the unconscious, 318
    and war, 238–41
    definition, 308–9
    James–Lange Theory, 310
    see also intuition
Epictetus, 296–98
Epicurus, 281–83

epistemology, xv, 1–83, 78–81
    empiricism 34–38, 25–27, 78–79
    infinite regress, 22
    justified true belief, 33–34, 78–79
    definition, 3, 20
    rationalism, 20, 25–27, 33–38, 78–79, 130, 132
    logic, 44–49
        deductive/inductive, 44–47
        fallacies, 47–49
    Plato's *Allegory of the Cave*, 27–33
    relativism, 23–24, 79
    scepticism, 22–23, 25–27, 79
    theories of truth, 39–40, 78
    coherence
    correspondence
    pragmatic theory
    phenomenology, 76–77, 131
    Pirsig, Robert M., *Zen and the Art of Motorcycle Maintenance*, 69–70
    science, 70–77
    scientism, 75–77
    intuition, 20, 38, 57–67, 106, 87, 129, 134, 170–71, 338, 359–60
    ways of knowing, 32, 38, 57–59, 131, 161, 169–73, 345, 375–76
    wonder, xiii xix, 2–6, 17, 81, 92, 99, 109–110, 290, 376
    wisdom, 4, 7–15, 211–12, 284–89, 291, 322
eudaimonia, 210, 284, 290–91, 327, 375
existentialism, 131, 340–43
    Buber, Martin, 136–37
    existential counselling, 322–23
    Gordon, Lewis R., 341–43
    Heidegger, Martin, 132–36, 259, 337–39
    Jaspers, Karl, 128
    Kierkegaard, Søren, 126–27, 229–30
    Ricouer, Paul, 138–39, 170
    Sartre, John-Paul, 196, 339, 341–42
    Weil, Simone, 128–30
    see also phenomenology

F

Fallon, Michael, 184–89
Feuerbach, Ludwig, 99, 101

Fiorenza, Elizabeth, 165
Francis, Pope, 217–23, 304, 336
Frankl, Victor, 322–23
Freud, Sigmund, 318
Friendship and happiness, 292
    and Aristotle, 293
    and Grayling, Anthony, 294–95
fundamentalism, 180–84

G

Gadamer, Hans-George, 170
Golden Rule, The, 197, 221, 268–69
God, existence of, 91–106
    and contemporary debates, 90, 103–111
    and miracles, 120–21
    argument from experience, 123–30, 229–31
    see also Swinburne, Richard; Plantinga, Alvin
    cosmological argument, 92–95
    ontological argument, 96–98, 100–101
    problems of suffering, 115–20
    teleological argument, 98, 102
    wager argument, 99, 101
    see also Dawkins, Richard; logical positivists
Gordon, Lewis R., 341–43
Gould, Stephen, 114
Grayling, Anthony, 17–18, 238, 294–95

H

Hanh, Thich Nhat, 260
Happiness
    and economics, 253–56, 329–32
    and emotions, 308–321
    and mindfulness, 354–57
    and religion, 299–307
    and well-being, 178, 278, 282, 301, 323–35
        counselling and CBT, 324–25
        existential counselling, 322–23

    positive psychology, 357, 326–29
    definition, 277–80, 284, 321, 375–76
    eudaimonia, 210, 284, 290–91, 327, 375
    existentialism, 131, 340–43
        Gordon, R. Lewis., 341–43
        Heidegger, Martin, 337–39
        John-Paul, Sartre, 196, 339, 341–42
    hedonism, 202, 280–84
    mysticism, 358–72
    Stoic philosophy, 295–98
hedonism, 202, 280–83
Heidegger, Martin, xix, 132–36, 259, 337–39
hermeneutics
    see also biblical hermeneutics
Hick, John, 89
Hilesum, Etty, 250
Hobbes, Thomas, 199
Hume, David, 21, 33, 36, 37–38, 45–55, 121, 208–9
Hursthouse, Rosaland, 213

I

infinite regress, 22
inquiry-based learning, xv–xvi,
intuition, 20, 38, 59–67
    and bias, 65-67
    and knowledge, 60–63, 338
    and morals, 64–65
    and relationships, 64–65
    and sacred text, 171
    and the divine, 38, 63–64, 87, 106, 129, 170–71, 359–60
    definition, 59–61
Islamic Golden Age, 92

J

James–Lange Theory, 310
James, William, 40, 123–25, 361–62
Jaspers, Karl, 128
John of the Cross, 363

INDEX

Joy, Morny, 138–40

K

Kahneman, Daniel, 65–67
kalam argument, 92–93
Kant, Immanuel, 38, 55–56, 72, 123, 130–31, 206–8
Kierkegaard, Søren, 126–27, 229–31
Kirkwood, Robert, 123
Kohlberg, Lawrence, 228–29
Kuhn, Thomas, 28, 73

L

language, 38, 122, 161–62
Lipman, Matthew, xvi
listening, xviii
    and attentiveness, 260, 137
    and contemplation, 260–61
    and relationships, 137
    and understanding, 134, 259, 170, 173
    practice, 263–65
    see also empathy
Locke, John, 61–62, 78
logic, 44–49
    deductive, 44–46
    fallacies, 47–49
    inductive, 46–47
logical positivist, 74, 121–22

M

Mackay, Hugh, 178
Magee, Bryan, 81, 123
market society, 253–57
Maslow, Abraham, 251
Merton, Thomas, 182, 227–28, 367–86
mindfulness, 354–56
miracles, 120–21
moral dilemmas, 226–27
mysticism, 358–72
    Christian
        Teresa of Avalia, 363,
        David Steindal-Rast, 370–72
        Merton, Thomas, 182, 227–28, 367–68
        see also, Kierkegaard, Søren
    Islamic
        Al-Ghazali, 364
        Rumi, 365–66
    Jewish
        Isaac Luria, 366–67
        see also, Buber, Martin;
    religious experience
        James, William, 123–25, 361–62
        Swinburne, Richard, 103–5
Mill, Stuart, 201–3

N

Nicomachean Ethics, 210, 212, 289–91, 293
Nussbaum, Martha, vi, 267–68, 313–14, 316
Nozick, Robert, 10–11, 283–84, 311, 314

O

Odgen, Steven, 115–20
ontological argument, 96–98, 100–101
Osiek, Carolyn, 166–67
Otto, Rudolf, 16, 111, 359

P

pacificism, 236
Paley, William, 98, 102
Pascal, Blaise, 99, 101
pedagogy, xv–xvii, xviii–xx
phenomenology, 76–77, 131, 135, 138
Picard, Max, 261
Pirsig, Robert M., 69–70
Plantinga, Alvin, 90, 105–6
Plato, 27–33, 35, 284, 345
    The Allegory, 27–33
    The Euthyphro, 215
    The Republic, 287
    The Symposium, 287–89

Popper, Karl, 58, 73, 75
positive psychology, 326–29
Putman, Ruth, 85

R

Rachels, James, 197
racism, 247–52
Ramanujan, Srinivasa, 63–64
rationalism, 20, 25–27, 35–38, 78–79, 130, 132
Rawls, John, 203–4
reason
    and *a priori* knowledge, 63, 130
    and ethics, 195–96, 204
        Kant, Immanuel, 206–8
    and emotions, 313–15
        Aristotle, 210–13
        Hume, David, 208–9
        see also CBT and positive psychology
    and happiness, *see also* Stoic philosophy; CBT; positive psychology
    and illusions;
        Plato's *Allegory*, 27–33
        sense perception/empiricism, 33–38, 25–27
        see also Descartes, Rene, rationalism
    and infinite regress, 22
    and its limitations, 54–57
    and justified true belief, 33–34, 78–81
    and logic, 44–49
        deductive/inductive, 44–47
        fallacies, 47–49
    and relativism, 23–24, 79, 196–99
    and religious faith, 19, 56, 81–82, 89–123, 140, 364–66
    see also God, existence of;
    and sacred text, 156, 170
    and scepticism, 22–23, 25–27, 79
    and the unconscious; Freud, Sigmund, 318
    and ways of knowing, 38, 57–58, 123, 161, 169–73, 375–76
    see also, epistemology; intuition; wisdom; wonder; Kant, Immanuel; Russell, Bertrand
refugees, 241
relativism, 23–24, 79, 196–99
religious faith, xviii, 16–19, 81–82, 85–86, 122, 140
    and atheism, 106–8
    and intuition, 38, 63–64, 87, 106, 129, 170–71, 359–60
    and miracles, 120–21
    and mysticism 358–72
    and objective/subjective truth, 68–69, 130
    and pluralism, 89
    and reason, 19, 56, 81–82, 89–108, 123, 140, 364–66
    see also God
    and religious experience, 19, 56, 104, 113, 123–30, 136–40, 229–31
    and science, 103–5, 106–114, 120–21
    and suffering, 115–20
    and *the mystery*, 108–111
    and wisdom, 7–8, 139
    and wonder, 6, 17, 81, 92, 99, 109–110, 360, 376
    epistemology of religion, 84–143
    existentialism and faith, 131–40
Regina v Dudley and Stephens, 209
religious communities, 178, 150–51
religious experience, 19, 56, 104, 113, 123–30, 136–40, 229–31
    see also mysticism
Ricoeur, Paul, 138–39, 170
Russell, Bertrand, 2–3, 6, 20, 57, 95, 63, 193

S

sacred text, 144–91
    and biblical hermeneutics, 156, 170, 173
        biblical criticism, 157–58
        historical criticism, 158–61
        language, 161–64
        redaction criticism, 164–68

sacred text (*continued*)
   and fundamentalism, 180–84
   and problems of interpretation, 147, 151–53, 162–68
   and reason, 156–71
   and religious communities, 178, 150–51
   and ways of knowing, 156, 161–62, 169–73
   definition, 145–47
Sandel, Michael, 253–57
Sartre, John–Paul, 196, 339, 341–42
scapegoating, 244–46
scepticism, 22–23, 25–27, 79
science
   and art, 345–46
   and imagination, 58
   and its limitations, 71–77
      problems of induction, 72
      confirmation bias, 72–73
      scientism, 75–76
   and method, 70–77
   and religion, 103–4, 106–114, 120–21
   definition, 70
   human sciences, 73–74
Scorsese, Martin, 85
Seligman, Martin, 326–31
Shields, Christopher, 295–96
Sidgwick, Henry, 214, 204
Singer, Peter, 204–6
Socrates, xiii, xix, 7, 23, 13–15, 29–33, 46, 81, 215, 284–86
Steyl, Steven, 238–41
Stoic philosophy, 10, 12, 295–98
Swinburne, Richard, 19, 103–5
Synderesis, 65

T

Tagore, Rabindranath, 253
technology and happiness, 332–39
   Heidegger, Martin, 337–39
   relationships, 335–36
   well-being, 332–35
teleological argument, 98, 102

Terry, Milton S., 173
Thiselton, Anthony, 156, 169–70
Tong, Samuel, 170–71, 173
tragedy of the commons, 200–201
truth, theories of, 39–40, 78

U

UNESCO. *Philosophy: A School of Freedom*, xvii
UNHCR. *Figures at a Glance*. 241

V

veil of ignorance, 203–4

W

wager argument, 99, 101
war, 231–43
   and emotions, 238–41
   and pacificism, 236
   causalities of, 241
   characteristics of, 238
   Just War Theory, 233–35
ways of knowing, 32, 38, 57–59, 131, 161, 169–73, 321, 345, 375–76
Weil, Simone, 128–30
well-being and happiness, 178, 277–78, 282, 301, 323–35, 375–76
Whelan, Michael, 227
wisdom, 4, 7–15, 211–12, 284–85, 291
Wittgenstein, Ludwig, 38, 122, 161–62
wonder, xiii, xix, 2–6, 17, 81, 92, 99, 109–110, 290, 360, 376

X

Xenophanes, 91

www.ingramcontent.com/pod-product-compliance
Lightning Source LLC
Chambersburg PA
CBHW071140300426
44113CB00009B/1035